In the Forest of the Blind

In the Forest of the Blind

The Eurasian Journey of Faxian's *Record of Buddhist Kingdoms*

MATTHEW W. KING

Columbia University Press
New York

Columbia University Press
Publishers Since 1893
New York Chichester, West Sussex
cup.columbia.edu

Library of Congress Cataloging-in-Publication Data
Names: King, Matthew W. (Matthew William), author.
Title: In the forest of the blind : the Eurasian journey of Faxian's record of Buddhist kingdoms / Matthew W. King.
Description: New York : Columbia University Press, [2022] | Includes bibliographical references and index.
Identifiers: LCCN 2021037596 (print) | LCCN 2021037597 (ebook) | ISBN 9780231203609 (hardback) | ISBN 9780231203616 (trade paperback) | ISBN 9780231555142 (ebook)
Subjects: LCSH: Faxian, approximately 337–approximately 422. Fo guo ji. | Asia—Description and travel. | Buddhism. | Buddhist pilgrims and pilgrimages—India.
Classification: LCC DS6.F353 K56 2022 (print) | LCC DS6.F353 (ebook) | DDC 915.04—dc23
LC record available at https://lccn.loc.gov/2021037596
LC ebook record available at https://lccn.loc.gov/2021037597

Columbia University Press books are printed on permanent and durable acid-free paper.
Printed in the United States of America

Cover design: Chang Jae Lee
Cover image: Figure in desert pathway. Digital copy of glass plate negative preserved in the Archives for Cinema, Photography and Sound Recording, Mongolia (1920s).

Contents

Contemporary Tibetan-style rendering of Faxian
Source: commissioned by author

Acknowledgments

This book has many moving parts. This is justified, I think, given that its subject is so many moving books. If thinking about them together is comprehensible, even interesting, this is not due to my meager scholarly abilities, but to colleagues and friends whose generous criticism has helped see this project through.

Unwisely, I decided to finish writing this book during the first year of the COVID-19 pandemic. The pandemic continues, emboldened and now endemic, as I submit final proofs for production. I open this book, framed by personal and global upheaval, by expressing my love and gratitude to Lyndsey and Esmie, whose support for this mad endeavor came while our family (and all families) weathered uncertain and distressing times. I would also like to thank my parents, Carol and Mike, for putting us up when during a surge in Los Angeles we escaped to Canada so that we could be safer. Being able to write a little during that time allowed me to finish this project.

I began to conceive of this book in 2017, when I first spoke about some of the relevant texts at a workshop at UC Berkeley. I am grateful for the feedback of the other participants, all of them wonderful colleagues whose comments helped get this project started: Profs. Vesna Wallace, Patricia Berger, Jacob Dalton, Uranchimeg Tsultem, Brian Baumann, Agata Bareja-Starzyńska, Isabelle Charleux, Hildegard Diemberger, Shen Weirong, and ErdeneBaatar Erdene-Ochir. While at Berkeley, Prof. Johan Elverskog suggested that I pursue a book project about Faxian and his European and Inner Asian interpreters, not an article as I had intended. He also urged me to dive deeply into the life and works of Jean-Pierre Abel-Rémusat, not only those of Dorji Banzarov and Zava

Damdin Lubsangdamdin. I am immensely grateful for this advice, since the exchanges and erasures shared among these three interpreters of Faxian became the story of these pages. My sincere thanks also to Professor Wayne Schlepp, who introduced me to classical Mongolian in 2008 based on close readings of two chapters from Banzarov's text, now explored in full in these pages.

Although I had been collecting and reading some of these texts since graduate school, the opportunity to focus on researching and writing this book full time came from two fellowships. In the spring of 2019, I joined the University of Leipzig's Centre for Advanced Study as part of the "Multiple Secularities in Pre-Modern Asia" Kolleg-Forschungsgruppe. I am extremely grateful for this opportunity, not only for the luxury of time and quiet to think but also because the work and feedback of the other fellows helped me expand the analytical focus of this project (and the next). The bulk of the writing for this book came later, during a yearlong Mellon Foundation second book fellowship in 2019–2020, administered by UC Riverside's Center for Ideas and Society. Though our fellowship year was rudely interrupted by a global pandemic, the support and comments of the other fellows and the CIS community were invaluable before and during our isolation. I would like to especially acknowledge the many insightful and encouraging notes given during a manuscript workshop by Profs. Georgia Warnke, Jody Benjamin, David Biggs, Marissa Brookes, Jade Sasser, and Stephen Sohn, as well as CIS's associate director, Katharine Henshaw. Other financial support for portions of this project came from the Committee on Research of the Riverside Division of the Academic Senate and from the University of California, Riverside Regents' Faculty Fellowship. I am also most grateful to UCR's Faculty Commons for collegiality, writing support, and a small grant that helped sustain and direct the revision of this book.

I must also thank colleagues and students in the departments of religious studies, history, philosophy, and art history at UC Riverside, whose comments on this book helped its evolution in myriad ways. I would especially like to thank Profs. Randolph Head, Ruhi Khan, Ana Bajželj, Melissa Wilcox, Pashaura Singh, Yong Cho, Muhamad Ali, Paul Chang, and graduate students including Elizabeth Miller, Samarth Singhal, and Sinjini Chatterjee. I also wish to thank Prof. Adam Harmer, who in addition to allowing me to ramble on about the story of these pages over years, shared his expertise in the life and philosophy of Leibniz in order to make sense of a faint but vital point of reference in the French works examined below. I am also most grateful to colleagues at the University of

California, Santa Barbara, for the invitation to share some preliminary ideas from this project in the spring of 2020 (as a cruise ship full of COVID patients idled ominously in the sea just off campus). As always, I am indebted to the mentorship, brilliance, and generosity of Profs. Vesna Wallace and José Cabezón, and to the other attendees at the UCSB event for their insightful feedback, especially Profs. Joseph Blankholm and Sangseraima Ujeed, Daigenga Duoer, Rory Lindsay, Jed Foreman, Michael Ium, and Patrick Lambelet.

My sincere thanks are due also to Prof. Amanda Lucia, for countless hours of wide-roaming and challenging conversations about this project (and much more!) over the last many years. I am also immensely grateful to Prof. Michael Alexander, who, for unfathomable reasons, offered to read an overwritten early draft of this book. I thank him in equal measure for his encouragement and gently worded criticism, as for his peerless example of collegiality and curiosity. Thanks also to my doctoral students Steven Quach and Alina Pokhrel, who read portions of the manuscript and offered many useful suggestions in the final leg of writing. I am most indebted to the novelist Liz Harmer, my dear friend, who kindly found time on several me occasions to help me reimagine the structure of this book and to become enamored again with its writing.

I would also like to sincerely thank three remarkable art historians and colleagues, Profs. Uranchimeg Tsultem, Sarah Richardson, and Wen-Shing Chou, for their generous assistance in exploring a possible depiction of Faxian from the Bingling Temple Grottoes. Sarah Richardson was also a reader of an early, convoluted draft of the introduction to this book and kindly helped me see all that needed to be changed. I am once again immensely grateful to Jody Butterworth, of the British Library's Rare Images Archive, and Mr. Bayasgalan Bayanbat, of the Monsound and Vision Foundation in Mongolia, for permission to use the image on the cover. I must especially thank Ven. Khenpo Kunga Sherab, a most remarkable scholar and friend. Khenpo-la found time in 2019 to help review my translation of several difficult passages in the Tibetan text examined below, locate a rare book in Lhasa, and connect me with the artist Ven. Tséwang Lama, the umdzé of Zurmang Monastery in Sikkim, whom I commissioned to invent a thangka-style depiction of Faxian that is reproduced in this book. I am also indebted to Kirsten Janene-Nelson, who brought her editorial skills to bear on the manuscript during a round of major revisions. I am forever grateful for her discerning eye, which always found a trail forward when I saw only bone-strewn desert and iced-over mountain passes.

Lastly, I would like to thank the blind reviewers of this book and the review board at Columbia University Press. I am very appreciative that they found merit in this project and offered such useful advice about how to clarify its structure and arguments. Also at Columbia University Press, as always, I am immensely appreciative of and grateful to the great Wendy Lochner for her interest in my work and for her support of this project. It has also been a joy to work again with all the staff at CUP. My thanks go especially to Lowell Frye and Leslie Kriesel for all their help (and patience) during editing and production.

Conventions

Tibetan

The transcription of Tibetan words in this book follows the Tibetan and Himalayan Library (THL)'s Simplified Phonetic Transcription of Standard Tibetan. The Wylie transliteration is usually given on first usage, either in an endnote or in parentheses in the text as appropriate. This book capitalizes the first letter of all Tibetan text titles, personal names, and place names, regardless of whether it is the root letter.

Mongolian

Keeping the spelling of Mongolian words consistent and not overly technical for the sake of nonspecialists is always challenging. For example, the Mongolian translation of Faxian's *Record* examined in these pages was written using the vertical literary script with classical Mongolian spellings and literary flourish, yet also informed by nineteenth-century Buryat conventions and in some cases, supplemented by twentieth-century spelling. In addition, the Mongolian secondary scholarship that accompanies these materials was written in Khalkha Mongolian using the Cyrillic script. To keep things as clear as possible, I transliterate the vertical script for all persons, places, and technical terminology, usually also giving equivalents in Sanskrit, Chinese, French, and Tibetan (marked in notes and parentheses as "Mong."). For the vertical script, I use the Tibetan and Himalayan Library (THL)'s simplified Mongolian transcription system, developed by Prof. Christopher Atwood, except that I keep γ instead of *ġ* or *gh* on the old Mostaert and Lessing models. For Cyrillic, I also use the Atwood system, except that I keep "v" for в on the Library of Congress model. Cyrillic Mongolian transliteration is marked in notes and parentheses as "Kh. Mong."

Chinese

According to convention, in these pages I give the pinyin spelling for all Chinese cited or translated in this book. When citing the work of the many seventeenth- to nineteenth-century French, German, English, and Russian scholars who appear in these pages, I have retained their idiosyncratic transliteration systems, though usually also providing readers with the pinyin and characters in endnotes or parentheses. I do the same for the Mongolian and Tibetan rendering of Chinese; whenever possible, I have provided the Chinese reference.

Foreign Terminology in Parentheses

Certain French terms, Buddhist technical language, and proper nouns are followed by transliterated equivalents in Tibetan and, as the case may be, Mongolian, Sanskrit, Chinese, French, German, or Russian. In each case, transliterated equivalents are given in parentheses or as notes with the respective language clearly marked, separated by a semicolon. The order of the equivalent terms changes in the course of the book, depending on the chain of translation being examined. For example: Tib. *Tun ha'ang*; Mong. *düng-huwang*; Fr. *Thun houang*; Ch. *Dunhuang* 燉煌.

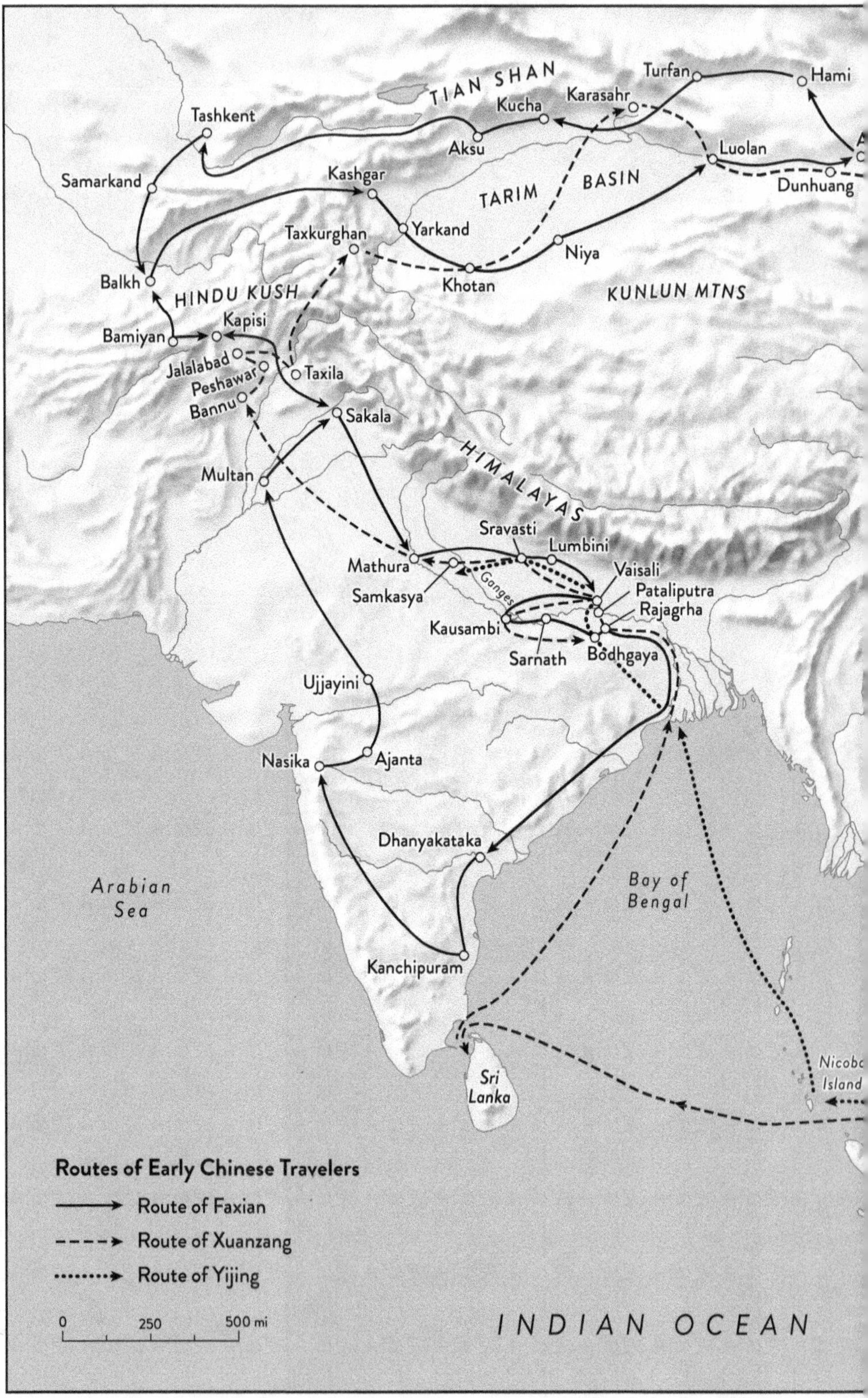

MAP 1. Faxian's journey across Asia

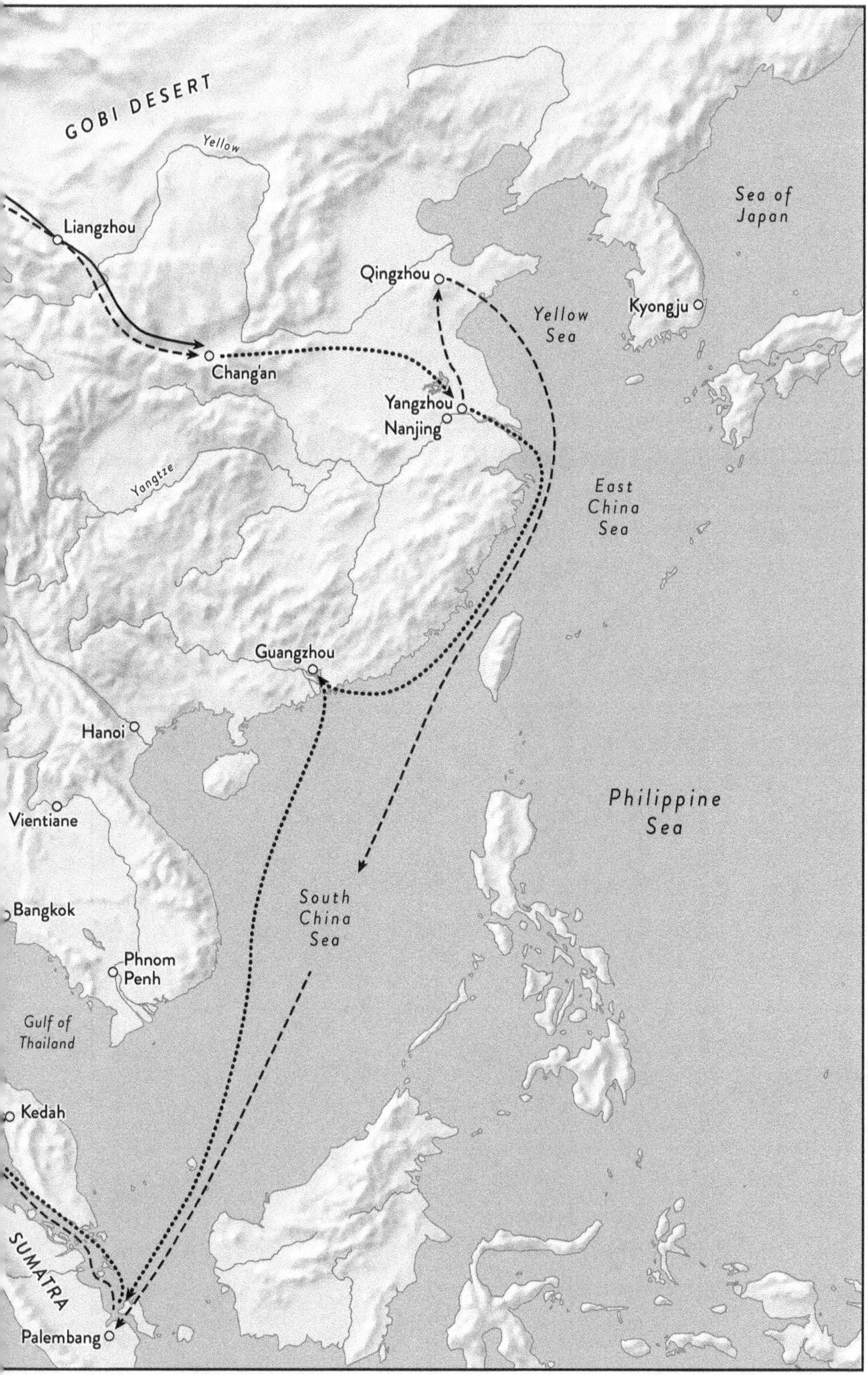

GOBI DESERT
Yellow
Liangzhou
Chang'an
Qingzhou
Yangzhou
Nanjing
Yangtze
Sea of
Japan
Kyongju
Yellow
Sea
East
China
Sea
Guangzhou
Hanoi
Vientiane
Philippine
Sea
South
China
Sea
Bangkok
Phnom
Penh
Gulf of
Thailand
Kedah
SUMATRA
Palembang

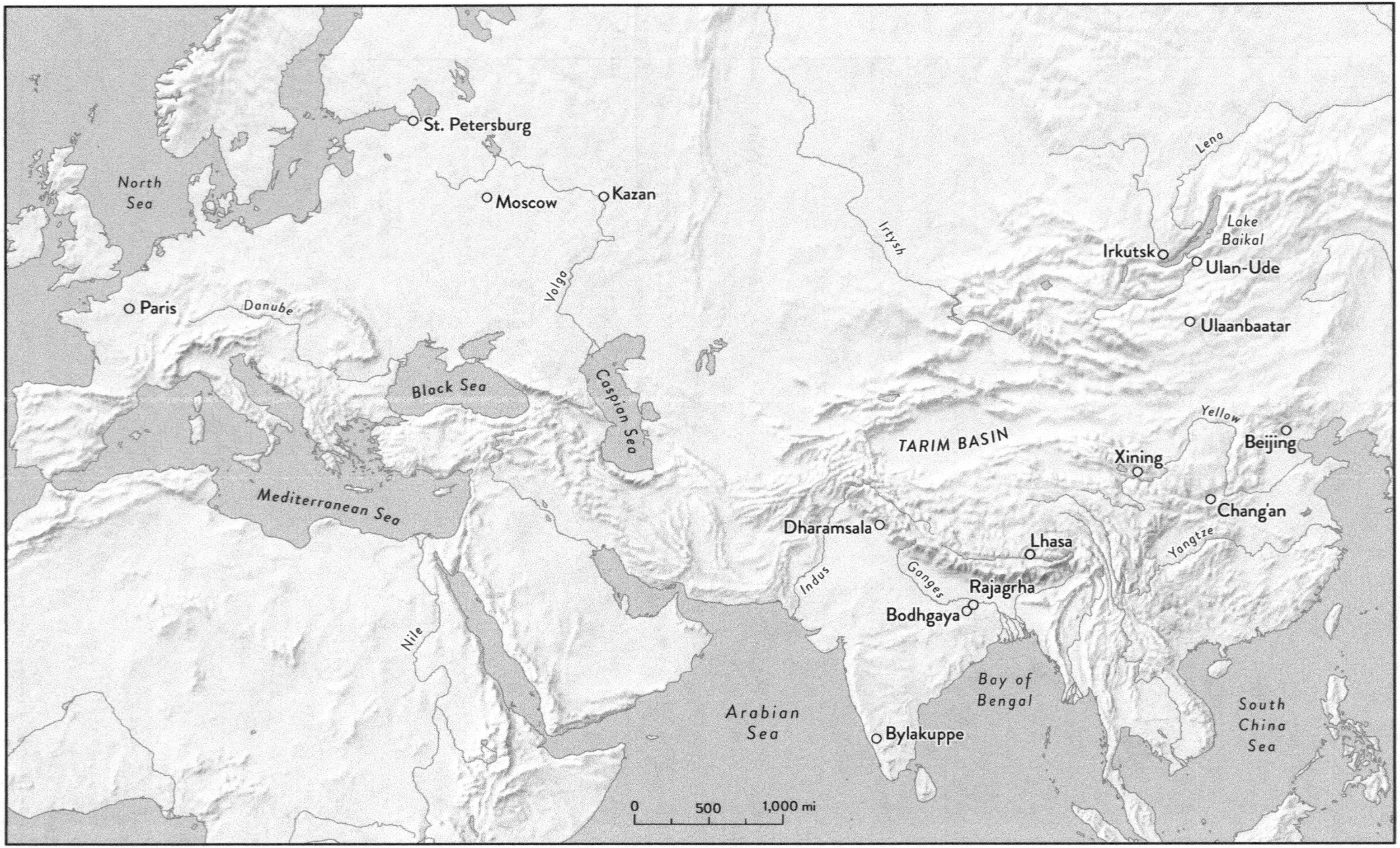

MAP 2. Eurasia, with key cities

In the Forest of the Blind

Introduction

༄༅ མཁས་པས་བཤད་ན་ཅི་ཡང་བདེན།

When explained by a scholar, anything is true.

—Tibetan proverb

> The astronomer is as blind to the significant phenomena, or the significance of phenomena, as the wood-sawyer who wears glasses to defend his eyes from sawdust. The question is not what you look at, but what you see.
>
> —Henry David Thoreau, journal entry on August 5, 1851

The savants of Paris whispered excitedly as they took their seats facing the empty podium.[1] It was mid-May of 1830. A highly anticipated mémoire would soon begin at the Institut de France, seat of the Académie des Inscriptions et Belles-Lettres. The speaker waiting to take the lectern was Jean-Pierre Abel-Rémusat (1788–1832). Just over forty years old, he was considered a master of the Orientalist's interpretative art. Those gathered knew him as "the first Sinologist in France, even in Europe, in the modern sense of the term."[2] But Abel-Rémusat had distinguished himself for much more. Using the language of fact and event, for decades he had pioneered scholarly practices to discipline "Bouddhisme," the "Bouddha," and "les Bouddhistes" as objects of history, geography, and philosophy. Paris was then the global hub of systematic Orientalism, and at the center of its *science de l'Orient bouddhiste* was Jean-Pierre Abel-Rémusat, its first professional practitioner.

In professional associations he had founded and in the pages of many books and articles, Abel-Rémusat had for decades specifically mapped "Buddhist Asia" (Fr. l'Orient bouddhiste) as a new continent of possibility for Europe. Without any precise physical location, its geography was not of the media of earth or water. Its sovereign territories were inaccesible to marauding imperialists manning salt-logged boats or weary caravans. The Buddhist Asia illuminated by Abel-Rémusat's scholarship was not any particular place, but an abstracted field of association among places. From its misted-over topography, Abel-Rémusat's disciplinary practices gleaned previously unknown moral and metaphysicial resources for the project of becoming modern in Europe.

Controversially among his critics, Abel-Rémusat had revealed the untrodden archipelagos and valleys of l'Orient bouddhiste outside of Indian texts and histories, and beyond Romantic visions of that original fount: "bouddhisme primitif." Instead, his methods surveyed its slopes and spires as they wound across Central, Inner, and East Asian scripts and dusted texts, many of them unknown in Europe. Out of the mire of the "Nonwest," that ill-defined and desire-satured object of Orientalist knowledge, Abel-Rémusat's methods set civilizations like Cambodia, Tibet, Java, and Japan in new analytic relation. Across their differences, they appeared now as sharing some deeply historical set of disciplines, ideas, and moral orders. "Bouddhisme," on this pioneering scholar's mosaiclike view, was spread across Chinese sources as much as Sanskrit ones. The life of the "Bouddha," which Abel-Rémusat and his milieu first presented to Europe, unfurled in Mongolian as much as in Pāli. While the philosophy of "la religion samanéen" surely originated in India—Abel-Rémusat himself had proven that the Buddha had been a man, in India, and not some avatar of Mercury, a meandering Egyptian, or a "kinky-haired" Ethiopian—the doctrinal substance of Buddhism could be illuminated only by rigorous comparison of interacting and connected ideas, histories, and literatures across Asia.

In these many ways, in a short swallow of time Buddhist Asia had emerged for European audiences as a logocentric order of conceptual equivalence and racialized difference. Tibetan and Burmese, Manchu and Cambodian, Uighur, Chinese, Mongolian, and Japanese: Buddhist Asia could be mapped only by thinking anew about interaction and mobility and language and ideas across oceans, deserts, and mountain peaks. For years before he took the podium that spring of 1830 in Paris, Abel-Rémusat mapped conceptual equivalencies across Buddhist literary artifacts, convinced that the structure of language imposed the limits of thought. His comparative examination of Buddhist "idiomes" was even supplemented by appeal to Persian or Turkic sources. Or Arabic ones. All this, in turn, was subjected to crisscrossed analyses against European eyewitness accounts and half-translations in Latin or Russian, German, French, English, Italian, or Portuguese. For his methodological innovations as much as for the content of his pathbreaking studies, Abel-Rémusat had become famous. His professionalized and systemic study of Buddhism had years before claimed the status of a science. The result was a new subfield under the umbrella of post-Napoleonic French natural philosophy.[3]

For these reasons, the rows of seats at the Institut continued to fill.

Many of those now seated lauded Abel-Rémusat as a genius—a luminary who had established a scientific field single-handedly. In public writing and oration about him from the 1810s to 1840s, he was often ranked next to Isaac Newton, Blaise Pascal, or Gottfried Wilhelm Leibniz as the singular wellspring of an entire field of science. But closer examination of his published works, his letters, and the impressions of those who knew him best reveals his debts. Like many other deified scholars of the eighteenth and nineteenth centuries, Abel-Rémusat's contributions were at their root about method; about standardizing and institutionalizing knowledge practices. His major innovations were in fact poached from several intellectual and literary traditions, including Eurasianist ones circulating from well beyond colonial Europe and the epistemic domains of the Enlightenment. Such were the generative conditions by which Buddhist Asia was not just "invented," but *disciplined.*

The first reservoir of practices used by Abel-Rémusat was a biblically derived philology applied for generations already to the "languages and literatures" of the Nonwest. As we shall see, Abel-Rémusat mastered these methods as a bedridden youth. Next was the contemporary, systematic, and professionalized Orientalism of the early nineteenth century, founded in mastery of primary languages and the technical excavation of primary sources. This, too, he mastered, under the patronage of Antoine Isaac Silvestre de Sacy (1758–1838), the famous Parisian architect of the new Orientalism. It was with Silvestre de Sacy's mentorship that Abel-Rémusat first undertook self-study of Chinese and Manchu. In time, not only could he read Chinese and "Tartar" (Manchu, Mongol, Tibetan, and Uighur), but also he offered Europe systematic grammars of all these languages.[4] For this he was appointed to the Collège de France as the world's first research chair in "les Langues et Litératures de Chine and Tartary-Mandchoes."

The next and most impactful methodological wellspring for Abel-Rémusat's science of Buddhist Asia was polylingual reference works produced in the contemporary Qing Empire (1644–1911). The sovereignty of the Manchu ruling elite and the nature of the Qing imperial formation—though never consensual and always in flux—were founded in overlapping models of Chinese, Manchu, Mongolian, Tibetan, and Uighur ethnicity, language, religion, history, territoriality, and right to rule.[5] Many dictionaries, vocabularies, and other translation tools published in the courts of the Kangxi, Yongzheng, and Qianlong emperors in the eighteenth century were collected by French envoys and deposited upon shelves of the Bibliothèque Royale, where Abel-Rémusat was appointed in 1824 as Conservateur des Manuscrits. But, as I will show, already as a student in the 1810s, he poached a comprehensive view of the form, languages, organizing concepts, and equivalencies of "Buddhist Asia" from Qing encyclopedias and translation guides. As his scholarly fame grew, still more Qing texts and resources were sent to him by colleagues around the world, from missionaries in Beijing to correspondents in Russia. Eventually, his interest would become piqued by references to an ancient wandering monk named Faxian in such a collection.

Abel-Rémusat's science of Buddhist Asia, not only his "sinology," thus owed a fundamental conceptual and methodological debt to Qing-derived models of language equivalency and flattened models of place, time, and pan-Asian connection. He was neither an "author" nor a "founder" of a science in the usual worshipful and linear sense of intellectual history. He was not, to repurpose Michel de Certeau's famous phrasing, a founder of his own place, heir of the peasants of earlier ages now working on the soil of language, diggers of wells and builders of houses. He was instead a traveler who never left Paris; he masterfully passed through lands belonging to others outside the sovereign political and epistemic territory of "the West," "like nomads poaching their way across fields they did not write, despoiling the wealth of Egypt to enjoy it themselves."[6]

While he is mostly forgotten by field historians outside of Sinology, over the course of two decades Abel-Rémusat's methodological principles and practices for the study of Buddhist Asia laid an enduring template still in use today in Asian and Buddhist studies: positivist evidentiary scholarship founded in language and literacy, examined in pan-Asian comparison, text criticism, and philological reconstruction. The result was a profound transition in analytical possibility in Europe. Using his methods, the "metaphysics and ethics" of a "Buddhist civilization" such as Japan could newly be abstracted and compared to the histories and languages of "civilizations" like not only Java or Afghanistan or Mongolia but also France or Britain or ancient Greece. Eurasia itself, very much including France and Western Europe, suddenly appeared as relational, in motion, and connected by this emergent constellation: l'Orient bouddhiste.

For all these reasons, the lecture hall at the Institut de France that spring of 1830 was bursting. And not only with Orientalists.[7] Philosophers, botanists, colonial administrators, chemists, and geographers pored over Abel-Rémusat's work. The entextualized continent of Buddhist Asia was revealed to them as a vast resource of possibility for natural philosophy—from ancient geography to political history and linguistics. No less than Georg Wilhelm Friedrich Hegel was a close reader and associate of Abel-Rémusat. From the latter's work, Hegel had (mistakenly) derived a stereotyped picture of Buddhist doctrine that buttressed his philosophy of "nothingness" (Ger. *Nichts*).[8] Schopenhauer and, later, Nietzsche would follow, each gleaning their nihilist versions of Buddhism from Abel-Rémusat and his milieu. The brothers Alexander and Wilhelm von Humboldt, Europe's best-known scientists, were exemplary of another sort of Abel-Rémusat's readers and interlocutors. For many years, Abel-Rémusat and Wilhelm von Humboldt publicly debated the nature of universal grammar: If Chinese possessed a structure comparable to German or French, did the Chinese then possess an analogous system of thought?[9]

And so, that hall at the Institut was so crowded, hushed, and expectant. Jean-Pierre Abel-Rémusat cleared his throat, arranged his notes, and filled the quiet of that long ago May.

Le Samanéen Fa-hien

After welcoming the audience and thanking his hosts, Abel-Rémusat announced that his lecture would divulge preliminary findings from a not yet written book.[10] His topic was a Chinese text as remarkable as it was enigmatic. He had first discovered it in a Qing imperial compilation shelved at the Bibliothèque Royale, where in the previous century it had been misnamed and miscatalogued by the fraud Sinologist Étienne Fourmont. Upon examination, Abel-Rémusat had identified the text as a turn-of-the-fifth-century travel account written by "un Samanéen nommé Chy Fa Hien"; a *śramaṇa,* or Buddhist renunciant, named Shi Faxian (釋法顯 337–422). Faxian was an ancient Chinese monk of the Eastern Jin dynasty who had been much disturbed by the incomplete state of the Buddhist canon in China. Specifically, he was concerned about the scarcity of available translations of the *vinaya,* or Buddhist monastic code. Without any sure textual firmament, dedicated Chinese monks like Faxian lived their disciplined lives with an uncertain connection to the Buddha's example. This was an untenable foundation for self-cultivation, a rutted-out and weeded-over path to enlightenment.

So, Abel-Rémusat continued, in 399 CE Faxian departed westward from the city of Chang'an 長安 in search of vinaya—on his way to becoming one of the ancient world's most ambitious travelers.[11] Faxian's destination was Tianzhu 天竺, roughly what today we call India and what Abel-Rémusat recognized definitively as the wellspring of Buddhism, "la religion Samanéen." At the end of the fourth century, Tianzhu was mostly terra incognita in Chinese thought and letters. Following perilous chains of exchange connecting the Ganges river basin to the loess-weighted lands of the Han, Faxian hoped he could retrieve vinaya and other scriptures missing from the Chinese proto-canon. And he did, completing a precarious passage over the course of fourteen years, along the way studying Sanskrit and collecting needed records of the Buddha's speech. Upon his return, Faxian had written an account of his travels, which fourteen centuries later a Manchu imperial court had compiled, and then a French envoy collected, and then this master Orientalist had deciphered.

How remarkable! Abel-Rémusat reminded his audience that no scholar in Europe had ever guessed that Indic languages and traditions were known or studied in China, nor among the pre-"Mohammadean" Buddhist nations of Asia's heartland. Here was an eyewitness account of language and ideas and disciplines of self- and community-making moving between China and the "Mongolian," "Tibetan," and "Turkic" societies ringing the Tarim Basin, into the valleys and high passes of the mountains of today's Afghanistan and Pakistan, and across the thriving, globalized monastic worlds of South Asia. All along his vast plane of connection and interaction, Faxian witnessed Buddhist monks studying Indic texts and intoned liturgies in Sanskrit, Pāli, or some prakrit. He came into the presence of monuments tethering the time of the Buddha, already a thousand years dead by Faxian's arrival, to the space of ancient India. Faxian's walking, when subjected to Abel-Rémusat's methods of analysis, traced lines around the physical, moral, and metaphyical contours of Buddhist Asia itself. And it wove Europe's project of becoming modern into the written lines of Faxian's antique account.

The audience held their breath.

Upon his return to China, the Frenchman continued hurriedly, Faxian was entreated by the ruling and monastic elite to write about all that he had seen. His account became best known as *The Biography of the Eminent Monk Faxian* (*Gaoseng faxian zhuan* 高僧法顯傳), or simply *The Record of Buddhist Kingdoms* (*Foguo ji* 佛國記).[12] Abel-Rémusat had determined that the *Record* had circulated widely in many redactions of varying length and focus. In time, Korean and Japanese translations followed over the centuries, and the *Record* became a widely read classic of East Asian literature. But until this Parisian spring, Faxian and his witnessing of Buddhist Asia were entirely unknown in Europe—and so, too, were the vast topography of exchanges and connections so described.

Abel-Rémusat explained: "I have not found any other bibliographic record of the *Fo-koue-ki*. As for its author, we shall see later that he was one of those who worked collaboratively to spread knowledge of the dogmas of Bouddhisme across the eastern stretches of Asia, to gather large collections of the sacred books of this religion in China, and to make known their contents by translating directly from the original Sanskrit."[13] Abel-Rémusat explained that Faxian had wandered farther afield into South Asia than had any Chinese monk before him. Of those who came after, the famous Tang dynasty traveling monks Xuanzang 玄奘 (c. 600–664 CE) and Yijing 義淨 (635–713 CE) were only the best known. Faxian and all who followed sought contact with the material relics of the Buddha's life and an education in the Indic heartland of Buddhist scholasticism—as well as to collect textual witnesses of the Buddha's seemingly inexhaustible teaching.

Abel-Rémusat declared triumphantly that his forthcoming translation and study of Faxian's *Record* would be the *summa* of his work to discipline Buddhist Asia as an object of Orientalist knowledge. For the first time, the Buddha's biography could be definitively set into place and time.[14] The spread of his followers could now be charted in trans-Asian constellation. The historical geography of Afghanistan could be roped to analysis of ethics in Japan; Chinese law to monastic institutionalism in fifth-century Java; Tibetan "lamaiste" iconography to liturgies intoned in ancient Ceylon. Decades before the invention of comparative religion, Abel-Rémusat was using Faxian's *Record* to render the fables of Buddhist chronicle into the facts of "Histoire." The fluid names and lost monuments of ancient India and Central Asia were being ordered into "Geographie." Buddhist moral orders and spheres of intellectual interactions fragmented in dozens of scripts and regional traditions were now being gathered and distilled into "Philosophie."

Still, Abel-Rémusat revealed, innumerable obstacles hampered completing his translation and study of Faxian's text. Though the *Record*'s style was simple, its contents resisted any easy interpretation. Its dispersed themes and references "are still very little known" in Europe. Faxian walked across more than thirty kingdoms, most of which had long since been smothered by sand and Islam. "India, like Tartary," he explained, "found itself partitioned (*morcelée*) into a great many minor, independent principalities."[15] And these were just the challenges faced in making geography out of the *Record*. In the matter of "Philosophie"—specifically, "métaphysique et éthique"—there was the herculean labor of decoding innumerable "doctrine," "dogme," "coutume," and "croyance."

> Absurd fables, mythological traditions, and observations about liturgies are certainly what [Faxian] intended to, and did, fill his book; but that does not stop him from occasionally collecting, from the names and relative positions of Indian states and villages, in a time for which we possess no other information, clues for which we search in vain in the writing of Occidentals, and maybe even in the writing of the Indians themselves. His itinerary is thus as precious for comparative geography as for the history of Oriental religions. One must simply surround oneself, to listen, with all the lights that history can provide, and to use criticism to trace such a long route across countries still so little known.[16]

The biography of the Buddha was like the vast interactional space of Buddhist Asia itself: described in the *Record* not chronologically but spatially, according to Faxian's meandering route. But with each translated line of the *Record,* with each equivalency drawn from some place or idea or figure across mosaics of linguistic registers, the frontiers of Europe's comparative science of Buddhist Asia were triumphantly extended, apace with Faxian's ancient and determined footsteps.

Even so, Abel-Rémusat sighed, much work lay before him. The *Record* had not been written for outsiders. And it was certainly not written for the savants and lettrés of nineteenth-century Europe. The *Record*'s intended readers were instead fellow monks, those living disciplined lives in long-ago worlds for whom "a single word" was "enough to refresh the memory" of their "sacred books."[17] Single words in the *Record*, moreover, called to their mind some ruin and some "wonder" (*prodiges*) from the life of the Buddha and myriad other "sacré," nearly all of them unknown to "Western knowledge (*connaissance occidentale*)."[18] Despite this, Abel-Rémusat promised the prestigious assembly that he would perservere. After ten years' toil, the *Record* had finally begun to divulge its fruit. Affirming a shared faith in the progressive trajectory of Orientalist knowledge, he vowed that the young science of Buddhist Asia would soon have its masterwork.

To loud applause, Abel-Rémusat left the stage. As he exited the Institut for the streets of Paris, however, a merciless scourge was rising in the "Asiatic world" and beginning already to wind its way to France. In a macabre mirroring of the pathway wandered by Faxian fourteen centuries earlier, the great cholera pandemic of 1817–1824 began in the west Indian Ganges Delta. Killing hundreds of thousands en route, it burned along trade and military networks across Eurasia, pushing westward to the Mediterranean and eastward to the Pacific.[19] Europe was at first spared, but commerce with Tsarist Russia proved a fatal failure in defense. A second surge of "Asiatic cholera" soon gathered force. Between 1826 and 1837, untold numbers were lost in China, Europe, the Middle East, and the Americas. In Paris alone, twenty thousand perished. Abel-Rémusat was among them, dying at home in the arms of his wife, Jenny Lecamus, at 10:45 in the evening on Sunday, June 3, 1832.[20] He was not yet forty-three years old.

Though two years had passed since his lecture at the Institut de France, Abel-Rémusat died leaving his work on Faxian's *Record* incomplete and unpublished. Two mourning colleagues, Julius von Klaproth and Ernest-Augustin Clerc de Landresse, resolved to bring it to print. Since Abel-Rémusat had finished the translation, Landresse and Klaproth focused on the magisterial footnoting. The result was published in 1836, four years after Abel-Rémusat's death (and a year after Klaproth's). It was titled *Foě kouě ki, ou Relation des Royaumes*

Bouddhiques; Voyages Dans la Tartarie, Dans l'Afghanistan et Dans l'Inde, Exécuté, à la Fin Du IV Siècle.[21] The translation of the Chinese text took up just fifty of its four hundred and fifty pages. Abel-Rémusat and his editors filled the remaining four hundred with fevered annotation. As Abel-Rémusat had promised the Parisian elite in 1830, the *Relation des Royaumes Bouddhiques* was a disciplinary triumph of the first order: an entire subfield of natural philosophy hung from nearly every Chinese noun in French translation.

Those hundreds of footnoted essays in *Relation* transformed Buddhist Asia into the object of a disciplinary knowledge in Europe: they staged a compendium of all scholarly knowledge about Bouddhisme and l'Orient bouddhiste then available, they promoted a small group of scholars in Abel-Rémusat's circle who employed his methods of polylingual comparativism, and they relentlessly exposed the pitiable work of amateurs and charlatans, including those with venerable positions in the Collège de France, as needing to be exiled from this new science.

Relation des Royaumes Bouddhiques was an immediate sensation. Exuberant reviews appeared in newspapers and journals in French, English, German, and Russian—their enthusiasm muted only by somber memorials for Abel-Rémusat's tragically shortened life.[22] In the many obituaries dedicated to him, Jean-Pierre Abel-Rémusat was remembered as indissociable from systematic knowledge about Buddhist Asia. Within a decade of its publication, however, Abel-Rémusat was already being forgotten for his field-building work. His poached methods were so quickly and universally adopted as to become invisible. His institution building at the Collège de France, the Société Asiatique, and the *Journal Asiatique* were soon disregarded. His pioneering insights were eclipsed and then muted by his successors, many of them his students.

Yet, I have not written this book to correct the record. The imperfect memory of normative disciplinary history does not concern me. I am not motivated to offer readers another example of "Buddhism" made ("discovered") in the desire-saturated scholarly and aesthetic ecologies of colonial Europe, the Orientalist academy, or some modernist circle of progressives in Asia.[23] This book is not about field building. While Abel-Rémusat held aloft his interpretation of Faxian's *Record* as the apogee of his disciplinary writing, this book explores the sources, silences, and shadows of his writing to see how his science, and "Buddhist Asia," was unmade in Eurasiansist exchange. An experiment in a critical Buddhist studies, this book rejects the linear vision of field history and looks instead for global histories of field erasure in the humanities. And *Relation*, Europe's first book-length study of Buddhist Asia, offers an excellent opportunity to pursue a global history not of the impact or influence of the humanities, but of its silencing.

Though we have begun at the Institut de France, we will follow the *Record* into and out of Chinese and the French, as Abel-Rémusat's masterwork of the science of Buddhist Asia was read, dismantled, and repurposed in Mongolian and Tibetan letters, including in Buddhist monastic settings well outside the epistemic and political sovereignty of Europe. And so we will move beyond the usual territory of field history and the Eurocentric memory of the humanities, following the play of silence and speech between Paris and the polylingual courts of the Qing Empire, the nascent Siberian academy, the Mongolian Buddhist monastic colleges, and the Tibetan refugee settlement.

Anti-Field History

Over the course of researching and writing this book, my organizing questions changed considerably. I began wishing to append an Inner Asian chapter to established scholarship about the *Record*'s well-known East Asian history. I then thought to put Abel-Rémusat's life and career into conversation with his later Inner Asian readers—his previously unstudied saboteurs. Although in what follows I have still pursued both these goals, I eventually realized that thinking these materials in relation to one another posed a far more challenging and interesting set of questions.

Who marks the frontiers separating the writing of Buddhist "superstition et dogme" from the writing of philosophy or history? What membrane cleaves "Asian" genres of writing the past (such as Chinese *gaoseng zhuan* 高僧傳 or Tibetan *chos 'byung* or Mongolian *teüke*) from Orientalist history? When does *lam yig* or *ji* 記 end and the geography of "pilgrimage" (*pèlerinage*) begin? Why does the universalism of natural philosophy in the Parisian academy subsume the world historical order of Qing polylingual sources or the *Kālacakra-tantra*? Where in "Jambudvīpa," the Rose-Apple Continent known to Buddhist canonical sources, is "Asia"? And how does the erasure implicit in rationalist, empirical treatments of primary Buddhist sources in the the work of Abel-Rémusat, but also in the setting of the world into text among Buddhist scholastics, or the imperial literary projects of Kangxi and Qianlong, or in my writing (and your reading), require the erasures of other contiguous knowledge traditions as a condition of speech? And what happens to our sense of disciplinary practice in Buddhist studies when we think such histories together as a chorus, however dissonant?

It is the wager of this book that by writing global histories of the ecologies of interpretation—ones that include, but do not, as in normative field history, privilege the humanities and its sovereign claims to knowledge—we can diversify and productively trouble field practice for those of us still daring to commit acts of history against "Buddhist Asia." The result of such inquiries are what I have come to call "anti-field history." This is an expanded examination of the disciplinary past, one that reconstructs the global chain of silence and speech that have made and unmade humanist knowledge. Here the humanities and contiguous knowledge traditions are treated as a single field of inquiry. Anti-field history looks beyond linearity and beyond origins, like a Foucauldian genealogy but well beyond the usual spatial and institutional scope of such investigation.[24] Here the aim is not to look past the fetish of the subject, but to find the disiplinary implications of centerless, overlapping, and mutually incomprehensible relations of knowledge-power that are coproductive but unbeholden to any specific relation of force (such as colonizer/colonized). The aim, ultimately, is to imagine new disciplinary futures in Buddhist and Asian studies by implicating the disciplinary present in a more diverse, global, subversive, and dispersed disciplinary past that is more attentive to negative space and absence than to impact or influence.

In the extended case study of the Eurasianist journey of Faxian's *Record* that follows, we will be regularly reminded that humanism, in content and practice, always operates in exchange with adjoining global knowledge traditions. This book attempts to straddle the margin of that perilous and porous boundary. To do so as clearly and simply as possible, I have adopted Prasenjit Duara's concept of "circulatory history" to organize my analysis.[25] Circulatory history is, in the first place, a refusal. It rejects the supposed universalism and naturalism of "linear, tunneled histories," which are always only ideological buttressing for such formations as the European colonial project, the modern nation state, and the globalism of market capitalism. In the Eurasianist chains of interpretation of Faxian's *Record*, we will see abundant examples of the "circulatory nature of historical ideas and practices" that are never "the exclusive property of a single community or entity."[26] Instead, the "historical profile of a community is crisscrossed and shaped—for good or bad—by numerous scales of interactions with circulatory networks and forces."[27] To think anew about humanist practice in such wider frames, in other words, is to think anew about silence and speech, about exile and return, that is implicit in the making of all knowledge.

I have been prompted by the Chinese, Manchu, French, Mongolian, and Tibetan sources treated below to seek out new models of descent and possibility that do not privilege the discursive arena of an imperializing science (the "West") over connected discursive arenas that dismantled and repurposed that science in trans-Eurasian circulation. These sources, as Michel de Certeau would put it, "'re-bite' (*re-mordent*) the space from which they were excluded; they continue to speak in the text/tomb that erudition erects in their place."[28] In this sense, this book studies the Eurasianist tombs erected for Faxian and his ancient witnessing, scattered between Paris and Yeke-yin Küriye, Beijing and India, between the 1830s and 1960s. In this way, to use Michel-Rolph Trouillot's pithy phrasing, otherwise disconnected pasts were transformed into radically different histories with Faxian's *Record* in hand: not only of Europe's intellectual, moral, political, and spiritual project of becoming modern by disciplining Buddhist Asia, but also of the continents of memory and erasure made in Inner Asia's bloody and contested experience of revolutionary modernity.

Against my earlier plans for this project, in what follows we will together explore, in Catherine Chin's sublime phrasing, the radiant "dreamer's art" of historical investigation: strange encounters with otherwise lives not usually included in the linear and bounded histories of humanism, Inner Asian monasticism, Orientalism, Qing intellectual culture, or Buddhist studies.[29] What does the social history of knowledge look like when it both includes and exceeds the gridding of the West/Nonwest binary, the ethnonational subject, the secular humanist gaze, and the moral narratives and metaphysical content of modernism?[30] When it produces and encompasses but also exceeds and erases any single knowledge tradition? When it decenters and troubles disciplinary certainty or epistemology in use today? Struggling with these questions over months and years, I was most helped by Lisa Lowe's absorbing counter-grain reading of the intimacies of colonial archives across "the four continents."[31] Like hers, my strange book tries as much as possible to "not foreground comprehensiveness and teleology, in either a historical or geographical sense, but rather emphasizes the rationality and differentiation of peoples, cultures, and societies, as well as the convergence and divergence of ideas, concepts, and themes."[32] My goal has been to examine such circulations as a single field of inquiry that also includes place of my writing (and your reading), and to reflect upon globalizing and pluralizing our disciplinary inheritance today in its refracted light. By this experiment, I hope that more scholars of Buddhist studies might begin to imagine as part of their disciplinary identity the requirement to have answers for Kuan-Hsing Chen's vital, de-imperializing, and decolonizing question: Why is "Asia" always an object, but never a generative condition or source, for theory and methodological innovation in the humanities?[33] Answers, I think, are to be found in thinking with the shadowlands made from circulations like that of Faxian's *Record*. Moving between interpretative sites spread across Eurasia, here we may sojourn stubbornly and make anew with great purpose in a centerless tangle of connection and interaction.

In the Forest of the Blind

I have come to think of those entangled objects and histories using a vegetal site described in Faxian's *Record*. The *Record* tells us that, years into their travels, the aged Faxian and his companion Daozheng arrived at the Jetavana Park already road weary. Jetavana Park had been a stage for many of the Buddha's most famous discourses, as recorded in numerous canonical records of his enlightened speech, such as in *sūtras* (Ch. *jing* 經; Tib. *mdo*; Mong. *sudur*) and *vinaya* monastic codes (Ch. *lü* 律; Tib. *'dul ba*; Mong. *vinai*). It was in search of the latter kind of scripture that Faxian had walked so long and endured so much. Now, arrived on the soil of Jetavana, Faxian and Daozheng stood immobile, pressed by the weight of the place. Tears wetted cheeks. Not awe but grief swept over them.

In the Tibetan translation (of the Mongolian translation of the French translation of the Chinese), Faxian and his companion wail:

> *E ma!* Just consider that the Principle of the World [the Buddha] lived in this place for twenty-five years! *Kyi hyud*! We have wandered to a great many blessed sites (*gnas chen*), and in order to come into worshipful contact (*mjal ba*) with this place, we joined with many companions upon the path. From among them, some have since returned to their homeland. Others have showed the fundamental nature of impermanence of the human life span. Though we two have arrived here today, the Buddha Bhagavān no longer abides here![34]

Reading farther into this section of the Tibetan *Record*—whose topic, like that of the circulatory history this book pursues, is absence and presence, exile and possibility—we come across another, vegetal site of loss and gain. This was the "medicinal land" (*sman ljongs*) called "The Forest of Restored Vision" (*Mig gsos pa'i nags*). Long ago, we read, five hundred blind people journeying to Jetavana Park took rest in this grove of cane trees. There the Buddha met them. He explained how his teachings, the Dharma, was a remedy for afflicted body and mind. By witnessing the truth of the Buddha's words, the one thousand eyes of these five hundred travelers became sighted. No longer in need of their walking sticks, they planted them deep in the rich woodland floor and carried on with their travels.

Later, roots grew from these abandoned walking sticks still standing in that quiet medicinal forest. The growing tendrils coiled into each other, becoming enmeshed and balled. Shoots pushed up as taproots felt deeply for unseen courses of water. Green sprigs and felted roots reached across the soiled underside of the Forest of the Blind. Woods of growth and rot multiplied in all directions, sustaining that grove of cane trees for a thousand years. "Later generations showed respect and never cut this wood," Faxian noted. "That is the reason it is known as the Forest of Restored Vision. There is a tradition among the saṅgha of the Jetavana Park that, after they take their meals, they retire to this wood to settle their minds into single-minded contemplation."[35]

This tangle of growth in the Forest of the Blind—and of the Sighted—exemplifies the centerless (and marginless) conditions for knowledge and disciplinary practice examined in this book. Mobile and interactive, like the coiled roots of those abandoned walking canes, the circulatory history of Faxian's *Record* encompasses vast networks of growth and rot, of speech and silence, of insight and ignorance. These exceed and complicate appeal to any linear conception of influence or origin, to any treelike notion of knowledge as having a hierarchical descent or simple origin. We see instead a Deleuze and Guattarian figure of the rhizome, in whose image I have sought to explore this circuitous and centerless story of compassing the present with Faxian.[36] In their famous formulation, rhizomes represent centerless and nonhierarchical connection, possibility, circulation, and creation. This is quite different from the "treelike" version of intellectual and field history we are accustomed to, where roots and origins explain the form and content of linear growth—so many straight trunks and limbs, replicated leaves.

As we shall see, everything about this story resists linearity, from the narrative structure of the texts involved to the interpretative resources each author drew upon to translate the *Record* and to see their present in Faxian's ancient walking. In the first place, the *Record* orders time by means of space. The Buddha's last act is giving his first teaching, a great many miles forward in time after his dying, which occurs long before he was born. In turn, the young history of the frontier of the Buddhist dispensation in China is told before the older history of Indian Buddhism. As Faxian's travels proceed westward from Chang'an to India, he walks into older and older nodes of the Dharma. The ruins marking the Buddha's descent from Tuṣita Heaven, where he went to teach his deceased mother the Dharma, arrive in the *Record* long before the story of how she bore him, or of how he entered her womb with the touch of a great white elephant. The Buddha's life and the deep history of Jambudvīpa, Faxian discovered, were fourteen years wide.

My task, as Deleuze and Guattari put it, is to adopt a kind of "perceptual semiotics" that does not impose precisely delineated hierarchies found nowhere in these sources.[37] There are no clear lines of descent in this circulatory history, no beginning or end; the interpretative ecologies of the Qing and Inner Asian monastic histories occur both before and after Parisian Orientalism, just as in the telling of Faxian's *Record* the Buddha dies before he is born. Each of the sites and sources examined herein, like the text that follows, is always already in the middle, made continually anew from silence and ruin and rot in lateral connection—not bequeathed by the West to the East, nor plotted by movement from tradition to the modern, Buddhism to Buddhist studies, legend to fact, chronicle to history, cosmology to geography, doctrine to philosophy.

To attempt all this, however imperfectly, this book first focuses on chains of Eurasianist interpretation that bound Faxian to the courts of the Qing Empire, the Parisian milieu of Abel-Rémusat, and the interpretative sites of Siberian, Mongolian, and Tibetan monastery and academy. I first introduce readers to what is known about Faxian's life, his walking, and his account about it. To avoid repeating narratives about him that are found elsewhere in the book, in the first chapter I present two separate biographical accounts written by Sengyou 僧祐 (445–518) and Huijiao 慧皎 (497–554), monk biographers who used Faxian's life to help time and emplace turn-of-the-sixth-century Chinese projects of canon building. Based on their colorful accounts, I also share some contemporary historical work about Faxian to help introduce readers to his life and times. Chapter 2 presents a fuller account of the Eurasian ecologies of Abel-Rémusat's science of Buddhist Asia. In chapter 3, we follow his *Relation des Royaumes Bouddhiques* in circulation out of Europe and into the hands of Dorji Banzarov, Zava Damdin Lubsangdamdin, and Ngakwang Nyima: Inner Asian translators and interpreters of Faxian's *Record* whose works silenced Abel-Rémusat's humanist account in order to radically extend Qing-inflected Mongolian and Tibetan historical traditions unbeholden to Europe.

In chapter 4, we come to the content of these connected analytical projects. We explore the vast topography of Abel-Rémusat's interpretation of nearly every person, place, and thing in Faxian's *Record*. This was his vast Commentaire, the prodigious footnotes that gave Europe its first book-length study of Buddhist Asia. In chapter 5, I look at chains of interpretation by which the Mongolian and Tibetan translations of Abel-Rémusat's French rendering of the Chinese opened completely new readings of Inner Asian history. Importantly, these extended not a European scientific gaze but a Qing synthetic one, made from the picked-over corpse of Abel-Rémusat's unnamed, unacknowledged, and discarded science.

Finally, I offer a complete annotated translation of the Inner Asian *Record*. Because of space constraints, the main body of the translation is of the Tibetan. Even so, each section (sometimes each line, or each word in a line) of the Tibetan is read carefully against the broken chain of silence and speech in Mongolian, French, and Chinese that preceded it. The ways forward that the Tibetan made with the Mongolian, and the Mongolian made with the French, and French made with the Chinese are noted and explored in full detail in annotation. Reading these four versions of the *Record* against one another, I have tried to provide a complete translation of the previously unstudied (and mostly unknown) Tibetan version of this classic Chinese text that also comprehensively treats the Mongolian and French versions. My notes not only supply comparative anaylsis among all four versions but also cross-reference the Tibetan with pagination in the Mongolian, French, and Chinese so that interested readers can easily follow along whichever language most interests them at any point in the text.

To borrow Saidiya Hartman's phrasing, by pursuing this circulatory history I hope to say something new about the Eurasianist journey of Faxian's *Record*, but also thereby to "illuminate the contested character of history, narrative, event, and fact; to topple the hierarchy of discourse; and to engulf authorized speech in the clash of voices."[38] For it is as true of writing the absent past as it is of the world's flora that, as John Muir put it, "when we try to pick out anything by itself, we find it hitched to everything else in the universe."[39] The humanities makes knowledge along porous boundaries always already hitched to contiguous knowledge traditions. Here is a rooted thicket of rot and new life in which I, and you, and Faxian, and the Gobi monks and Parisian Orientalists and Tibetan refugees whom we shall meet, are already entangled. So let us tear out our eyes, sift through the dirt of this enmeshed and rooted forest floor, and think anew about disciplinary futures in the shadow of this centerless disciplinary past.

1

Chang'an to India

There are many ways to fix a life in text. One may start, as Faxian did in the *Record*, by infilling the space of a person. In that fifth-century account , Faxian's desires, virtues, and holy longing draw forth the crabbed lines of his written life. French, Mongolian, and Tibetan translations followed fourteen centuries later, though painted using different palettes and roped to dissimilar horizons. In all accounts about Faxian, including some current scholarly ones I introduce in this chapter, the scale of adversity that measures his achievements matches only the scale of his purpose. Setting out to find all that was missing in the Chinese Buddhist canon, for example. Or suffering ice-walled passes. Foreign babble. The sea.

There are many ways to fix a life in text.

The earliest of Faxian's known biographers were two lettered monks of the sixth century. Within fifteen years of each other, Sengyou 僧祐 (445–518) and Huijiao 慧皎 (497–554) wrote complementary biographical collections. Their protagonists were "caravan leaders" (Skt. *sārthavāha*): those who hauled the Dharma eastward across centuries onto the floury loess plateau of China's northwest. Sengyou was a popular teacher and master of the monastic code who, later in life, resided at Dinglin Monastery 定林寺.[1] Emperor Wu 武帝 (r. 502–549) of the fledgling Liang dynasty 梁朝 (502–557) revered this monk and reserved a place for him at court.[2] Sometime around 515, a few years before his death, Sengyou composed *Compilation of Notes on the Translation of the Tripiṭaka* (Chusanzang jiji 出三藏記集).[3] This is the earliest extant catalogue of Chinese Buddhist scriptures and one of the most impactful literary products of its time. Faxian haunts *Compilation of Notes.* Across its pages he is recorded as collector and translator of many dusty and sea-salted sūtras and vinaya texts. Sengyou also included a dedicated biography of Faxian in the fifteenth scroll of *Compilation of Notes*. There, Faxian is numbered as the sixth of ten exemplary Chinese "Dharma Masters" (*fashi* 法師) who laid the firmaments for the still-embryonic monasticism of the Liang period.

Sometime around the year 530, that other early and still existing account of Faxian's life was set to ink. This was Huijiao's *Biographies of Eminent Monks* (*Gaoseng zhuan* 高僧傳). Huijiao was a monk of Jiaxiang temple 嘉祥寺 perched upon Mount Kuaiji 会稽山.[4] The well-known *Biographies of Eminent Monks* organized lives from across four and a half centuries.[5] This was a personality-driven picture of the arrival of the Dharma into China, presenting 257 "eminent" but not "famous monks" (*mingseng* 名僧), including An Shigao, Kumārajīva, Dao'an, and Faxian.[6] *Biographies of Eminent Monks* was based in part on Sengyou's earlier work, though Huijiao occasionally expands certain episodes in Faxian's life in relation to narrative histories of the Māhāyana canon as it was coalescing in Liang-period China.[7]

Taken together, Sengyou's and Huijiao's biographical portraits of Faxian are distinct from the autobiographical *Record*. As the historian Yuna-ju Liu puts it, these two sixth-century biographies "provide fuller, more detailed representations of Faxian's life by narrating the various events in Faxian's journey as the story (*gushi*) of a single character."[8] In this chapter, I introduce the story of Faxian, based mostly on the unique memorializations of Sengyou and Huijiao, as context for the nineteenth- and twentieth-century Eurasianist circulation of the *Record* that will occupy the remainder of this book.

Birth and Death and the Monastery Place

In the year 337, Faxian was born into a family named Gong 龔. He was the fourth son but the first to live long enough to suffer teeth pushed through gums.[9] Faxian and his dead brothers were people of Wuyang 武陽, then administered by Pingyang city 平陽 along the Fen river in southern Shanxi 山西.[10] To guard his still-living son from whatever unseen force had killed his other children, the Gong patriarch sent a three-year-old Faxian to ordain as a Buddhist monk.[11] Perhaps the shroud of vows proved to be efficacious medicine, since Faxian would live eighty-three more years.

Still a child and still a monk, Faxian later returned to his natal home and the polluted world of the laity. While he was living again with his parents, some ailment stalked and then took hold of him. Away from the purifying space of the monastery, Faxian came close to following his brothers along those paths that come after dying. Terrified, Faxian's father rushed his boy back to the monastery, where over ten days he recovered.[12] Faxian would never again leave the monastery nor mix with the laity. Much distressed by his departure, Faxian's mother installed herself near the monastery gates, longing only to lay eyes upon her son. He, however, refused to be seen.

Sengyou and Huijiao both tell us that when Faxian was ten or eleven years old his father died. A grieving uncle implored his nephew to quit the monastery and take over Gong family affairs. Faxian flatly refused. He would live permanently as a renunciant within the saffron folds of the saṅgha (the Buddhist monastic community).[13] The uncle acquiesced, and the Gong family stopped trying to force Faxian away from the monastery. As if to affirm his monastic commitments and the Buddha's teachings on impermanence, Faxian's mother died soon after. Faxian emerged to bury her, then walked back through the monastery gates.[14]

On some later day, according to Huijiao, Faxian was toiling with other monks in rice paddies when a posse of food-starved bandits arrived to rob them of their grain. All the monks fled in a scene that Erik Zürcher notes encapsulates the civil unrest and "sheer terror" of the Later Zhao period 後趙 (319–351 CE).[15] All the monks fled, that is, except for Faxian. "If you desire grain," he told them, "Take as much as you wish. However, not practicing giving (*bushi* 布施, Skt. *dāna*) in the past has caused you to suffer hunger and poverty in the present. Now you are again thieving, and so I fear that you will similarly suffer in future lives. I, a humble monk (*pin dao* 貧道), am concerned in advance on your behalf!"[16] With karmic framing suspended weightily in the air, Huijiao tells us, Faxian turned and calmly walked away. The bandits fled, empty-handed.

In the years that followed, Faxian took higher ordination as a fully ordained monk, or *bhikṣu* (Ch. *biqiu* 比丘).[17] In the late fourth century, however, China was as yet without translated monastic codes or any authoritative lineage of monastic transmission.[18] What did taking higher ordination mean, monks like Faxian wondered? The historian John Kieschnick helps contextualize Faxian's worry, explaining that Buddhist monasticism developed in China during four distinct periods.[19] The earliest began in the first century of the Common Era, when Central Asian and Indian monks and merchants working with Chinese collaborators produced early translations, often more like sketches, of Buddhist scriptures and liturgical texts. Merchants and monks walking from Central Asia then brought the Buddha's Dharma to Chinese societies via texts (oral and material) that presented foundational teachings of the Buddha, including some sūtras. Some particularly inspired men and women later began to organize embryonic monastic institutions on Chinese soil. They distinguished themselves from the laity by shaving their heads and wearing robes, as well as by shirking filial responsibility and productive labor. Scandously, they propagated prayer, text, and liberation instead of children, soldiers, and taxes.

The next period, which Kieschnick describes as the formative era of Chinese Buddhist monasticism, encompasses the third to fifth centuries. In the third century, these early Buddhist practitioners increasingly sought to shape their monastic lineages according to Indian models, though these were still poorly understood. During the reign of Prince Qi of the Wei state 魏 (220–265), for example, a Central Asian monk named Dharmakāla 曇柯迦羅 (c. 249–253) arrived in Luoyang.[20] Aghast that Chinese "monastics" did not follow the vinaya other than in outward appearance, he founded a tradition of ordaining locals. He also translated into Chinese a pithy vinaya text titled *Mahāsāṃghika-vinaya-hṛdaya* (a portion of the much longer *Mahāsāṃghika-vinaya*), thereby introducing a version of the rules and procedures that ought to discipline a Buddhist monastic community. After two centuries without monastic codes, translated vinayas began appearing all around. A Parthian monk named Dharmakīrti translated the *Dharmagupta-karman* in Luoyang, for example, while another unknown monk translated the *Bhikṣuprātimokṣa*, or *Rules for Fully Ordained Monks*. But these fragmentary texts, translated with uneven ability and no agreed-upon conventions, did not form a complete monastic code. Without a single complete monastic code in Chinese, there could never be a legitimate saṅgha. And without a legitimate saṅgha, the dispensation of the Dharma from India into China would lack foundation, like water pouring through the fingers of the thirsty into baked sand.[21]

By Faxian's time, in the next century, aspirational heirs of Śākyamuni in China still lived their lives as best guesses. Were they just impersonating actual monastic followers of the Buddha? Down what karmic pathway would their future mind tumble on account of their transgressions? We read that although Faxian lived most of his life enclosed by the walls of a Buddhist monastery, and his days and nights were disciplined in the company of many fellow monks, he was "despondent" (*kai* 慨). He knew their lives rested precariously upon only a ribboned scriptural firmament of *sūtra* and *vinaya* (*jing lü* 經律).[22] Their waking, eating, praying, and dying were as yet imperfect and imperfectable.

Many other Chinese monks were similarly concerned, and an upswell of projects to systematize and complete the Chinese canon were under way around him. In the year 374, when Faxian was about thirty-seven years old, the monk Shi Dao'an 釋道安 (312–385) published the epochal *Comprehensive Catalogue of Sūtras* (*Zhongli zhongjing mulu* 綜理眾經目錄).[23] This was China's first catalogue of its first translated Buddhist scriptures. Hailing from present-day Hebei, Dao'an became a disciple of the Kuchean monk Fotudeng 佛圖澄

(232–348). He later settled in Chang'an 長安, where Faxian also lived. There he became the personal teacher of Emperor Fujian of the Former Qin 前秦.[24] In *Comprehensive Catalogue of Sūtras*, Dao'an provided a hierarchical template for ambitious scholar monks like Faxian. Here was a map of which texts were known and translated in China and which were not. *Comprehensive Catalogue of Sūtras* also modeled how to rigorously vet scattershot Chinese translations from previous ages: what was authentic (*zhen* 真) could now be distinguished from what was suspect (*yi* 疑) or false (*wei* 偽).[25]

Guidelines like these were written over generations, as they were in most Buddhist societies when trying to order an inheritance of Indic scripture. Sengyou, in the same sixth-century work that contains Faxian's earliest extant biography, instructs readers to determine "whether a text did not come from 'Western regions' (as in Central Asia or India) or whether a text had not been translated by a 'Western guest.'"[26] Here were essential *spatial* qualifications of textual authenticity in these early centuries of Chinese Buddhism. Could a line be drawn incontrovertibly between a text and the place of the Buddhadharma's origin? Had a translation been made, moreover, in the presence of a Western guest? Or had a Chinese translator walked the route to distant India, and there read and collected it? In the years after Dao'an and generations before Sengyou, Faxian strove after both markers of authenticity. With sturdy shoes and iron determination, he would join the "Central Lands" of India to China anew in space and text.

Walking West

Faxian was most likely sixty-two years old when he resolved to undertake the perilous passage to India. "That the Dharma spread into the eastern land is clearly the merit of the translators [who] crossed the dangers of the sand or drifted about among the huge waves," writes Huijiao, by way of introducing Faxian and the lives of China's other early traveler-translators. "[They] all did not consider [their] lives in order to die [for the sake] of the Way, [and] dedicated [their] lives to spreading the Dharma. China became enlightened only because of them, [and] their virtues should be venerated. Therefore, [I] put them at the beginning of this work."[27]

We do not know if Faxian considered death or companionship, but the monks Daozheng (道整), Huawei (慧嵬), Huijing (慧景), and Huiying (慧應) accompanied him at the outset. Despite the assumptions of European translators so many centuries later, including Abel-Rémusat, their journey was not a "pilgrimage" in any recognizably Christian sense of the word. These Chinese monks' preparedness to endure sand-choked desert and cruel mountain passes came instead from "striving for the Dharma" (*qiufa* 求法); striving, as Jacques Gernet has it, "to determine the true doctrine and bring back a greater number of texts from 'Buddhist kingdoms.'"[28] Faxian an early example of Chinese traveler-translators who survived and left accounts of their journeys. Many more died en route or never put ink to paper to tell their story.

Faxian departed Chang'an in 399 CE.[29] He and his companions walked westward, crossing the Long Mountains to reach Qiangui. They spent the summer rains retreat (*xia zuo* 夏坐) there and then pressed farther west through the Yanglou Mountains.[30] In time, they arrived at the garrison town of Zhangye, situated on the border of what is today Inner Mongolia and Gansu province. Zhangye was then enmeshed in some military conflict, however, so they could not proceed. Happily for them, both Sengyou and Huijiao write, the local prince hosted the stranded monks, providing food and shelter while they awaited safe passage. Before long, additional parties of wayward monks arrived and took shelter.

FIGURE 1.1. Possible painting depicting Faxian (center left) from Cave 169, Bingling Temple Grottoes, China
Source: *Foguang shan Buddhist Dictionary*

FIGURE 1.2. "Travelling monk 行腳僧圖" from Magao Caves, Dunhuang, Tang dynasty, late 9th century CE
Source: British Museum, Ch.00380

Isolated together, Faxian and his extended company undertook another summer rains retreat in the long eye of that arid frontier.

By the end of their summer retreat, armed conflict had subsided and the monks could travel. Faxian and companions headed westward once again, the party now also including the other marooned monks who had been waiting in Zhangye. In time they reached the garrison town of Dunhuang in northwestern Gansu province, where they stayed for one month. Outfitted by the governor, Faxian and his four original companions split from the other monks and crossed the Gansu corridor, which for Huijiao was the "moving sands" (*liusha* 流沙) and for Sengyou "the river of sand" (*shahe* 沙河).[31] Whatever its name, death was the topography of this cursed place. "There were no birds in the sky, no beasts upon the land.[32] Looking about, they saw nothing but vast, immeasurable land. [Only] by observing the sun . . . could they determine east and west. Only the sight of human bones marked their path. There were frequently scorching winds and malevolent ghosts; those who happened upon them by chance would definitely perish."[33] Though it is skipped over by Sengyou and Huijiao, Faxian wrote in the *Record* that after this perilous passage he and his party arrived in the kingdom of Shanshan. They rested a month in the city of Loulan, long since vanished but likely located near the seasonal salt marshes of Lop Nor.

In Shanshan, Faxian made note of the fraying edge of his familiar Chinese world in the fraying edges of tunics and robes. Though these locals dressed in nearly the same costume as Han people did, the Shanshan were clothed in coarser cloth and pressed felt. Faxian marveled especially at Shanshan thriving monastic scene, which was supported by a devoted prince and bloated with monks living disciplined lives on opulent campuses and appropriately based in the vinaya monastic code. "While dialects differed from region to region," Faxian observed in the *Record*, "all the monastics there studied Indian texts and languages." Faxian and company continued beyond Shanshan to the oasis and merchant cities ringing the Taklamakan desert. En route, we read, they marveled that Buddhist monasticism had found such fertile and enviable soil in this life-denying basin.

In Shanshan, a few of Faxian's companions left their weary party to follow other tributary merchant trails, such as those leading to Kāśmīra. Faxian continued doggedly over the course of many weeks, from Khotan to Kukyar, through the high passes and steep mountain walls of what we now call Ladakh. In time, Faxian's wayward companions reunited with him in the kingdom of Khaśa, where a local king was hosting a *pañcavārṣika* ceremony. This was a great quinquennial gathering for feasting and public monastic ritual performances founded, according to tradition, by the great Mauryan king Aśoka (c. 304–232).[34] In the high mountain light of this Dharma festival, we read, the trials of our monks' desert travel passed from weary feet and life-drained bones to quivered memory.

Continuing from Khaśa and stopping often along the way, Faxian, Daozheng, and Huijing traversed the mountainous barrier and entered the Ganges plains of Central India. Sengyou and Huijao both record that in the stark peaks of the Pamirs—known to them in Chinese as the "Onion Mountains" (*Cong ling* 葱嶺)—more than cold and altitude threatened Faxian's progress.

> The peaks accumulate snow in winter and summer. There are malevolent dragons there that spit poison and cause rain, snow, and sandstorms. The mountain paths are perilous, the cliff faces a thousand *ren* 仞 high.[35] In times past, people carved steps into the rock of the cliffsides; altogether [Faxian and companions] had to cross these in more than seven hundred places.[36] They further had to cross rope bridges suspended over rivers in more than ten places.[37]

On barren trails untrodden before by any of their Han countrymen, Faxian and Daozheng lost their dear companion Huijing. He had been silently leading their party through the throes of some glacial tempest along the narrow corridors of those hellish mountains. Suddenly, he collapsed. "I will die," he told Faxian, who had rushed to his side. "You must continue on; we cannot both perish!"

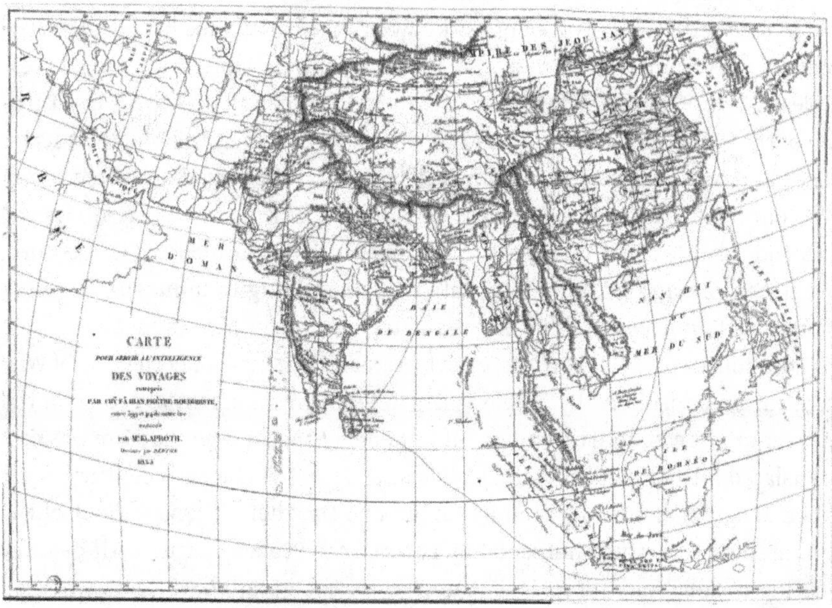

FIGURE 1.3. "Carte Pour Servir a L'Intelligence des Voyages Entrepris par Chy Fă Hian, Prêtre Bouddhiste, Entre 399 et 414 de Notre Ère," drafted by Julien Klaproth
Source: *Relations Des Royaumes Bouddhiques,* plate 426

These were his last words. Caressing Huijing's hand as he died, Faxian quaked. "Our intended journey will no longer be realized. It is destiny (*ming* 命). What else is there to do?"[38] There was only to continue. Picking frozen tears from their eyes, Faxian and Daozheng left Huijing's corpse laid upon the ice and rock and descended into what is now Afghanistan.

Their interminable alpine descent—down mountain cliffs, across perilous rope bridges strung over black water, and through steep valleys—led eventually into lush, rain-soaked plains and cropland. They had finally drawn near to the warm, fertile, life-giving climes of Madhyadeśa, the "Central Land" of India, the heart of Buddhist monasticism and the wellspring of the Buddha's word.[39]

Vulture's Peak and Wisdom, Perfected

Unlike in extant versions of the *Record,* Sengyou and Huijiao both write that the wearied but inspired Faxian and Daozheng immediately sought shelter at a monastery some thirty *li* (里) from the city of Rājagṛha (*Wangshe cheng* 王舍城) near

Vulture's Peak (*Qishejue shan* 耆闍崛山).[40] Soon after his enlightenment, according to received versions of events as known to Faxian and his biographers, the Buddha Śākyamuni had first taught the famous Four Noble Truths to five disciples at Deer Park in Sarnath. This was eventually counted as the "First Turning of the Wheel of the Dharma." According to later Mahāyāna Buddhist scriptures and communal memory, the Buddha's teachings on the "Perfection of Wisdom" (Skt. *Prajñapāramitā*) were delivered at Vulture's Peak. This was the "Second Turning of the Wheel of the Dharma." In Sengyou and Huijiao's account, but not in Faxian's *Record,* immediately upon arriving in India our traveling monk sought out Vulture's Peak, the staging ground for the Mahāyāna.[41]

The Chinese proto-canon was, even by Faxian's time, full of Perfection of Wisdom sūtras, considered by Mahāyānists to be the most essential record of the Buddha's most essential teachings.[42] It is thought that the *Diamond Sūtra* was first translated into Chinese by Kumārajīva at the start of the fifth century, right when Sengyou and Huijiao tell us Faxian and Daozheng staggered out of the mountains and arrived immediately at Vulture's Peak.[43] By the sixth-century writing of Sengyou and Huijiao, the story of the great charioteers who had brought the Buddhadharma to China prominently featured the translation of those texts. So important was the idea of Faxian's contact with that primal site of the Mahāyāna for his Chinese biographers that Huijiao makes it the centerpiece of his biography, though it is only a muted, shorter, and much later narrative in Faxian's *Record.*

Faxian and Daozheng had just arrived in Rājagṛha and were eager to make the short journey to Vulture's Peak, Huijiao writes, but the abbot of their host monastery had only words of caution for them.[44] The road was treacherous. Its pathways were stalked by lions with a taste for human flesh. No matter, replied Faxian. "One's lifespan is unstable, the future unsure. How can one abandon a vow made years ago, at the very moment of realizing its aim? Though it may be dangerous and arduous, I remain unafraid. There is no one who can stop me!"[45] And indeed, no one could. Leaving Daozheng behind and proceeding with two local monks as reluctant guides, Faxian realized his aim—Chinese contact with the wellspring of the Mahāyāna—and walked to Vulture's Peak.

Arriving at sundown, Faxian prepared to spend the night. His two guides, terrified at the prospect of never again seeing daylight, made a hasty retreat to the sanctuary of their monastery. Faxian arranged a seat in the dark upon the very stone where the Buddha had turned the wheel of the Mahāyāna. Faxian then burned fragrant incense and paid homage (*libai* 禮拜).[46] Overcome by reverence for the Dharma at this ancient site, we read, Faxian felt as if he were in the presence of the Buddha himself. Just then, three black lions appeared with wet lips and twitching tails. Faxian, focused single-pointedly on recollecting the

FIGURE 1.4. "Sākyamuni Preaching on the Vulture Peak 靈鷲山釋迦說法圖,"
Tang dynasty, 8th–9th century CE
Source: Stein painting 20, British Museum

Buddha (*nian fo* 念佛), continued chanting sūtras and ignored them. In his presence, the lions dropped to their bellies and fell asleep. Faxian later addressed them serenely while stroking their fur. Had they come to devour him? If so, they would need to await the end of his recitations. Had they come to test his resolve? If so, they would be wise to see the futility of their task and look elsewhere for meat. Late into the night, the lions slipped quietly back into the shadows, their stomachs empty.[47]

In the light of early morning, Faxian walked the return path to his host monastery. Along the way, he came across a ninety-year-old monk heading up the trail. Though the elderly monk wore tattered robes and scowled, Faxian recognized some holiness about him. This impression was confirmed when later he asked a young monk also walking up the trail if he knew the old man. "It is Dhūta Kāśyapa, the grand disciple," replied the young monk.[48] Otherwise known as Mahākāśyapa, he had been the foremost disciple of the Buddha Śākyamuni when the World Teacher walked these trails a thousand years earlier. According to the shared tradition of the Chinese and Indian monks walking past one another on the trail to Vulture's Peak (and of Huijiao and Sengyou writing about it a century later), Mahākāśyapa had been tasked with overseeing the First Council, when the recently deceased Buddha's body of teachings were systematized and set to collective memory.

Faxian stood dumbfounded in front of the young monk. He had just unknowingly crossed paths with the apparently deathless compiler of the Buddhist canon. Turning to rush back up the trail and prostrate himself before Kāśyapa, Faxian was blocked by a boulder that had tumbled across the path. Crying out of frustration, he resigned himself to lost opportunity and turned to continue downtrail to the monastery.[49] In Huijiao's telling, it was in this silent and fleeting encounter upon the slopes of Vulture's Peak, not in his reverential practice on its summit, that the vast space of Faxian's journey—and his young Chinese monasticism—was tethered to the vast time of the Buddhist dispensation.

Although Faxian had made contact with the site of the Perfection of Wisdom and the person who had compiled the Buddhist canon, Huijiao and Sengyou emphasize for their later readers that it was not on Vulture Peak but in Madhyadeśa, or "Central India" (*Zhong Tianzhu* 中天竺), that Faxian finally began to collect the scriptures needed to complete the Chinese canon.[50] Faxian dutifully obtained his first copies of the vinaya at the Mahāyāna monastery named Devarāja (*Tianwangsi* 天王寺), near a stūpa erected by King Aśoka in the city of Pāṭaliputrā (*Balianfu* 波連弗, modern Patna) in Magadha (*Mojie* 摩竭).[51] There, Faxian copied an entire edition of the vinaya belonging to the Mahāsāṃghika school (*Mohesengzhi lü* 摩訶僧祇律), as well as sections from the vinaya of the Sarvāstivāda school (*Sapoduo lü* 薩婆多律).[52] Also in Pāṭaliputrā, Huijiao and

Sengyou explain, Faxian obtained Abhidharma texts (*Apitan* 阿毘曇), part of a "basket" of scripture focused on itemizing and organizing references made elsewhere in the Buddha's discourses.[53] He also acquired various sūtras, such as the *Detailed Parinirvāṇa Sūtra*, one of a corpora of texts that describe the Buddha's passing and quintessential teaching that would remain widely influential in Chinese Buddhism thereafter.[54]

Though Faxian acquired texts in Magadha, even more notably, he devoted himself to the rigors of Sanskrit learning in order to read, copy, and translate Indian texts into Chinese ("to study the Indian spoken language and texts" 學梵語梵書, according to Huijiao, or as Sengyou puts it: "studying barbarian texts and the barbarian dialect" 學胡書胡語).[55] After many years in India, Faxian journeyed on to the lush shores of Ceylon. There, Sengyou and Huijiao tell us, he was beset with some bitter loneliness and scrutinized his shadow, his only remaining companion.[56] "Unexpectedly [one day], in front of a jade statue of the Buddha, he observed a merchant raising a round Chinese fan made of white silk as an offering. Involuntarily (*bujue* 不覺), Faxian became distraught and began to weep."[57] Though suffering from homesickness, the now septuagenarian Faxian stayed on in Ceylon for two years.[58] In the *Record*, he writes that he spent his time exploring various ritual traditions and holy sites. Predictably, Huijiao's and Sengyou's canon-focused biographical accounts have him only acquiring texts. According to the colophons of the later Chinese canon, in Ceylon Faxian did indeed obtain a copy of another vinaya, that of the Mahīśāsaka school (*Mishasai lü*彌沙塞律).[59] He also acquired collections of sūtras: the "Longer Discourses,"[60] the "Connected Discourses,"[61] and the *Saṃyuktāpiṭaka-sūtra*;[62] none of which, Sengyou notes, had as yet been translated into Chinese.

With so many prized texts in hand and the silk fan playing upon his melancholic mind, Faxian and his shadow began to look eastward toward China.

Return

Some thirteen or fourteen years after his departure, Faxian returned home aboard a merchant vessel that set off to sea intending to sail directly from Ceylon to China. He stood on deck watching the green island retreat toward the horizon. a clutch of holy texts carefully stowed away alongside the possessions of his two hundred fellow passengers. Many of them, we read in the *Record*, looked suspiciously upon Faxian. They worried that this monk, or perhaps the powerful but frightening objects he had stored below deck, could upset the unseen elements and beings who controlled the plains of salted water and wind before them. Benevolence and permission were required for safe passage, and this Chinese monk was out of place.

As Ceylon retreated from view, when they were at the full mercy of the ocean, a brutal squall overtook them. Terror added dangerously to suspicion and blame. Faxian's wrapped scriptures, the passengers soon decided, had brought this wicked weather upon them. Despairing that he and his texts would be thrown overboard into the hysterical sea, Faxian prayed to the bodhisattva of compassion, Avalokiteśvara (Guanshiyin 觀世音). In Huijiao's account, notably, he also took refuge in "the saṅgha of China" (*hantu zhongseng* 漢土眾僧).[63] While the boat, Faxian, and his texts stayed above water, the storm blew them far off course. They were eventually marooned on the island of Yavadvīpa (*Yepotiguo* 耶婆提國), which we recognize today as Java, a volcanic island in the center of Indonesia.

Faxian remained stranded there for five months before boarding another merchant vessel headed to Guangzhou 廣州. Only twenty days into that voyage, another gale struck, wreaking havoc upon this second vessel. As before, the crew quickly pointed to Faxian and his peculiar luggage as the culprits. "Because of carrying this monk onboard, we are facing difficulties!"[64] Another passenger jumped to the monk's defense. They would have to kill him as well, otherwise he would report Faxian's murder to the emperor of China, a devoted Buddhist, who would severely punish them. Pale-faced, the crew left Faxian alone and focused on navigating the furious water. After a hellish journey that again blew them far off course, a ribbon of earth appeared on the horizon. Drawing closer, they ecstatically identified Chinese fruits and other crops. But just where in China were they? Consulting the locals, they discovered they had washed up at the commandery of Changguang 長廣 to the south of Mount Lao 牢山. This was in the province of Qingzhou 青州, approximately 1,100 miles from Chang'an.[65] The local governor, a fervent devotee of the Buddha, learned that a far-traveled monk was stranded on deck in his harbor. He rushed to escort Faxian and his texts ashore, thus closing that long circuitous journey that had begun while walking westward into hostile desert and now ended with a salt-caked Faxian rowed ashore out of the Pacific, with vinaya in hand and many stories to tell.

In a strange twist of history, during the long years of Faxian's walking—in which he faced death and loss and enormous struggle—the complete vinaya had been translated already into Chinese. At least four complete vinayas, in fact, had been separately translated into Chinese while Faxian walked Eurasia chasing after the monastic code.[66] Neither Sengyou or Huijiao, nor the *Record*, tell us whether, upon learning this fact, Faxian collapsed to his knees.

Local officials at Changguang requested Faxian to stay on as their esteemed guest, and the weary monk at first acquiesced.[67] In time he began to travel more widely, his fame apparently spreading. From examining a variety of contemporary records and inscriptions, the historian Yuan-ju Liu proposes that Faxian's route from Changguang was most likely as follows: he stayed in either Jingkou 京口 or Pengcheng 彭城 in Jiangsu province from the winter of 412 through the summer of 413 before heading south to Yangzhou, either by land or by following the Yangzi River, past Gusu 姑蘇 (present-day Dangtu 當塗), arriving, at the invitation of the great monk Lushan Huiyang 盧山慧遠 (334–416), at the latter's namesake Mount Lu in present-day Jiujiangshi 九江市.[68]

The *Record* and the Buddha's Word

It appears to have been at Mount Lu, in the year 414, that Faxian began to compose the *Record*.[69] He likely started while at Mount Lu in the community of venerable Huiyang, perhaps even at that master's request. After two years, Faxian returned to Daochang in the capital Jiankang, possibly with an early draft of the *Record* already completed. There, in the company of the Indian monk Buddhabhadra 佛陀跋陀 (d. 429), he began to translate works he had collected in India, such as the *Mahāsāṃghika-vinaya*. Several of Faxian's translations of vinaya and sūtra are extant in the Taishō Canon: the aforementioned *Mahāsāṃghika-vinaya* in forty fascicles and the *Mahāsaṅghabhikṣuṇi Vinaya* in one fascicle;[70] the *Mahāparinirvāṇa-sūtra* in six scrolls[71] and the "Hinayāna" *Mahāparinibbāna-sutta* in three scrolls;[72] the *Vaipulyaparinirvāṇa-sūtra*;[73] the *Saṃyuktābhidharmahṛdaya-śāstra*;[74] and the *Kṣudraka-sūtra*, a short biographical anthology about such figures as the Buddha's chief disciples, Śāriputra and Maudgalyāyana.[75] According to one catalogue, a translation of an Abhidharma text in thirteen fascicles bearing the title *Za ebitan xinlun* is also attributed to Faxian and Buddhabhadra—but the text had already been lost by Sengyou's time. Two other Sanskrit texts acquired by Faxian were later translated into Chinese—the *Mahīśāsaka-vinaya*, which Faxian collected in Ceylon, was translated by Buddhajīva and Zhu Daosheng,[76] and the *Saṃyuktā-āgama* ("*The Connected Discourses*") was translated by Guṇabhadra[77]—both during the Liu Song dynasty (420–479 CE 劉宋).

It seems possible, as Liu has suggested, that the *Record* would have been completed in 416 using the communal procedures by which canonical texts were then translated and compiled at Daochang. In this scenario, Faxian would have sat at the center of an assembly of lettered monks and laity, including foreigners hailing from the Western Regions. The *Record* would have passed from memory to lips and to text only after collective scrutiny and verification. "The audience would have numbered upwards of one or two hundred members, among whom were Buddhabhadra, Huiguan, and Baoyun. There would also be numerous foreign monks, a number of whom would have had significant knowledge of the religions, geography, and customs of the Western Regions and India. The audience members certainly would have had numerous chances to question details in Faxian's account."[78] The *Record* that we know, and that Abel-Rémusat and his Inner Asian readers struggled to know, is likely a later recension of an original work forged using this public, critical process of text building.[79]

Much like Abel-Rémusat's early nineteenth-century science of Buddhist Asia (examined in chapters 2 and 4), and like the inter-regional world of Tibetan and Mongolian monastic colleges in the late and post-Qing that unmade Abel-Rémusat's work (examined in chapters 3 and 5), the original *Record* probably took shape in a community of authorized critics and associates. They made collective use of agreed-upon standards of truth and evidence, employing technical procedures of text criticism and comparison across multiple linguistic, historical, and spatial frames. It is little wonder that, as we shall see in chapter 4, the Parisian Orientalists saw a humanist, even an Orientalist philologist, in Faxian; and that the Inner Asian monks saw a distant echo of their own scholastic identities as writers of society and history in the long narrative shadow of canonical Indian scripture.

Conclusion

Faxian dedicated much of the remainder of his life to translation.[80] Some of the works, such as the *Mahāparinirvāṇa-sūtra,* had been unknown in China prior to his contribution. The six-scroll translation of this sutra that he and Buddhabhadra completed in 418 became the basis for an enduring (and decentered) exegetical movement in Chinese Buddhism known as the Nirvāṇa school (*Niepan zong* 涅槃宗), which was based in the sūtra's exposition of a personal, everlasting, and pure nature of liberation from saṃsāra.[81] After translating this later work, note Huijiao and Sengyou, "Faxian propagated and taught" what was contained in the *Nirvāṇa-sūtra*, "and all came to know of it."[82]

In 418, Buddhabhadra and the translation workshop at Daochang Monastery moved on from texts acquired by Faxian. Sengyou notes, "that which did not get translated numbered something approaching millions of words." Huijiao, who included Faxian in his list of exemplary translators, wrote that Faxian's translation work "transmit[ed] to later generations in millions of characters."[83] Here we again see these two scholars' different narrative interests in Faxian's biography—in text acquisition and translation, respectively.

By 418, Faxian's *Record* was likely verified and complete. By then eighty-one years old, Faxian made his way to Xin Monastery 新寺 in Jingzhou 荊州, contemporary Hubei province.[84] There, say Huijiao and Sengyou in chorus, Faxian died in some unwritten way, and the entire world wept.

In the China of Faxian's day, the Ganges plains—the homeland of the Dharma—was known in Sanskrit as Madhyadeśa, the "Middle Country," and translated into Chinese using no less than the name for its own sense of imperial centrality, the Middle Kingdom, *Zhong guo* (中國).[85] Such "borderland complexes," Antonio Forte writes, had Chinese monks until the seventh century feeling like outsiders to their own tradition—a pervasive decentering that Janine Nicol notes challenged "the entire Chinese understanding of the cosmos and man's place in it."[86] Chinese Buddhists during Faxian's time understood themselves as living in the intellectual and soteriological borderlands (*biandi* 邊地) of the Buddhadharma and its dispensation. Such was the situation of so many Chinese traveler monks between the late fourth and tenth centuries, and of so many Tibetan traveler monks between the eighth and fourteenth centuries, and of so many Mongolian and Siberian pilgrim monks between the sixteenth and twentieth centuries, and of so many scholars of "Buddhist Asia" between the eighteenth and twenty-first centuries.

Faxian's toil was, as Max Deeg argues, to journey from an intellectual and Dharmic periphery to a center *and then to return*: "a 'transportatio' rather than a 'transmission.'"[87] By such transport, peripheries became centers. And, indeed, this is what the record indicates occurred between the Jin (265–420), the time of Faxian's journey, and the first half of the Tang dynasty, the time of Xuanzang (seventh–ninth century). In this transitory period straddling two dynastic orders, "Chinese Buddhists no longer accepted the happen-stance transmissions of Buddhist texts by Indian or Central Asian Buddhist masters but were actively looking for specific textual and doctrinal authentic traditions (Faxian: Vinaya; Xuanzang: Abhidharma, Yogācāra, and other texts)—or in the case of the Sino-Korean monk Huichao 慧超 (first half of the eighth century), esoteric practices as well—at their claimed places of origin, mostly in Magadha in East India."[88] Thus Faxian's life, travels, writing, and death became entrenched in the always evolving histories of medieval Chinese Buddhist literary cultures.

However, never in the fourteen centuries that separated Faxian from its nineteenth-century treatment was the *Record* known or read in Siberia, Tibet, Mongolia, or Europe. Its circulatory history occupies the remainder of this book and begins with the Eurasianist contexts for the life and work of Jean-Pierre Abel-Rémusat, who disciplined Buddhist Asia in Europe by means of Faxian's ancient witnessing.

2
Beijing to Paris

Jean-Pierre Abel-Rémusat was devoted to antiquity and to the world's green flora. A surgeon's son, he first became a surgeon. Though he tethered the faraway world to writing, he lived and died and loved and learned only in Paris. Memorialists often called him a *génie*, a genius whose accomplishments derived from some inborn and inscrutable talent. In reality, his career was driven by disciplinary practice and site-specific conditions of possibility. Like many scholars of influence, he was born into advantageous social conditions that shaped, rewarded, and amplified his industry. And he was aided by silent women—a widowed mother and a young bride—about whom we know little.

To this day, Abel-Rémusat's life story has mostly been written by Sinologists, those who look for something of themselves in his long-ago "modern" and "professional" scholarship about Chinese language and literature. We could follow suit and trace more lines from his work to "modern" and "professional" Buddhist studies or New Qing studies (as Mark C. Elliot has done so eloquently).[1] We could pull down tangles of names and ideas and places once recorded by his pen, examining them in the treelike mode of field history: grabbing their leaves and tracing back their branches in the language of "origin" and "impact." It is a matter of convention and genre to write about Abel-Rémusat's work in this way.

But that is not the project of this chapter, or of this book. Here I am after the silence that is a condition for speech; for the centerless rounds of Eurasianist knowledge from which Abel-Rémusat poached his methodological innovations and disciplined Buddhist Asia as an object of systematic knowledge in Europe. And then, in the remainder of this book, the hunt continues to see how his science, in the form of his magisterial translation and study of Faxian's *Record,* was itself stripped and gutted, silenced and repurposed in the Siberian academy, the Mongolian monastic college, and the Tibetan refugee camp. My aim here is the refusal of circulatory history, the uncentered becoming of antifield history. Here we inquire after exchanges that both created and denied disciplinary identities and practices. Our work is to illuminate that raw plane of combination, connection, and exchange that made and unmade the disciplinary practice of Buddhist and Asian studies, Qing-inflected global historical orders, and the time and place of Mongolian and Tibetan experiences of modernist erasure and exile.

So let us first consider the circulatory knowledge and practice collected by a crippled boy lying bedridden in Paris, a surgeon in a field hospital belonging to Napoleon's army, and an awed young man staring upon the hieroglyphics of Chinese text. From such centerless sites of speech and absence, Faxian's ancient walking became the object of an emergent science in Europe before then becoming a condition for its erasure.

Youth

Jean-Pierre Abel-Rémusat was born in Paris on September 5, 1788. The family Rémusat, chronicled in Provence since the fourteenth century, had previously lived in distant Marseille.[2] His parents were Jeanne-Françoise Aydrée and Jean-Henri Rémusat, "one of the King's six select surgeons."[3] As a boy, Jean-Pierre was admired for "a just and observant spirit." He possessed a "buoyant memory" and "rare sagacity," quick to submit "everything to strict analysis."[4] His voracious curiosity was nourished by classical thought and natural philosophy, as was expected of privileged youth in Paris at the close of the eighteenth century.

In the reminiscences of Abel-Rémusat's eulogists, especially those who knew him personally, his scholarly accomplishments later in life were rooted in childhood tragedy. Once, while playing with friends, Jean-Pierre fell from a terrace onto the unforgiving stone of the Quai des Tuileries, along the Right Bank of the Seine.[5] The rest of his childhood was dedicated to healing. Though he was bound for years to bed and books, "his mind and his imagination . . . were free." His intellectual formation, moreover, "profited from the sacrifice which he was obliged to make of his pleasures."[6] By all accounts, Jean-Pierre was insatiable in his learning while bedridden. The study of natural philosophy engaged him most; in the style of the day, this encompassed not only plant and animal life but also the study of language, history, geography, mathematics, and philosophy.

FIGURE 2.1. *Abel-Rémusat, Portrait lithegraphié, par Devéria, Le Collège de France (1530–1930): Livre jubilaire composé à l'occasion de son quatrième centenaire* (Paris: Presses Universitaires de France, 1932), 355

After he recovered, Jean-Pierre kept to his cossetted life. As one colleague later remarked, "The young Rémusat knew no secondary school (*lycée*) other than his paternal home, no teacher other than himself." From bed, Jean-Pierre taught himself to not only write but also speak Latin "as if it were his mother tongue." Sunlight crept across his wall as he compiled a "substantial mythological dictionary over the course of this long retreat."[7] He was not, however, "content to confide all [his learning] to memory." Jean-Pierre strove instead to "distill" all knowledge "into a system" and "into writing."[8] His father eventually decided that the world's names and grammars were insufficient; his son needed formal education in analysis and criticism.[9] Jean-Pierre dutifully joined the École Centrale at the Collège de Quatre-Nations. Though he was only a teenager, "His piercing acumen was working already to track the progress of nations, to observe their customs, to study the influences that shaped them."[10] Using a system of his own invention, he continued to collect, dry, and catalogue botany at the École Centrale: "while not that of science," observed one of his later collaborators, "[his taxonomy] was lacking in neither method nor lucidness."[11] This idiosyncratic but systematic study of botany in his youth, many later agreed, provided methodological footing for the rigor and improvisation of Abel-Rémusat's revolutionary treatment of "the Orient," specifically, the Buddhist Nonwest.

Brittle human life, however, once again intervened to disturb childhood wonder. Jean-Pierre's father died unexpectedly in 1805. The teenager and his mother were suddenly without financial security, and Jean-Pierre saw no option but to soberly commit to a well-paid career in medicine. He enrolled at the École de Médecine de Paris just over a decade after its founding in 1794. He undertook his training while new medical faculties were created as part of the systematizing and disciplining of such institutions as the Université Impériale de France. Abel-Rémusat's entry into medicine began while France was upturned. In the previous year, the Sénat Conservateur had crowned Napoleon Bonaparte Empereur des Français, inaugurating the French Empire period (1804–1814, 1815). As one of his later colleagues put it, Jean-Pierre and other young Parisian elites were formed intellectually "in this terrible, insane, monstrous era, when . . . philanthropy and social virtues were what we practiced the least, perhaps because we spoke about them the most."[12] Even so, Jean-Pierre's desire for "knowledge of all things and an indefinite perfectibility" remained untamed and unnourished by the narrower focus of his medical training.[13] But as with many crossings examined in this book, horizons inverted suddenly. Destinations became origins.

A blink, and the cold scalpel became the Orientalist's pen.

Among those who recognized Jean-Pierre's intellectual abilities was Antoine-Isaac Silvestre de Sacy (1758–1838), professor of Persian and master Orientalist of France.[14] Already by the turn of the nineteenth century and then under Napoleon's imperial patronage, Paris emerged as the global center of systematic Orientalist scholarship. Around the time that Jean-Pierre tumbled to the stone as a boy, Orientalist fields of knowledge and aesthetic sensibilities in France were much amplified by then-general Napoleon Bonaparte's invasion of Egypt and Syria (1798–1801). Soon lavishly funded "imperial" research programs were devoted to the ill-defined, desire-saturated, and self-referential "Orient," such as the Institute de l'Egypte in 1798. Long before this, in the reign of Louis XIV (r. 1643–1715), court-patronized scholars examined the contemporary Ottoman and Qing empires.[15] By the dawn of the nineteenth century, France had for generations pursued access to the Qing "through the empire's diverse Inner Asian territories."[16] Eighteenth-century French strategists had long conspired "to plan bold ventures in diplomacy, trade, proselytization, and academic research" in the Qing from its Mongolian, Tibetan, Uighur, and Manchu edges.[17]

By Abel-Rémusat's student days, a cadre of scholars from the French Commission on the Science and Arts accompanied Napoleon on his conquests. They were known as the general's "learned division of the army," running lockstep behind the artillery with notebooks in hand.[18] Such developments were driven in untold ways by Antoine-Isaac Silvestre de Sacy. As Edward Said put it evocatively in *Orientalism*, Silvestre de Sacey was "a self-aware inaugurator . . . he acted in his writing like a secularized ecclesiastic for whom his Orient and his students were doctrine and parishioners respectively."[19] Sometime early on in his medical studies, Abel-Rémusat met de Sacy. He suitably impressed the master and then converted faithfully to the doctrine of the Orient. In their interimperial world and upon the wave of Napoleonic enthusiasm for scientific knowledge about the Nonwest, Silvestre de Sacy began to direct Abel-Rémusat's aspiration. The restless student now longed to exit the blooded floor of the surgery and to climb the tiered podiums of the French academy.

An opportunity came in 1805. Then, Silvestre de Sacy introduced Jean-Pierre to a storehouse of artifacts of the Orient: the curios collection of Charles Philippe Campion, the Abbé de Tersan (1736–1819).[20] By the dawn of the nineteenth century, the abbé's collection was an edifice to the material traces of the Nonwest; therein were displayed "different monuments of barbarism and of civilization, the infancy and the development of the arts among the world's different peoples."[21] A great many opaque objects pulled from this collection, which previously had resisted all categorization and analysis, were now being made to

FIGURE 2.2. Abbaye-aux-Bois, location of the Abbé de Tersan's curios collection and where a young Jean-Pierre Abel-Rémusat acquired the Chinese *materia medica*
Source: "Préau du cloître de l'abbaye-aux-Bois, Paris, France," Bibliothèque Nationale de France

speak the language of science. This labor was being done by those among the Napoleonic generation who became, under Silvestre de Sacy's mentorship, professional interpreters of the Orient.[22] Abel-Rémusat's career would take similar root, which after thirty years of poaching and writing would find expression in the first European arrangement of objects and texts and histories and placesunder the sign of "L'Orient bouddhique."

When first visiting the Abbé de Tersan's collection, Jean-Pierre became enamored with a bound Chinese text. The riot of indecipherable characters in the text were accompanied by images, which indicated to Jean-Pierre that it was a *materia medica*, a catalogue of medicinal plants and their therapeutic application. His abilities in botany and fascination with languages apparently inspired the abbé to gift him the text. In the reverential telling of his young life that came after his young death, that gift of the Chinese *materia medica* became an icon of the passage from ignorance to science, from the Nonwest to the West, in both Sinology and the professional study of Buddhist Asia.[23] This was due to the methodological principles Jean-Pierre developed to decipher it, which drew in original ways upon his childhood obsession with systematic analysis of the natural world. "Botany," recalled Silvestre de Sacy, "was thus the first cause of his love for Oriental languages, even the most difficult, such as Chinese, Tibetan, and Tartar."[24]

When Abel-Rémusat received the abbé's gift of the Chinese text, European knowledge about China was, according to the field historian David Honey, a "haphazard and aimless individual effort, vitiated by fantastic theories and lacking method."[25] Leaving the curios collection, Abel-Rémusat resolved not simply to learn Chinese but to unearth its grammar, to systematically name its literary genres of expression, to fit it with history and with place. And, by sheer tyranny of will, he did just that.

From the Surgery to the Academy

From the time he set to work on the Chinese *materia medica*, Abel-Rémusat's career took shape in the shadow of a trio of eighteenth-century French Orientalists. The first was the famed professor of Arabic, Étienne Fourmont (1683–1745). The other two were Fourmont's pupils: the Sinologist and Turkologist Joseph Deguignes (1721–1800) and Fourmont's nephew, Michel-Ange-André Le Roux Deshauterayes (1724–1795). Connected to the story of these pages, the latter was the first to present Europe with a Tibetan vocabulary and the Manchu alphabet. He was also a vocal critique of Deguignes's thesis that China was an

Egyptian colony and the author of *Histoire Générale de la Chine* in 1783 (which Abel-Rémusat's study of Faxian's *Record* regularly references and corrects).[26] Nearly everything Abel-Rémusat wrote and all of his field-building activity was defined against the legacy of these three. He considered them to be at best amateurs and at worst frauds. The disciplinary rigor that he later modeled and institutionalized in the study of China, "Tartary," and Buddhist Asia was founded in boundary work that specifically excluded this famous trio.

Fourmont was an early collector of Chinese materials for the Bibliothèque Royale.[27] Though he was recognized in his lifetime as a self-taught genius of the Chinese language, he knew little more than the radical system. What he gleaned of classical and vernacular Chinese came from time spent studying with Arcadio Hoang (*Huang Jialüe* 黃嘉略, 1679–1716),[28] a well-read Chinese Christian convert who was brought from Fujian to Paris by the Missions Étrangères around 1704.[29] A living curiosity among the erudite of Paris, Arcadio Hoang married and helped catalogue Chinese materials in the Bibliothèque du Roi.[30] He also began work on a grammar of Chinese and a dictionary using the "Kangxi radical" system (Kangxi bushou 康熙部首).[31] When Hoang died suddenly in 1716, Fourmont infamously published Hoang's work as his own.[32] Fourmont later published the unexceptional *Grammatica sinica* (1742), which in 1825 Abel-Rémusat exposed as still another fraudulent work (Fourmont had copied it directly from the Spanish Franciscan Francisco Varo's [1627–1687] *Arte de la lengua mandarina* of 1682).[33]

While the disciplinary weakness of this previous generation would preoccupy Abel-Rémusat later in his career, it was Joseph Deguignes's son who blocked his progress when the eager medical student set out to decipher the Chinese *materia medica*. Chrétien-Louis-Joseph Deguignes (1759–1845) had served as translator for a Dutch mission at the court of Qianlong from 1794 to 1795. At Napoleon's bidding, the junior Deguignes was to compose a Chinese-Latin-French dictionary.[34] In preparation, the many Chinese-Latin dictionaries written by generations of missionaries and merchants and collected at the Bibliothèque Impériale were put on hold for his personal use. Abel-Rémusat, a lowly medical student, was prohibited from accessing any of them. As he later recalled, "the Bibliothèque Impériale, which contains immense riches in all genres, has at most between sixteen and eighteen Chinese dictionaries. [. . .] Circumstances did not allow me to consult them. I never held them in my hands, I never even saw a single dictionary composed by missionaries in China and sent to Europe."[35] Although Deguignes had reserved all dictionaries in European languages, Abel-Rémusat was permitted access to the library's collection of dictionaries, vocabularies, and encyclopedic works in exclusively Asian languages. The most relevant of these had been acquired by European missionaries and merchants from the printeries of the Kangxi (康熙, r. 1661–1722), Yongzheng (雍正, r. 1722–1735), and

Qianlong (乾隆, r. 1735–1796) rulers of the Qing Empire. The blush of patronage for such polylingial reference works in the Qing court itself was aimed at systematizing and reforming education, administration, and translation of this vast polylingual empire.[36] The topics of these works were as diverse as celestial maps and Manchu and Chinese studies of the lunar eclipse, Chinese language encyclopedias for children, revised dictionaries, editions of the Confucian classics, Manchu dictionaries compiled under Qianlong, sundry collections of poetry and drama, and a great many parallel vocabularies and texts in Chinese, Mongolian, Tibetan, Sanskrit, and Manchu.[37]

Mårten Söderblom Saarela has illuminated the vast trans-Eurasian circulation of philology and history making connected to the study of Manchu language in the two centuries preceeding Abel-Rémusat's career. This "global philology" connected the early-modern world, very much including the sites of natural philosophy in Europe.[38] As Saarela shows, between the seventeenth and eighteenth centuries, scholars in Chosŏn Korea, South China, Tokugawa Japan, France, and Russia set to work deciphering Manchu in order to extend regional knowledge traditions.[39] Although they were focused on mastering the Manchu script, their aim was to open the treasury of Qing literary cultures to strategic inquiry elsewhere. For this reason, the Bibliothèque was full of Manchu works and polylingual collections patronized by the Qing court. In order to read the Chinese *materia medica*, Abel-Rémusat acquired Manchu-Tibetan-Chinese grammars and dictionaries and—by candlelight, after his day of medical studies—worked character by character to decipher it. He laboriously found equivalencies between Chinese characters and Manchu words, constructed his own vocabularies, drew up grammatical models, and slowly began to render meaning from its characters. In the process of working from these primary language sources, he found the mechanism of Chinese itself opened to him.[40] "Sinologues will appreciate," he later recalled dryly, "the difficulties which detained me while translating Chinese texts using an entirely Chinese dictionary."[41] Over the course of five years, the basis of a systematic Sinology, and a methodological standard for the study of the Oriental Nonwest generally, took form.

Abel-Rémusat's progress was disrupted not only by duplicitous gatekeepers in the Parisian academy but also by political upheavals in Napoleon's France. As caregiver for his widowed mother, Abel-Rémusat had been exempt from military conscription. In 1808, however, he was unexpectedly called to lay down books and take up arms. The Rhine and the Scheldt, the Alps and the Pyrenees were about to be crossed by Napoleon's armies—for which three hundred thousand men were needed immediately.[42] Silvestre de Sacy, intervening on his prodigy's behalf, ensured that Abel-Rémusat would avoid the front lines and be assigned instead to a Paris-based hospital for wounded soldiers.[43] The "painful study" of his *materia medica* continued, however, in between the rigors of work on his medical degree and the horrors of the surgery. In 1811—after five years of study and war service, and still without a medical degree—Abel-Rémusat published the results of his self-driven learning in Chinese. This was the epochal *Essai sur la Langue et la Littérature Chinoises,* cited by field historians to this day in their treelike field histories as the roots of modern Sinology.[44]

In its pages, Abel-Rémusat proved to Europe that Chinese possessed a grammar and, as such, complex structures of thought.[45] This was paradigm shifting, but the *Essai* did more: it was a work modeling a new kind of systematic methodology. It was written explicitly with field building in mind, a pedagogical instrument providing techniques for other Orientalists to work directly from Chinese sources.[46] Abel-Rémusat referenced this fact in the opening pages, wherein he characterized his labor with a quote from Confucius:

> There are those who cannot act, or who lack patience: let them persevere.
> What others do in a day, they do in a hundred;
> What others do in ten days, they do in a thousand.[47]

Lacking access to the "sole authority of European authors,"[48] Abel-Rémusat had used the polylingual reference works of the Qing, such as the *Kangxi Zidian* 康熙字典, as the basis for a comparativist methodological practice founded in technical mastery of primary sources.[49] (This is not to say that his original method was without faults, nor that the merits of the *Essai* with stood the test of time; the author himself realized this later in his career.)

The *Essai* was recognized and celebrated almost immediately among European Orientalists,[50] not due to its contents alone, but because Abel-Rémusat had based its claims in sources "made for the use of natives."[51] And he had produced a study meeting the rigorous standards of Silvestre de Sacy's systematic Orientalism. Abel-Rémusat, writes Denis Thouard, "a physician and naturalist by training, was of a generation who saw in the French Revolution the possibility of breaking with onerous religious and cultural traditions and to orient more willingly on the model of the exact sciences."[52] With the *Essai,* scholarship in Europe graduated from the amateur "mental *chinoiserie*" of Fourmont and his disciples to a science in the professionalizing Orientalism of the Napoelonic era.[53] Despite being entombed in field histories of Sinology down to today, the *Essai* was indebted to a new kind of interpretative practice, quite beyond Abel-Rémusat's "genius" or institutional developments at the Collège de France. This was a methodological innovation in the context of Sylvestre de Sacy's systematic Orientalism, based upon gleaning equivalencies and conceptual structues from polylingual Qing reference works. As we shall see, Abel-Rémusat's poaching from Qing sources was not limited to Sinology. It was also one of the fundamental disciplinary practices of his science of Buddhist Asia, whose apogee would be a translation and exposition of Faxian's ancient walking.

Soon after its publication in 1811, Abel-Rémusat was selected by "royal munificence" for a professorship in the Collège de France. He was appointed on November 29, 1814, during the Restoration—just months after the abdication of Napoleon, his brief exile to the island of Elba, and the re-enthronement of King Louis XVIII. A minister "who was a friend of the arts and sciences" convinced Louis to create two research chairs at the Collège de France: one in "Chinese and Manchu-Tartar languages and literatures" and the other in Sanskrit. Abel-Rémusat was appointed to the former and Antoine-Léonard de Chézy (1773–1832) to the latter.[54] This made Abel-Rémusat Europe's first professional scholar not only of Chinese but also of the languages, philosophies, literatures, and political structures of the Manchu-ruled Qing Empire (Tibetan, Mongolian, Manchu, and Uighur). In the imperial gaze that organized Abel-Rémusat's milieu and all his scholarship, not just the Chinese but these "Tartar" communities too "owed" the newly appointed Abel-Rémusat "all intellectual culture, from the alphabet to metaphysics."[55]

Abel-Rémusat's inaugural lecture at the Collège de France, in 1815, was titled "Programme du cours de langue et de littérature chinoises, et de tartare-mandchou." Later published, it reverberated widely in Europe, described for example in the Anglo *Asiatic Journal* as heralding the destruction of long-held European misunderstandings about "the philosophical character and literary genius of the Chinese nation."[56] He opened the 1815 "programme du cours" with more immediate, methodological issues in mind: "We have no model to follow, no hope for counsel; we must, in a word, suffice for ourselves and draw everything from our own provisions."[57] In the eighteen years that he held this research chair, from ages twenty-six to forty-four, "the study of Chinese in France (and later, elsewhere in Europe) was beginning to take the form it was to hold for the next 150 years," which "set high standards of scholarship which was to become the hallmark of the French school of sinology, known by its preference for philology and translation."[58]

As the editors of Abel-Rémusat's monumental *Mélanges Asiatqiue* put it in 1825, with his "numerous dissertations upon points of criticism or philosophy, mémoirs of small scope, fragments pulled from works written in the languages of Asia, and delivered to the knowledge of Europeans . . . M. Abel-Rémusat is one of those who drew from these methods (*moyens*) the most advantageous portion."[59] In this sense, Edward Said's description of Silvestre de Sacy, Abel-Rémusat's mentor, applied equally to his mentee during his seventeen years as research chair: "because his work virtually put before the profession an entire systematic body of texts, a pedagogical practice, a scholarly tradition, and an important link between Oriental scholarship and public policy . . . [Here] was a self-conscious methodological principle at work as a coeval with scholarly discipline."[60] Abel-Rémusat's revisionist project was similarly focused. However, in nearly all his scholarship he extended his mentor's "self-conscious methodological principles" in original ways by making use of textual artifacts from "the conquering Tartars of the Heavenly Empire," or the Qing.[61]

Though it is largely forgotten among field historians today, at the Collège de France Abel-Rémusat's lectures and quickly accumulating publications focused not only on "China" but also the systematic study of Inner Asia, such as surveys of Mongolian chronicle and astrological systems, Manchu ritual texts, and the structure of Tibetan "lamaist hierarchies."[62] Abel-Rémusat also wrote critical works on the grammatical structure of the languages of the other ethnic groups of the Qing Empire—Mongolian, Tibetan, Uighur, and Manchu—as well as their inter-Asian historical relations.[63] One early and influential work (published alongside the *Essai* in 1811) was "On the Study of Foreign Languages Among the Chinese," which appeared in several popular publications, like the *Journal des Savants* and *Extrait du Magasin Encyclopédique*.[64] Abel-Rémusat revealed to an incredulous Orientalist readership that Indic languages had been widely studied in China for millennia, especially Sanskrit and other "sacred languages" (*l'idiome sacré de l'Inde*) grouped together as the *langage de Fan*, the language of the Buddha.[65]

In recent decades, scholars contributing to revisionist turns in the study of late-imperial Chinese history, such as the so-called "New Qing history," have discovered the value of Manchu sources and have understood the Qing as an imperial formation made along its Inner Asian frontiers. But as Mark Elliot noted in a lecture delivered to the Collège de France celebrating the two-hundredth anniversary of Abel-Rémusat's appointment, this turn to Inner Asian sources on Chinese history is only a rediscovery of methods pioneered by Abel-Rémusat: "Abel-Rémusat helped lay the foundations of both modern Sinology and modern Manjuristics."[66] So too did he lay the methodological foundations for what would later be called Buddhist studies, from his first work on the historicity of the Buddha to his final work on Faxian's *Record*.

Disciplining "La Religion et les langues de Fo"

In his extended introduction to the 1836 *Foĕ kouĕ ki, Ou Relation des Royaumes Bouddhiques*, Ernest Augustin Xavier Clerc de Landresse memorialized the deceased

Abel-Rémusat's immense contribution to the academic study of Buddhist Asia in Europe.

> Twenty years ago, when M. Rémusat began to occupy himself with Buddhism, there were no models to follow; there was neither counsel nor hope for assistance. This celebrated religion had been the subject of only a very few essays, whose results were in any case limited by haphazard comparison and reckless conjecture. We were hardly occupied with its moral abstractions and metaphysics, and of those who were tempted to glance in that direction, some gave up and others failed to make them sensible. Too often these were rendered using expressions that do not correspond to any of ours, which group differently together, and which are made from so many metaphors taken from material or sensory objects other than those which formed our figurative language. "Emptiness" for "spirit," "ignorance" for "material" (*matière*), "appearance" for "the body," the five "roots" for our organs, the five "obscurations" (*poussières*) for our senses, the five "heaps" (*amas*) for our faculties, and innumerable other terms of the same kind; all must be taken in a sense so far removed from the ordinary sphere of our ideas, that for a long time they were able to elude even the most exact understanding of the texts.[67]

European missionaries had for centuries documented the life and exotic ideas of *la religion de Fo*, and in many cases translated short sections of texts into Latin and other European languages. But it was Abel-Rémusat who transformed the newly invented "Buddhist Asia"—a continuous field of "Oriental" interaction and relation across time and space—into the object of a comparative "science," a term only just being cleaved off from "natural philosophy" in the European academy.[68]

But how? According to his colleagues across Western Europe and its colonies, as well as in Russia, Abel-Rémusat had successfully disciplined Buddhist Asia using methodological innovation, a prolific publication record, and institution building. As Eugène Jacquet (1811–1838), himself a pioneer in the study of Indian numerals, said in a eulogy, while "a science hoisted toward its perfection is always the labor of more than a century, the fruit of competition between so many great minds (*grands esprits*)," Abel-Rémusat had hoisted his science of Buddhist Asia toward its perfection in only a little over two decades, and largely by individual effort.[69] As Silvestre de Sacy put it reverentially, Abel-Rémusat's scholarship was always "justified at minimum by proofs and examples predicated on reading and examining a great number of original texts."[70] In the shadow of his labor, not only Sinology, the study of Inner Asian languages and literatures, and Buddhist studies but also Asian studies generally would develop over the course of the middle and late nineteenth century.

A complete picture of the European understanding of Buddhism when Abel-Rémusat took his position at the Collège de France in 1815 is beyond the scope of this chapter.[71] However, a quite relevant glimpse comes from Michel-Ange-André Leroux Deshauterayes (1724–1795), the disciple of the fraud Fourmont introduced above. Abel-Rémusat sought to edit and publish Deshauterayes's mostly unpublished eighteenth-century essays during the 1820s, though largely without success (they were too unfinished and too problematic). An exception is the 1780 essay "Recherches sur la religion de Fo," prepared and published by Abel-Rémusat in the *Journal Asiatique* in 1825. Therein, Deshauterayes summarizes eighteenth-century European views on the "doubled nature" of the religion of "Boudh or Bouda so well-known in China under the name *Fo,* and in Japan under that of *Chaka.*" Buddhism, writes Deshauterayes, possesses an external aspect focused on "the worship of idols, teaches the transmigration of souls, and prevents from eating that which has had life," and it possesses an internal aspect that "asserts nothing but voidness or nothingness, does not recognize penalties or rewards after death . . . [and] is a doctrine that in this regard is entirely moral, for its object is the victory of the soul over her dissolute afflictions, if only there could ever be a morality where nothing exists that is real."[72]

From his post at the Collège de France, at the center of institutional Orientalism in Paris, Abel-Rémusat complicated the old suppositions of Europeans as sketched by Deshauterayes. The dualistic external idolatry and internal philosophy, Abel-Rémusat would show, was only a superficial impression. His disciplinary effort sought instead "to trace effects to causes and from idolatry to metaphysics" in "Buddhist philosophy," and to "distinguish the exterior doctrine, which is only an allegorical polytheism, from the interior doctrine, which consists in a few simple dogmas, such as the unity of God, the spirit opposed to matter, and in a physicalist explanation of natural phenomena."[73] Buddhism thus appeared in Abel-Rémusat's pioneering reading not as some exotic nihilism but rather as a life-affirming form of idealism, a mystical union even.[74] Hegel, Schopenhauer, and Nietzsche all came to know about Buddhism by reading Deshauterayes, Abel-Rémusat, and those in the latter's disciplinary sphere of influence, like Julius von Klaproth, Stanislas Julien, Isaac Jacob Schmidt, and Eugène Burnouf.[75] Buddhism, on Abel-Rémusat's view, appeared as a kind of "Oriental" systematic inquiry legible to, and thus a resource to help expand, European natural philosophy. But Abel-Rémusat's disciplinary efforts were focused not on the content of Buddhist philosophy but on a rather new and quite more expansive object: the geography and history of l'Orient bouddhiste.

Conceiving "Buddhist Asia" with Leibniz and the Qing

In addition to his debt to eighteenth-century philology and the technical rigors of his mentor's systematic Orientalism, Abel-Rémusat's disciplining of Buddhist Asia depended upon a methodological practice of polylingual analysis in order to draw forth models of equivalency and hierarchies of difference. That practice had two specific, though only rarely acknowledged, sources. First was a pre-Darwinian model of racialized and nationalized descent derived explicitly from the great German philosopher and mathematician Gottfried Wilhelm Leibniz (1646–1716). The second were methodological principles derived from Qing polylingual reference works and models of language and "philosophical" equivalency.

Abel-Rémusat understood his nineteenth-century scholarship about Buddhist Asia as extending Leibniz's seventeenth-century work to model human similitude. Though Abel-Rémusat references Leibniz in a number of his published works, a concise summary comes in the former's long review of Julius von Klaproth's *Asie Polyglotte* (1823, 1831), a monumental contribution to the classification of Asian languages .[76] Leibniz, in Abel-Rémusat's view, was the first to understand that from the comparison of languages comes knowledge of "the origin of nations."[77] Before Leibniz, just as before Abel-Rémusat in the matter of Buddhist Asia, research had focused upon "objects that were too narrow" and pursued scholarship only "in the interest of a [limited] system." Such pitiable analysis could only produce "partial or indecisive" results.[78] After Leibniz, just as after Abel-Rémusat's field-building work, a more universalist, comparative attention was fixed on "ideas about the descent of populations (*peuples*), the diffusion of diverse families in Europe and Asia, and their proximate relations (*rapports de consanguinité*)."[79] By such "means" (*moyen*), Abel-Rémusat exulted, European scholarship about human difference had come to understand, "with the degree of certainty desirable in such matters," the "mix of races which melded together to form most modern nations."[80]

Using "the same procedure," Abel-Rémusat and his colleagues had similarly "recognized the original community of tribes now separated by extraordinary distances" and produced an "almost complete genealogical table" of the original communities that populated ancient Eurasia.[81] Leibniz's project on universal characteristics, which understood all diversity as mirrored and relational, proposed that all difference could be translated into a single grammar using the appropriate means. So too, Abel-Rémusat and his closest colleagues, like Klaproth, approached Buddhist Asia as a vast continent of similitude overlaid by only superficial difference. Its mosaic of scripts, peoples, and ideas masked vast networks of relation, interaction, and mobility. Using the appropriate scientific means, Abel-Rémusat and his close colleagues had made history, philosophy, and geography from finding and translating mirrored-language and concepts in such "*idiomes*" as Chinese, Sanskrit, Manchu, Mongolian, Pāli, Tibetan, Burmese, and Korean.[82] It was in this Leibnizian frame that Abel-Rémusat imagined his scholarship, not only of Chinese and Manchu languages and literatures but especially his science of Buddhist Asia.

An example is his 1831 "Ouvrage Sur Le Bouddhisme," one of his last major works on this topic before the posthumous publication of his study of Faxian's *Record*.[83] In "Ouvrage," Abel-Rémusat describes a Leibnizian model of descent, diffusion, and proximity in this newly imagined relational continent: "four large missions spread into countries bordering Hindoustan; the faith (*la foi*) was established in eastern Persia; the inhabitants of the kingdoms of Kachemir and Kandahar received it and introduced it to Ceylon." In a second period, zealous missionaries spread Buddhism in India "below the Ganges, in Ava, in Siam, among the Birmans; others in Bactria, in little Boukharia, in Chine, in Korea all the way to Japan." This was the world inhabited and described by Faxian at the turn of the fifth century. A third dispensation came, according to this pioneering tableau, with "Lamaism, or reformed Buddhism"; at the start of the fifth century, "samanéisme, which is primitive Buddhism, had already penetrated into Tibet, without being able to maintain itself; two hundred years later, it was the dominant religion." From there, because of "frequent incursions of the Tartars into the northern part of China" and the military successes of "the tangouse race" across Central and Inner Asia from Khotan to the Pacific Ocean, Buddhist Asia was formed.[84] In such ways, Abel-Rémusat traced his "genealogical tables" of l'Asie bouddhiste, vast surveys recovering likeness from only apparent historical, geographical, linguistic, and philosophical difference.

Within that project, Abel-Rémusat had more immediately used his methods to persuade Europeans that the Buddha had been a man in history. For generations—indeed, centuries—prior, the Buddha had been known among Europeans only in the mix of a primitive ether of names and ideas, unrooted from any specific place and torn from any specific history. This was not the hierarchical, evolutionary primitivism of Tylor, Bruhl, or any of the social Darwinist authors of Nonwestern difference who came decades later in the professionalization of sociology and anthropology. This was the earlier primitive of the Nonwest imagined in European natural philosophy: "a uniform space-time continuum that constituted the substrate of history—a first, ageless, self-sufficient world where unity supposedly reigned . . . Despite the disparity in customs and the diversity in appearances, the same beliefs were present everywhere."[85] With this assumption, there was no impulse to differentiate, define, or specify. The need was only for unsubstantiated equivalence and half-hazard comparison. Against this centuries-long trend, Abel-Rémusat defined, specified, compassed, and traced the Buddha—a man, in history—and Buddhist Asia—a plane of interaction and relation beyond any particular place or time. He did so by inventing new, "scientific" ways to read primary sources in multiple registers against one another, thereby unearthing a startlingly vast, interactional topography. Its concrete forms could now be construed in the language of fact and event, defined against the abstracted field of the Nonwest.

Indeed, just as Abel-Rémusat worked tirelessly to teach himself Chinese, beginning in the 1810s he used the same kind of polylingual Qing sources to draw equivalencies between the names of Buddhist Asia. Among other European scholars at this time, those unequipped with his comparative methods, the Buddha remained interchangeable with the god Mercury. Or he was Odin. Or he was Ethiopian, since in some missionary accounts his statues were said to have curly hair and "thick lips." Or, like much of the Oriental Nonwest for a time, the Buddha was said to be of Egyptian lineage just as India and China, alternatively, were considered to be an Egyptian colony and, as Deguignes stubbornly maintained, Chinese characters were derived from Egyptian hieroglyphics.

In 1816, a year after Abel-Rémusat had taken his chair at the Collège de France, George Stanley Faber could write with supreme confidence in *The Origin of Pagan Idolatry: Ascertained from Historical Testimony and Circumstantial Evidence* (whose three volumes open with the epigraph: "Every reasonable Hypothesis should be supported by a fact") such things as: "The twenty two Buddhas, like the fourteen Menus, may all be reduced to two, Adam and Noah: for Buddha is the very same person as Menu" or "Buddha is at once confessed to be an Avatar of Vishnou, and pronounced to be no other than the mystic Om by which name the Trimurti is wont to be designated."[86] The primitive Nonwest was not only placeless, timeless, and interchangeable; it existed already within the knowledge traditions of the West. For Faber, the Buddha was as available to the European gaze among the Celts and Goths as in "Thibet" and Siam.

While Abel-Rémusat carefully traced his tableaux from Qing reference works, appeals to the ether of the Nonwest in order to identify the Buddha and Buddhism were already beginning to lose currency among Europeans. Some, like the British Orientalist Sir William Jones (1746–1794), considered that the Buddha might have been a historical figure, but insisted along with generations of missionaries that he was "a negro" of African, most likely Ethiopian, stock. In 1817, Michel-Jean-François Ozeray published *Recherches sur Buddhou ou Bouddhou, Instituteur Religieux de l'Asie Orientale.*[87] Though unremarkable in its scholarship and fanciful in much of its content, Ozeray's widely read book made one vital claim: the Buddha had been a historical figure and a philosopher, not only an idol, whose teachings later washed over Asia in a great many languages.

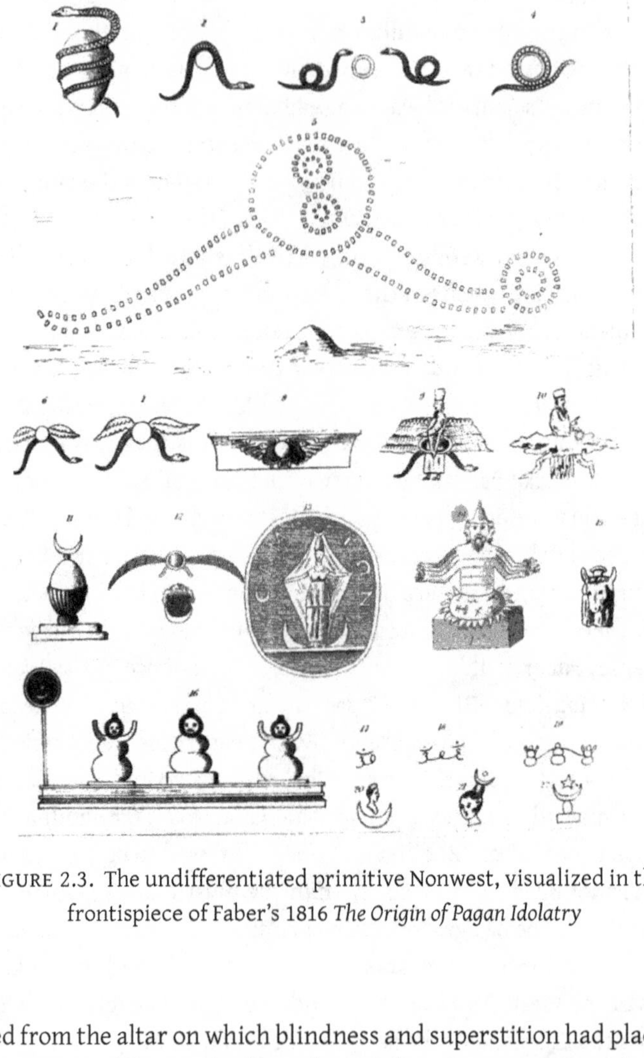

FIGURE 2.3. The undifferentiated primitive Nonwest, visualized in the frontispiece of Faber's 1816 *The Origin of Pagan Idolatry*

"Removed from the altar on which blindness and superstition had placed him," Ozeray wrote, "Bouddha is a distinguished philosopher, a sage born for the happiness of his fellow creatures and for the good of humanity. A deified man, he is the foremost of religious law-givers of eastern Asia." But Ozeray's analysis was undisciplined. His claims lacked method, were unaccountable to any field, and were presented without evidence.

In an 1819 article entitled "Note Sur Quelques Épithètes Descriptives Du Bouddha," Abel-Rémusat disproved the "Black Buddha" thesis and fitted Ozeray's unscholarly conjecture with evidence derived from a variety of textual sources in, among other languages, Chinese, Manchu, Mongolian, and Tibetan. The qualities of the Buddha's body represented in statuary and paintings were not "African," he revealed, but rather so many physical manifestations of enlightened realization well attested and widely explained in the textual and visual traditions of Buddhist Asia.[88] In dozens of major publications over the 1820s, Abel-Rémusat continued to outline the archipelagos of its connected and mobile histories. The Buddha had been a man, in history, who had lived in India. For centuries, even millennia, Indian linguistics, rituals, and philosophical forms had been known and widely studied across Eurasia. Japan could be thought of in new spatial and temporal relation to Cambodia, or Java, or Ceylon, or Mongolia. The ethical and metaphysical teachings of the Buddha Śākyamuni were preserved, fossil-like, in Indic languages but also in such languages as Korean, Manchu, Tibetan, Thai, Uighur, and Persian. Here were the dispersed Eurasianist methodological sources of the disciplining of Buddhist Asia.

A good example is a Qing reference work available to him in the Bibliothèque Nationale, which he used, as far as I have been able to tell, at the very start of his study of Buddhist Asia. In Abel-Rémusat's hand-copied edition, still extant in the archives of the Bibliothèque Nationale de France, it is titled the *Man, han, si-fan tsi yao, Vocabularium pentaglottum, Samskriticum, Tangutanum, Mandschuanum, Mongolicum et Sinicum, cum latina interpretation Essential Collection of Manchu, Chinese, and Tibetan Words.* This was the *Man han xi fan ji yao* 滿漢西番集要, which used three scripts to write Buddhist technical terminology in five languages (Mongolian and Sanskrit added to the three listed in the title). Abel-Rémusat understood the provenance of this text from the writing of the great Jesuit missionary to the Qing court, Jean Joseph Marie Amiot (1718–1793). Amiot lived in Beijing for forty years and was a confidant of the Qianlong emperor. He was an early European authority on "Chinese philosophy" and a translator of Qing imperial literature.[89] According to Amiot, the "dictionary or vocabulary" was composed by order of the Qianlong emperor "to assist those among his subjects who, because of polity (*état*) or employment, are obligated to correspond with Tibet."[90] Various lettered Manchu and Han Chinese, as well as Tibetan and Mongolian lamas, set to work.

Having traced over its lines and added French and Latin to the chain of meaning, Abel-Rémusat became convinced that the *Man han xi fan ji yao* was in fact "a kind of theological, philosophical, and moral collection, for use among sectarians of the Bouddha in Hindoustan, Tibet, Tartary, and China."[91] He gleaned from its arrangements of ideas and themes an entire doctrinal treatise of Buddhism, "la religion de Fo." And he saw in the language equivalencies of the Qing both a model and a source for methodological practices in the scientific study of Buddhism: an "authentic synonymy" listing the proper names and "the particular philosophical expressions of this cult" across the many "langues de Fo" and rooted in the "original Sanskrit."[92] As always for Abel-Rémusat, in the Leibzinian frame, finding "native" models of language equivalency from

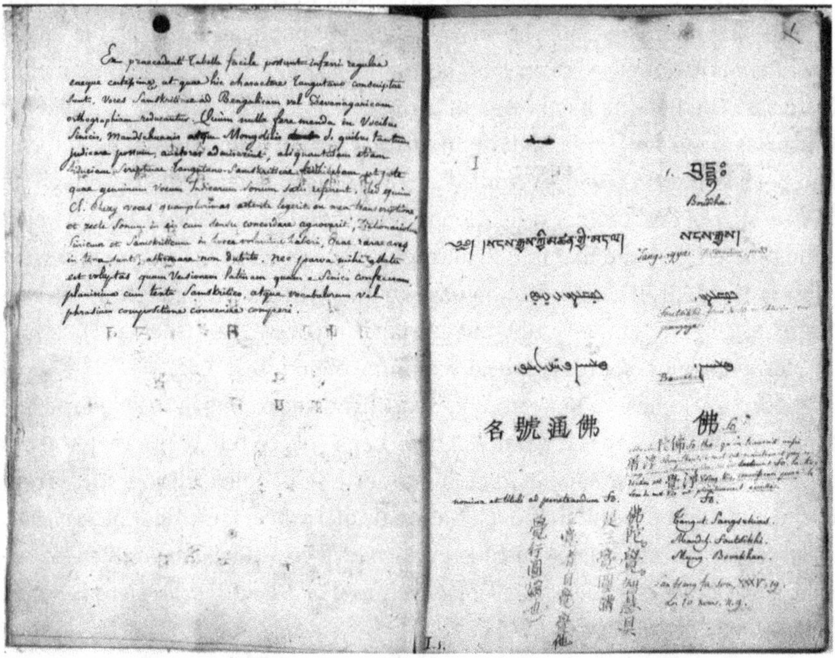

FIGURE 2.4. “Abel-Rémusat’s 1812 handwritten names of ‘Buddha’ in Chinese, Tibetan, Manchu, and Mongol from *Man han xi fan ji yao.*” *Vocabulaire bouddhique pentaglotte copié et traduit par Rémusat. Sanscrit, tibétain, mandchou, mongol, chinois*
Source: Bibliothèque Nationale de France. Département des Manuscrits. Sanscrit 1758

the Qing Empire was considered the same as uncovering the conceptual unity, shared histories, and continuous plane of doctrine of “Buddhist Asia.” Here was a “philosophical system of Indian origin, that serves as the basis of the religious convictions of all the people of eastern Asia.”[93]

This pentaglot Buddhist vocabulary from Qianlong’s court supplied Abel-Rémusat with comparative principles and resources that he used in his earliest and most influential work. As revealed in an introductory essay to the *Man han xi fan ji yao* in 1825 , Abel-Rémusat wrote his groundbreaking 1819 “Note sur quelques épithètes descriptives du Bouddha”—which proved to Europe that the Buddha had been a historical figure in India—by summarizing sections from this Qing text on the bodily attributes and epithets of the Buddha in five languages. This was the reference and methodological model by which he disciplined Buddhist Asia and disproved the likes of Sir William Jones’s belief that the Buddha “had to have been a negro come from Ethiopia to Hindoustan.” With the *Man han xi fan ji yao* in hand, Abel-Rémusat—still in the early years of his career at the Collège de France—could show that the Buddha had been born in Central India; a "fact established by too many witnesses."[94] And years later, with Faxian's *Record* in hand at the end of his life, Abel-Rémusat would give Europe its first master statement of his science of Buddhist Asia, also using references and methodological resources overwhelmingly derived from the Qing Empire.

Faxian's *Record*

Hauling primary texts across the epistemic frontiers of the West and Nonwest, Abel-Rémusat and his milieu disciplined Buddhist Asia into the object of a science. Working in the frame of Silvestre de Sacy's systematic Orientalism, he charted the continent of Buddhist Asia through the lens of Qing reference works, all in order to fulfill Leibniz's vision of a comprehensive, universal grammar of human linguistic, racial, and philosophical difference.

The apogee of Abel-Rémusat's project was his translation and study of Faxian's *Record*, the first European scholarly study of Buddhist Asia. In one of the few notes in a field history on this vital but forgotten work, Donald Lopez comments in passing that "For the European view of the life of the Buddha, it was the first concerted attempt to identify the places in the Buddha's biography with actual locations in India . . . Abel-Rémusat's work represents the most detailed life of the Buddha to appear in Europe up to that time."[95] Max Deeg adds, "It is clear that this astonishing achievement at that time, which is often referred to as the beginning of scientific Sinology, can no longer do justice to the current state of research. The reaction of contemporary scholars, however, showed that the meaning of the text for Buddhology, which was still in its early stages, was well recognized."[96]

Abel-Rémusat supplied some of the backstory for his Faxian project in his 1830 lecture at the Institut de France, which opened this book.

> [The *Record* was] unknown to me other than from the short extract made by Deguignes, and from a few passages reported in the historical and geographic compilations of emperor Qianlong when I transcribed a fairly long portion, related to the monasteries and religious celebrations of the kingdom of Khotan, in the history of this city extracted and translated from Chinese writings.[97] This fragment pointed to a text wherein I should find precious notes on the state of Bouddhisme in the central regions of Asia; but the era about

> which it reported was only vaguely suggested, and even the title of the work from which [the extract] was taken left, due to the Chinese construction, room for doubt whether, under the name *Kingdom of Fo,* it referred to one or more states.[98]

Unperturbed, Abel-Rémusat told his learned audience, he later discovered the Chinese text itself in a "voluminous collection in the Bibliothèque du Roi, which Fourmont had taken for a collection of treatises upon 'a cabal and the philosopher's stone' (*la cabale et la pierre philosophale*), but which in reality contained a very great number of tracts (*opuscules*) related to historical, geographical, and literary topics."[99]

This collection was the *Jin dai mi shu* 津逮秘書 by the Ming scholar Mao Jin 毛晉 (1599–1659). We can still find and hold and scrutinize the very copy used by Abel-Rémusat in the holdings of the Bibliothèque Nationale de France.[100] Buried in the footnotes of chapter 16 in *Relations des Royaumes Bouddhiques* is the only other reference by Abel-Rémusat to his sources: while pondering a particularly difficult passage, he notes that perhaps his translation will require correction, "but that it is the same in the two texts I have before my eyes" (*mais il est le même dans les deux textes que j'ai sous les yeux*).[101] These "two texts" seem to have been the excerpts found in the Qianlong history and the full version of the *Record* catalogued, but misidentified, by Fourmont.

The latter *Record* was forty-four pages long and included in the collection's tenth volume. Therein it was identified as having been written

> under the Soung dynasty [i.e., the Liu Song dynasty 劉宋朝], which began its reign in 420 A.D.], by Chy-fa-hian [i.e., Shi Faxian, "the monk Faxian" 釋法顯], the leading pilgrim who undertook this extraordinary journey, and then revised during the Ming dynasty by two authors named *Hou-tchin-heng* and *Mao-tsin.*[102] I have not found any other bibliographic record of the *Fo-koue-ki.* As for the author, we shall see at the end of his memoirs that he was one of those who worked together to spread knowledge about the dogmas of Bouddhisme in the eastern regions of Asia, to gather large collections of the sacred books of this religion in China, and to make known their contents by means of translations made directly from their original Sanskrit.[103]

It too, like so much of his scholarship on the relational, interactive continent of Buddhist Asia, was transformed into the object of a science through circulations between Europe and the Qing.

In his 1830 public lecture, Abel-Rémusat provided a further introduction to Faxian:

> The Chinese samanéen [i.e., Faxian] speaks of different kingdoms and states; he even boasts (*vante*) of having passed through more than thirty. The epoque in which he voyaged was not one of any great dominion, and India, like Tartary, found itself partitioned into many independent, small principalities . . . The names that he records are spelled in the Chinese manner, which is to say they are almost always altered, and sometimes rendered unrecognizable. Nevertheless, for a few years great progress has been made in the art of *restoring names* transcribed by the Chinese. Comparison of a great many words of this variety has allowed us to recognize the most usual mode of alteration, and to follow a sure method to render them into their *original form* (*forme primitive*). I applied this to many of the names of people and places of Transoxania and Persia in a study read, a couple years ago, to the Académie, and to the lists of synonyms I have come to obtain with the help of colleagues (*l'assentiment des savants*). . . . In the case that occupies us here, the value of many Sanskrit words given by Fa-hian provided me with the means to subject such a return according to fixed rules, and the clarifications kindly supplied by M. E. Burnhouf leave no doubt about the results of this operation.[104]

Abel-Rémusat "applied himself particularly to not lose anything original or ingenuous (*d'original et de naif*)." In the estimation of Landresse, Abel-Rémusat "produced a more literal than elegant translation so as not to alter this quality of sincerity and truthfulness (*bonne foi et de véracité*) which one notices even in its smallest expressions, and which each word carries with him, so to speak."[105]

But about what did Faxian and Abel-Rémusat speak in this layered voice? First, at the start of the fifth century CE, Buddhism was established in "Central Tartary," to the west of the great desert, in the environs of Lop Lake, among the Uighurs, in Khotan, and in all petty kingdoms north of the Himalaya. Monasteries bursting with monks there celebrated "Indian ceremonies" and basked in Sanskrit learning. Second, Buddhism flourished west of the Indus River, in the "completely Indian" states of Oudiana, Gandara, Beloutcha, Tchioudasira, and so forth in the mountains of Afghanistan. What's more, local traditions had adopted the ceremonial pomp of Buddhist India and events related to the life of the Buddha, his travels, and "the second redaction of the sacred texts." Abel-Rémusat and his colleagues marveled that Buddhism had circulated so far east: "Fa hian makes its existence indisputable, helps us know the period and origin, and provides scholarship with the materials it lacked to explain the mixture and combination of many Oriental doctrines."[106]

Third, Central India is the "true homeland of Buddhism" (*la veritable patrie du boudhisme*), which was then transported to southern Bihar. Śākyamuni was born in Kapila to a titular prince of the king of Magadha, resident of Patalipoutra. He had done his preaching (*prédication*) north of the Ganges, and he finished his career north of Patna in the mountains of Nepal. All of his activities, either ignored until now or whose sense had been displaced, correct errors of those, like Deguignes, who placed the Bouddha's birth in Cachemire or, like the English scholars, had him born in south Bihar, near Gayā.

Fourth, Buddhism enjoyed political superiority over Brahmanism going back to the tenth century BCE. By the fifth century CE—centuries into Buddhist history, when Faxian walked—many of its original monuments still stood. Others were plainly visible in ruins, "confirming the tenacity of these traditions" (*confirmaient la teneur de ces traditions*). Fifth, Buddhism once penetrated in Bengal and the Deccan and, sixth, did so as early as the early generations of the followers of "Chakia-mouni." Seventh, Buddhism dominated Ceylon when Faxian passed through—reckoned by Abel-Rémusat to be 1,497 years after the nirvana of Śākyamuni. Recent textual finds, such as Eugene Burnouf's examination of the "Singhalese chronicles," confirmed this deep history. Eighth, in light of this, the search was on to acquire Buddhist texts, for "the study of sacred languages, to complete the collection, and facilitate the understanding of religious texts. Abel-Rémusat has obtained a great many in the province of Aoude, in Patna, in Bénarès, and in Ceylon."[107]

But Abel-Rémusat would never see this project to print. On June 3, 1832, a few months before his forty-fourth birthday, he died in the merciless second wave of a cholera pandemic that ravaged Eurasia. Cholera took several of the great Parisian Orientalists that terrible summer, including Chézy, the Sanskritist who had been appointed to the Collège de France with Abel-Rémusat in 1814. We know almost nothing about how Jean-Pierre's young bride and widowed mother endured his death. There is a record of his wife Jenny's auction of Abel-Rémusat's formidable library, but then—silence.[108] The loss extends to the fact that many of Abel-Rémusat's major projects were unfinished when he died, including a planned translation and study with Eugène Burnouf of the Qianlong emperor's Buddhist vocabulary, the aforementioned *Man han xi fan ji yao,* that had been the basis for his work to convince Europe that the Buddha had been a man in history and in India.

And there was his magisterial study and translation of Faxian's *Record,* still incomplete. Several of Abel-Rémusat's close collaborators committed to bringing it to print. Though this required few additions to the translation itself, Abel-Rémusat had footnoted only half of the text. Julius von Klaproth and Ernest Clarc de Landresse set to work. The result was published four years later, a year after von Klaproth's death, as *Foĕ Kouĕ Ki, ou, Relation des Royaumes Bouddhiques: Voyage Dans la Tartarie, Dans l'Afghanistan et Dans l'Inde, Exécuté à la FinDu IVe Siècle*. Klaproth had divided the French translation of the *Record* somewhat arbitrarily into forty chapters—much like books in the Bible, as David Jaspers once noted.[109] Klaproth also completed Abel-Rémusat's unfinished Commentaire, with a few additions by Landresse (though Klaproth adopted what Landresse lamented as an idiosyncratic transliteration system for Chinese, one quite at odds with Abel-Rémusat's scientific standards).[110]

Once printed, *Relations des Royaumes Bouddhiques* was almost universally praised as the first book-length masterwork about Buddhist Asia, illuminated by Abel-Rémusat's pioneering methods. "What is more remarkable," marveled Landresse in characterizing the work of his deceased colleague, "than to see the same ideas about universal emanation (*emanation universelle*), the perfectibility of the human soul, the identity of its nature with that of the divinity, propagated, over centuries, with their own language and legends which consecrate them, from India to China, Bengal to Tibet, the deep valleys of the Himalaya to the center of the snow of Siberia? And in the domain of Oriental literature, what is there of more importance than to penetrate the profound obscurity which envelopes the history of India before the conquest of the Musulmans?"[111] As Burnouf put it severely to readers of *Journal des Savants*: "What is more worthy of attention in the intellectual history of our species than to pursue the walking of this 'reverent traveler' (*culte voyageur*)?"[112]

In *The Journal of the Royal Asiatic Society* in 1839, H. H. Wilson praised Abel-Rémusat's extraordinary disciplinary contributions, noting how, on his methodological example, "both ends" of Asia—India and China—could now be conceived of in relation to each other. Abel-Rémusat's magisterial analytical treatment clarified that Sanskrit and Pāli learning flourished "from Khoten to Ceylon, and Buddhist works studied over the same tract."[113] While Buddhist communities appeared to be in decline in its center, Faxian witnessed Buddhism in efflorescence "on the borders of the Great Desert, prosperous on the upper course of the Indus, on either bank, declining in the Punjab, and in a languid state, although existing, on the Jumna and Ganges" and then onward in Ceylon.[114] As Abel-Rémusat's student Karl Friedrich Neumann put it in a review from 1840, "If India is the sun, then China is the moon which abundantly reflects the light to where it originated."[115] Now, known in relation to one another, the "written monuments of the Bouddha" that lay "conserved"—as if patiently awaiting the rational gaze of Europe—in Nepal, Tibet, and Mongolia; in Ceylon and in the mosaic of Indian kingdoms, could be rendered into the facts and events of history, philosophy, and geography.[116]

Conclusion

Nowadays, Abel-Rémusat is usually remembered in passing by specialists who use his life to bookend a historical transition from amateur to "professional" scholarship about Chinese language and literature in Europe. Practitioners of what would later be called Buddhist studies long ago forgot him.[117] This appears to be due to at least two factors. One is that his methodological impact was so widely and quickly embraced and adopted as to become invisible in the years after his death (in the sense of no longer being uniquely attributed to his scholarship). The second is that the field identity of Buddhist studies largely came to side with the Indophilia favored by Abel-Rémusat's few critics, who deplored that the Parisian master had focused upon the later, "degenerated," "derivative," and polluted "secondary" Chinese, Manchu, Mongol, Tibetan, and Uighur sources on Buddhism over the "pure," "original," and "primary" Sanskrit and Pāli.

The primary objectors to Abel-Rémusat's sources and methods were the British colonial Orientalists, among whom Brian Houghton Hodgson (1800–1894) was the most vocal. Though Abel-Rémusat counted the Englishmen among the rarified field of colleagues who met his high standards (which outside of Paris also included such figures as Alexander Csoma de Körös and Isaac Jacob Schmidt), Hodgson publicly rebuked Abel-Rémusat's armchair scholarship, the trans-Asian breadth of his sources, and the comparative nature of his analyses.[118] Hodgson saw the Frenchman's approach to Buddhist Asia, so influenced by the Qing imperial looking glass, as anathema to a more suitable scholarly practice of collecting original Indic witnesses to original or "primitive" Buddhism. As he once put it acerbically, "the Chinese and Mongolian works on Buddhism, from which the continental *savans* have drawn the information they possess on that topic, are not *per se* adequate to supply any very intelligible views of the general subject [of Buddhism]."[119] Hodgson insisted instead that the philological reconstruction of the original meanings of Sanskrit and Pāli texts was the most suitable method for serious scholarship about Buddhism.

Hodgson's vitriol seems to be in response to rather prickly jabs at the too narrow methodological practices of the Anglo Orientalists, which the Parisians characterized as impressionistic and too beholden to material artifacts. It was precisely by making use of those sources that Abel-Rémusat had publicly rebuked and humiliated the guesswork and conjecture of no less than Sir William Jones, grandfather of British Orientalism, over the matter of the "Black Buddha." Such Indocentric attitudes took over even among "the continentals" a decade after Abel-Rémusat's death, thus further marginalizing him in the memory of the synthetic discipline he had created and instituted at the Collège de France, in the Société Asiatique (which he cofounded in 1822 and helped lead until his death), and in the pages of *Journal Asiatique* (which he founded that same year and helped edit).[120]

As M. Biot wrote dismissively in an introduction to Eugène Burnouf's 1844 *Introduction à l'histoire du bouddhisme Indie*, quoted in an article from an 1845 issue of the *Journal des Savans*: "Unfortunately, A. Rémusat had for too long dedicated the force of his intelligence to try and reconstruct the incoherent material of all the periods of Buddhism that the Chinese texts provided him into a unique system."[121] And because of such changing opinions, Abel-Rémusat's transregional science of Buddhist Asia—derived from Leibniz, Silvestre de Sacy, and what Prasenjit Duara calls the loosely bounded, unstable, discontinuous, and essenceless "language games" of Qing sovereignty—began to fade from view.[122] Today he is remembered only in passing by field historians of Buddhist studies, if at all, either for giving Europe its first biography of the Buddha or for revealing the utility of "Chinese" sources for Orientalist research.[123]

But it is not the many European inheritors of Abel-Rémusat's methods and projects that concern us. It is to other readers, sites, and interpretative operations normally invisible in field history—East and Inner Asians disparaged by Hodgson and the Anglo Orientalists for their polluted and derivative Buddhist inheritance, and Mongols and Tibetans whose boundary-crossing predecessors authored the Qing reference works mined by Abel-Rémusat that gave Europe the "Buddha" and "Buddhist Asia."

For soon after *Relation des Royaumes Bouddhiques* was printed in Europe, it took flight. Abel-Rémusat's masterwork of the science of Buddhist Asia circulated out of the halls of the Orientalist academy, out of the discursive arena of a science, out of the epistemic and political sovereignty of Europe, beyond the West as site and source of universal history and knowledge. In circulation, its disciplinary apparatus—so celebrated by those mourning Abel-Rémusat's death—would be muted. History, geography, and philosophy would become the condition for chos 'byung, and teüke, and rnam thar, and lam yig, and grub mtha'. Buddhist Asia would be scrubbed from Jambudvīpa. In circulation into Asia's heartland, there would be a reversal of Trouillot's phrasing: the past would be made anew from history.

3

Buddhist Asia to Jambudvīpa

As we have seen, Abel-Rémusat and his colleagues mapped Buddhist Asia by transforming models of time, place, and community they read in polylingual primary sources into the objects of philosophy, geography, and history. Making use of comparative analysis, text-criticism, and models of language equivalency, they produced and disciplined the homogenous orders of Buddhist Asia ("Buddhist doctrine," "Buddhist history," "Buddhists"). Long before the invention of comparative religion as a scholarly field and long before the impact of Darwinian-inflected evolutionism on the human sciences, Abel-Rémusat's scholarship and methods carved Buddhist Asia, a new continent of relations and interaction, out of the primitive ether of the Nonwest. Using the disciplinary language of fact and event, he successfully claimed the status of a science for his analysis.

But speech is always also a condition for silence, writing a condition for erasure. The world historical order of the Qing sources Abel-Rémusat poached needed to be buried in his published work so that the universal frameworks of his Orientalist scholarship could be extended. But in circulation, after his death, the masterwork of his science—*Relation des royaumes Bouddhiques*—would itself be muted. Rooted networks of vast scale and complexity connected the Qing court to the Parisian academy to the Gobi monastery to the Tibetan refugee camp. They formed an understory of possibility rarely explored in siloed humanist field history, in histories of Orientalism, or in the intellectual and social history of knowledge in nineteenth-to-twentieth-century Inner Asia. So many threads enveloped and fused in nonlinear, centerless, nonhierarchical webs of connection, exchange, and coproduction.

This chapter follows Abel-Rémusat's study and translation of the *Record* as it moved across the perilous frontier of humanism and its contiguous knowledge traditions, and as its disciplinary apparatus was dismantled so that others could be assembled. As Claude Lévi-Strauss once put it, "the progress of knowledge and the creation of new sciences take place through the generation of anti-histories which show that a certain order which is possible on one [chronological] plane ceases to be so on another."[1] Here we will meet some of the interpretative communities of those Inner Asian scholars who brought Faxian's *Record,* by means of Abel-Rémusat's French translation, into the late- and postimperial republic of Tibetan and Mongolian letters and historical imagination. In chapter 5 we will see the details of their remaking of Faxian's ancient witnessing into distinct and quickly expanding historical traditions. And in "The Inner Asian *Record,*" we will read complete translations of their oftentimes radically different Mongolian and Tibetan translations, read against the French and Chinese.

Here is circulation, exchange, rot, and new life. Here is the Forest of the Blind, that centerless and continuous plane of Eurasian exchange and interpretation, all by looking over Faxian's shoulder and trying to name his long-ago world, one that would become radically familiar in Mongolian and Tibetan translation.

Into Siberia

From Paris, the next leg of the Eurasianist journey of Faxian's *Record* into Siberia depended upon a little-known but influential scholar named Dorji Banzarov (1822–1855).[2] This ethnologist and philologist was born to a family of peasant Buryat Cossacks in Transbaikal Oblast. After succeeding in his studies at the Troitskosavsk Mongol-Russian military school, in 1835 Banzarov was sent to the gymnasium at Kazan. In this, he followed other influential Buryat intellectuals of his day, such as the Buddhist monk Gomboev. Kazan was then "the cultural as well as the political forefront of Russia in Asia, and an important center of oriental studies."[3] Much like Abel-Rémusat, who was filling lecture halls in distant Paris, Banzarov was prodigious in his study of language, classics, and science. He defined himself especially in the pursuit of Latin, French, English, Turkish, and Russian, as well as mathematics, geography, and logic.[4]

In 1842 Banzarov matriculated to Kazan University and joined the department of Oriental Studies. There "he got a thorough education in the humanities and proved a person of brilliant scientific abilities."[5] His 1846 dissertation, *The Black Faith, or Shamanism Among the Mongols* (Rus. *Chernaya vera ili shamanstvo u mongolov*), was the first study on "shamanism" produced in any language,

FIGURE 3.1. Dorji Banzarov (1822–1855)
Source: National Museum of the Republic of Buryatia

which as such attracted attention across Russia.[6] Other of his scholarly works included monographs in Mongolian on geography and grammar as well as two translations: *The Travels of Tulishen* (from Manchu) and *Ubashi Khung-taidzhi* (from Oirat Mongolian). Though these manuscripts were carefully archived by the great Polish Orientalist Jósef Kowalewski (1801–1878), they were burned in the Warsaw fire of 1863.

After *The Black Faith,* Banzarov moved to St. Petersburg. There he took a research position at the Asiatic Museum while a request to be exempt from mandatory military service due to his Cossack heritage was considered.[7] He later served as an official of special missions under the governor-general of Eastern Siberia from 1850 to his death in 1855. During this trying period, he developed relations with the Decembrists while enduring "the grim conditions of serfdom and Tsarist autocracy . . . deprived of the opportunity to carry on his research."[8] In 1855, when only thirty-three, Banzarov died of some unnamed illness.

Though his career was short, like Abel-Rémusat, Banzarov was widely known and his contributions celebrated for both their descriptive content and their methodological rigor. The Russian Orientalist P. S. Saveliev, for example, wrote of his deceased colleague in 1856: "He was the most literate person among Mongols and Europeans. He was a brilliant researcher of the East."[9] Banzarov was formed in a transregional and prolific intellectual environment. The historian Nikolay Tsyrempilov includes among its population so many lamas, Russian imperial officials of various levels, Orthodox missionaries, Buryat national activists, St. Petersburg Orientologists, modern Buddhist reformers and conservatives. But by extension, this seventeenth-to-early twentieth-century community was deeply bonded to both Qing models of world historical order and evolving Orientalist scholarship in Western Europe.[10]

Banzarov was specifically one of the first of what Robert Rupen called the "Buryat Intelligentsia," a multigenerational and loosely affiliated group that included the aforementioned Galsan Gomboev (1818–1863); the ethnologist, Buddhist studies scholar, and pioneering documentary explorer of Tibet, Gombojab Tsybikov (1873–1930); the great Mongolist scholar and author of the Mongolian People's Republic's revolutionary platform, Tseveen Jamtsarano (1880–1942); the folklorist and archaeologist Matvei Khangalov (1858–1918), the Buddhist reformist Badzar Baradin (1878–1937); and the tragic monastic scholar, diplomat, and modernist Agvan Dorjiev (1853–1938). Though their specific goals were often at odds with one another, these figures made use of circulating Orientalist scholarly methods from Europe to circumscribe, unify, and nationalize Buryat, Mongol, and pan-Mongolian peoples (that included Tibetans and Manchus, in some iterations). Their work, and in some cases their leadership, would shape revolutionary modernist movements in the ruins of of empire across early twentieth-century Inner Asia.

As intermediaries among Russian, Mongolian, and Tibetan spheres of possibility, they engaged in research and espionage on topics ranging from folk songs and Buddhism to drafting the socialist platform of the Mongolian People's Party.[11] Banzarov created the early conditions for these increasingly revolutionary developments through his training, his mastery of Orientalism's methods, and the field-building implications of his work. The Buryat Intelligentsia's wide-ranging interests were inspired by a particular brand of progressive nationalist politics, but they also drew deeply upon late imperial Buddhist scholastic cultures that by the nineteenth century connected Central Tibet with North China, all Mongolian societies, and Siberia on both shores of Lake Baikal. According to the Soviet Mongolist Byambyn Rinchen, Banzarov's translation choices and calligraphy skills suggest he was himself trained as a monk, or *lam,* in his youth. Indeed, many early members of this profoundly influential (and profoundly understudied) group had trained as Buddhist monks earlier in life, or else remained ordained as monks over the course of the imperial–socialist transition.

Working in the disciplinary spaces opened by Banzarov, the Buryat Intelligentsia focused on Mongolic languages (including Buryat), pan-Mongol folk traditions, epic and historical traditions, literature, and ritual life (which in many iterations included Tibetan and Manchu peoples). Banzarov and his milieu were motivated by an "increased consciousness of 'Mongol-ness.'"[12] Much like the nearly contemporaneous Abel-Rémusat in distant Paris, Banzarov was a methodological pioneer whose synthetic scholarly practices helped solidify certain problematic biases in the study of Inner Asian religions that continue to influence research on Asia and Buddhism even today.[13] Christopher Atwood credits Banzarov's *Black Faith* for helping to cast a misshapen template in the study of Mongolian religions, one laden with "dubious first principles"—for example, that a foreign "Lamaism" rooted in Tibet could mask but never erase enduring shamanist sensibilities that were inextricable from the Buryat and Mongol character.[14]

In addition to writing original ethnographic and philological studies, Banzarov undertook many translations of works in European arts and sciences. When still a student at Kazan, sometime between 1842 and 1846, Banzarov discovered Abel-Rémusat's *Relation des Royaumes Bouddhiques.* Apparently moved by this reading and drawing connections between Faxian's ancient walking and the "Buryat and Mongolian" national character that occupied his scholarship, Banzarov decided to translate *Relation* into Mongolian. According to Byambyn Rinchen, himself a Buryat Mongolist working a century later in the Soviet era, Banzarov completed several drafts of his translation of *Relation.* Rinchen learned from oral history about the rather grand circulation of Banzarov's handwritten drafts and the many handwritten copies later made of them. Several manuscript editions were treasured among scholars in St. Petersburg, Siberia, Mongolia, and eastern Europe long after Banzarov's early death. Yet these were fragile and singular, much like those innumerable manuscript copies of sūtras and vinaya texts moved perilously over sand, snow, and sea to China in Faxian's time. As mentioned, some of Banzarov's manuscripts burned in the 1863 Warsaw fires, along with much of his other work. And still more burned in an earlier fire at Kazan University.[15]

Some drafts of Banzarov's Mongolian translation of Abel-Rémusat's *Relation* survived the nineteenth century, ending up in personal collections across Slavic Russia and in Siberia. One handwritten reproduction, made on March 8, 1844, was kept in a Buryat community along the banks of the Selenge in the hands of the elders of the Bulgad clan (Kh. Mong. *Bulgad ovogt*). Decades into the socialist period, working between the Soviet Union and the Mongolian People's Republic, Byambyn Rinchen acquired this manuscript and published a lightly edited version in 1970.[16] It is this edition, published some 125 years after Banzarov's composition, that I have used in the translations and studies that follow (despite my best efforts, I could not locate any extant manuscript editions).

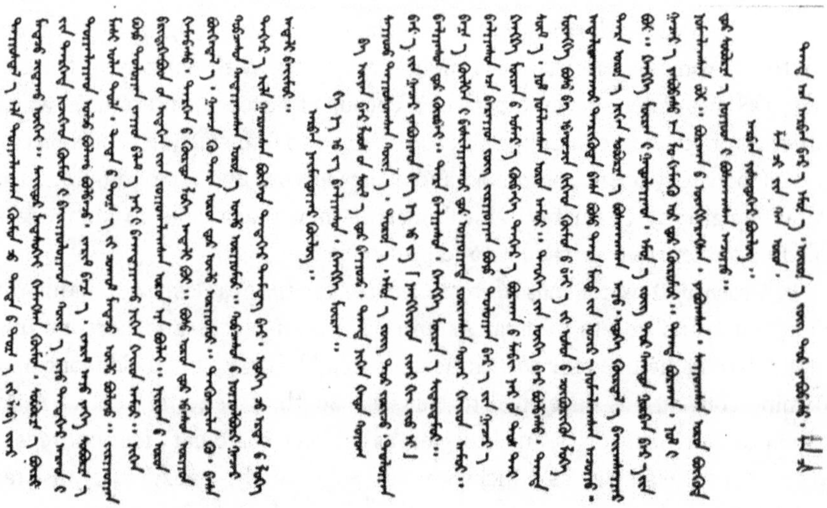

FIGURE 3.2. Example of parentheses (just left of center) in Dorji Banzarov's *Account of Travel to Lands Where the Buddha's Scriptures Flourished* (Mong. *Burqan-u nom delgeregsen ulus-nuγud-tur ǰiγulčilγsan bičig*), 22.

Banzarov's Mongolian translation of Faxian's *Record* is titled rather straightforwardly: *Account of Travel to Lands Where the Buddha's Scriptures Flourished* (*Burqan-u nom delgeregsen ulus-nuγud-tur ǰiγulčilγsan bičig*). As Rinchen put it in the long introduction that accompanied his 1970 publication, Banzarov chose from among the many varieties of written Mongolian to translate Faxian's *Record* into "the language of the scriptures" (Kh. Mong. *sudrîn khel*), as befitted the subject matter.[17] Impressed by the young Buryat's abilities in this technical variety of literary Mongolian, Rinchen was convinced Banzarov had undertaken his translation while still in gymnasium, before entering the University of Kazan. There he had encountered a learned monk named Galsang who would later become a widely known Buryat intellectual, the aforementioned savant, Galsan Gomboev, from whom the young Buryat must have learned his Mongol letters.[18]

In all, Banzarov's translation of the *Record* is remarkably filial to Abel-Rèmusat's translation. It follows the Frenchman's narrative without any introduction, annotation, or clarification. In the manuscript published by Rinchen, at least, none of the magisterial footnoting from the French is translated. However, as I will show in chapter 5 and the appendix of this book, there is clear evidence that Banzarov had read the French Commentaire and used that staging of the science of Buddhist Asia for his radical departures in the body of his Mongolian translation. The only explicit disruption of Banzarov's reproduction of Abel-Rémusat's *Relation* are occasional parenthetical notes. These appear to be clarifications by Rinchen (as shown in figure 3.2) and not anything from the original 1844 manuscript itself. With Banzarov's translation, Faxian's *Record* became part of a corpus of European literature—which ranged from David-Léon Cahun's *La Bannière Blue* to Daniel Defoe's *Robinson Crusoe*, introductory science textbooks about the weather and astronomy, and the Altaic epigraphy of Gustav John Ramstedt—newly available to Mongolian-reading audiences over the late and postimperium.[19]

In *Account of Travel to Lands Where the Buddha's Scriptures Flourished*, Banzarov does not transliterate Central Asian and Indian places and persons into Mongolian as he does for the Chinese. Instead he draws upon old Mongolian naming conventions developed to translate South, Inner, and Central Asian canonical works, histories, and liturgies "as has been customary for hundreds of years."[20] For example, as Rinchen notes approvingly, Banzarov translated "Avaloketiśvara"—the embodiment of the compassion of all the buddhas—as "Khoshim Bobisad" in Rinchen's Khalkha gloss, or "Qongsim bodisadu-a" in Banzarov's rendering in *Account*. Likewise, Prajñāpāramitā, the "Perfection of Wisdom" deified as the mother of all buddhas, appears as "Bilig barimid." Even so, dozens, perhaps hundreds, of new Central and South Asian places, peoples, and things witnessed by Faxian and laboriously rendered and interpreted by Abel-Rémusat required creative treatment in Banzarov's Mongolian. The old translation conventions could not help him.

And as we shall see, in his creative renderings of Faxian's opaque references, via the French new worlds emerged in Mongolian and Tibetan translation. From their broken chain of meaning, spread between Paris and Siberia and then later Khalkha Mongolia and Tibetan refugee settlement, the time and place of Faxian's ancient walking transformed. From a reservoir of facts about "Buddhist Asia," Faxian's account became with Banzarov a new exposition upon the historical experience, mobility, and interaction of "the Mongols." Then, in the next node of this circulatory history, Banzarov's reader and translator Zava Damdin Lubsangdamdin extended the trading of silence and speech, using Faxian's witnessing to expand the horizon of his Tibetan-language historical tradition.

Faxian, Tibetan, and the Revolutionary Modern

As we have seen, fire and untimely death left Banzarov's Mongolian translation of Abel-Rèmusat's French translation of Faxian's *Record* unread for nearly a century. It was only by chance that it survived at all. In the early twentieth century, an unnamed Inner Mongolian scholar made a hand copy of a surviving manuscript edition. That copy in turn was collected in 1921 by the Mongolian Institute of Scripts and Letters (*Sudar Bichgiin Khureelen*), the early socialist-era precursor to the Mongolian Academy of Sciences founded in Ulaanbaatar city, the capital of Mongolia.[21] In 1921, the very year of the founding of the Mongolian People's Republic, Asia's first experiment with state socialism, the Institute of Scripts and Letters adopted a wide-ranging program to both produce original scientific research and widely disseminate European arts and sciences in the Mongolian language.

According to Rinchen, that copy collected by the Institute of Scripts and Letters became the basis for the entrance of Faxian's *Record* into Tibetan translation and, in turn, for its reinterpretation in (and of) the early twentieth century.[22] Rinchen's dating, however, is contradicted in the colophon of the Tibetan text itself, which claims that it was completed in 1917 (or, less likely, 1918; the Pingala year he gives is usually the fifty-first year of a rapjung cycle, but he or his scribe identified it erroneously as the fifty-second). By the turn of the twentieth century, Tibetan had long been the dominant literary language of monastic networks among the British, Russian, and Qing empires. Before this complete translation of the *Record* into Tibetan in early twentieth-century Mongolia, to my knowledge Faxian had been named in Tibetan script only twice in the previous sixteen centuries. In the eighteenth century, the Mongolian scholar Güng Gombojab referred in passing to Faxian as "Thözung" (Tib. *Thos bzung*) in his monumental *History of the Dharma in China* (Tib. *Rgya nag chos 'byung*).[23] Faxian was referenced in passing in Gö Lotsawa Zhönnu-pél's 1476 *Blue Annals* (Tib. *Deb ther sngon po*).[24]

But it was only in this 1917 translation and reinterpretation that a full account of Faxian's ancient journey would come into the literary and conceptual worlds of Tibetan letters. As mentioned, the scholar responsible for this was the great Khalkha polymath abbot, historian traveler, yogi, logician, and tantric master Zava Damdin Lubsangdamdin (1867–1937). Lubsangdamdin was heir to generations of boundary-crossing Mongolian and Siberian Buddhist monks working across the Sino-Tibetan-Mongol-European frontiers. His unenviable task, as I have extensively explored in another book, was to make sense of a series of profound upheavals that tipped imperial Inner Asian into the tumult of revolutionary modernity.[25] For example, he worked wildly to fix with time and place the British invasion of Tibet in 1904, the collapsing Qing and Tsarist empires in the 1910s, the rise of radical nationalist and socialist movements in the 1920s, and the escalation of state annexation and violence against Mongolian monasticism.

In what I have called "countermodern" forms of writing and interpretation, Zava Damdin Lubsangdamdin deeply engaged circulating intellectual currents through the lens of his Géluk Buddhist scholastic tradition. He sought specifically to extend Qing frames of reference and equivalency, such as reference works and vocabularies made in the courts of Kangxi and Qianlong under the supervision of earlier generations of Géluk monks from the Sino-Tibetan-Mongolian frontiers: monks like Thuken Chökyi Nyima, Changkya Rolpé Dorjé, and Sumpa Khenpo Yéshé Dorjé, and lay intellectuals like Güng Gombojab. As we shall see, when Lubsangdamdin sought to bring Faxian into his Tibetan language monastic historiography, he turned to the interpretative and narrative precedent of those eighteenth-century scholars in another centerless resonance with Abel-Rémusat's use of polylingual Qing sources to discipline Buddhist Asia, and Faxian's *Record,* in Paris.

Lubsangdamdin completed his translation of Faxian's *Record* some six years after the Qing collapse, during the dissolution of the autonomous Buddhist theocracy that rose in its ruins. After he completed the Tibetan *Record,* Lubsangdamdin would undertake other more formidable historical work to make sense of, and survive, the post-Qing ruins and, after 1921, the rise of an increasingly aggressive state socialism. He did this via institution building (such as directing the founding of several scholastic colleges during the 1920s and 1930s) as well as by orchestrating large public tantric transmissions and ritual practices (such as mass recitations of the *maṇi* mantra). He was also compelled by a range of Tibetan and Mongolian religious and political leaders, as well as a member of the Russian Bakhtin circle, to set the Qing collapse into time in a variety of Tibetan language monastic histories. The apogee of that project was his 450-folio masterwork, the 1931 *The Golden Book* (Tib. *Gser gyi deb ther*; Mong. *Altan debter*).[26]

In the *Golden Book,* Lubsangdamdin drew upon his earlier translation of Faxian's *Record* to produce the oldest historical frame for Mongolian and Tibetan social continuity and Buddhist dispensation. As we shall see in chapter 5, this was made possible because of a great many interpretative and translation choices made by Banzarov in the 1850s and then in Lubsangdamdin's own Tibetan translation in 1917. Like Abel-Rémusat, but unburdened by the conceit of a West/Nonwest binary or the emerging discursive arenas of scientific discipline, Lubsangdamdin's approach to translating the *Record* was directly in conversation with centuries-long synthetic, polylingual, genre-bending forms of scholastic knowledge forged along the frontiers of the Qing. These brought Indian Buddhist canonical sources and scholastic traditions of the imperially favored Gélukpa school into conversation with new forms of medical, astronomical, historical, geographical, artistic, military, and cartographic traditions.[27] In Lubsangdamdin's translation of the *Record,* these alterations come

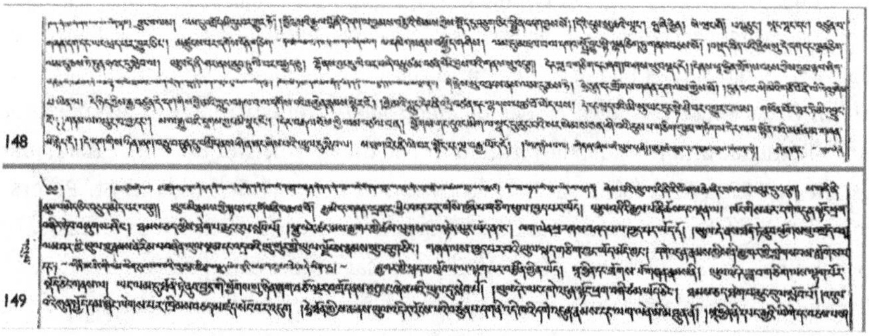

FIGURE 3.3. Example of interlinear notes in Lubsangdamdin's *Emanated Mirror* (pp. 148–49). Larger text is the body of the translation, the small text is the translator's asides and citations of other texts.

in substitutions within the body of the text itself. But more commonly they come in extensive interlinear annotations, much like Abel-Rémusat and his editors staged their science of Buddhist Asia in the footnotes to the translation.

Foremost among his influences in the matter of making Faxian legible to his historical tradition was the aforementioned Üjümüčin Mongol nobleman and scholar Güng Gombojab (Tib. *Mi dbang mgon po skyabs*; Ch. *Gongbu Chabu* 工布查布, d. eighteenth century). Born and raised in Beijing during the Kangxi reign, Gombojab inherited the imperial rank of *gong* 公 (Mong. *güng*) and married into the Manchu aristocracy. Gombojab exemplified the kind of polyglot, boundary-crossing intellectual movements that linked frontier Inner Asian scholasticism and literary practices to Qing cosmopolitanism and multiethnic representational discourse. Gombojab's translations into Tibetan and Mongolian of a variety of previously unknown Chinese religious and historical material widely influenced eighteenth- and nineteenth-century scholastic cultures along the Sino-Tibetan-Mongolian frontier.[28]

Gombojab was also a lexicographer involved in dictionary projects, such as the *Merged garqu-yin orun*, connected with the imperially sponsored translation and printing of the Kanjur and Tengyur. In another example of the circulatory histories that bound Abel-Rémusat's science of Buddhist Asia to Tibeto-Mongolian scholasticism, the Moravian missionary Isaac Jacob Schmidt (1779–1847) used Gombojab's dictionary as the primary source for his pioneering studies of Tibetan, Mongolian, and Manchu grammar and literature.[29] Schmidt's studies—along with his 1829 German translation of Saγang Sečen's 1662 chronicle *Erdeni-yin tobči*; his 1828 *On the Relationship of Gnostic-Theosophical*

Teachings with the Religious Systems of the Orient, Especially Buddhism (*Über die Verwandtschaft der gnostisch-theosophischen Lehren mit den Religions-Systemen des Orients, vorzüglich des Buddhaismus*); and his 1831 *On Some Basic Teachings of Buddhism* (*Über einige Grundlehren des Buddhaismus*)—were primary references for Abel-Rémusat and his Parisian milieu in the disciplining of Buddhist Asia, just as the work of Abel-Rémusat was known and used by Schmidt in St. Petersburg.[30] Klaproth especially turned to Schmidt's work (and, by extension, to Gombojab's) in order to complete Abel-Rémusat's footnoting of Faxian's *Record*. Inner Asian scholastic cultures thus helped produce and erase the science of Buddhist Asia in Europe, with Gombojab as interpretative fount.

Much like Leibniz's interactions with the intellectual currents at the Qing court, and Abel-Rémusat's disciplining of Buddhist Asia based on Qing encyclopedias and dictionaries, Gombojab's scholarship not only helped lay the groundwork for the science of Buddhist Asia in Europe. It also, in its reception and interpretation of European humanism in the form of *Relation des royaumes Bouddhique*, opened new narrative and interpretative territory for nineteenth- and twentieth-century frontier Buddhist scholastics like Lubsangdamdin in the matter of translating and incorporating Chinese-language materials into Inner Asian monastic literature. This is especially true of new visions of the deep history of Mongolia culled from Chinese and Tibetan sources and pertaining to any Central and Inner Asian peoples north of the Great Wall.[31] In this ecology, humanism first entered Asia's heartland with Faxian's *Record*.

Two of Gombojab's texts were most explicitly referenced by Lubsangdamdin in his translation and, as we shall see, often quite transformative interpretation of Banzarov's Mongolian rendering of Abel-Rémusat's rendering of Faxian's Chinese *Record*. The first was Gombojab's aforementioned "history of the Dharma" (Tib. *chos 'byung*) entitled *History of Buddhism in China* (Tib. *Rgya nag chos 'byung*), which introduced Chinese Buddhist lineages, figures, doctrine, and events to Tibetan scholarship. The other was Gombojab's Tibetan translation of the famous seventh-century travel account of Faxian's successor, Xuanzang (玄奘, 602–644), known to Tibetan letters thereafter as Tangsen Lama (*Thang san bla ma*). Xuanzang's orginal Chinese account is most recognizably titled *Datang xiyu ji* 大唐西域記, the *Record of the Western Regions of the Great Tang*. Gombojab titled his Tibetan translation *A Record of the Arrangement of India During the Great Tang Dynasty* (*Chen po thang gur dus kyi rgya gar zhing gi bkod pa'i dkar chag*).[32]

Just as Abel-Rémusat, Klaproth, and Landresse widely used Xuanzang's *Record of the Western Regions* to decipher Faxian's *Record* in the discursive arena of their science at the Collège de France, in another ellipses of this circulatory history I explore in this book, Lubsangdamdin similarly relied on Gombojab's translation of Xuanzang's account to further weave Faxian's text—via Paris and

Siberia—back into an expanded, Qing-inflected vision of Inner Asian history. As Lubsangdamdin puts it in the concluding line of his translation of the Tibetan *Record*:

> It is said in [Gombojab's] *The History of the Dharma in China* (*Rgya nag chos 'byung*):
>
> I have not seen any extensive travel guides (*lam yig*) composed by Tibetan translators. It is very difficult to trust the embellishments and descriptions of gold and musk sellers!
>
> [There] are several [Chinese] works about pilgrimage (*gnas mjal skor*). There is Xuanzang's abbreviated edition in two sections (*bam po*) and the extensive edition in ten sections. I have abridged the meaning of the latter and presented it in these pages. Furthermore, regarding both India and China, the erudite monk Faxian (*Hwa shang yan tsung*) prepared a narrative geography in ten chapters about the Land of Noble Ones. If one studies his tenth chapter (*le'u*) and the tenth section (*bam po*) of Xuanzang's work describing the geography of India, you are left feeling that you have yourself traveled to the Land of Noble Ones!
>
> O knowledgeable one, in addition to these two great texts [by Faxian and Xuanzang], please allow to ripen in the sphere of your wisdom mind that you should search for the work of the great translator Yijing (*Yi kying*), who traveled across India for twenty-five years. Should you find it, translate it into Tibetan![33]

Other important references that were centered in Lubsangdamdin's Tibetan translation and reinterpretation of Faxian's *Record* included Indic and Tibetan prophetic works, some of which were canonical, most notably the *Abhidharma*, the *Kālacakra-tantra*, and the *Root Tantra of Mañjuśrī*; but also less-referenced canonical texts such as the *Prophecy of the Land of Li Sūtra* (Tib. *Li yul lung bstand pa'i mdo*) and the *Oxhorn Mountain Prophecy Sūtra* (Tib. *Glang ru lung bstan pa'i mdo*; Mong. *Qutuγ-tu üker-ün aγulan-dur vivangirid-i üjegülügsen sudur*). And indeed, despite Rinchen's claims in the introduction to his 1970 publication of fascimilies of Banzarov's and Lubsangdamdin's translations, the latter pays no debt to the new "science of history" promoted by the socialist state nor to any continuous "pan-Mongolian historiography" to which Banzarov and Rinchen both were beholden. Rather, Lubsangdamdin frames his Tibetan translation in far more global, inter-Asian terms:

> Concerning this, the fourth of the one thousand guides of this fortunate aeon, the matchless teacher Śākyamuni, was born here in Jambudvīpa as the son of

King Śuddhodana[34] in India, land of Noble Ones, when the lifespan of human beings was one hundred years.

When the emperor of Zhou (*Co'u dbang*), fifth in the line of the Te'u kingdom (*Te'u rgyal srid*), was twenty-six years old, an omen appeared on the eighth day of the fourth month of the Wood Male Tiger Year in the form of a great mass of light that arose from the southwest border of China. Seeing this, the king conferred with diviners (*ltas mkhan rnams*) who determined that this was a sign that a Great Being[35] would be born in that region. After a thousand years had passed, what they had theorized (*grub mtha'*) came to be here in this land. So it had been prophesied. Moreover, this is also established in (various) writings.[36]

Some one thousand years later, during the reign of Emperor Ming Di of the great Han dynasty, the precious teachings of the Buddha began to flourish in the easterly kingdom of China.[37] Since that time roughly three renowned figures (this master, Xuanzang,[38] and the great translator Yijing[39]) have emerged from among the Indian arhats and paṇḍitas and the Chinese monks and translator-scholars.

As for the first of these, the great Han dynasty monk named Faxian, it is recorded in the great translator Güng Gombojab's *History of Buddhism in China*:

> The master named Thö-zung [Faxian] went to India in the company of four companions.[40] In Magadha they studied the Indian language and some of the auxiliary fields of knowledge.[41] Enduring many hardships, they journeyed all the way to Siṅghala. Although they saw a direct disciple of the Elder Kāśyapa, they did not have the opportunity to request Dharma teachings.[42] After his companions died, the master was left all alone. In the company of a merchant he continued along his journey. He produced his own translations (rang 'gyur) of many Dharma texts, including the Mahāsāṃghika Vinaya.[43] He greatly benefited sentient beings again and again. When he was eighty-six, he departed for the Pure Lands.

It is clear that this refers to [Faxian].[44] The Dharma histories of India, China, and so on illuminate how such journeys, full of hardships, were undertaken back and forth between different lands for the sake of the Dharma. Just so, from those pages it is clear that the names of authentic Chinese monks are recorded in the biographical literature of the Land of Noble Ones [India].

The biography of one such great being who journeyed to the Land of Noble Ones survives in the Chinese language. A foreign European[45] [i.e., Jean-Pierre Abel-Rémusat] discovered (that text) and translated it into his language. [. . .]

> Consequently, since [this text] has passed through the vernaculars (*skad cha*) of so many regions, specific names for a great many of the environs and beings have become corrupted (*zur chags*). Even so, here I left them unchanged, just as I found them. Please keep in mind that in the future it will be necessary to edit these names by examining other texts and visiting (the sites described herein) (*gtugs shing*).[46]

Lubsangdamdin's translation and interpretation of Faxian's *Record* was an extension of Qing precedents. These had remade, far from Central Tibet, Géluk scholastic fields of knowledge by leveraging textual hermeneutical practices that, as we read above, could strategically reconstruct the distortions of "vernaculars" (*skad cha*) and "corrupted names" (*mingzur chags pa*) in order to establish "authentic" (Skt. *pramāṇa*; Tib. *tshad ma*; Mong. *kemjiy-e*) knowledge and persons; a category in which, Lubsangdamdin concluded in the early twentieth century, Faxian and his ancient witnessing should be counted, just as Gombojab had decided of Xuanzang in the early eighteenth century).

By further expanding what José Cabezón has described as the Géluk scholastic imperative not simply to ignore but rather to refute or synthesize new knowledge using various hermeneutic (and philologically derived) dialectic strategies, Faxian's *Record* afforded new perspectives on the deep history of the Buddhist dispensation and Buddhist societies within Tibetan and Mongolian societies.[47] Faxian's witnessing, oftentimes wildly remade in Tibetan letters, transformed the territorial and historical picture of the "early dispensation" (*snga dar*) of the Buddhadharma into Mongol lands. Despite Lubsangdamdin's disdain for the revolutionary politics of his day and the complete censure of any reference to post-Qing nationalist or political formation, much of his work to reconstruct the deep time of Mongolian and Tibetan societies, including his translation of the *Record*, was used by others to invent a Mongol nationalist historiography. A good example is Anandyn Amar's (1886–1941) use of Lubsangdamdin's monastic histories, including those sections referencing Faxian's just discovered and translated *Record*, as the sole Tibetan-language source for what became an early and influential national history of socialist Mongolia: the 1934 *Brief History of Mongolia* (Mong. *Mongγol-un tobči teüke*).[48]

For Lubsangdamdin, however, Faxian's *Record* was not a piece of "nationalist history." It was most legible in the Tibetan genre of "travel narrative" or "travel biography" (*'grims pa'i rnam thar*) that told of the "liberated life story" (*rnam par thar pa*) of Faxian, imagined as a pioneering bodhisattva in the Buddhist dispensation to China and a great witness of the thriving "Mongol" and "Tibetan" Buddhist worlds of Central Eurasia. Lubsangdamdin specifically decided to fit his translation into the well-worn genre of a "travel guide" (*lam yig*) to holy sites (*gnas chen*) in such places as India, "Land of Noble Ones" (*'phags pa'i yul*), or Lhasa, Wutaishan, or Kathmandu. Even so, he understood his reception of Faxian's *Record* as coming from a trans-Eursian circulation. As he puts it in the introduction:

> There exists a Chinese-language biography of one such great being who journeyed to the Land of Noble Ones. Having found [that Chinese account], a European foreigner[49] translated it into his own language. The meaning of what was described [in that text] helped to verify authentic research already undertaken on India. A Buryat lama-lotsawa[50] translated that [foreign translation] into the Mongolian language. The present [text] is a translation of that [Mongolian translation] into the Tibetan language.[51]

According to Rinchen, it was at the Institute of Scripts and Letters that Lubsangdamdin completed his translation diligently alongside Buryat and Russian Orientalists to produce, among other projects, the Tibetan version of Faxian's *Record*, entitled *The All-Illuminating Emanated Mirror That Reflects the Source of the Victor's Teachings: The Story of the Great Han-era Monk Faxian's Journey to the Land of Noble Ones* (*Chen po hān gur gyi btsun pa phā hyin gyis'phags pa'i yul du'grims pa'i rnam thar rgyal bstan'byung khungs kun gsal'phrul kyi me long*).[52] And yet Lubsangdamdin dates his translation to 1917—"during the virtuous waxing moon period in the tenth month of the Pingala year"—which was four years before the founding of the institute. He also makes no mention of Buryat or Russian Orientalists or the Institute of Scripts and Letters, and claims that his translation was completed at his main monastic seat within the nearby compound of Gandentegchenlin Monastery.

What matters here is not this discrepancy, but the way Lubsangdamdin times his work—and thus himself and the scholastic site wherein it was made. His date of completion does not refer to the new nationalist and later socialist polity in which he lived. It was not timed by the European calendar, but rather in the deep historical vision of the trans-Asian Buddhist dispensation.

> As for *The Emanated Mirror That Completely Illuminates the Source of the Victor's Teachings* . . . it was translated, edited, and finalized by the bhikṣu Aśvaghoṣa [i.e., Lubsangdamdin] in the great land of Mongolia in the north of the world, at that great monastery prophesied by the Buddha in the center of the Glorious Tā Khurel [i.e., Yeke-yin Küriye], when according to trustworthy Chinese texts 2,943 years had passed since the Buddha was born in India. Nowadays, based on the inscriptions of Aśoka's pillars, Europeans claim that more than 2,500 years have passed since the Buddha's birth.

> According to the Puk system (*Phugs lugs*), 2,300 [years have passed]. According to the New Astrology of Genden (*Dge ldan rtsis gsar*), [2],200 years have passed, and according to the Golden astrological system (*Gser rtsis*), more than [2],400 years have passed. Since the jewel of the Buddha's Teachings spread into the land of Mahā China, more than 1,900 years have passed. Since the venerable Faxian of the Great Han dynasty traveled to Central India, 1,500 years have passed. According to the Kālacakra system, [Faxian's journey] occurred in the 52nd year of the 15th *rapjung*, in the later part of the *mindruk* (*smin drug*) month of the Mouse Year.
>
> By all this, may the door of the precious teachings of scripture and realization of the King of Subduers, the Supramundane Victor, spread everywhere in the ten directions, and may it increase for a very long time to come! *Dzayantu!*[53]

Lubsangdamdin's translation thus served to "clarify" (Tib. *bsal*) and "order" (Tib. *bkod*) this vast story of Eurasian exchange and connection in ways quite apart from the Chinese, the French, or the Mongolian.

Conclusion

The circulatory history of the *Record*'s nineteenth-to-twentieth-century Eurasian transit is thus not so simply the passage of representational discourse about Buddhist Asia forged in Europe into other places that were not Europe. The story is organized not simply by the narrative alterations and reframing that attended this transit (though we will see in detail how such alterations occurred) but rather by a chain of site-specific and differing orientations to knowledge itself—of treatments for traces of the past, of methodology. And here my own treatment—as well as your reading—become implicated in this centerless and marginless circulation, in webs of interaction and the play of possibility and erasure that propels the story of the French *Record* out of the epistemic and political sovereignty of Europe and into Asia's heartland. The past, as Michel-Rolph Trouillot reminds us, is never "a fixed reality," and knowledge about it is never "a fixed content."[54] And the conditions of possibility for making history from the past are not only mutable but also mobile. They are nonlinear, circulatory, and centerless.

We have now encountered Faxian, his walking and writing, and been introduced to some of the ways these were disciplined as the object of a science between Qing and European spheres of influence in the work of

Jean-Pierre Abel-Rémusat and his clique. We have also seen how the masterwork of Abel-Rémusat's young science of Buddhist Asia, the *Relation des royaumes Bouddhiques*, escaped the halls of the Collège de France, the universalist categories of Orientalism, and the epistemic and political sovereignty of the West. In the hands of Buryat and Mongolian interpreters, Faxian's *Record* was remade from the French and the distant Chinese as the basis for an emergent Mongolian nationalist historiography and then a Qing-derived scholastic historiography in the vast republic of Tibetan letters.

We will now move to explore the specific ways that in French, Faxian's ancient walking was made into the object of a science, and thus claimed as sovereign territory by the universal forms of knowledge and history of the Orientalists. In the language of fact and event, Faxian's ancient witnessing was made into objects of philosophy, geography, and history. Then, in chapter 5, we will look more closely at chains of interpretation in the Mongolian and Tibetan that, in various ways, decentered humanism and silenced the West to extend forms of historical imagination in Inner Asia.

4

Jambudvīpa to Science

The publication of *Relation des Royaumes Bouddhiques* in 1836 was a sensation. Reviewers across Europe and its colonies lauded it as a masterwork, the founding document of a scientific field, the marker of an epochal transition in the practice of Orientalist scholarship. Readers were astounded by Abel-Rémusat's scholarly ability. Here was a magisterial display of comparative analysis, trans-Asian historiography, and philosophical excavation. However, leaving aside the sources of Abel-Rémusat's "genealogical" map of Oriental similitude, his "genius," and the effects of his Qing-derived methodologies, what exactly did his readers consider that they had *learned* from interpreting Faxian's *Record*?

This chapter focuses on the themes, topics, events, and processes from the *Record* that Abel-Rémusat and his editors, Klaproth and Landresse, considered most important for their science. We glean the content of these discoveries most clearly in the great Commentaire: the hundreds of pages of notes hung from nearly every noun of the French translation of the *Record*. Abel-Rémusat and his editors organized their historical and philosophical exegesis spatially, in the circuitous footsteps of Faxian's ancient walking. Also in those footnotes, Abel-Rémusat and his editors performed their boundary work: a select few scholars from the seventeenth to nineteenth centuries, such as Leibniz, the Italian Antonio Agostino Giorgi, and the French Jesuit Amiot, were anointed as methodological predecessors in the science of Buddhist Asia. Frauds who had shamelessly borne the mantle of Orientalists, like Fourmont and his heirs, were eviscerated and exiled. With this pioneering monograph, Buddhist Asia was disciplined in Europe.

Faxian: Human and Optimist

When *Relations des Royaumes Bouddhiques* finally came to print in 1836, much was assumed in Europe about the supposed nihilism, inaction, and pessimism of "Bouddhisme" and "les bouddhistes."[1] As Abel-Rémusat's interlocutor Georg Wilhelm Friedrich Hegel had recently put it in his 1827 *Lectures on the Philosophy of Religion* (*Vorlesungen über die Philosophie der Religion*), the Buddha's Dharma supposedly maintains that "the ultimate or highest [truth] is . . . nothing or not being." For Buddhist practitioners, Hegel determined, "the state of negation is the highest state: one must immerse oneself in this nothing, in the eternal tranquility of the nothing generally."[2]

Though Abel-Rémusat's works were widely read by major figures in nineteenth-century continental philosophy, Hegel's gloss of Buddhist philosophy, as well as those of Schopenhauer and Nietzsche, unselfconsciously reproduced biases from centuries of missionary writing. "[The Buddhists] teach that a Vacuum or Nothing is the Principle of all things . . . to live happily we must continually strive for Meditation . . . to become like *Principium,* and to this end accustom ourselves to do nothing, to desire nothing, to perceive nothing, [and] to think on nothing."[3] These were the words of Jean Baptiste Du Halde's 1736 *Description Géographique, Historique, Chronologique, Politique, et Physique de l'Empire de la Chine et de la Tartarie Chinoise,* cited by both Abel-Rémusat and Hegel. There was also Deshauterayes's eighteenth-century summary of the doubled nature of Buddhism: an "external idolatry" and an "internal nihilism." The European invention of Buddhism as the doctrine of nothingness (Ger. *Nichts*) could only persist if ignorance of Buddhist sources reigned. Though Abel-Rémusat's scholarship and field-building work did not disabuse the German *Philosophen* of their misunderstandings, his novel comparative reading and analysis of Buddhist sources complicated the nihilist expectations of the philosophers and missionaries.

And indeed, Abel-Rémusat and his colleagues often remarked in their footnoting that Faxian's *Record* was hardly pessimistic. Why would Faxian cry, kneeling upon the snow, when his companion died on the frozen trailside? Why did he become so bitterly homesick upon seeing a Chinese fan offered to the Buddha? Why would terror seize him when sailing, water lashed and praying to the buddha of compassion for safe passage? Should he not have better "accustomed" himself, as Hegel would have it, "to do nothing, to desire nothing, to perceive nothing" at home in Chang'an and not on the heel in a perilous passage across l'orient bouddhiste?

Unlike the great philosophers of nothingness, Abel-Rémusat recognized in the *Record* an abundance of some species of idealism. "However attached [Faxian] may have been to his cult," he reflects in a footnote, "he had not yet reached that point of idealism." And what counted as the "idealism" of Buddhist monks for these Parisian Orientalists? It was that "degree of perfection where rest is considered the abode of the soul (*la demeure d l'âme*), where the absence of all qualities is the terrain of reason (*l'absence de toute qualité est le propre de la raison*). Inaction is far from being its entire morality and contemplation its only virtue." Faxian's struggles in frigid desert and alpine passes appeared now as admirable pursuits of moral ideals and disciplines of self-cultivation. Buddhists apparently did something, desired something, perceived something, and thought about something.

Abel-Rémusat and his editors were also struck by how recognizable Faxian appeared to their humanist ideals across the chasm of centuries. "With pious motives," wrote Landresse as introduction to *Relations des Royaumes Bouddhiques*, it seemed clear that Faxian was entirely beholden to "the obligations of his apostolate"; a world-affirming tapestry of yearning guided his countless thousands of steps and his meticulous writing. What occupied him most were "those wonders whose memory endures in certain places, the relics that are preserved there, the ceremonies that are practiced there, the temples and the monasteries that are raised there, and the number of the pious."[4] In the French translation and its footnoting, Faxian was driven by awe, striving, grief, and exaltation. He was flawed and earnest and beholden to blood and bone and doubt and fear. And he appeared recognizably and admirably rational: "He is superstitious without being fanatical. Even among monastics, exaltation could not encompass all feelings, control all impressions, silence all the weaknesses of the man; and these weaknesses make us love him more, inspire more sympathy in us for his person, more interest in his actions and in his words."[5]

In stark contrast to his Inner Asian readers' response, as we shall see, nowhere did Faxian appear more human to the Parisians than when he stroked Huijiao's pinched face as he died. "His description of the dangers from which he had escaped while traversing the impassable marches (*les défilés impracticables*) of the Indian Caucauses, the tears he shed for his companion who succumbed in the middle of the Himalayan snow . . ." Weeping over his dead companion, buckling at the sublime thought of arriving to sites once inhabited by the Buddha, or fearing ocean tempests and the violence of desperate sailors: according to Landresse, readers meet Faxian in the *Record* full of "touching traits of candor and genuine sensitivity." Across fourteen centuries, this Chinese traveler appeared in French in remarkably human ways, full of doubt and pain, spirit and creativity, and a bare moral compass quite apart from a "pilgrim's" inspiration or the nihilist's reverie.

Mirroring the humanist expectations of his Parisian translator and interpreters and their own scholarly identities, Faxian was often praised by them as a scrupulous, comparative collector and "critic" of Buddhist Asia. In Faxian, in effect, Abel-Rémusat found not only an object for the Orientalist's interpretation but also a pseudo-practitioner of such interpretation, separated by fourteen centuries. Memorialists of Abel-Rémusat in the 1830s often underscored the resonances between their deceased colleague and this fifth-century wanderer, his muse. Faxian, they often remarked, emphasized as Abel-Rémusat had "research into these texts" that he had collected in India. Faxian, like Abel-Rémusat, mastered "the study of the different formulations (*idiomes*) in which they were written" and categorized "knowledge about the doctrine and the facts which they record."[6]

Much like the Buddha appeared in the lens of this science of Buddhist Asia as a human wellspring of metaphsyics and ethics comparable to the Greek philosophers, so too did Faxian mirror Abel-Rémusat as a "critique" and rational interpreter of Buddhist Asia. Though the latter had lived and died only in Paris, he had wandered after Faxian in order to render Buddhist Asia as a racially organized, genealogical tableau of similitude and descent.

A Day's Walk

In the Chinese *Record*, Faxian measured the space of his walking with time. One *li* 里, for example, was a measure of both distance and the duration spent crossing it. Fifty yards of precipitous rock and two miles of flat trail could each be one *li* long. A hobbled monk with frozen toes and white froth bubbling from his mouth might count immeasurable *li* separating him from some dry and warm place, whereas an able-bodied companion stroking his face might count only a few. This was a refusal of the empty and homogenous space produced by the disciplinary practices of Geographie. And it profoundly troubled the exacting, cartographic impulses of Abel-Rémusat as he set out to map Buddhist Asia in Faxian's footsteps.

To remedy the confusion of space and labor in *li* and other measuring devices in the *Record*, Abel-Rémusat relied upon his comparative methodological practices. "Mountain chains, well-known rivers, and villages whose actual name I managed to recover, provided me a few fixed points," he revealed at the Institut de France about his ongoing research. "On more than one occasion, history came to the rescue of geographical relations (*combinaisons géographiques*)."[7]

But *li* also demanded such disciplinary treatment. "[M]easures using days walked when journeying in Tartary, in the deserts, and in parts of his route that he crossed by water, whether upon the Ganges or whether upon the Indian or

Chinese seas. This mode is very imperfect; but the uncertainty inherent in it causes regret in only two or three places of the itinerary. When the distances are very small, the traveler expresses them using the Chinese *li*, an inconstant measure, as we know, especially when it is a question of foreign countries, and which can be estimated at the two hundred and fiftieth part of a degree, or perhaps to a fraction smaller."[8]

Once Faxian arrived in India, Abel-Rémusat was relieved to report later in his footnoting to the *Record*, the ancient monk began to measure his stride more reliably using "the Indian *yeou-yan* or *yodjana* [Skt. *yojana*]." A *yojana*, the Indologists had already decided, is of a length "estimated at 4 *krosas*, that is to say, at 4½, 5, or even 9 English miles." And yet, this disciplinary work to rationalize the space compassed by Faxian's fourteen years on the heel was still frustrated. Many of Faxian's measures, Abel-Rémusat continued, "seem overstated," and a few quite exaggerated. "On several occasions, he is fooled by faulty and somewhat legendary reports."[9] Closely referencing H. H. Wilson's Indological work, Abel-Rémusat hazards a well-reasoned median sense of space for Faxian's *Record*: "We believe we can adopt, as an average term for the value of a yojana in the *Fo-koue-ki*, the smallest of those spoken of by M. Wilson, which is to say that of 4½ English miles or from fifteen to the degree, which applies exactly to the best-known points, and whose synonymy will be established below in an incontestable manner."[10]

Translating a time-based measure of space was not Abel-Rémusat's only challenge. The *Record*'s space-based measure of time was equally opaque. Measured by Faxian's progress across it, Buddhist Asia was fourteen years wide. For clarity, the Parisian Orientalist turned often to "the Tibetan and Tartar races" who had "divided and fought over the land that currently forms the provinces of Shanxi (*Chen-si*) and Gansu (*Kan-sou*)." These "Tibetans" and "Tartars" controlled Chang'an by the time Faxian departed upon his voyage. Their measure of time, Abel-Rémusat decided, was written as both reign year and heavenly movement. In the *Record,* Faxian leaves Chang'an in both 399 and 400 "of our era"; Faxian's doubled walking was thus emplaced in the empty and static march of Histoire.[11]

Khotan

As Abel-Rémusat put it in the opening pages of his landmark 1820 monograph, *Histoire de la ville de Khotan,* "[Khotan's] vicinity was covered by Buddhist monasteries where Buddhists from countries farther east came to search for sacred texts and the lineages of their faith (*les traditions de leur croyance*)."[12] From the study of Chinese sources about Khotan, "we can succeed in tracing the history of the cult of the Bouddha in Tartary, and construct a picture of the circulations (*révolutions*) that have carried the Samanéens so far from the land of their birth and extended the influence of the religions, institutions, and languages of Hindoustan into northern regions."[13] Just a few years after he had proved that the Buddha had been a man in India and in history, Abel-Rémusat turned to Khotan as a microcosm of the relational and interactive continent of Buddhist Asia.

But where do the ruins of Khotan's Buddhist past lie buried?

By consulting several Chinese sources and a Qing imperial almanac in Manchu from 1769, from the Qianlong reign period, Abel-Rémusat discovered that the ancient Chinese name for Khotan, "The Kingdom of Yu thian" (i.e., Yutian guo 于闐國), was equivalent to "*Khotiyan-ni-ilitsi*" (or *Hotiyan-i gurun* in Manchu).[14]

He tried to emplace Khotan using what he calls the *Täi-thsing-i-toung-tchi,* which must refer to the 1723–35 *Unification of the Great Qing* (*Da qing yi tong zhi* 大清一統志) and "the new edition of the geography of the Manchus."[15] His research for his earlier 1820 book revealed that "the Tartary Buddhist language" used in ancient Khotan was saturated with Sanskrit words, and that there was a vast new frontier of Indic learning extending into not only Central Asia but also China. Indeed, Khotan was a mediating point in Abel-Rémusat's analysis, enticing monks from the east to receive "pious training (*pieux enseignements*)" in South Asian languages and scripture.[16]

Assembling traces of Buddhist Khotanese history from a variety of Chinese, Manchu, Tibetan, and Mongolian sources in *Histoire de Khotan,* Abel-Rémusat developed a completely new, paradigm-shifting perspective. This concerned not only the routes through which Indic thought and community organization had traveled beyond India's borders or the degree to which China had been engaged globally since antiquity. It was the very topography of Buddhist Asia itself, conceived as a vast new continent of relation, exchange, and Eurasian possibility. As Landresse put it later in the introduction to *Relation des Royaumes Bouddhiques,* "Ideas about reincarnation, for example, were only adopted by followers of Laozi (*Lao tseu*) since the introduction of Buddhism, and M. Rémusat held the opinion, based on so much evidence, that China must have received from the West the Platonic dogma of *Reason*, of *Unité-trine*, of the breath of harmony which unites spirit and matter, etc."[17]

In the footnotes of the French *Record,* Abel-Rémusat could confidently claim that "the village of Khotan" was "one of those in Tartary where Buddhism seems to have been established the earliest and practiced most magnificently."[18] For

Klaproth, elsewhere in the footnotes to the French *Record*, Khotan represented no less than "the metropole of Buddhism" mediating the Sino-Tibetan-Mongol-Indic-Persian crossroads. As always, Klaproth was overjoyed to add his expertise in Mongolian languages to Abel-Rémusat's analysis: "The word Khotan, or, as we normally write it without the pleonastic -n, *Khotà*, is not of Mongol origin, but is one of numerous Sanskrit terms that were introduced into Mongol. It is in fact *Kótta*, which signifies a fortified place, like *Khotà* does in Mongolian, since a 'village' in general is called *Balghasoun*[19] in this language."[20] Could Abel-Rémusat or Klaproth have imagined that these footnotes would soon be read by Mongols keen to emplace Khotan in their own monastic chronicle tradition? That, because of their scientific treatments, Faxian's ancient walking would depart the discursive arean of Orientalism and enter the Inner Asian historical imagination, fitting the upheaval of imperial collapse and socialist state erasure with time and place and moral purpose? That monks would see themselves not just in Faxian but in ancient Khotan, in the shadow of modernist erasure?

The Towers of Gandhāra

In the *Record*, it was not only, or even most frequently, monasteries or statues or saffron-robed saṅgha that helped Faxian mark his travels, but reliquary stūpas (Ch. *ta* 塔; Tib. *mchod rten*; Mong. *suburγan*).[21] Stūpas contain relics (Skt. *śarīra*), the remains of teachers, and other holy objects such as scriptures and mantras pressed millions of times in ink. In the *Mahāparinirvāṇa-sūtra*, one of the most consequential texts Faxian brought to China, the Buddha instructs his followers to enshrine his relics in a stūpa erected at a crossroads, and to visit and honor it with offerings as if it were the body and the mind of the enlightened. Stūpas organized time. They provided material conditions wherein living communities understood themselves in relation to the life of the Buddha, the continuous river of lineage and transmission, and circuitous progress toward their own future enlightenment.

Of the hundreds of stūpas Faxian encountered, many were made of mudded stone, decorated in gold, and festooned with incense and crisp paint. As often they were chipped, cracked apart, and lying upon the ground. Faxian and Abel-Rémusat used stūpas in any state of disrepair to transform the past into history.[22] Most regularly in the *Record*, stūpas communicate about events in the Buddha's life, which by Faxian's arrival was already a thousand years in the past. This constellation of stories, organized by stūpas, was structured not chronologically but spatially. In the *Record*, their collective narrative is consequently

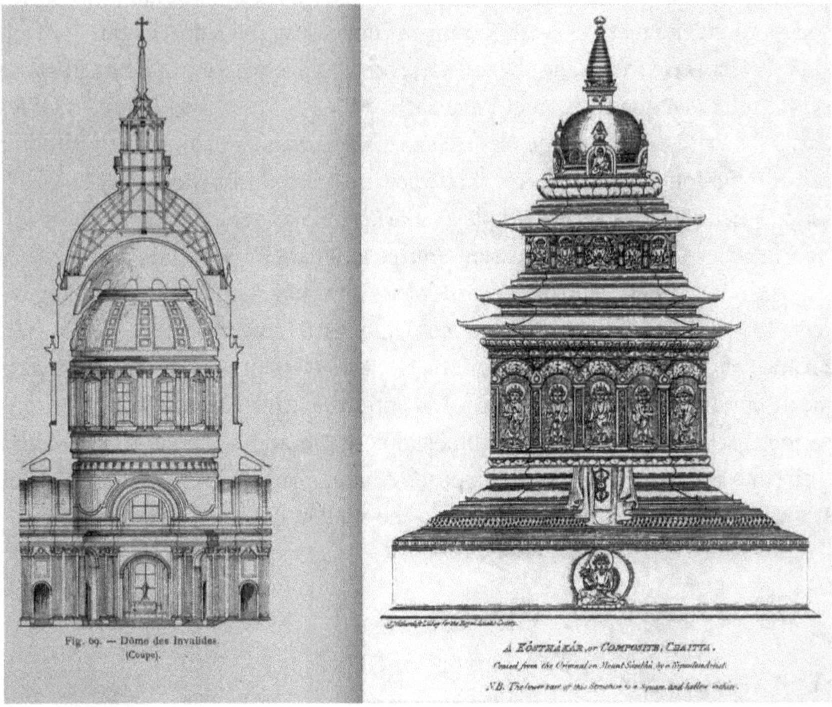

FIGURE 4.1. Left: "Dôme des Invalides." Right: "A Kósthákár, or Composite, Chaitya." Sources: *Relations Des Royaumes Bouddhiques.* Anatole de Baudot, *L'architecture. Le passé.—Le présent* (Paris : H. Laurens, 1916), 119; Hodgson, *Sketch of Buddhism; Derived from the Bauddha Scriptures of Nipal*, plate v

told piecemeal. Faxian marks the distance between stūpas and tells each element of the narrative not in chronological order but according to the path of his wandering. In the *Record*, and in the field-building explanations of the Parisian Orientalists that followed along after its narrative, the Buddha dies before he travels to see his deceased mother in Tuṣita and before he is born from her side.

For Abel-Rémusat and Klaproth, the devotional act of Buddhists visiting a stūpa required explanation. The same was true for other Europeans engaged in Orientalist work about Buddhist Asia in the 1820s and 1830s, such as the Englishman Brian Houghton Hodgson in Nepal.[23] In footnotes rooted to early passages about Faxian's walking, Abel-Rémusat writes: "[Faxian] speaks of a tower found in the country of *Gandhâra* that was 700 Chinese feet in elevation, or about 216 meters, more than twice the height of the spire of the Invalide in Paris."[24] In order to compass Buddhist Asia for his European readers, Abel-Rémusat often drew upon the material facts of contemporary Paris to fit the opaque references of the *Record* with scale, relation, and presence.

Bouddhisme as Vehicle

When Faxian wrote about the Buddhist city states that dotted the desert throughways of Central Asia, he noted most regularly the virtue of their kings, the number of their monasteries and monks, and their doctrinal affiliation. In the latter case, the difference that he noted most often was between monks of the "Great Vehicle," or the Mahāyāna, and those of the pejoratively named "Lesser Vehicle," or Hīnayāna.[25] As he wrote about Shanshan (from the French translation): "The kingdom of *Chen chen* (Shanshan) is a mountainous and undulating (*très-inégal*) country. The earth there is poor and infertile. The customs (*moeurs*) and clothing of the inhabitants are vulgar and resemble those found in the land of the Han . . . The king of this country honors the [Dharmic] Law. There are approximately four thousand monastics in this state, all of them attached to the study of the *little transfer* (*petitetranslation*)."[26] Doctrinal and institutional distinctions such as "little transfer"—Abel-Rémusat's rendering of Sanskrit Hīnayāna (Ch. *xiao cheng* 小乘; Mong. *baγ-a külgen*; Tib. *theg dman*)—pepper Faxian's *Record* without any further explanation. His readers, after all, were monks, or else the lettered faithful. But for Orientalists fourteen centuries later, such references required not only explanation but also an accounting of centuries of European bewilderment. Such was the descriptive and field-building task of Abel-Rémusat's final work.

Relational concepts like "greater" or "lesser" were clear to European audiences, of course. But what about "transfer" (Fr. *translation*), which Abel-Rémusat uses for Sanskrit "vehicle," or *yāna*? Confusion had long reigned on this matter among missionary writers, and the few previous Orientalist scholars who had attempted to define *yāna* had done so too narrowly, based on idiosyncratic readings of specific texts in specific places and used by specific communities. Most recently, Joseph Deguignes had lectured on the topic in Paris, but in Abel-Rémusat's acidic appraisal, "[he] in fact knew the meaning only imperfectly and could not locate its origins."[27] Wielding his comparative methods, as always, Abel-Rémusat offered a sober correction in his footnotes to the *Record*: "We say in Chinese *ta tching*, the great revolution; *siao tching*, the little revolution. *Tching* is a word that means *transfer, passage from one place to another, revolution, a tour,* and also any means for transportation, like a *chariot* or a *mount*. It is equivalent to Sanskrit *yâna*, which encompasses all the same meanings."[28]

Another erroneous interpretation of *yāna* was in Isaak Jakob Schmidt's aforementioned *Forschungen im Gebiete der älteren religiösen, politischen und literärischen Bildungsgeschichte der Völker Mittel-Asiens, vorzüglich der Mongolen und Tibeter.* In this otherwise laudable study, which Abel-Rémusat counted in the library of the science of Buddhist Asia, Schmidt had mistakenly translated *yāna* as "tradition" (Ger. *Überlieferung*).[29] Abel-Rémusat's corrective not only provided Europeans with a clear-sighted and sourced picture of Buddhism as process, as cultivation, as verbal, but also drew new links among structures of doctrine, hierarchies of of beings and practitioners, and the nature of liberation.

> [Yāna] is a mystical expression that designates the action that an individual soul (*l'âme individuelle*) can and must exercise upon itself, in order to transport itself into a superior condition. Since there are several degrees of such action and its results, they distinguish two, three, or a larger number still of *yānas*, in Chinese *tching* [*cheng* 乘], in Mongolian *kulgun* [*külgen*]; and following that they direct their efforts toward a more or less elevated perfection, they belong to the small, medium, and the greater *transfer* or *revolution*.[30]

Common to all Buddhist "transfers," he continues, is contemplation upon the "four truths" (*quatre vérités*)—which he calls pain, reunion, death, and the doctrine—as well as of the "twelve links" (*douze enchaînements*). From this, "men are transported beyond the enclosure (*enceinte*) of the three worlds and the circle of birth and death."[31]

Abel-Rémusat clarifies that there is, properly speaking, only a single vehicle: that taken by the Buddha himself, which he then entreated others to follow, each according to their capacity. Thus beings pull themselves out of "the ocean of the suffering of birth and death, to disembark upon the other shore, which is that of the absolute." And while the Buddha would have preferred to assign a vehicle to each being, Abel-Rémusat writes, three general vehicles are recognized across Buddhist Asia: the vehicle proper to the passage of the "listeners," or *śrāvakas* in Sanskrit (Fr. *Shrawaka, Ching ven*; Ch. *shengwen* 聲聞); the vehicle of those with "distinctive intelligence," the *pratyekabuddha* (Fr. *Pratyeka-Bouddha*; Ch. *yuanjue* 緣覺); and the vehicle of the bodhisattvas (Ch. *pusa* 菩薩), "those beings much closer to absolute perfection," who escape from the three worlds to nirvāṇa (Fr. *nirvân'a*; Ch. *niepan* 涅槃).[32]

The first of these, the "listeners," explains Abel-Rémusat, is represented ideographically by Buddhists as a chariot drawn by a sheep, an animal who will run ahead without ever looking behind to see if the herd follows. "It is so with the śrāvakas, who search to depart from the three worlds by observing the four realities, though only while focused upon their own salvation, without regard for other men."[33] The second is represented by a deer-drawn chariot. The deer may bound ahead while keeping track of the herd behind; likewise, the pratyekabuddhas cultivate their knowledge of the twelve "causes" (Fr. *Nidânas*; Skt. *nidāna*) that bind beings to cyclic existence, and by this "pass beyond the enclosure of the three worlds, and think of the salvation of other men."[34] The third is the ox-drawn chariot, which represents "the bodhisattva men of the doctrine of the three *piṭakas*," the Buddhist canon, about which Abel-Rémusat promises a more thorough explanation in a later note. Just as the ox bears patiently whatever load he is burdened with, so too do bodhisattvas "practice the six means of salvation and think of nothing other than to bring others out of the enclosure of the three worlds, not ever thinking of themselves."[35] Thus were the grounds and paths uniting Buddhist Asia illuminated for Europe in the sober discursive arena of a comparative science.

But first these "raw" sources needed to be "cooked," as the social historian of knowledge Peter Burke would put it, paraphrasing Lévi-Strauss. They needed to be "transferred" across the boundary of the West/Nonwest, to be rendered from the reservoir of facts and events and case studies of Buddhist Asia into the stuff of metaphysics and ethics. "To translate all this into European language, we can say that the *little transfer* consists of morality and the exterior cult; that the *middling transfer* is undertaken by spontaneous or traditional psychological permutations (*combinaisons psychologiques*), and that, as its base, the *great transfer* possesses an obscure theology, a refined ontology, a most exalted mysticism."[36] Translating doctrine into geography in his Leibnizian-derived, racially inflected picture of Buddhist Asia, Abel-Rémusat surmises that, "according to their more or less contemplative dispositions and the degree of their intellectual culture," Buddhist peoples of various rank "must stop more or less up the scale of *translations.* The peoples of the north, in the testimony of the Chinese, have always preferred the *little translation*, which is to say morality and mythology, which alone accords with nomadic habits and belligerent inclinations. Middling nations, submissive to the influence of the climate and more taken by scholarly reverie, have usually aspired to the *great translation* and to spread it among their neighbors."[37]

And, Abel-Rémusat assumed, this semiracial distinction among the peoples of Asia—a mix of meteorology, moral compassing, and acumen—was recognized by Buddhists about themselves, and used to classify their scriptural traditions. "We understand the distinctions as well that the Buddhists establish between their sacred books, according to whether they contain expositions of dogmas most relevant to their theology, or else to their moral principles and the myths of their symbolism."[38] It was for this reason that, in French, Faxian would so scrupulously record the sorts of monks who sat murmuring and meditating in the desert and mountain city states and lonely temples. Entering, by this clarification, into new territory in the intellectual history of Europe, Abel-Rémusat provides a schema of Buddhist persons, practices, doctrines, scriptures, cosmology, and "moral philosophy" that are still taught in world religions classrooms today.

Maitreya and "the Mysterious Revolution"

Maitreya, the "Benevolent One," abides patiently in the Tuṣita heaven. For Mahāyānists like Faxian, as for his Inner Asian interpreters a millenium and a half later, Maitreya is considered the historical Buddha Śākyamuni's enlightened successor, the next to turn the Wheel of the Dharma in Jambudvīpa.[39] In Buddhist societies, Maitreya has for more than twenty centuries been pulled from the geologic dignity of thousands of hundreds of millions of years and been made to measure the toil of individual human lives or, as commonly, the beginning or end of so many human polities and conquests.

In the *Record*, Faxian uses Maitreya to time the spread of Buddhism into "the East." Having stumbled out of the mountains onto the banks of the Sindhu River, Faxian made sure to note that no previous Han Chinese traveler, not even the intrepid Zhang Qian or Gan Ying of the Han dynasty, had ever come so far.[40] Local Indian monks were amazed at the sight of him: "Can you explain when the Buddha's teachings began to flourish in the East?" they asked. Faxian replied that monastics had come to China bearing sūtras and volumes of the vinaya—in the Mongolian and Tibetan translation, the general "monks" (*Cha man* in Abel-Rémusat's French) becomes the far more local "lamas"—just when a local Maitreya statue was built. Calculating on his feet, Faxian continued, "this occurred during the reign of Emperor Ping 平王 of the Zhou family 周氏. Another account is that the holy Dharma started to spread continuously into the East the very moment this [Maitreya] statue was built. Either explanation is acceptable."

"This personage, who must succeed Shâkya mouni as the terrestrial Buddha, was, under the name *Ayi to*, among the disciples of the latter," Abel-Rémusat wrote in his footnotes about Maitreya. "Others assure us that he was born in the sky during the time when Shâkya embraced the religious life."[41] Here are those dizzying numbers so loved by Buddhist authors and, in written accounts about him, loved by the Buddha. Like the billions of microorganisms that inhabit a single square foot of turf, or, at this exact moment, the parasites inhabiting guts, skin, and brains that make up a staggering one tenth of all life, unthinkable

FIGURE 4.2. "Maitreya and entourage" from Gandhara
Source: Ostasiatische Kunst Museum

numbers have been part of Buddhist authors' descriptions of Maitreya. According to predictions made by Śākyamuni, explained Abel-Rémusat, Maitreya will take the human stage in some distant age, when the human life span is eighty-four thousand years. Opening his trusty *Encyclopedie Japonais*, he adds, "That is to say, five thousand six hundred and ten million years" from today.[42]

In his 1830 introduction to his research on the *Record* at the Institut de France, Abel-Rémusat walked his audience through the historical implications of Faxian's statements about this Maitreya statue. "The pilgrims stated that the most remarkable feature of this township (*canton*) was an eight-story wood giant representing *Mi-le-Phou-sa* (the bodhisattva Maitreya), a colossus that was the object of veneration for all the kings of neighboring regions. This statue was erected three hundred years after the *nirvân'a* (ecstasy or the death) of Fo, which corresponds (*se rapporte*), says the author, to the time of Phing-wang of the Tcheou family (771–720 B.C.). This tradition would postpone the event in question to the year 1071 or 1020 B.C. We shall see, before the end of this mémoire, a Singhalese dating that nicely matches this one."[43]

After explaining the bodhisattva Maitreya's identity, Abel-Rémusat emphasized the astonishing web of connection and coproduction that made up the object of his science. "It is remarkable that Fa-hian puts three hundred years between the death of Shâkya-mouni and the fabrication of the statue of the bodhisattva, an event that seems to mark the conversion of the people of western India and of eastern Persia to the Buddhist religion."[44] For European readers, as for Central Asian societies in the fifth century and Inner Asians in the nineteenth and twentieth centuries, referencing Maitreya in Tuṣita helped unfurl the immeasurable cloth of time that stages the Buddhadharma, whether as event in history or in the longue durée of saṃsāra.

The Xiongnu and the Golden Man

Zhang Qian 張騫 (d. c. 114 BCE) was a famous envoy of Emperor Wu 武帝 of the Han dynasty (r. 141–87 BCE) who journeyed to the Yuezhi 月氏 territories (Indo-Scythia). According to a well-worn tale in later sources, the former returned from the Western Regions with either the first Buddhist scripture or the first Buddha image to arrive in China. Abel-Rémusat was tasked with identifying this figure and this event to a European audience. Since the early eighteenth century, well-read Tibetan and Mongolian monastic historians had known about the story of Zhang Qian, Emperor Wu, and the arrival of Buddhist material culture to China from such sources as Güng Gombojab's early *History of the Dharma in China*. Without these monastic sources in France, Abel-Rémusat had to contend with a contemporaneous misinterpretation: Deguignes had mistakingly read Zhang Qian 張騫 as *Tchang kiao* and erroneously published about him under that name in his much-maligned 1756 *Histoire des Huns*.[45]

Zhang Qian, Abel-Rémusat corrected in his footnotes to the *Record*, had in fact been sent on expedition to Central Asia "in the year 122 before Jesus Christ."[46] Though he aimed to make contact with the Yuezhi (Fr. *Yuě ti*), Zhang Qian was captured by Xiongnu forces (Fr. *Hioung nou*) and detained, during which time

FIGURE 4.3. Zhang Qing taking leave of Emperor Wu, Magao Caves, Dunhuang
Source: Zhang Qing taking leave of Emperor Wu. North wall fresco in Mogao Cave 323, Early Tang. Dunhuang Academy

he married and had children. After ten years, he famously escaped and journeyed farther west, past *Ta wan* (Farghana) and *Khang kiu* (Sogdiana), before arriving in the lands of the Yuezhi. Returning to China via *Khiang*, which Abel-Rémusat identifies as "Tibet," Zhang Qian was recaptured and escaped again, finally arriving home after thirteen years. "I have thought to delve into these details because they relate to the first discovery of India by the Chinese," Abel-Rémusat wrote. Here we must remember that before Abel-Rémusat's scholarship—such as his pioneering 1811 *De l'Étude des Langues Étrangères chez les Chinois* and the 1820 *Histoire de La Ville de Khotan*—the prevailing European view was that China had no developed knowledge or interest in foreign lands or foreign tongues.[47]

From this tangle of legend telling about Buddhism's arrival to China, Abel-Rémusat revealed, "we have a custom of placing its introduction in . . . [China] to the year 61 before Jesus Christ."[48] The year 61 CE dated a dream that famously disturbed the sleep of Emperor Ming 明帝 (28–75 CE) of the Han dynasty 漢朝 (202 BCE–9 CE/25–220 CE). The ancient emperor, Abel-Rémusat explains, "saw a man the color of gold and of great height, his head encased by a white, luminous halo and flying over the top of his palace."[49] Shaken, Emperor Ming consulted with officials at court, who told him "in the Western Regions there is a Being (*esprit*) named Foĕ."[50] Emperor Ming dispatched two officials to "retrieve information about the doctrine of Foĕ, draw a temple of Feou thou (temples and idols), and collect the precepts."[51] His envoys returned to Luoyang with two monks. "By this, the Middle Kingdom came to possess Samanéens and to observe rites of paying homage (*génuflexions*). A prince of the Zhou named Yng was the first to embrace the new religion. Yng also procured the book of Foĕ in forty-four chapters and images of Shâkya. Ming ti had religious images painted and placed them in the tower of purity. The sacred book was deposited in in a stone edifice."[52] Abel-Rémusat's European readers thus learned, in the manner of the Indian monks staring with mouths agape at Faxian, how Buddhism had officially arrived in the public life of China.

Faxian's explanation to the monks about the time of Buddhism in China inspired Abel-Rémusat not only to relay such official histories in his footnotes. He was working entirely from Chinese sources, especially the early fourteenth-century *Comprehensive Examination of Literature* (*Wenxian Tongkao* 文献通考), which, like the Buddhist texts that Zhou royalty deposited unread into stone towers, were found on the shelves of the Bibliothèque Nationale but never read in Europe. "But isolated events, the trace of which was only vaguely conserved, attest no less that Bouddhisme penetrated into diverse provinces in previous ages and was established obscurely without being noticed." In the "twenty-ninth or thirtieth reign year (or 217 years before Jesus Christ) of Chi houang ti of the Thsin dynasty, a monk from the western regions named *Che li fang* along with eighteen monastic companions arrived in Hian yang carrying Sanskrit scripture."[53] They addressed the court, "but the emperor, shocked by their strange mannerisms, put them in prison. Thereafter Li fang and companions began to recite the *Maha pradjña paramita,* an effervescent clarity (*un vive clarté*) filled the entire prison, and immediately after a genie the color of gold and six feet tall, armed with a mace, burst through the doors and absconded with the prisoners."[54]

But it was Abel-Rémusat's next citation of the "obscure" and only vaguely recorded arrival of the Buddhadharma into China that bore a remarkable resonance with Inner Asian monastic strategies during the late Qing. "Near the year 11 before Jesus Christ, the expedition of general *Hou khiu* against the Hioung ngu [Xiongnu] brought the Chinese into a country named *Hieou thou,* situated beyond the mountains of Yarkland. The king of the country offered sacrifices to a statue of a golden man. This statue was taken as bounty and brought to the emperor in 121."[55] To render such legends into history, Abel-Rémusat was forced to read this story against the grain of other, critical Chinese sources. "Yan sse kou remarks on this subject that this was made in gold in order to represent the prince of the celestial genies, and that this was the origin of the statues of Foě in use today." It was then, in the small offerings made to this statue in the Chinese court, "that the introduction of the religion of Foě began."[56]

Though earlier traces of Chinese contact with Central Asian Buddhist societies "established in the north of Tibet and in Boukharie" abound in Chinese sources such as the above, continued Abel-Rémusat, Faxian "was the author who recorded this [Central Asian] tradition most precisely and interestingly." Following him and returning to his exchange with the incredulous monks, Abel-Rémusat expanded the historical record still further: "the Bouddhistes of the banks of the Indus (i.e., Sindhu) understood that their religion had spread from beyond this river, with the help of Indian renunciants, just when the colossus of the bodhisattva Maitreya was erected, and that this event took place three hundred years after the Nirvân'a of Shâkya, during the era of Phing wang of the Tcheou dynasty."[57]

With all this in mind, Abel-Rémusat offers readers of the French *Record* a timeline of the history of Buddhism in China and Central Asia not known before in Europe.[58] "Phing wang started his reign 770 years before Jesus Christ and died in the year 720. To say briefly in passing here, this indication reports the death of Shâkya—which occurred three hundred years prior to the erection of the colossus, according to the author—to the year 1020 [BCE] or earlier. Or, without entering here into a discussion of all the dates assigned by the Bouddhistes of diverse nations to this event as well as by the Chinese, the birth of Shâkya may be placed in the year 1027 or 1029, and his death to the year 950."[59] Abel-Rémusat notes that other Chinese sources, such as *Wenxian Tongkao,* contradict Faxian and place the Buddha's birth in the year 688 BCE. This was the widely held European view of his day that there were in fact two Buddhas, one from the earlier date cited by Persian and South Asian authors—and in Abel-Rémusat's earlier work and his present study of the *Record,* by Faxian as well—and then another of a more recent vintage used by Tibetans, Chinese, Sinhalese, Nepalese, and the Japanese.[60]

Internal Paths

In Abel-Rémusat's commentary to the French *Record,* European readers were frequently presented with accounts of the tripled external world conceived in Buddhist cosmology and the *mārga,* or "path," that maps the internal cultivation conceived in Buddhist soteriology. At best, these were meagerly understood constructions of the person and environment in Europe. For all but a few, they were unknown entirely. "All beings find themselves placed at greater or lesser distances from the primitive actuality (*être primitif*), from the absolute, with more or less of a disposition to draw nearer to it, or, to speak the language of the Bouddhistes, to traverse the river of life and death and win the other shore."[61] And what, readers of *Relations des Royaumes Bouddhiques* must have wondered, could possibly lie upon that other embankment? The "soul is freed of that which alters its nature; it departs from this secondary and deceptive state where illusion, altered in a thousand ways, has produced dependence, variation, duration, individuality, the relations that follow upon this, thoughts, emotions, and the passions. By nature indestructible, *extinction* is the goal we must reach: meditation is the means."[62] Here is extinction without nihilism, a moral program for "salvation" without pessimism.

In the footnotes of the French *Record,* Landresse adds that "purified men," whether arhats or buddhas or bodhisattvas, "incarnations of the first and second order," no less than *devas,* "that class of beings the Bouddhistes retained from the Brahmanical cult," are not gods, "in the sense attached to the word in Western mythology," but rather "souls engaged in, and more or less distant from, the route to perfection."[63] Such grounds and paths described the inner landscape crossed over in Buddhist contemplation, but what was the form of that dusty and ice-choked external world trodden by Faxian?

As they would elsewhere in works by Abel-Rémusat, such as the posthumous *Essai Sur la Cosmographie et la Cosmogonie des Bouddhistes,* readers of the French *Record* learned that the world was not one but three uncountable, overlapping,

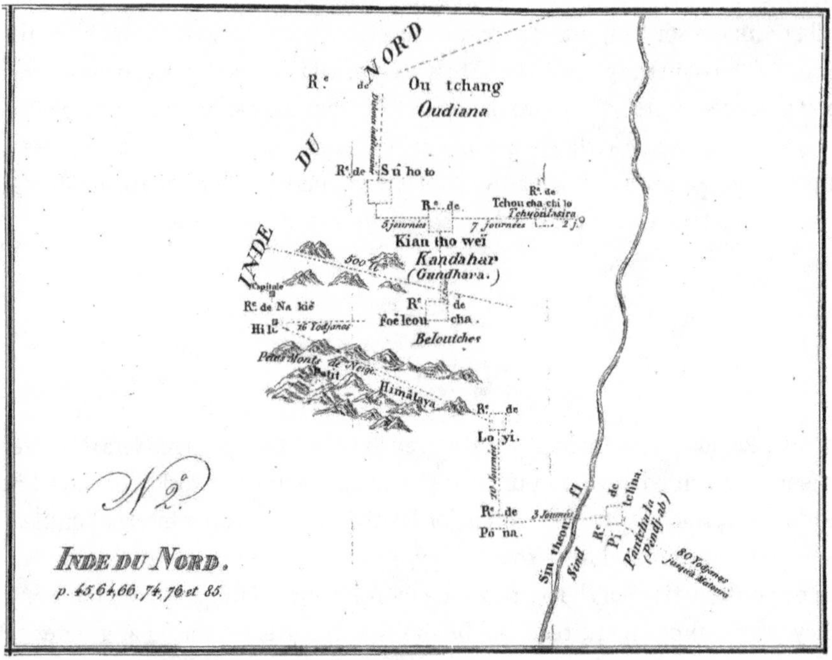

FIGURE 4.4. "Inde du Nord," drawn by Julien Klaproth
Source: *Relations Des Royaumes Bouddhiques,* plate iii

and simultaneous iterations.[64] "The imaginary powers are grouped by the millions and the billions, in the space that the view of man can hold from the earth to the sky, and in the diverse levels of the superimposed universe whose number even the mental perception of the most powerful (*puissant*) cannot conceive of. That which they occupy, the role that they play, are determined by the degree of their moral and intellectual perfection, and the duration of their life is proportionate to their rung in this mythological hierarchy . . . [W]e cannot ignore, at the base, the idea, well determined, strongly designed, and vividly recommended, about the production of all things by a primordial and absolute actuality (*être*). Innumerable worlds spring up in all directions and in an immeasurable space, within this divine substance, and the authors of legends never tire in piling up the most foolish exaggerations to enhance still more this idea."[65]

Buddhist cosmogony, in this early reporting, "apparently rests upon the doctrine of a single actuality (*un seul être*) to which all is reduced by the successive and reciprocal action of two principles of knowledge: a supreme intelligence and ignorance or mistakenness, or, in other terms, spirit and matter."[66] This sort of dualism was known already to Europeans from the writing of Jesuit missionaries. But it was Abel-Rémusat, in the view of his colleagues, who had first understood that "within this dualism, the universe and its parts, once formed, develops, taking their growth and configuration; abides, alters, and degenerates according to a kind of internal and spontaneous action, without any intervention on the part of a first principle."[67] Errors, passions, and vice "circumscribe, limit, and extend the phenomenal world; its duration is subordinated to the morality of the actions of living beings that either prolong their individual existence or else reunite them finally with the universal substance."[68] What is formed is destroyed. What is destroyed is reformed. A beginning and an ending succeed each other indefinitely. "This is unimaginable!"[69]

The Buddha's Birth

At the Institut de France in 1830, Abel-Rémusat had promised the lettered of Europe that by subjecting Faxian's *Record* to his methodological treatments, the birthplace of the Buddha ("a thousand years before Christ") would finally be emplaced. The geography of the Buddha's life, like the geography of Buddhist Asia generally, had never been mapped with certainty in Europe. In Abel-Rémusat's French rendering of the *Record,* Faxian named that natal place "the village of Kia-'weï-lo-'weï." This was, he determined, in the vicinity of the antiquarian Indian city of *Aoude* (i.e., Skt. Ayodhyā, in today's Uttar Pradesh). Ayodhyā was, Abel-Rémusat elaborated, "one of the principal theaters for the preaching (*prédication*) of le bouddhisme primitif." Here were geographic and historical facts made about the Buddha Śākyamuni's historical birth, carefully purified from "the fanciful" legends and superstitions about him and the thousands of other buddhas whose appearance and disappearance periodize the unfolding of time.

"The village of Kia-'weï-lo-'weï" (Skt. *Kapilavastu*), Abel-Rémusat continued, was the birthplace of the historical Buddha but also near what he called Na-pi-kia (Skt. *Nābhika*), a city also visited by Faxian and considered the birthplace of what Abel-Rémusat called "the fanciful" Buddha Krakoutchanda" (Skt. *Krakucchanda*). Just to the north was the birth site of "another buddha, equally mythological, Kanaka-mouni" (Skt. *Kanakamuni*).[70] Consigned to myth, these sites and their eminent but imaginary historical sons, the legendary population of previous buddhas, were exiled from the facts and events of the historical and geographical science of Buddhist Asia disciplined by Abel-Rémusat. But Kapilavastu was another matter entirely: "Here we must gather all the means at our disposal to fix the location of a site that was the theater of *one of the most remarkable events in the history of Oriental religions*, and which until now has been shrouded in obscurity. I wish to speak to you of the birth of Shâkyamouni, who became, by the force of

FIGURE 4.5. "The Birth of Shâkya mouni," drawn by Julien Klaproth
Source: *Relations Des Royaumes Bouddhiques,* 501

austerities and moral perfection, Bouddha, that is to say a saint *par excellence*, superior among men, among geniuses, and equal to the gods."[71]

Lost between myth and event, superstition and religion, the Nonwest and the West, the misidentification of the Buddha's birthplace had dogged the short history of Abel-Rémusat's methodical, professionalized science of Buddhist Asia. In what sense, he and his close colleagues had long wondered, was Śākyamuni "historical" while the previous four (or six buddhas) of this universal age were "mythic"? Wasn't all their speech recorded in text? Weren't they all assigned birthplaces in "actual" Indian sites? Are there not still-standing shadows, imprinted hands, ruins, and relics as artifacts of each of their lives? What analytical approach could render events and biography for some but not all?

The *Record* provided an opportunity. In his 1830 lecture, Abel-Rémusat first refuted the identifications of the Buddha's birthplace by previous authors, which provides a sense of what Abel-Rémusat and those in his milieu (Giorgi, Klaproth,

Schmidt, Landresse, Burnouf, etc.) considered their field in the 1820s and 1830s. Other authors had at best been "very vague on this subject." In the previous century, for example, Deguignes had ignorantly emplaced the Buddha's birth in Kashmir.[72] Langlès had it first in Tartarie and then Ethiopia, a claim Abel-Rémusat had disproved already in 1819. Others, like the Englishman William Jones on the authority of an Indian author (who confusingly also advocated the Black Buddha hypothesis) put it in the ancient kingdom of Kikata, understood to be a forest close to Gayā.

What other references were known? Abel-Rémusat turns to the sixteenth-century *Ain-i-Akbari* (Fr. *Aïn-akberi*), the final volume of a sixteenth-century Persian record of Emperor Akbar's administration of the Mughal Empire, titled the *Account of Akbar* (Per. *Akbarnama*). The *Ain-i-Akbari* identifies the Buddha as a prince born in Bihar. "Most recent authors identify his father as a king of Magadha, in southern Bihar, without any other explanation."[73] Abel-Rémusat's

FIGURE 4.6. "Mythic" and "historical" buddhas reproduced in Hodgson's 1827 *Sketch of Buddhism* (plate iv); rare visual depictions in an era before widespread use of photography that were widely referenced by Abel-Rémusat and Klaproth to interpret Faxian's *Record* in *Relations Des Royaumes Bouddhiques*
Source: Hodgson, *Sketch of Buddhism; Derived from the Bauddha Scriptures of Nipal*

comparative reading showed that Chinese authors, whose writing otherwise illuminates so many facts about Buddhist Asia, had misled European and Near Eastern authors on this important point for centuries. Deshauterayes, for example, had erroneously followed his Chinese sources in identifying the birthplace of the Buddha as *Kia-pi-lo-weï*. So too had Persian translations of Chinese histories, some of which had been known to European scholars since the late seventeenth century.[74] Finally, the "Chronology of the Buddhist Patriarchs," a Chinese text upon which Abel-Rémusat had previously published, named the Buddha's birthplace *Kia-pi-lo*.[75] All of these Chinese transcriptions, declared Abel-Rémusat, point clearly to "Kapila," which had been identified by Wilson in his Sanskrit dictionary as "a country which we believe was situated in the north of India."[76] Available Singhalese sources were equally imprecise.[77] Such was the rather pitiable extent of European knowledge about this fundamental fact of the Buddha's life, only pulled from the ether of the primitive Nonwest in 1817 by Ozeray and in 1819 by Abel-Rémusat.

In 1830, Abel-Rémusat spoke of this mystery as hiding one of the primary events in the "history of Eastern religions." Here only Faxian could help. The Chinese traveler was, after all, "the most ancient author to speak upon this region, and the one whose authority is most decisive, as he was present in these places to learn about Buddhist antiquities."[78] With the *Record* in hand, Abel-Rémusat triumphantly declared that the Buddha had been born in Kapilavastu.

> I thus regard as a sure point that the birthplace of Bouddha must be placed in the northern reaches of Ayodhyā (*la province d'Aoude*), to the southwest of

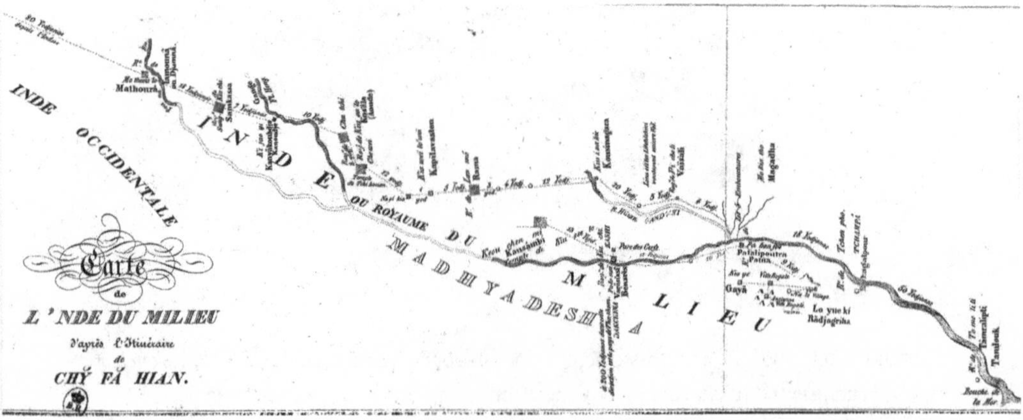

FIGURE 4.7. "L'Inde du Milieu," or Madhyadeśa, drawn by Julien Klaproth
Source: *Relations Des Royaumes Bouddhiques*, plate iv

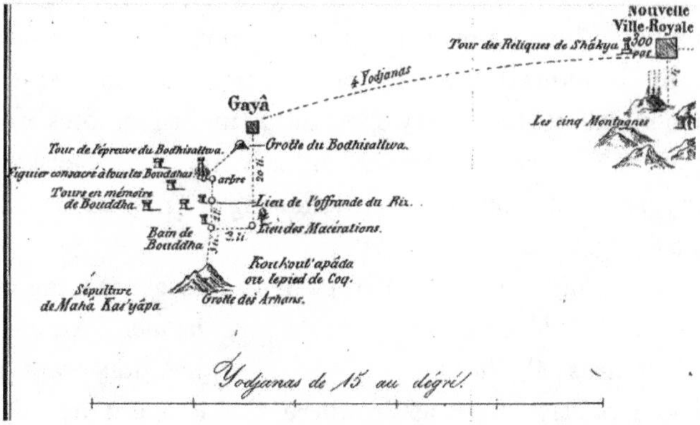

FIGURE 4.8. Portion of "Environs de Gayâ, Selons Chy Fă hian," drawn by Julien Klaproth

Source: *Relations Des Royaumes Bouddhiques,* plate iii

> Nepal, not far from the mountains that separate India from this latter country, some thirty leagues north of the Ganges, and more than sixty leagues to the northwest of Gayā, where we have regularly placed [the Buddha's birthplace] until now. We may thus no longer assign southern Bihar as the theater for this event, nor even the kingdom of Magadha . . . With this change, all of the facts related to the first preaching of Bouddhisme are much better explained.[79]

Working against the misrepresentations by previous scholars, such as the simplistic modeling of ancient Indian geography into a center and four cardinal regions, "as was said by the learned scholar" Deguignes, Abel-Rémusat reported that his "science" had determined that "Bouddhisme was born in Central India, though the place of its origin reaches to the borders of North India."[80] Here were the wellspring of the Buddhadharma and the places of the Buddha's life, arranged not in chronological time but in the circuitous space of Faxian's excited walking.

Saṅgha

When Abel-Rémusat spoke of Buddhist Asia, it was as a vast sphere of relation in the Nonwest bonded by a universal language that structured its metaphysics and ethics. Unbeholden to any specific location, Buddhist Asia was a relation among places in time. But who were its inhabitants, those "followers" (Skt.

pariṣad) of the Buddha in trans-Asian exchange, those ascetic members of "the Samanéen religion," whose movements, translations, and inter-Asian affiliations made up the interactional, relational continent of Buddhist Asia?[81] Abel-Rémusat and his editors took every opportunity in the footnotes of the French *Record* to present European readers with an early and comprehensive picture of the Buddhist community, or, in Sanskrit, the saṅgha (Fr. *Sanga*; Ch. *sengqie* 僧伽; Tib. *dge' dun*; Mong. *bursang, sangga*).

In the most rudimentary sense, European readers learned, the saṅgha was fourfold: monks (Skt. *bhikṣu*), nuns (Skt. *bhikṣuni*), laymen (Skt. *upāsaka*), and laywomen (Skt. *upāsikā*). The saṅgha was cleaved these four ways "according to a moral point of view." Here, as elsewhere, Abel-Rémusat drew deeply from his previously published work: a landmark study in the pages of *Journal Asiatique* just a year before his death and widely read across Europe: "Observations Upon a Few Points in the Doctrine of the Samanéene, and in Particular, Upon the Names of the Supreme Triade Among Different Buddhist Peoples."[82] The clean-shaven and saffron-clad monastics of Buddhist Asia, Abel-Rémusat revealed in one of several substantive footnotes on the subject in the French *Record*, are described in Antonio Agostino Giorgi's 1762 *Alphabetum Tibetanum* as "named in Tibetam *dGe slong*."[83] Moving dizzyingly between sources, periods, and languages, Abel-Rémusat unfurls the many names of monks, *bhikṣu*, and *bhikuṇi* nuns across Buddhist Asia. In Chinese, renunciants are

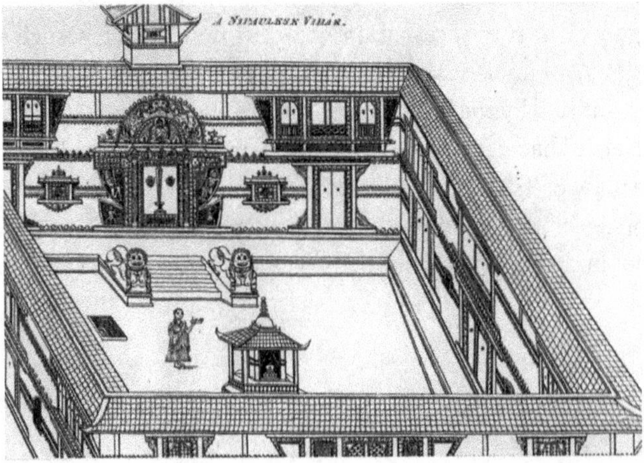

FIGURE 4.9. Section of "A Nipaulese Vihár." A rare visual rendering of a Buddhist monastery and monk from Hodgson's 1827 *Sketch of Buddhism* (plate vii), referenced on several occasions by Abel-Rémusat and Klaproth to illuminate the kinds of monasteries and monks Faxian would have witnessed in "north India" and "central India." Source: Hodgson, *Sketch of Buddhism; Derived from the Bauddha Scriptures of Nipal*

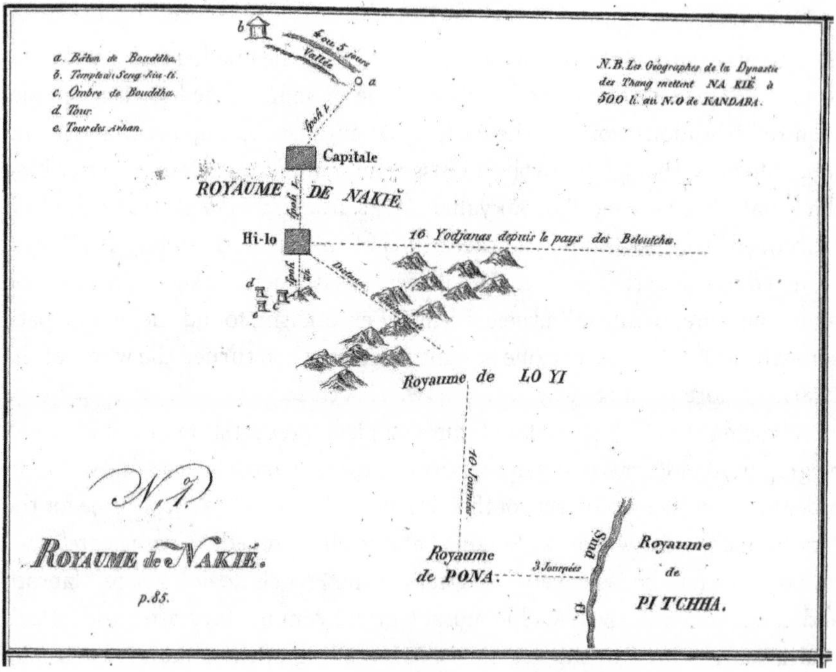

FIGURE 4.10. *Royaume de Nakie,* drawn by Julien Klaproth
Source: *Relations Des Royaumes Bouddhiques,* plate iii

known in general as "the race of Shâkya"; since the time of Dao'an (312–385), family names of monastics have been dropped for the clan name of the Buddha, Śākya (Ch. *shi* 釋). Indeed, Faxian was so named. The erasure of kin and blood in favor of lineage and saffron was also the work of monasticism in India. "When four rivers flow into the sea," he wrote, translating previously unread Chinese reference material from the back shelves of the Bibliothèque Nationale, "they may no longer reappear bearing their river name."[84] When men of the four castes become śramaṇa, they are named anew as kin of Śākyamuni.

And what are the names for the renunciant life monastics then lead? "Those who devote themselves to this kind of life must practice twelve kinds of observances that are named *theou tho,* from a Sanskrit word that means to shake up (*secouer*), since the observations serve to shake off the dust and stains of depravity (*la poussière et les souillures du vice*)."[85] Excavating from still more Chinese sources dedicated to the topic, Abel-Rémusat's naming of the life of an ideal monk mirrors that of the vinaya itself: "coming hither" into monkhood or nunhood, one lives, eats, sleeps, walks, and dies in twelve named ways and no others.

(Extinguishing) the Buddha's Life

The dozens of sites visited by Faxian associated with the Buddha's life, marked by so many imprints of feet and hands in stone or some ruined ancient temple, required strenuous work for the Parisian Orientalists to emplace in space and time. Much of this labor involved cross-referencing long passages describing the usual "Twelve Deeds" of Śākyamuni (Skt. *Dvadaśabuddhakārya*) as he first descended from Tuṣita, played the drama of taking birth among the Śākya, indulged in the extreme of worldly pleasure, saw the four sights, took to the renunciant life, indulged in the extreme of asceticism, found the middle path beneath the Bodhi tree, became enlightened, and then turned the wheel of the Dharma before passing away between two śāla trees.

Following Faxian's spatial, not chronological, presentation of the Buddha's biography, Abel-Rémusat and his editors needed to name its places and events in order to claim them as objects of their science. What was the Latin name for the "Bodhi tree" under which the Buddha became enlightened? It was *ficus religiosa*. In footnotes for the last twenty chapters of the French *Record*, where Klaproth and Landresse took over Abel-Rémusat's grand commentary after the latter's death, sources used to supplement Faxian's telling of the Buddha's biography moved from Chinese and Japanese (with regular turns to Sanskrit and Pāli with the help of the younger "Mr. Eugène Burnouf") to Mongolian and Tibetan.[86]

One of the primary tasks for these pioneering European biographers of the Buddha was to distinguish the man from fable. First, they had to transmute the fanciful tradition describing the Buddha's previous lives as a bodhisattva, as recounted most famously in the *jātakas* (Ch. *bensheng jing* 本生經; Tib. *skyes rabs*; Mong. *čadiγ*), and the usual stories of the Buddha's miracles, such as his ascent to the Tuṣita heaven, into event and biography, the objects of history and geography. Abel-Rémusat makes this distinction characteristically in a footnote to Faxian's account of Gandhāra that reads "when the Buddha was a bodhisattva": "that is to say, in his existences prior to his existence that he recognized as historical, where Shâkya mouni had already arrived at the next-to-last degree of moral and intellectual perfection, and obtained the quality of a Bodhisattwa."[87] Abel-Rémusat later clarifies that the Buddha is named "the Bodhisattwa" (Bodhisattva) "in several adventures of his earthly life, related to that portion of his life when he had not yet become the Bouddha, which is to say before his thirtieth year.[88] The *jātaka*, part of the "legendary" component of the Buddha's life, were "little known [in Europe], and form, if I may say so in this manner, the *prior-staging* (*l'avant scène*) of the life of the Bouddha."[89]

And what of the *after-staging*? What of the *parinirvāṇa*, or passing beyond, of the Buddha as he lay among weeping disciples in the shade of śāla trees, leafed

FIGURE 4.11. The Buddha's descent from Tuṣita Heaven into the womb of Mayadevi and birth. 20th century woodblock print from Kham
Source: *Himalayan Art Resources*, n. 87502

witnesses to an iconic moment in "the history of Oriental religions" at Kuśinagarī? Abel-Rémusat is careful to transmute even those trees witnessing the Buddha's passage, like the Bodhi tree and the death they shaded, into the taxonomical language of his science. Śāla trees were *cissampelos hexandra,* he determined.

And what was the name and nature of that great "extinction"—nirvāṇa—that begins Buddhist history under the Bodhi tree and, later practitioners expect, will end their personal story of cyclical existence? In a footnote to Faxian's witnessing of Puruṣa (Peshawar), Klaproth writes that nirvāṇa is in Chinese *pan ni houan* (i.e., *banniepian* 般涅槃). "*Ni houan,* or *extinction,* is easily recognizable as a transcription of Sanskrit *nirvân'a.* But in Chinese texts we frequently find this expression preceded by the syllable *pan* [i.e., *ban*]: it is always when it is a question, not of annihilation or ecstasy in general, but of the passage from actual and relative life to the state of absorption achieved by a buddha. *Ni houan* [nirvāṇa] is the state to which saints aspire; *pan ni houan* [parinirvāṇa] is the act by which they arrive."[90] Klaproth records consultations with Eugène Burnouf, which illuminated the Sanskrit source of *pan ni houan*, and the great many Qing sources whose comparative reading ordered words, and thus ideas, and thus difference within the unity that Abel-Rémusat invented as the Buddhist Nonwest.

But what of the Buddha's personal nirvāṇa? Faxian retrieved for China its first version of the *Mahāparinirvāṇa Sūtra*, that famous and widely influential account of the Buddha's final teachings.[91] In its many Sanskrit, Chinese, and Tibetan versions (but not the Pāli), the *Mahāparinirvāṇa Sūtra* illuminates key Mahāyāna doctrines concerning the "buddha nature" that underlies the mental continuum of all sentient life, various extended views about the experience of buddhahood, a grand historical schema of the decline of the Buddha's teachings, and the abundances of the world in general, beginning seven centuries after the Buddha's passing.

The state of European thinking about the dating of the Buddha's death at the time of Abel-Rémusat's *Relations des Royaumes Bouddhiques* can be gleaned from an 1827 article in the *Asiatic Journal* entitled "On the Eras of the Buddhas."[92] Here the dates proposed by European scholars are prefaced by, and set on equal footing to, a variety of Tibetan scholastic positions as collected by the Hungarian Orientalist Alexander Csoma de Kőrös (1784–1842) from the sixteenth-century works of the Tibetan polymath Kagyu lama Padma Karpo (Padma dkar po, 1527–1592). The work in question, though not named in the *Asiatic Journal*, is this lama's 1575 text *History of the Dharma, entitled Sun Which Spreads the Lotus of the Teachings* (*Chos 'byung bstan pa'i padma rgyas pa'i nyin byed*).[93] Padma Karpo supplied twelve separate chronologies of the Buddha's death current in Tibet between the seventh and sixteenth centuries, adding a separate thirteenth dating according to his own reckoning. These thirteen schemes range from 4,247 years to 2,885 years between the Buddha's death and the publication of this issue of *Asiatic Journal* in 1827. "The Era of Buddha," wrote its author, "is a subject of as much uncertainty in Tibet, as it is in India and Europe."[94] Indeed.

Averaging this Tibetan schema, Klaproth writes in his footnotes to the *Record*, the Buddha lived 2,959 years before the life of Jesus of Nazareth. The varied dating, however, suggested a multiplicity of buddhas; "there is great reason to believe [that the older estimation] refers to an Elder Buddha, one who is called in the Tibetan translation of the *Amera Cosha*, according to Mr. De Körös, Buddha Gan tan Khas-pa, or Buddha, an old and wise man."[95] Abulfazi was the grand vizier of the aforementioned Mughal emperor Akbar.[96] In his famous encyclopedic history, the *Akbarnama*, writes Klaproth, Abu'i-Fazi gave an entry on "Bauddha," which opens: "The founder of this rational system of faith is known as Buddha, and is called by many names."[97] This Persian source dates the

Buddha's death to 1366 BCE. Chinese sources, referenced by Deguignes and Couplet, have it as circa 1030 BCE.

Several well-known European scholars broadly concurred, such as Giorgi (959 BCE), Bailly (1031 BCE), Jones (1027 BCE), and Bentley (1081 BCE). Klaproth, in his 1824 *Vie de Bouddha, d'Après les Livres Mongols,* consults with Chinese sources and concurs with William Jones. Abel-Rémusat, in a 1821 article in *Journal des Savans*, also makes use of Chinese sources and dates the Buddha to 970 BCE. However, South and Southeast Asian Buddhist literature (or more precisely, the living South Asian paṇḍitas who advised the Anglo Orientalists) proposed a more recent chronology. The Burmese (546 BCE), the Siamese (544 BCE), the Singhalese (619 BCE), and the Peguers (in Burma, 638 BCE) were all more or less in agreement, which "bears testimony to the existence of a similar personage—a Buddha, or revival or that legislator, in a more recent period."[98] Even the Chinese source consulted by Klaproth gives a second, nearer date for the Buddha as 688 BCE.

In addition to referencing scholarship as diverse as a German study of Japanese iconography by "M. le docteur de Siebold" and a Chinese account extracted by Deshauterayes, Klaproth appeals to the aforementioned Chinese monk Xuanzang's seventh-century travelogue, which like Faxian's *Record* maps the site of the Buddha's passing as so many steps from Kuśinagarī.[99] (Abel-Rémusat's successor at the Collège de France, his student Stanislas Julien, would follow his teacher in publishing a French translation and study of Xuanzang's travelogue in 1854.)[100] What mattered for Klaproth was the scene in this text where Xuanzang walks slowly through the largely ruined site of the Buddha's passing to gaze at a painting depicting the scene upon a dilapidated temple wall. There he pauses to read an inscription scratched into the stone of a still-standing tower "some two hundred Chinese fathoms (*toises*) high": "Bouddha, age eighty, entered into nirvāṇa at midnight on the fifteenth day of the *Fei la ti kia* moon (Vaîsakhâ)."[101]

Like the doubled dating of Faxian's departure from Chang'an, deciphering this inscription read from the notes of a seventh-century Chinese monk occupied the best historical minds of nineteenth-century Paris (just as it would those interpreters of Faxian in Inner Asia, as we will see in the following chapter). In Klaproth's rendering of Xuanzang's reflection on that inscription, "Regarding the time of the Buddha's nirvana, the various [textual] collections differ in their determination. Some have it more than 1,200 years ago, others more than 1,300, and still others at more than 1,500. There are even those that assure us that it had been but 900 years, and that not even 1,000 years have passed since this event."[102] Klaproth interjects to help Xuanzang with the math: "Hiuan thsang [Xuanzang] wrote around the year 640 after Jesus Christ; it is thus to this year that these calculations are made, which puts the death of Shâkya mouni in the years 560, 660, 860, and even 360 before our era."[103]

Later, commenting on Faxian's account of the tooth procession ritual he witnessed in Ceylon ("the same relic which, by all appearances, was destroyed by the Portuguese viceroy more than a thousand years later") and the cremation of an eminent monk, Abel-Rémusat's editors remark: "The details of these two ceremonies are infinitely curious for the history of Buddhism in Ceylon. A fact that we learn from his narrative is that the *samanéens* counted, in the springtime of the year Fa-hian visited the island, 1,497 years since the nirvana of Bouddha; the traveler spent two years in Ceylon; he then took seven months to return to his country, where he arrived during the year 414 A.D. The death of Bouddha, according to these *samanéens*, corresponds to the year 1084 or 1085 before our era [i.e., B.C.]. This is a new date to add to all those that we have collected for this event, and we should compare it with other Singhalese dates that have been discussed by MM. E. Burnouf and Lassen, in their research upon the sacred language of the Bouddhistes."[104]

FIGURE 4.12. The Buddha's parinirvāṇa between two sāla trees, 20th century woodblock print from Kham
Source: *Himalayan Art Resources*, n. 87509

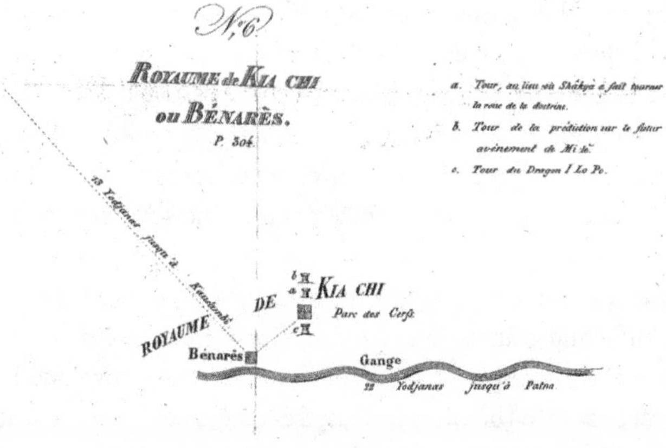

FIGURE 4.13. "Royaume de Kia chi ou Bénarěs," including site where the Buddha turned the first wheel of the Dharma (a), drawn by Julien Klaproth
Source: *Relations Des Royaumes Bouddhiques,* plate iv

In one of the many remarkable resonances of the Parisian treatment of Faxian's *Record* and those of Inner Asian scholasticism we will encounter in chapter 5, Klaproth hangs another note about nirvāṇa, extinction, and history upon Faxian's rather uneventful visit to Nālandā, a provincial town in the fifth century but by the seventh-century visit of Xuanzang already on its way to being the biggest monastic university in world history. Nearby, according to Faxian, the Buddha's disciple Śāriputra had achieved nirvāṇa. To illuminate the reference, Klaproth draws on the Mongolian historiographic tradition, providing a version of Śāriputra's nirvāṇa from the *Uliger-ün dalai,* or *Ocean of Parables.*[105] Within two decades, the product of this master statement of disciplinary knowledge about Buddhist Asia in Europe would be dismantled, its ruins and parts remade in order to extend not the epistemic and political sovereignty of the West but of the world historical orders of tantric prophecy, the Abhidharma, Chinggisid genealogy, and Qing historiography.

One wonders how Klaproth and Abel-Rémusat would have viewed their contribution and erasure in the chronicles of Asia's heartland.

Conclusion

"Is it not a great and astonishing spectacle," Landresse once said , "to see that religious doctrines, or morality and metaphysics, cosmogony and psychology, are continually confused, then established and perpetuated far from their birthplace and beyond the causes that produced them; united by the most abstract philosophical system, peoples located at two extremes of civilization, as if they were on two ends of Asia, and separated less by considerable distances, so difficult to cross, than by the differences of their climates, customs, and languages?"[106] Precisely this model of mobility, erasure, exile, connection, and new growth described the circulation of Faxian's *Record* into the sovereign territory of Europe and its sciences.

But as we shall now see, so too did this model describe the exit of Abel-Rémusat's study and translation of the *Record,* out of the Orientalist academy, beyond the imperializing association of universal knowledge and history with the West, and back into the Qing-inflected ecologies of interpretation of Asia's heartland. In the republic of Mongolian and Tibetan letters and imagination, the humanities were silenced so that other histories might speak. Buddhist Asia would soon become Jambudvīpa once again.

5

Science to History of the Dharma

On March 17, 1959, under the cover of darkness and in disguise, the twenty-three-year-old Fourteenth Dalai Lama, Tenzin Gyatso (Bstan 'dzin rgya mtsho, 1935–), fled the besieged Potala Palace for sanctuary in India. His escape came after a months-long occupation of Lhasa by the Chinese People's Liberation Army (PLA) and a week-long "Lhasa uprising" against what was seen as his imminent arrest.[1] As mass violence loomed, the Dalai Lama took flight dressed as a soldier in the company of bodyguards, senior monastic advisors, and government officials. Over a period of years thereafter, tens of thousands of Tibetans also fled, staggering out of Himalayan passes as refugees headed for welcome but dismal camps in India. The Indian government settled the early Tibetan refugees in places like Bylakuppe, in the southwestern state of Mysore.[2] Many died from tuberculosis, the stolid heat, or the toil of the road building that was required of them in compensation for their sanctuary.[3] The stream of refugees following the Dalai Lama widened during the terror of the Cultural Revolution (1966–1976). They still come, more than sixty years later, walking by night over ice and snow and alpine passes.

For some of the early waves of refugees fleeing the PRC annexation of Tibetan cultural regions, this was only the most recent phase of a doubled or even trebled crisis. In the late 1930s, Mongols who had survived the even greater mass extermination of monasteries and monastics by the Mongolian People's Revolutionary Party had fled to the eastern and Central Tibetan "mother monasteries" of their shared Gélukpa tradition. Among that Mongol contingent were some Kalmyk and Buryat monks who even earlier, in the 1920s and 1930s, had fled to Mongolia under the Soviet repression of their monastic tradition in Siberia. They

FIGURE 5.1. A group of early Tibetan refugees in Northern India, 1960s
Source: Courtesy of The Tibet Museum/DIIR

continued fleeing socialist state violence southeast from Mongolia to Tibet—and then, in the 1950s and 1960s, to India as well.[4]

For the wearied Inner Asian refugee community housed in the Indian Tibetan settlements of the early 1960s, what *time* was the violence of their twentieth century?[5] How did displaced ethnic and linguistic groups from Siberian, Mongolian, and Tibetan societies *emplace* their loss in relation to one another? What "regimes of historicity" governed their dizzied present?[6] In early Tibetan settlements like Lugsung Samdupling and Dickey Larsoe, the historical frame of the refugee diaspora was unclear at best.[7] One strategy developed by the exiled Tibetan leadership—with roots in mostly failed diplomatic strategies by the Lhasa-based Ganden Potrang government going back to the early twentieth century—was to evoke the language of a nation state and its right to sovereignty. Many monk historians in the early refugee camps, however, sought a historical frame for their diaspora experience in terms other than the national subject. They drew instead upon their millennia-old traditions of writing local and global history according to the precedents and expectations of genres like *chö-jung*, "history of the Dharma" (Tib. *chos 'byung*), or *nam-thar*, a "liberated life story" (Tib. *rnam thar*).

As far as I have been able to determine, the earliest author of a *chö-jung* in the Tibetan refugee community was a Buryat abbot and revered scholastic named Ngakwang Nyima (Tib. *Ngag dbang nyi ma*; Mong. *Agvaannyam*, 1907–1990).[8] Over the course of his unseated life, Ngakwang Nyima wrote prodigiously on all manner of scholastic subjects. His 1965 history *The Lamp of Scripture and Reasoning Dharma History* (Tib. *Chos 'byung lung rigs sgron me*) was the first major monastic history published in the Tibetan refugee community.[9] Therein, Ngakwang Nyima does not engage the nationalist narrative of the government-in-exile. He draws instead upon a variety of synthetic works from the Sino-Mongol-Tibetan frontiers of the Qing Empire by go-between scholar monks: authors we have met already like Güng Gombojab and Zava Damdin Lubsangdamdin, as well as other Géluk scholastics working in the synthetic frames of the Qing frontiers. Dzaya Paṇḍita Lubsangperlei, Sumpa Khenpo Yéshé Peljor, and Thuken Chökyi Nyima, for example, all emplace and time Jambudvīpa in canonical works such as the *Prophecy of Li Sūtra*, the *Root Tantra of Mañjuśrī*, and the *Kālacakra-tantra*.

In sections of *The Lamp of Scripture* where Ngakwang Nyima writes about the deep history of the Inner Asian twentieth century, however, he looks past these well-worn works and well-known events and actors from the Inner Asian historical record. Unexpectedly, the usual litany of Buddhist kings and khans, Manchu emperors, and luminary Tibetan and Mongolian monks are reordered. The refugee experience of socialist state violence and refugee diaspora among Siberian, Mongolian, and Tibetan communities is instead set into time by appeal to the wandering of a fifth-century Chinese monk named Faxian.

> What's more, the route through which Indian *paṇḍitas* and *siddhas*,
> Chinese monks, and so on
> journeyed to and fro while composing scriptures,
> passed through Khotan, part of the territory of the Uighur-Mongols.
>
> Faxian (*Phā hyin*), Xuanzang (*Thang zin bla ma*), and others—
> those who uniquely observed all this for themselves while traveling across Mongol dominions
> on their way to the Land of Noble Ones—
> made record of it all in their writings.
>
> *The Travel Guide* [i.e., the *Record*][10] reports that
> during Faxian's journey to the Land of Noble Ones,
> more than two hundred years before Xuanzang,
> the Dharma traditions he witnessed
> in Upper Sok [Tokhara and Khotan, claimed as "Mongol lands"]
> followed Indian traditions.
>
> When the King of Subduers[11] and his spiritual heirs blessed Khotan,

three hundred and fifty-three lotuses emerged from an ocean
[bearing] buddhas and bodhisattvas with resplendent bodies.

[The Buddha] prophesied that in the future
there would be as many great monasteries founded here and
there in this land
as there were lotuses [sprung from that ocean].
The knowledgeable accept that this prophesied event has now
concluded.

Based on that, if I were to guess, most of the Mongolian
population
are the rebirths of creatures who lived in that ocean.
Likewise, the sūtras record that the pure land of Ākāśagarbha[12]
is located in the borderland where the sun rises.

By appeal to Faxian's walking as written in *The Record of Buddhist Kingdoms*, Ngakwang Nyima presented his refugee readership with an encompassing vision of hereditary place now lost. In the 1960s, exiled to India in a tragic reversal of Faxian's ancient travels, pining for lost worlds on the Himalayan plateau just as Faxian had longed for home upon seeing the Chinese fan in Sri Lanka, he understood Faxian's *Record* as witnessing Tibetan and Mongolian history. Indeed, the version of the *Record* Ngakwang Nyima held in his hands in the Tibetan refugee settlements did tell this history, but only after a century of Mongolian and Tibetan reinterpretation—not of Faxian's original Chinese, but of Jean-Pierre Abel-Rémusat's *Relations des Royaumes Bouddhiques,* Europe's first book-length study of "Buddhist Asia." In that century and a quarter, *Relations* had circulated out of Europe, out of the epistemic sovereignty of humanism, into late imperial frameworks unbeholden to the discursive frame of a science or the West/Nonwest binary of Orientalism.

This chapter shares the major Inner Asian interpretations of Eurasian history that mark the unmaking of the science of Buddhist Asia between the time that *Relations des Royaumes Bouddhiques* left Paris after 1836 to Ngakwang Nyima's writing during the 1960s. As mentioned in the previous chapters, there are remarkable synchronicities in the topics and interpretative strategies that mark their deciphering of Faxian's *Record* in Siberia, upon Mongol steppes, and in refugee settlements —even though the content of their interpretation is radically divergent. As for Abel-Rémusat and Klaproth, the timing of the Buddha's life, the place and status of Khotan, and the nature of Faxian's personhood occupied Dorji Banzarov and Lubsangdamdin. With the *Record* in hand, however, neither was concerned with extending a Leibniz-derived model of racially inflected global similitude, or to fulfill the modernist promise of the human sciences. Rather, they leveraged their scholastic interpretative practices and the bulk of Inner Asian knowledge about East, Inner, and South Asian history in order to clarify (Tib. *gsal*), order (*bkod*), and connect (*'brel*) narrative fragments in sources like the *Kālacakra-tantra*, the Abhidharma, various Mongolian and Tibetan chronicles, and two centuries of Qing-inflected models of

FIGURE 5.2. Contemporary Tibetan-style rendering of Faxian
Source: commissioned by author

world history. Like Abel-Rémusat and his edtors, Lubsangdamdin did so by extensively annotated his translation with interlinear notes.

The substitutions of Inner Asian references into the writing of Faxian himself (*lamas* for monks, *Bön* practitioners for Indian non-Buddhists, *Mongol* kings for foreign rulers, and so on) transformed Europe's first book-length statement of the science of Buddhist Asia into a monastic illumination about the deep time of the Buddhadharma and the Tibetan and Mongolian communal experience. In conditions of possibility sprung from silencing humanism in Asia's heartland, Faxian was identified as an enlightened bodhisattva, Khotan was claimed as "Mongol," mountains and deserts through which he passed were identified as pilgrimage places still visited by the Tibetan faithful, non-Buddhist *Bön* practitioners were found in ancient India, and references to Buddhist canon and doctrine were interpreted through the lens of Lubsangdamdin's Géluk scholastic tradition. By this, Faxian's ancient wandering became remarkably familiar. It helped to time and emplace the forced mobility experienced by Inner Asian peoples weathering the violence of revolutionary transition to modernity in Asia's heartland.

Faxian the Mahātma

Do the enlightened weep when watching life drain from the eyes of a friend? Do even their lips tighten as they resign themselves to karmic law? What is born, dies. What is gathered, disperses. In their written lives, do buddhas and bodhisattvas know tragedy or sorrow? When and in what sense can the emotional, or emotionless, lives of the enlightened compass the present of the contemporary reader? Marpa Lotsawa, the great eleventh-century Tibetan tantric master whose life story was well known to Lubsangdamdin and Ngakwang Nyima, covered his head and shed many tears when his son was killed in a riding accident.[13] Marpa's students were bewildered by his emotional display. What should one do when the guru cries and grieves and beats his chest? "Have you not taught us that death is illusory?" they asked him. "Yes," sobbed Marpa, "death is illusory. But the death of one's child is an even greater illusion!" Inner Asian authors have spent one thousand years pondering what he could have meant.

In the black-stroked Chinese of the *Record* pored over by Abel-Rémusat, Faxian had often cried and wailed and suffered bone-deep ache for home. Among Parisian Orientalists and later generations of European translators influenced by humanism and Romanticism specifically, the emotional landscape of Faxian was often discussed. How "human" this ancient monk must have suddenly appeared to "modern" readers recognizing his tears! This transhistorical sign of "devotion," "piety," and the "religious impulse" found in the emotional intensity of Faxian's walking promised Orientalists rare access to the "individuals," "facts," and "events" of Buddhist Asia. In learning of Faxian's grieving next to his companion's corpse, his bitter contemplation of a shadow, his tears fallen upon the ruins marking the long-ago wandering of the Buddha, Abel-Rémusat and milieu found evidence for a human life so often obscured by superstitious adulation and mythic exaggeration in the vast literary heritage of "the Orient."

In contrast, in Lubsangdamdin's Tibetan translation of Banzarov's Mongolian translation of Abel-Rémusat's French, Faxian is made to fit genre expectations as a protagonist of a "liberated life story" or *nam-thar.* Such characters were, in general, expected to be already enlightened figures (or figures on the path to enlightenment) performing a human drama in order to draw forward the frontiers of the Dharma. In the thousands of folios of auto/biography Lubsangdamdin wrote between 1900 and 1936, there are almost no examples of ordinary individuals—only ordinary collectivities who are as fields for the enlightened activity of others ("Mongols," "Tibetans," "Chinese"). And Faxian is no exception, altered in Tibetan translation from the Parisians' view of him as a rational human full of awe, doubt, fear, and a neophyte's aspiration for "idealism." In the topography of Tibetan letters, Faxian becomes a bodhisattva, an advanced practitioner weathering saṃsāra in order to haul the Dharma from the "Middle Kingdom" of India to the "Middle Kingdom" of China.

As it had for the European interpreters, Faxian's reaction to Huijing's death in the iced passes of the Little Snowy Mountains offered opportunities to rewrite the content of his person. Suffering terribly from the cold, Huijing had lost bodily vigor rapidly, with "white foam [coming] from his mouth." With his dying breath, he had pleaded with Faxian to complete their journey and not die slopeside with him. In Abel-Rémusat's French, just as in the Chinese, Faxian caresses Huijing as the latter passes into another life. Seeing that he was dead, "[Faxian had] cried and deeply bemoaned that their shared mission was running *contraire à la destinée.*"[14] Overwhelmed by the bald fact of human frailty, Faxian nonetheless "gathered his strength." He left Huijing's corpse and descended through the peaks and valleys of French letters into India, the horizon line of "destiny."

When the *Record* was made in Tibetan, Faxian was rarely a man; he was more often a "Great Being," or *mahātma* (Tib. *bdag nyid chen po*), an enlightened one deserving the honor of an inscribed life.[15] In Lubsangdamdin's account, the "human monk" so recognizable to Parisian Orientalists is left to die alongside Huijing. In the Tibetan, Faxian still holds Huijing's cold hand, but he neither cries nor grieves.

> In those conditions, only Huijing could not endure the intensely savage cold (*grang ba'i ngar rtsub*). As he journeyed in front, his bodily vigor (*lus stobs*) began to decline. Bubbles dribbled from his mouth. He spoke thus to Faxian: "Now there is no way I can survive. You all must quickly move on! There is no reason that we all should die here!" With those words, he passed away.
>
> Though many means were used to console Faxian, he expressed no mournful lamentation. He deliberated instead upon the meaning of what had occurred: "This is the general karma of sentient beings as well as my own bad karma arising as an obstacle. Though unhappy, there is nothing I can do."[16]

For Tibetan readers thereafter—like Ngakwang Nyima, global historian of the refugee camp—Faxian was not the individualized agent shaping his own destiny through moral and rational means recognized by nineteenth-century humanists. Nor was he a mirrored image of Abel-Rémusat: a sober, rationalist Orientalist seeking truth in the opaque lines of foreign text. Bearing himself appropriately as an advanced Buddhist practitioner or bodhisattva, Faxian the mahātma throughout the Tibetan *Record* endures the suffering wheel of *saṃsāra* with dry eyes and enlightened vision.

Finding Khotan

For Lubsangdamdin writing in revolutionary Khalkha Mongolia, Faxian's *Record* allowed for an entire reimagining of Inner Asian scholastic historiography centered on new, ethnicized histories of Central Asia—focused especially on the city-state of Khotan as being Mongolian. In several publications from the 1820s and 1830s, we will recall, Abel-Rémusat and Klaproth had set Khotan into the homogenous space of their historical geography and explored its throughways as a microcosm of the relational continent of "Buddhist Asia." The status, location, and identity of Khotan were also topics of long-standing debate among scholastic thinkers in Tibet and Mongolia. Monastic scholars from across Inner Asia had for centuries debated about Khotan, and especially about its relationship to "the Land of Li" (Tib. *li yul*): the setting for several famous accounts about the teaching and prophecy-giving activity of the Buddha.

Faxian's *Record* allowed Lubsangdamdin to authoritatively identity Khotan as the "Land of Li." He could thereby rewrite not only the religious, social, and political history of the Mongols, but also the Buddhist history of India, Central Asia, Tibet, and China from a newly buttressed Mongol-centric worldview. He elaborated these claims in a great variety of ways in many texts, such as his monumental *Golden Book* from 1931 (all of which are quite beyond the present study).[17] Of relevance here is that in the Tibetan *Record* Faxian did not center Khotan as "the metropole of Buddhism" at the Sino-Tibetan-Mongol-Indic-Persian crossroads (as the Parisian Orientalists had); rather, he centered "Mongolia" as the crossroads of Buddhism moving between India and China.

The following is from Lubsangdamdin's annotations to his Tibetan translation of Faxian's visit to Khotan:

> It is said in the *Prophecy of the Land of Li Sūtra* (Tib. *Li yul lung bstan pa'i mdo*):
>
> > When my beloved place
> > becomes the Land of Li,
> > at the Dharmarājan Stūpa (*Chos kyi rgyal po'i mchod rten*)
> > in that beautiful abode of Gomatrī (*'Gu ma ti ra*),
> > the buddhas of the Fortunate Age
> > will establish the vinaya.
>
> This [land described by Faxian] is actually the place referred to in the prophecy.[18]

And then soon after:

> Concerning this Jowo procession, the *Ox-Horn Sūtra* (Tib. *Blang ru lung bstan pa'i mdo*) states:
>
> > Moreover, in this land a great statue of my form will be carried about by chariot and installed inside a palace called "Possessing Virtue," where it will become a great object of offering.
>
> It is clear this prophecy refers to this [Jowo procession witnessed by Faxian in Gomatrī].[19]

The implications of Lubsangdamdin's substitution of Khotan for "The Land of Li" become even more apparent in the opening lines of chapter IV of the *Record*, which describe Faxian and company departing from Dunhang for Zihe. In chapter III, Lubsangdamdin gives a Tibetan spelling for the Mongolian

Kotung—which is Banzarov's rendering of Abel-Rémusat's *Royaume d'Yu thian* for Faxian's *Yutian guo* 于闐國. In chapter IV, Lubsangdamdin simply provides *Li'i yul* for Khotan, never betraying his heavy hand other than to underscore that the Land of Li represented an ancient "Mongol" connection to the life and teaching career of the historical Buddha.

> When Khotan's (*Li'i yul*) fourth-month procession of holy objects (*rten gyi gling bskor*) was complete, Sengshao (*Se wang sho'u*) departed alone toward Jibin in the company of a scholar. Faxian and his other companions journeyed on toward the country of Zihe,[20] arriving after twenty-five days.
>
> [This was the land of the Yi he kho khān (i.e., Mong. *Yekeqoqan*), a group belonging to the southern Mongols (*Sog po lho sde*). Xuanzang similarly recorded how these people greatly served him as well. It appears most likely that this is the Kardo (Skar do) region prophesied in the *Prophecy of the Land of Li Sūtra*].[21]

Lubsangdamdin retained Banzarov's Mongolian in this spot: "When Khotan's fourth-month procession of holy objects was complete." Thus did Faxian walk into the prophetic time of Buddhist monastic historiography in post-Qing Mongolia.[22]

But "Mongols" and later, "Tibetans" would not stop appearing in Faxian's journey in Inner Asian translation. Banzarov and Lybsangdamdin would find them again and again in distant India, and as virtuous patrons nearby in the city-states of Central India at the northern frontiers of the Land of Noble Ones. But first Faxian needed to cross a familiar bone-strewn desert.

Finding the Gobi Desert

It was Abel-Rémusat's colleague Julius von Klaproth who carved Faxian's *Record* into forty chapters with subheadings, not found anywhere in the Chinese. Following the French, Banzarov and Lubsangdamdin adopted this organization and titling in the Tibetan and Mongolian. Yet their obedience to Orientalist structure was only superficial; the subheadings in many cases were subtly transformed in Mongolian and Tibetan so that Faxian's ancient walking would be through more recognizable Inner Asian topographies.

The earliest example comes in a rather broken chain of subheadings in chapter 1. The opening of the *Record* in the French, Mongolian, and Tibetan is framed by reference to the desert expanse of the Hexi Corridor and Lop Nor through which Faxian passed as he moved westward from Chang'an. In the French translation from 1836, Klaproth added the final subheading *Désert de Sable,* or "the Sandy Desert." In the intermediary Mongolian translation, Banzarov uses "the sandy Gobi" (Mong. *elesütü γobi*), whereas in the later Tibetan translation Lubsangdamdin offers "Sandy Wilderness" (Tib. *bye ma can kyi 'brog*). By gently silencing the French *Record* long enough to slip in the decidedly familiar and localized Gobi Desert, Banzarov allows Faxian's tale to speak more directly to Mongolian readers and thus offer them a new historical perspective on their deep history. This departure is just the first of many nativizing choices that enabled Banzarov and especially Lubsangdamdin to coax Faxian's *Record* into telling radically familiar stories about Mongolian and Tibetan places, peoples, and histories.

But recall that Lubsangdamdin translated Banzarov's translation. How did the former depart from the latter back toward the original French without seeing the French? According to Byambyn Rinchen in 1970, Lubsangdamdin and his collaborators never had access to the French text. And yet, both extant editions of Lubsangdamdin's Tibetan text skip over Banzarov's Mongolian "Sandy Gobi" and translate directly from the French, which he supposedly never knew, to produce "Sandy Wilderness." In fact, references to French footnotes or translations that are absent in the Mongolian text occur elsewhere in the early chapters of the later Tibetan rendition. Most likely, Lubsangdamdin had access to different drafts of Banzarov's work in 1917 than Rinchen did in 1970, perhaps including some with partial translations of the great footnoted Commentaire.

Once Faxian and company were far enough west of Chang'an, they were—in Abel-Rémusat's French—swept to Shanshan upon a "River of Sand" (*le fleuve de sable*). This is a literal reading of the Chinese *sha he* 沙河—a current of grit haunted by evil spirits and flesh-melting winds. Such attributions in the Chinese required rationalization in the French, where the work of ghosts was muted in order to appeal to the mechanical working of nature. By such silencing, the West/Nonwest binary was reproduced and the events and facts of an imperializing science were made. But such empirical expectations of Europe were unknown or irrelevant for these Inner Asian interpreters of Faxian. The Chinese *Record* specifically names this malevolent devil population of the desert as *egui* 惡鬼, or hungry ghosts (Skt. *preta*). Lubsangdamdin does not lose this opportunity to bend the reference to more recognizably Inner Asian "demons" (*bdud*) and the local disease-giving "tsan spirits" (*btsan*).

For readers of the Tibetan *Record,* such seemingly minor translations would have enormous historical implications: tsan spirits, for example, are regional beings famously commanded by a native class of protective deities who were the chief opponents of the Dharma arriving in Tibet in the seventh century. In the narrative arc of most post-eleventh-century "history of the Dharma," the memory of the Indian tantric master Padmasambhava's subjugation of these antagonistic local spirits and protectors and their vow to thereafter protect the Dharma frames a vast history of Buddhism's spread out of India into "Tibet and Mongolia." So do the demonic spirits, demons, and serpent-spirit nāgās that tormented the body of Köten Ejen, the grandson of Chinggis Khan. In another oft-repeated episode in the dispensation of the Dharma from Tibet to Mongolia, the thirteenth-century Tibetan polymath Sakya Paṇḍita exorcised the spirits and demons inhabiting Köten's flesh. Thus purified, he and the Mongols generally are remembered to have become devotees of the Sakya lama and patrons of the Dharma arriving from Tibet. In the Tibetan *Record,* Faxian walks across similarly occupied landscapes of sand and ghosts enlivened by familiarly named demons and spirits. So too were some of the mountains that lined Faxian's westward passage to India; in Tibetan translation, they mark familiar horizons and bear already known names.

Finding "Tibetan" Mountains

According to the Chinese *Record,* after leaving a summer retreat spent in Quiangui, Faxian and companions passed near the Long Mountains into the dominion of the Tufa Rutan. Heading for the garrison town of Zhangye, the monks next traversed the Yanglou Mountains (Yanglou shan 養樓山).[23] Though only mentioned in passing in the Chinese *Record,* these bare peaks received abundant interpretive attention in the French, Mongolian, and Tibetan. Where was the Yanglou range to be found on the tenuously webbed maps moving elliptically among readers and writers in France and Inner Asia? By what names was it now known? What communities dwell in its shadow?

The Parisian Orientalists drew deeply upon forms of language equivalency derived from the Inner Asia–facing Qing Empire. As Faxian walks from *Si ning* (Xining) to *Kan tcheou* (Gansu), Klaproth offers in a long footnote: "[Faxian] must have necessarily passed the large mountain range perpetually covered by snow, which separates the districts of *Kan tcheou* and *Liang tcheou* from the large valley through which runs a river called (*Oulan mouran*) by the Mongols, and *Houang choui* or *Ta thoung ho* by the Chinese. This high range was named by the ancients Hioung nou [Xiongnu] *Khi lian chan.* Nowadays the neighboring Mongols name its highest peak, formed of a colossal glacier, *Amiye gang gar oola,* which is to say, 'grandfather's mountain, white with snow.' "[24] Klaproth locates this mountain between the cities of Xining and Ganzhou, both of which are part of the Sino-Tibeto-Mongol Amdo cultural region (Tib. *A mdo*) that is today mostly partitioned into Qinghai and Gansu provinces of the People's Republic of China.

The "Mongol name" Klaproth cites—"Amiye gang gar oola"—is in fact a compound of Mongolian and Tibetan. What he writes as "oola" is "mountain" in Mongolian (*aγula*), while his "Amiye gang gar" represents the Tibetan "Amyé Gangkar" (*A myes gang dkar*), making together "the White Snow Mountain of Amyé." Banzarov's Mongolian follows Abel-Rémusat's French verbatim ("les monts Yang leou" = "yang-lu aγula") while Lubsangdamdin departs from the Chinese, French, and Mongolian translation altogether. In Tibetan letters, Faxian does not walk past *Yanglou shan*, *les monts Yangleou*, or *Yang-lu aγula*, but "the

FIGURE 5.3. Tibetan thangka painting of Amnyé Machen, Buddhist regional protector resident of, and coterminous with, Mount Amnyé Machen. Mid-twentieth century, Amdo
Source: *Himalayan Art Resources*

mountain range of Amyé Gangkar," the identification given also by Klaproth a century earlier in Paris. But just where were these peaks in the spatial reckoning of the Tibeto-Mongolian scholastic imagination?

Lubsangdamdin offers a tentative interpretation, and in so doing ropes Tibetan and Mongolian histories even deeper into the tale. "Although this appears to be a region in Amdo," he writes in an annotation, "nowadays it remains unidentified; even so, I am thinking it may refer to a snowy region to the north of Serkhok (*Gser khog*)."[25] The Amyé Gangkar of Klaproth's identification, Lubsangdamdin decides, must be that very well-known sacred mountain in Inner Asia named Amyé Machen (Tib. *A mye rma chen*; Ch. *Ani ma qing shan* 阿尼玛卿). This is one of eastern Tibet's most popular pilgrimage destinations, in the east of today's Qinghai province in the PRC. Moreover, the "Serkhok" in Lubsangdamdin's note seems to refer to one of the great Géluk monasteries of Amdo.[26] In the shadows of Mount Yanglou—or should we say Amyé Gangkar? Or Amyé Machen?—Faxian walked further west. A millennium and a half later, Mongolian and Tibetan readers discovered themselves anew in each named peak, river, and temple. So too did they find themselves among the desert and mountain peoples of the Western Regions Faxian had passed fifteen centuries earlier.

Finding Uighurs

Moving westward from Shan-shan, Faxian and his party continued to move through Buddhist kingdoms. Their rulers patronized thriving monasteries whose abundances set the half-built monastic world of Buddhist China into sharp relief. At one point in these early descriptions, Faxian comments upon how similar each of these kingdoms was to the others, "except that in each country the barbarian language differs 唯國國胡語不同."[27] The term Faxian used for "barbarian" is a common one: *hu* 胡. As elsewhere in the circulatory history of the *Record* examined in these pages, this single word *hu* opened sightlines for Inner Asian readers to find themselves.

Abel-Rémusat translated the Chinese faithfully into French: "except that in each country the barbarian language differs."[28] In footnoted reflections about Faxian's reference to "barbarian languages" that hangs from this passage, Abel-Rémusat does something noteworthy.

> Faxian's remark [about "barbarian languages"] gives us reason to think that the tribes (*peuplades*) who lived west of Lob Lake up to the edge of Khotan all

> belonged to individual races and had different languages, not speaking the same as the Hindous from whom religion had been introduced in these countries. The languages in question were certainly Tangusic (*tangutain*) or Tibetan, Turkish, a few Getic vernaculars (*dialects gétiques*), and other unknown languages. It is doubtful that during this era a single Mongolian people had spread in this direction.[29]

"Hindous" and the Chinese are here understood in relation to one another and, in the same breath, to the Tibetans and Turks of antiquity. Arranged on the newly discovered continent, these disparate peoples were "certainly" connected to one another: in time and space, in matrices of language, race, political formation, and religion, in the relational landscape of "Buddhist Asia." For Abel-Rémusat, these were all open to careful reconstruction in the linear and empty time of history, transmuted into facts in the empty plane of geography, and read as shared philosophy only superficially encased in different scripts and tongues.

FIGURE 5.4. Fragment of Uighur scripture recovered from Dunhuang (Magao Cave Complex)
Source: Princeton East Asian Library

In the Tibetan version of the French and Chinese passages (which both read "except that in each country, the barbarian language differs"), Lubsangdamdin does not use the expected Tibetan word for "barbarian" (*kla klo*) to translate the tongues heard by Faxian. In the Tibetan, the different languages Faxian heard in the deserts west of Shan-shan become "Uighur" (Tib. *yu gur*). Lubsangdamdin explains in an annotation couched in the flow of the Tibetan narrative:

> As they departed this region and journeyed to the west, each successive country along the path was like the one before; they all resembled the territories of the Uighur (*Yu gur gyi yul ljongs*). [This seems similar to a small kingdom connected by royal succession to the Uighur called Ka'u chang, clearly described in Xuanzang's *Guidebook*]. Though each region possessed a distinct local language, the monks read Indian texts and endeavored in particular to study the Indian language.[30]

But how did Lubsangdamdin have Faxian walking across the territories of the Uighur, a people he claimed in the grand pan-Mongolian family, when in the Chinese and French Faxian merely notes that he heard "barbarian languages"? The answer comes from chains of silencing and interpretation in the Mongolian and Tibetan out of Abel-Rémusat's footnotes, the staging ground of his science of Buddhist Asia.

In the body of his French translation, Abel-Rémusat gives "le royaume de Ou i" for the Chinese "country of Yanyi 焉夷國," referring to Qarašahr.[31] Abel-Rémusat apparently misread the first character as 烏 (*wu*) ("*oi*" in his transliteration system) instead of 焉 (*yan*).[32] Combined with the second character 夷 (*yi*)—meaning "barbarian"—Abel-Rémusat's wording reads "the barbarians of Ou." But who were they? Neither the Frenchman nor his editors could find any reference to the *Ou i*. In a footnote, Abel-Rémusat came up with a guess: *Ou i* "is easy to recognize with the help of a simple correction. Instead of 夷 *i* [*yi*], barbarian, it should read 胡, *hou* [*hu*], which has the same meaning."[33] Some Chinese editor, Abel-Rémusat decided, had likely "substituted one word for the other," since 夷 and 胡 share the same meaning. "These kinds of substitutions frequently occur," he assures his readers. And indeed, in his earlier research about the historic Buddhist city state of Khotan, Abel-Rémusat had come across a Chinese editor making precisely this switch while quoting the *Record*. The result, in the transcription of the French text, is thus not "the country Yanli," but "the country of Ou hou ." And so, Abel-Rémusat concludes in his footnote, "*Ou hou* would be the name of the Uighurs (Fr. *Ouïgours*)."[34]

Banzarov, who had access to Abel-Rémusat's footnotes, takes up Abel-Rémusat's guess and simply writes "Uighur" without comment into the body of his Mongolian translation. From this, in the Mongolian *Record* Faxian walks from society to society between Shanshan and Yanli observing that "each was similar to the Uiγur nation" (*uiγur ulus büri tor busud eče ilγaburi nigen qari qala baymui*).[35] Reading Banzarov's Mongolian generations later, Lubsangdamdin simply amplifies this narrative in the Tibetan. Therein, Faxian walks westward from Chang'an to north India, passing through societies that are not "similar" to the Uighurs but *are* Uighurs. This is significant since—according to monastic historical convention developing the Inner Asian frontiers of the Qing since at least the time of Gombojab in the eighteenth century—the Uighurs (and Sogdians and Xiongnu and Turks and Khotanese) were increasingly claimed as part of the vast Yeke-Mongγol Ulus, the Great Mongolian nation. In the Tibetan *Record*, because of a misguided guess by Abel-Rémusat in Paris a century earlier, Faxian witnesses a shared pan-Mongolian past. And thereby, in the tumultuous revolutionary upheaval of the Qing ruins, the Europe's first study of Buddhist Asia helped buttress a brand of Géluk scholastic interpretation developed over the course of the Qing; therein, all peoples beyond the Great Wall, including in the Western Regions, were "Mongol" and "Buddhist."[36]

Finding "Mongol" Kings

Reading Inner Asian places and peoples into the *Record* because of Orientalist interpretation was not limited to identifying "Tibetan" mountains or "Uighurs." In the Chinese *text*, the ruler of Zhangye sheltered Faxian and companions during a time of violence and unrest, acting as their benefactor. At this juncture, Abel-Rémusat duly supplies the etymology and doctrinal significance of Buddhist patronage, charity, and giving—teaching European readers that such giving (Skt. *dāna*) was counted as one of the "perfections" (Skt. *paramita*; Ch. *boluomi* 波羅; Mong. *baramid*; Tib. *pha rol tu phyin pa*) whose practice propelled practitioners of Mahāyāna Buddhism to enlightenment. Here was holy action in the webbing of karma along the path to emancipation: "Whosoever practices beneficence," he cites from a sūtra, "crosses over the sea of poverty."[37]

Unlike Abel-Rémusat, for whom Faxian's witnessing was an opportunity to explain Buddhist "metaphysics and ethics" to uninformed European readers, in the Tibetan *Record* Lubsangdamdin did not need to make Faxian's shelter at Zhangye an opportunity to explain perfected giving. What he saw instead—as he did in so much of Faxian's journey to India—was an opportunity to develop historical arguments about the "Mongol" and "Tibetan" places, people, and histories Faxian witnessed. Now altering the body of the translation itself, he has

Faxian and companions finding shelter and appropriate kingly munificence in what "appears to be Mongolian territory"[38]—thereby assigning a new geography to the soil of ancient Zhangye.

Faxian's walking from Zihe to Mount Congling inspired additional substitutions. The Chinese reads simply: "To the west of the desert until India 沙河已西迄于天竺."[39] Abel-Rémusat's French follows the Chinese faithfully: "After passing the River of Sand (*le fleuve de Sable*) in the west, he reached India."[40] Banzarov follows Abel-Rémusat filially in the Mongolian, summarizing Faxian's passage as leading through "the River of Sand in the west" (*barayun jüy-dur elesün mörin*).[41] Lubsangdamdin, however, departs from Banzarov in the Tibetan: "In the westerly direction of the setting sun, he passed through many desert mountainous passes and valleys in *Mongol territories* in order to reach India" (*Nyi ma nub phyogs su hor yul gyi bye ma'i la lung mang po brgal ba'i rjes su rgya gar du slebs po*).[42] In chains of interpretation and erasure, Banzarov and Lubsangdamdin once again subtly transform the *Record* into an ancient witness of Inner Asian history. By such play of silence and speech in the circulatory history of the *Record*, Ngakwang Nyima and his readers, in the squalor of the Tibetan refugee camps during the 1960s, could find themselves and thereby set into time and place all that had been lost to Soviet, Mongolian, and PRC state violence.

Following his description of the four-month procession in "the Land of Li" (i.e., Khotan) described earlier, Faxian elaborates on the ornate public ritualism promoted in this polity. We read of magnificent gold-covered statues of the Buddha in unspeakably beautiful temples. In the ways these translators chose to identify devotees at these events, we find still another transformation of Faxian's *Record* from the object of a science in Europe into a witness of synthetic monastic history forged in the Qing and its ruins. Compare the chain of translation from the Chinese to French, Mongolian, and then Tibetan.

FAXIAN: "The six kings of kingdoms to the east of the mountain range 嶺東六國諸王" come regularly to make offerings.[43]

ABEL-RÉMUSAT: "The princes of the six kingdoms to the east of the mountains send offerings of the most precious substances of all they possess" (*Les princes des six royaumes qui sont situés à l'orient de la chaine des montagnes, y envoient en offrande tout ce qu'ils peuvent avoir de plus précieux*).[44]

BANZAROV: "Princes of six lands" (Mong. *jirγuγan ulus-un qatun*) from east of the Pamirs and their notable offerings.[45]

LUBSANGDAMDIN: "The kings of some six Mongolian kingdoms (*hor sog gi yul ljongs*) to the east of the mountain range offered whatever valuables they had to this place."[46]

In the Tibetan Lubsangdamdin has injected radical substitutions in the many annotations and in the main body of the text.[47] As with Amnyé Machen and Serkhok Monastery (in the "Traversing 'Tibetan' Mountains" portion above), in Lubsangdamdin's Tibetan language telling Faxian trod through territories and temporalities already of the late- and post-Qing scholastic worlds of Inner Asia, where the great imagined community of Mongols, the Yeke Mongɣol Ulus (Tib. *chen po hor gyi yul*), was being made and unmade as a national subject—a Buddhist one—aching for revolutionary emancipation.

Maitreya and the Hidden World

In the body of the French *Record* of 1836 and the Tibetan translation of 1917, the "great master" Maitreya helps time the present in altogether different knowledge ecologies. When Faxian and his companions arrive in India, along the banks of the Indus River, incredulous local monks interrogate them. From where did they come? When and how did the Dharma spread so far east? In Abel-Rémusat's French, Faxian replies to the Indian monks by reflecting upon the place of Maitreya, the future buddha, in the young history of the Dharma in China:

> Without the help of this great master *Mi lĕ* (Maitreya), who could continue the work of *Chˇy kia* (Śākyamuni) and transmute (*réduit*) his laws into practice? Who else could have been capable of spreading knowledge of the Three Precious Ones (*trois êtres précieux*) and have them penetrate as far as the inhabitants of the edge of the world, by teaching them to know with certitude the origin of the mysterious revolution (*revolution mystérieuse*)? This was not an effect of any human operation. This was the cause of the reverie of *Ming ti* of the Han dynasty.[48]

Though Banzarov's Mongolian follows the French faithfully, compare the above with Lubsangdamdin's scholastic rereading in Tibetan:

> If not for this great teacher Maitreya (*Byams pa*), who else could we identify as establishing the tradition of Śākyamuni? As facilitating the study of the scriptures? As propagating (*rgyas*) the explanation of the Three Jewels into the ends of the world? [As illuminating] hidden phenomena and the end of

> activity (i.e., right conduct, [*yang dag pa'i*] *las kyi mtha'*)? As being powerful enough to translate the scriptures and their commentaries to foster excellent understanding and study? Ordinary people hardly have the ability to accomplish such activities at their leisure! This is why Emperor Ming of the Great Han dynasty was beset with such marvelous dreams.[49]

The great divergences of the *Record*'s circulatory history are laid out in such passages. Note the difference in translation and implication between Abel-Rémusat's "origin of the mysterious revolution" and Lubsangdamdin's "As illuminating hidden phenomena and the end of activity." In his explanatory footnotes, Abel-Rémusat provides essays on the "Three Precious Ones (*trois êtres précieux*)"—the three objects of refuge: Buddha, Dharma, and Saṅgha—and Emperor Ming's dream. There are no essays, however, upon the mysteriously translated *revolution mystérieuse*.

Lubsangdamdin, however, inserts a very specific Géluk scholastic reading of Banzarov's Mongolian rendering of the French *revolution mystérieuse*. Without acknowledging the addition, he first supplies the technical term "hidden (phenomena)" (*lkog gyur*, i.e., Skt. *parokṣa*). According to his dispersed late-Qing scholastic tradition, "hidden" and "evident" (Skt. *Abhumukhi*; Tib. *mngon du'gyur ba*) make up the two fundamental classifications of phenomena. The latter refers to objects of knowledge available to sense perception and thereby to most human beings; the former refers to objects that can only be known through inference. The difference, to use a well-worn example in Buddhist epistemology and logic (Skt. *pramāṇa*; Ch. *liang* 量; Mong. *kemjiy-e*; Tib. *tshad ma*), is between a fire seen directly and a fire inferred from detecting smoke wafting over a mountain ridge.

The opportunity to learn the difference, "not an effect of any human operation," had come to Eemperor Ming of the Han, and to the people of China, and later to Tibetans and Mongolians. It would, however, remain a mystery in the first masterwork of the science of Buddhist Asia.

The Xiongnu and the "Golden Man"

Abel-Rémusat hunted the "vague" and poorly recorded instances of early Chinese and Indian contact, as well as the arrival of Buddhism into "the East." Similarly, from his Mongolian monastic college, Lubsangdamdin developed much of his historical writing about the deep history of Inner Asian Buddhism by pursuing the witnessing of poorly known Chinese sources available to him in Mongolian translation. Like Abel-Rémusat and his milieu, Lubsangdamdin was especially interested in finding narratives related to Emperor Ming's long military and economic engagement with the Xiongnu 匈奴. "At that time, it happened that [the Chinese] robbed a large golden statue of the Teacher Buddha, [which had been] a sacred object (*nang rten*) of the Xiongnu."[50] Just like Abel-Rémusat and the Parisians, and building directly upon the interpretative precedents of his eighteenth-century forebears, such as Rašipungsuγ's 1775 *Crystal Rosary* (*Bolur erike*) and Gombojab's *History of the Dharma in China*, Lubsangdamdin writes, "This is renowned as the first image of the Buddha to have arrived in China. As such, it clarifies just how the Buddhadharma spread into Mongolia (*Hor yul*) before [it spread into] either China or Tibet."[51]

For both Abel-Rémusat and Lubsangdamdin, the historical references in Faxian's exchange with the monks on the banks of the Indus were critical pieces of evidence for making Buddhist Asia into the object of scientific history and geography. For Lubsangdamdin, the implications were for identifying and claiming vast swaths of Central and Inner Asian religious, social, and political history through the Qing looking glass. In either case, their new evidentiary knowledge drew upon the very same Chinese historical sources; not only Faxian's *Record*, but also records of the emperors of the Zhou and Han and their encounters with "Tibetan" and "Mongols" among the Xiongnu, Khotanese, Bokharians, and Sogdians.

Finding "Bön" Practitioners in India

As we have seen, Dorji Banzarov and Lubsangdamdin often found opportunities to populate Faxian's *Record* with Inner Asian themes and agents. These came in chains of erasure and elaboration enmeshed with the French footnotes seen by Banzarov (and possibly Lubsangdamdin). Such elaborations came most often in passages describing Faxian's travel across the deserts and mountains west of Chang'an and before arriving in India. In both Mongolian and Tibetan, as we have seen, "Mongol" princes suddenly appear as celebrated patrons of Buddhist societies witnessed by Faxian. Yutian guo 于闐國 became not only Khotan but "the Land of Li" (Tib. *Li yul*), a Buddhist society visited by the Buddha, recorded in various canonical sūtras, and for Lubsangdamdin most assuredly a "Mongolian" place. On his way to India, furthermore, Faxian had apparently wandered devotedly past mountains like Amnyé Machen, which Tibetans in the twentieth century still recognized as a place to be circumambulated, touched, placated, and propitiated. Examples of Banzarov and Lubsangdamdin having Faxian encounter ancient "Tibetans" and "Mongolians" in India are rarer, but hardly absent. Throughout the Inner Asian appropriation of Faxian's *Record*, opportunities came not just from the lines of the French translation but also from the apparatus of the footnotes, especially from Klaproth's layering of Mongolian references atop Abel-Rémusat's magisterial annotation essays.

In chapter XXII of *Relations des Royaumes Bouddhiques*, Faxian describes King Aśoka's centuries-old encounter with a nāga in Central India. He also describes in passing the elephant caretakers of the Rāma Stūpa. About the Rāma Stūpa, Abel-Rémusat translates: "There were *Tao sse* from various countries who came to make their adorations of this tower (*Il y eut des Tao sse de diverse pays qui vinrent pour faire leurs adorations à cette tour*)."[52] Klaproth hangs a fascinating correction to the above line, drawing upon Mongolian and Tibetan "chronicle" in ways that, a century later, would bring the science of Buddhist Asia back into that Inner Asian chronicle tradition. "It is quite remarkable," writes Klaproth, "that in his itinerary Fă hian speaks so regularly about the Tao szu who, in his time, existed not only in Central Asia but also in India."[53] Moving past Klaproth's stubborn use of idiosyncratically transcribed Chinese words, at odds with Abel-Rémusat in the very same lines of the same text (from *Tao sse* to *Tao szu*!), it is Klaproth's historical certainty that matters. "It seems," he writes, "as though the doctrine of this philosophical sect was already widespread since long ago in the countries to the west and south-west of China."[54]

The "Tao szu" devotees witnessed by Faxian in fifth-century Central India were for Klaproth not just possibly but quite certainly Bön practitioners (Tib. *bon po rnams*; Mong. *bon-nar*). And though this "philosophical sect" was an opaque reference for French readers, it was immediately legible to Inner Asian readers, and triggered a rush of familiarity and opportunity among the Mongols and Tibetans. Bön is a non-Buddhist tradition that developed a distinct but parallel identity in Tibet alongside Buddhism in the "renaissance period" of the eleventh to twelfth centuries. The story of the mirrorwork of Bön and Buddhism in Inner Asian monastic chronicle is vast.[55] Indeed, fundamental themes in Inner Asian Buddhist monastic histories—such as subjugation (Tib. *'dul*), contact (Tib. *mjal*), and purificatory place (Tib. *gnas*), as well as landscape enlivened by mundane and supramundane presence and agency—are meaningless without Bön frames of reference.[56] In the conventions of Tibetan language writing among Mongolian Buddhist monastics over the course of the Qing, very much including in Lubsangdamdin's wider oeuvre, indigenous non-Buddhist traditions such as Mongolian Böge-yin šasin had been glossed in Tibetan as Bön for generations.

We will recall that, in still another exchange in this circulatory history, it was Dorji Banzarov who would influentially call Böge-yin šasin "shamanism" in his article *The Black Faith, or Shamanism Among the Mongols*.[57] Such a heterogenous phenomenon is named "shamanism" in comparative religion textbooks to this day. And in Banzarov's and Lubsangdamdin's translations of the *Record*, Bön practitioners appear in ancient India as pilgrims who see a ruined temple and stūpa commemorating the life of the Buddha, tended by devoted elephants who clean and make offerings. But how? As usual, in the Eurasianist making and unmaking of historical knowledge from the footnotes of the great French Commentaire.

"The 士道 *Tao szu*," opines Klaproth in his footnote, "are named in Tibetan བོན་གྱི་ཆོས་ *Bon ghĭi tsiōs* [i.e., *bon gyi chos*], which was the ancient religion of Tibet (*Tubet*); it prevailed until even the ninth century, the period of the general introduction of Buddhism in this country; still today, there are a great number of these sectarians in *K'hams youl* [i.e., *Khams yul*] or Lower Tibet (*Tubet inferieur*)."[58] And here we come to the interpretation apparently picked up by Dorji Banzarov as he brought the *Record* into the republic of Mongolian and Tibetan letters—and in so doing projected Inner Asian identities onto the ancient *dao ren* witnesses to the marvels of elephant devotees. "There are many texts that contain descriptions of their doctrine, which the Mongols call *Bom bò-ūn nom*. ག་ཤེན་རབས་*Chen raeebs* was its founder."[59]

Here Klaproth is making use of Alexander Csoma de Körös's *Essay Towards a Dictionary of Tibetan and English*, published after Abel-Rémusat's death in 1834, to confidently reframe the entirety of this section of the *Record*.[60] From Csoma de Körös, Klaproth moves to his familiar haunt: Isaak Jakob Schmidt's German translation and study of Sayang Sečen's seventeenth-century Mongolian chronicle *Erdeni-yin tobči*, entitled *History of the Eastern Mongols and Their Princely Houses* (*Geschichte der Ost-Mongolen und ihres Fürstenhauses*). According to this text, the Bön were present in the courts of the Tibetan Yarlung Empire. Elaborating upon Schmidt's interpretation in *Geschichte der Ost-Mongolen*, "*Bon bò* means 'lord' (*seigneur*) in Tibetan. I believe here the reference is to inhabitants of mountains and valleys," Klaproth muses, deciding that they could have spilled south into the Indic plains and thus into the misted past of Buddhist Asia.[61] With this rather careless connection—a misreading of the Chinese and an interpretation of a fifth-century Chinese text making use of a seventeenth-century Mongolian chronicle read through an entry in Europe's most recent Tibetan dictionary—the Bön arrived in India clad in the clothes of *dao ren*, 道人 (a "person of the Way").

Later in the Inner Asian versions of the *Record*, we see a similarly anarchic chain of interpretation, with Bön practitioners appearing in the main body of Banzarov's Mongolian and Lubsangdamdin's Tibetan translations. In the section about Faxian's arrival to Mount Kukkuṭapāda, we read in the Tibetan: "The residences of the arhats lay upon the western slope of this mountain. Scholars and Bön practitioners from every country come here to prostrate to Kāśyapa. People with uncertainty about the meaning of the scriptures come each evening to hold discussions with the arhats."[62] The Chinese, however, simply reads: "Devoted people (*dao ren* 道人) from other kingdoms come year after year to make offerings to Kāśyapa 諸國道人年年往供養迦葉."[63] Abel-Rémusat translated this into French as: "les *religieux de la raison* de tous les royaumes de ces contrées."[64] Similar to what we saw above, Abel-Rémusat's "the scholarly religious" (*religieux de la raison*) becomes in Banzarov's Mongolian "Bön practitioners" (*bumbu-ner*). This was then reworked in Lubsangdamdin's Tibetan as "scholars and Bön practitioners" (Tib. *mkhas pa dang bon po rnams*).[65]

Such is the centerless play of silence and speech, erasure and writing, in the Forest of the Blind that made and unmade Europe's first book-length study of Buddhist Asia.

(Extinguishing) the Buddha's Life

In 1923, a few years after he had finished his translation of Faxian's *Record*, Lubsangdamdin was contacted by Agvan Dorjiev, the great Buryat monastic scholar and confidant of the Thirteenth Dalai Lama and Tsar Nikolai II. Dorjiev asked the Khalkha master to comment upon the contradictory dating of the Buddha's life between their shared Inner Asian scholastic tradition and the chronologies of European Orientalism. Here the reference is to a popular genre of scholastic historiography, in which Lubsangdamdin also wrote, known as ten-tsi (Tib. *bstan rtsi*) or "chronologies of the teachings," though such dating was often embedded in "histories of the Dharma" (*chos 'byung*) and other genres of monastic historical writing.

By the 1920s, scientific chronologies of "foreign Europeans" (Tib. *phyi rgya ser pa*) were increasingly becoming available in revolutionary Siberia and Mongolia, severely challenging received chronologies of the monastic tradition. But it was not only French, English, German, or Russian scholarship but also Chinese and Japanese sources and ancient Central Asian text being pulled from deserts and caves that offered competing temporalizations of the Buddha's birth and death. Chinese texts translated into Mongolian and Tibetan during the Qing Empire, for example, in Gombojab's *History of Buddhism in China*, indicated that 2,943 years had passed since the Buddha had emerged from his mother's right side and declared, "Thus have I come for the well-being of the world!" Against the Chinese and European timing of the Buddha's life, Lubsangdamdin's post-Qing monastic calendars gave him several competing dates from across Tibetan traditions. According to the Puk system, 2,300 years had passed; according to the New Astrological System of the Genden, 2,200 years had passed; while according to the Golden Astrological system, more than 2,400 years had passed.[66]

Reconciling these competing dates was a dominant matter of debate among monks in revolutionary Mongolia and Siberia. In 1923, Dorjiev wrote to Lubsangdamdin, a scholar known for his command of several historical traditions, to ask for a definitive dating of the Buddha's life and death. Agvan Dorjiev wrote:

> Of great consequence for us Buddhists
> are contributions to "chronologies of the teachings" (*bstan rtsi*)
> made by Europeans who have determined that the Buddha
> was born a little more than two thousand five hundred years ago
> by examining inscriptions found on the stone pillars of the
>   Dharma King Aśoka.
> Since this [view] completely contradicts our [own],
> it is essential that we refute it using scripture and logic.
> If we cannot, we will have to accept [their position].
> Concerning all this, we ought to seek the sure counsel
> of our own Lords of Learned Ones.[67]

In his extant response (written a year later, in 1924) Lubsangdamdin emphasizes the sort of relativist position on European truth that had long been the interpretative procedure of his frontier Géluk scholastic forebears from the eighteenth and nineteenth centuries, such as Sumpa Khenpo Yéshé Peljor.

> Concerning matters such as the year of the Buddha's birth:
> Since for us time and place are suprasensory objects of
>   knowledge (*skla ba'i don*),
> we must establish [this fact] by means
> of valid cognition based on scriptural sources.[68]
> Yet, since there are so many explanations of scripture,
> Indians, Chinese, Tibetans, and other scholars hold various views.
> From among these, just one is correct while all the others are not.
> Regardless, our tradition will only accept what is proven.
> Except for us, no one else will trust [our conclusions].
> Leaving that aside, if whatsoever disciple
> were to follow the Buddha's teachings,
> [they] could attain higher rebirth, liberation, and enlightenment.
> Therefore, those wishing for liberation should be impartial [in
>   this debate].

According to foreign European calculations from stone inscriptions,
it has been more than two thousand five hundred years.
Alternatively, following the Phuk [astrological] tradition,[69]
it has been [an additional] three hundred years.
Following the New Genden Calculation [System],[70]
it has been two hundred [years more].
And there are more systems still.
These measurements come from using rationality (*rig stobs kyis dpog pa tsam*).
Since there are no proofs available to direct perception,
whether you wish to refute another's tradition and prove your own tradition,
or whether you wish to refute another's objection and prove your own position,
it remains uncertain whether the stone inscriptions
in the Land of Noble Ones may lead to valid knowledge.
For example, two inscribed pillars are on the stone stūpa
that was built where the Teacher achieved parinirvāṇa.
There, two systems recording just when he "went beyond" appear.
One says he "went beyond" on the fifteenth of the second month,
while the other says it was the ninth day of the eighth month!
Xuanzang describes all this.
Besides, the emanations of the Teacher's three secrets are unthinkable.
Because of this, perhaps the Buddha appears
to be born and to pass away at different times
according to the experience of individual disciples?
For these reasons, Glorious Candrakīrti said:

> In terms of karmic causes and their results,
> [the Buddha] objected to using logical reason.[71]

Also, the Venerable Rendawa has said:

> The doorway to the process by which
> the Saṃbhogakāya Pure Land is formed is unthinkable.[72]

Do not, therefore, think about it![73]

But Lubsangdamdin had thought about it, and quite deeply, five years earlier when trying to interpret Faxian's *Record.* There he tended to favor another view, that of the *Kālacakra-tantra* system. According to the *Kālacakra*, Lubsangdamdin had finished translating and interpreting the *Record* 1,900 years after the Dharma first came to China, and 1,500 years after Faxian's walking "in the fifty-second year of the fifteenth *rapjung*, in the later part of the Mindruk (*smin drug*) month of the Mouse Year."[74]

In the final section of Faxian's *Record* that deals with dating the Buddha's life and death (in Ceylon while witnessing the tooth relic procession), Abel-Rémusat and Lubsangdamdin do not agree. The former has Faxian dating himself in line with the Chinese, which reads: "One thousand four hundred and ninety-seven years have passed since [the Buddha's] parinirvāṇa 泥洹已來一千四百九十七歲."[75] The latter has: "In these ways, countless beings were liberated from saṃsāra into nirvāṇa, and then he passed to nirvāṇa. Since he passed to nirvāṇa, one thousand four hundred and sixty-seven years have passed. When the Eyes of the World were closed, all sentient beings were profoundly grieved."[76]

Eyewitnessing

Lubsangdamdin's historiography, like that of his frontier scholastic forebears of the Qing, increasingly expanded upon, sought evidence for, or rejected received textual history by appeal to eyewitness accounts, oral history, and material culture.[77] He explored this empirical evidence in many of his annotations to Faxian's *Record.* Here we see fascinating and important evidence about the understudied connections between Siberia and Mongolia and the major pilgrimage sites in India in the early twentieth century. Everyday laity, monks, and lamas were apparently traveling to and fro; indeed, in another of Lubsangdamdin's writings—a praise biography for his recently deceased root lama, Sanjaa (i.e., Tib. *Sangs rgyas*)—we read that this master traveled to Nepal and India, though he never wrote of his journey.[78]

In his *Record*, Faxian used many examples of personal communications to elaborate both upon the narrative and upon the extensive appeals to textual authority elsewhere in his annotations (the *Root Tantra of Mañjuśrī*, Xuanzang's *Guidebook*, etc.). Similarly interrupting Faxian's description of visiting Vulture's Peak—that critical episode so emphasized by Sengyou and Huijiao in the sixth century—Lubsangdamdin inserts: "Although Xuangzang recorded many blessed temples there, pilgrims who visit today report that there are only a few caves, the ruins of some houses, and the stone throne. Other than these, nothing remains."[79] Later, when Faxian arrives at Vārāṇasī, in the kingdom of Kāśī, Lubsangdamdin includes a long firsthand account of its present condition, ending with: "In short, from the temple of the Teacher Buddha to the flesh eaters of the charnel ground (*dur khrod kyi khrod kyi sha za*), the people of Kāśī say that there are thirty-three million different statues and temples! I have heard that nowadays they claim these still remain! Even today, the king of that region is known as the Hindu Mahārajā and is very famous all across the world."[80]

Lubsangdamdin jumps into Faxian's telling about Ceylon (i.e., Siṃhala) to share: "I have directly heard from many Tibetans and Mongolians who have gone on pilgrimage to Siṃhala. They tell me that the power and wealth of Siṃhala island, its temples, their three supports, the manner in which the saṅgha study and practice, and the old demon fort (*sngon gyi srin mo'i rdzong*) all remain the same today."[81] Describing the luminosity of the jewel fixed into the peak of the stūpa housing the Buddha's tooth relic in Ceylon, Lubsangdamdin writes, "People say that even nowadays you can see this from *Kalikata* (Calcutta), which is part of the Bangala region. I once even received a picture of this amazing Gandhola into my hands."[82] But it is another, much longer personal intrusion that is the most arresting.

> Long ago, a Buryat Khenpo named Chödzin (*Chos'dzin*) went by boat to this island. He met Paṇḍita Sumangala. This Khenpo explained the style of his Buddhism to [the paṇḍita]. Then the paṇḍita asked, "Who do you believe created this universe?" He answered, "We believe that the many different types of worlds are created by karma." Happy, [the pandita] asked, "Has the Buddha's teaching spread into your region?" He answered, "Yes, it has spread, but it has spread more into Tibet." He responded, "Even nowadays, the Buddha's teaching is spreading into many regions, but in terms of maintaining the Dharma discipline (*vinaya*), this is the only place where it is carefully followed." He continued, saying, "Although I have heard that the Buddha's teaching has spread to the north, there it is mixed with many Buddhist and non-Buddhist [traditions]."
>
> Then [Chödzin] requested the local saṅgha to do an auspicious *sojong*. He offered a handful of silver thamka coins, but no monks would accept it. He was shocked, and when laypeople came they took it. He was so embarrassed. This last teaching of that paṇḍita had a very profound meaning, and exposed our shameful secret (*mtshang thog tu'ang babs 'dug*).
>
> I think based on all this, when people say, "The Mahāyāna teachings do not exist in Siṃhala," this is just uninformed babble.[83]

Appeals to eyewitness accounts—personal impressions of "the many types of worlds created by karma" as a buttress for, or escape from, textual legacies—do not situate Lubsangdamdin's remaking of Faxian's *Record* as a progressive "scientific" historical account, though many Soviet-era scholars (like Byambyn Rinchen, who published his translation along with Banzarov's Mongolian in 1970) would say otherwise.

Here instead is the Forest of the Blind: the extension of Qing-inflected models of world historical order made from the erasure of European humanism, itself made in fundamental ways by appeal to Qing models of equivalency and meaning. Like his ancient walking, this Eurasianist journey of Faxian's *Record* is made and unmade in circulation, in the play of silence and speech.

Conclusion

In the Eurasian circulation of silence and speech, of erasure and writing, explored in these pages, shared topics of concern emerged unexpectedly. What was the nature of Faxian as a person (or enlightened being)? Why did he walk westward from Chang'an? What was the historical significance of the city-state of Khotan? What was the identity and influence of the ancient Yuezhi and Xiongnu nomads? How could the opaque references in Faxian's *Record* be correctly interpreted by appeal to Xuanzang's later travelogue? What was the scale of space and distance of Faxian's walking in relation to the place of interpretation (Chang'an, Paris, Lhasa, Yeke-yin Küriy-e)? What measure of time could exactly date the Buddha's life and death?

And yet their interpretations, ever entangled like centerless rooted mesh, worked to wildly different interpretative ends. What helped reproduce the West/Nonwest binary in the Collège de France was used to extend the cosmological order of the *Kālacakra-tantra* in the Tibetan diaspora community. What could be explained to affirm racial hierarchies of Nonwestern difference in Paris could be used to claim a deep historical transmission of the Buddhadharma among ancient "Mongols" or "Tibetans" in Siberia. All was the tangled mass of rot and new life that is the Forest of the Blind, wherein humanism and its contiguous traditions are made and unmade.

In the seventh issue of *Journal Asiatique* is a short report about a séance from February 7, 1831. We read that at that meeting notice was given about Jean-Pierre Abel-Rémusat's forthcoming work on the *Record.* "M. Abel-Rémusat has translated in its entirety from the Chinese the record of Faxian, so curious for the ancient geography of India, and the understanding of Buddhist traditions.

The clarifications that he has included in his translation, which make known other voyages in the same genre, and which contain much information upon the state of Hindoustan in the fourth and fifth centuries, will form a fourth volume."[1]

Digging still deeper into this 1831 issue of the *Journal*, buried among news and miscellany in its back pages, we come to the record of another séance of the Société Asiatique, from April of that year, that includes: "Notice Upon the Cholera Epidemic Observed in China."[2] Eyewitnesses in China, Calcutta, and "Tartary" were reporting a second upswell of the pandemic. Though European observers were struggling to assess its scope and impact, news about it was ominous. A previous global outbreak had started in Bengal and burned through India in the 1820s. Hundreds of thousands had died, including ten thousand British soldiers. It then spread to Southeast Asia before diminishing. Now, apparently, it had returned.

Soon it would wreak havoc across the Qing Empire, Russia, and Egypt. Within a year, it would arrive in Europe. Hungary and Germany would be desolated. Fifty-five thousand would die in the United Kingdom, and after it passed over the Atlantic, hundreds of thousands more would perish in North America, from Quebec to Mexico. As we know, France would not be spared. One hundred thousand would die there. In Paris, one out of every thirty-three residents would be lowered into the earth because of it. Among them would be Jean-Pierre Abel-Rémusat.

As noted in my acknowledgments, this book was largely written during the COVID-19 pandemic that began in 2020. The experience of writing it—through social isolation and fear, upheaval and insecurity among loved ones, and profound suffering and loss in our broader community—has forced a double movement of alienation and familiarity. As it did for Abel-Rémusat, the pandemic suddenly and unexpectedly wrenched most of the world from normal livelihoods, routines, and acquaintances. At the same time, this moment has forced a dizzying reacquaintance with the harsh particularities of our everyday. On a collective level, we have seen the pandemic lay bare the preexisting, indefensible structural inequalities that continue to organize our communal lives, whether locally or globally. Individually, we have been forced to sit with the square footage of our housing, habits, relationships, desires, and fragilities. This is our sublime particularity, the harsh but undeniable reality of our minute lives, rolling over from birth to death. Full of beauty and poetry, yes; but unfolding only in the small space between our eyes and a wall at the end of our nose.

I have thought often about the historical anthropologists Bernard Cohn, who worked on colonial India, and Michel-Rolph Trouillot, who worked on, among other things, slave societies in the Caribbean. Both argued for an analysis that treated the site of scholarship and the object of scholarship as united fields of inquiry.[3] And both looked to the insights of Michel de Certeau, as I have, for modes of doing humanist work that accounts for the place of one's own analysis and the practice of one's writing as indissociable from the objects of study. Indeed, the materials examined in this book and the complex circumstances of its writing seemed always to implicate my own space into the story. The myth of distanciation and sovereignty that still organizes our disciplinary knowledges seemed ever more apparent, and ever more unstable.[4]

At its minimum, I hope this book is an example of how to fill a lacuna described by Rens Bod in his history of the humanities, "the historiography of separate humanistic disciplines are often confined to the Western tradition . . . [A] history of the humanities from a global perspective is difficult because many sources are not yet accessible or remain untranslated."[5] I have also written it to add to the strangely small body of scholarly works dedicated to the reception of Orientalism among "Orientals," a topic ignored by Edward Said but taken up much later in such revisionist works as Zeynep Çelik's examination of Ottoman and early Turkish Republican critiques.[6] We might also include in this category scholarship about the inversion of Orientalism among "Buddhist Modernist" movements in colonial and imperial Asia.[7] As Sudipta Kaviraj puts it: "What Said described and analyzed was not what is called colonial discourse in the narrow sense. His work was concerned primarily with European, and subsequently, Western representations of the Orient. He rarely concerns himself with the reception of these ideas in the very different context of colonial societies."[8] The story I have pursued in these pages, however, has tried to go far beyond "reception." It has followed circulations outside of any specific colonial or imperial relations of force, and beyond the epistemic sovereignty of the West as site and source of universal history and knowledge.

I have pursued this circulatory history as anti-field history without any clear precedent. Well-worn and widely studied historical examples of colonial and imperial zones of contact, exchange, go-betweens, split consciousnesses, or margins simply do not apply. For example, scholarly studies of the "middle ground" traveled by boundary-crossing figures—like Leo Africanus (al-Hasan al-Wazzan) or Arcade Huang, or so many colonial migrants, murdered (or redeemed) slaves, settlers, merchants, commercial brokers, religious converts, or diplomatic interpreters in the Ottoman, Tsarist, Qing, British, French, Dutch, or Spanish empires—are different from the place-bound, static, and divergent actors and contexts wherein this story of Faxian's *Record* unfolds.[9] Rather than focusing upon figures that "moved between different polities, made use of different cultural and social resources, and entangled or separated them so as to survive, discover, write, make relationships, and think about society and [themselves]," this story instead has connected place-bound interpreters of the *Record* who hardly knew of each other and who began anew from the silence of analytical practices staged elsewhere.[10]

In this case, models from world history and transcultural studies—which tend to foreground the interplay of material conditions of knowledge, writing, and diaspora in the rubric of translation, mediation, exchange, and network in *colonial relations of power*—obscure more than they reveal.[11] For example, Homi Bhaba's examination of the relation of Indian colonizer and colonized as "hybridity" or Michel-Rolph Trouillot's and Bernard Cohn's pioneering approaches of uniting colonial poles of domination into a single field of inquiry cannot account for the making and unmaking explored in these pages.[12] Nor can otherwise admirable models—such as Richard White's exploration of the middle ground that facilitated exchanges between Indigenous peoples and the British who settled on their ancestral lands; or Natalie Zemon Davis's work on the associations of European women "on the margins" among Iroquois, Algonquin, Carib, and African women in colonial zones of contact and exchange; or Paul Gilroy's work on the webbed relations of the Black Atlantic, which rejected clear partitioning of diaspora and national perspectives—offer any clear analytical template.[13]

It is my hope that by instead attending to the spiraled and the circulatory, the rhizomatic, the play of silence and speech, we might not just learn something new about Faxian's *Record.* We might also, as Brian Keith Axel once put it, "advance to the limits of conventions and epistemologies [and] expose the margins at the center of our institutionally defined disciplines."[14] Interpreting the centerless but connected present of each author through the lens of Faxian's *Record* is what Saidiya Hartman and Fred Moten call "the resistance of the object": that opaque hieroglyphic, what Michel de Certeau calls the perpetual absence of the dead. This was the very condition for this Eurasianist chain of learned interpretation of Faxian's ancient walking. So too is it the condition for my writing. And for your reading.[15]

I finish this book convinced of the timeliness of leaning into these sites of epistemological and disciplinary precarity. There are more than simply decolonizing, deimperializing, and de-Orientalizing possibilities here: of troubling the treelike memory of our disciplines, tracing their histories to include field creation and field erasure, and thinking collectively about new disciplinary identities and practices that arise from these more global disciplinary histories. I have called this kind of inquiry, rather simplistically, anti-field history: an occupation of the porous frontiers of the humanities and the contiguous knowledge traditions upon which it depends, and across which much is always moving.

It is vital to remember and celebrate that our imperfect disciplinary epistemologies and scholarly practices are fragile. We can do this simply by looking at their histories in wider circulations of erasure and production. It is vital, as we renew Buddhist and Asian studies and the humanities generally, to ask what more plural, decentered, participatory, and less sovereign model of the Real is presenting itself to us—for example, in circulatory histories that followed after Faxian's walking sixteen centuries ago, and in the ones upturning our current world.

If nothing else, I hope I have shown that the countless connections and erasures that propelled the Eurasianist circuit of Faxian's *Record* examined in this book were never beholden to any "original" source or knowledge tradition, and that thinking them together requires rethinking field history and field practice. Writing anti-field history of the making and unmaking of disciplinary knowledge admits pluralism, multivocality, heterogeneity, and erasure into not only our disciplinary past but also our present. As Linda Tuhiwai Smith puts it, "To hold alternative histories is to hold alternative knowledges." So too is it to hold alternative knowledge practices. What *refusals* of the purificatory gestures of the human sciences emerge for us today in thinking in circulatory fashion? What outside of the epistemic and political sovereignty of the modernist staging of "the West" emerges? How might scholarship about "Buddhist Asia" (and what this concept excludes) proceed?

While transference, impact, and influence is a central theme in the history of knowledge, according to Johan Östling, "the very concept of circulation is in need of both elaboration and theorization."[16] In the circulatory histories of Orientalist and Buddhist studies scholarship, an example of which I have shared in these pages, are opportunities to illuminate what Alejandro Vallega has called the "radical exteriority" of the human sciences.[17] Chains of interpretation and repurposing in such histories insist upon what Walter Mignolo calls "acts of epistemic disobedience" that "de-link" scholarly epistemologies from the universalist claims of the Western modern.[18] Attempting to disrupt accepted analytics of division and isolation, this inquiry into the circuit of Faxian's *Record* is just an example (of what must be hundreds of such circulations) of trying to think outside the very notion of territorialized "areas" of ethnonational units, which Arjun Appadurai reminds us is the product of European exclusion (always territorylessness) in the doing of analysis in the human sciences.[19]

The Eurasianist circulation of the *Record*—this chain of silence and speech that binds otherwise distinct knowledge traditions intimately to one another—reminds us at least that history may never be consigned to a single point of view. To acknowledge the fact is a critical performance of what Phillipe Boutry calls "plural readings" ever responding to a "plurality of logics." What good methodological trouble and opportunities arise from this? What acts of epistemic disobedience and methodological mischief might we pursue on its basis? What de-linking from the modernist staging of the West, from indefensible claims to epistemic sovereignty, from the fictional neutrality of the secular humanist gaze and metaphysics of the modern, in the doing of the Asian humanities might we find?

A revisionist Buddhist studies committed to the critical Asian humanities might respond to such questions by modeling the work of João Biehl and Peter Locke and their anthropology of becoming. Biehl and Locke, like Deleuze and Guattari, insist, among other things, on leaving behind those totemic authorities "without place" (and without first names)—Marx, Mahmood, Freud, Foucault, Asad, Weber, and the like—and writing human difference using orientations to time, place, agency, and knowledge produced by those with place, first names, and positions radically outside Enlightenment-inflected orientations and traditions,[20] Can Faxian's or Lubsangdamdin's practices of writing time and place be a generative condition for producing methodological practices and theoretical approaches in the humanities, and not just always its object? After all, the torn lives filling Ngakwang Nyima's refugee community or the questions that astonished Banzarov exist already as cause and effect across the perilous frontier of primary and secondary sources, of the object and subject of humanism, of the West/Nonwest binary.

We now have many rigorous scholarly descriptions of the colonial-derived, Eurocentric genealogies of the many sciences of the Nonwest: philology and ethnology, for example, as well as Orientalism and Buddhist studies.[21] We teach such scholarship in our courses. We tend to reference them as part of our professional sociality, to comfort ourselves that we are acknowledging the power-laden location and relations of our field. *But do we have a single example as yet of scholarship in "Buddhist studies" that disowns this intellectual legacy?* Have we even contemplated what Buddhist studies would look like by disavowing its colonial and imperial conceptual apparatus? How can doing the Asian humanities, focused on whatever era and on whatever place, de-link from what Prasenjit Duara alleges is the dominant, perhaps even singular, object of the humanities and social sciences: "the rise of the West"?

Instead of simply continuing to name the Eurocentric genealogies of this clumsy object called "Buddhist Asia," what kinds of analysis and writing and "dreaming arts" allow us to lean into new spaces of the imagination? We might further find occasion for analysis focused not on past events or biographies but on the production of disparate categories of people in the representational strategies of political discipline: moving beyond negotiating representations of "Buddhist" life as such, or of its supposed inaccuracies, or of the "real" relationship of text and context, to what Ann Laura Stoler describes in another revisionist context, "the changing force fields in which these models were produced . . . from the high gloss print to the darkroom negative, from figure and event . . . to field and ground" in the continued scholarly reproduction of the Nonwest.[22] What might a book about these unruly and confounding concepts and connections be capable of if they were described nonlinearly, nonhierarchically, outside of the frame of center and periphery, West and the rest, origin and influence, all subsumed into new connections evolving "by subterranean stems and flows, along river valleys or train tracks; . . . like a patch of oil"?[23] How might we think of all this as relation unbonded from rigid geographic, national, imperial, and intellectual boundaries? Beyond comparative religion? Beyond field history?

In each movement and connection, in each act of speech in the site of some previous silencing, we might entice otherwise meanings and epistemic possibilities to return, like the repressed, "in order to haunt and disquiet contemporary organizations of meaning" that can illuminate new horizons of disciplinary practice today.[24] We might see such possibilities even in the tangle of names flung over the robed shoulder of a Chinese monk who once walked west from Chang'an.

Appendix

The Inner Asian *Record*

Technical Note

The following is a complete, annotated translation of the Tibetan *Record.* It is read line by line against the Mongolian, French, and Chinese, with page numbers and notes about continuities and discrepancies across all four versions provided in the endnotes (my own Commentaire, I suppose). Lubsangdamdin's extensive interlinear notes to the Tibetan *Record,* which he titled *The Emanated Mirror That Completely Illuminates the Source of the Victor's Teachings,* are preserved in the way that they are included in the two extant editions of his text: as reflections, comparisons, and messages to readers inserted within the body of the text as interlinear notes.

To preserve this doubled narrative in my translation, the main body of the Tibetan *Record*, is regularly interrupted by Lubsangdamdin's authorial intrusion. I do as he did: shorter notes are included in the flow of the *Record*'s sentences in brackets. Lubsangdamdin's longer notes, which sometimes are paragraphs long, are included as indented, bracketed, and bolded blocks of text. To keep the flow of the narrative as clear as possible, I only occasionally include Tibetan (and, less commonly, Chinese, Mongolian, and French) terminology in the body of the translation. More often, I include it in endnotes, along with many explanatory notes, and my own reflections and analysis.

To situate these previously unstudied Inner Asian redactions and reinterpretations of the *Record* most clearly in relation to the original Chinese and its related East Asian intellectual (and travel) traditions, in the endnotes I have included references to page numbers in the canonical version of the *Record* in the Taishō Canon pagination for the Chinese. As with my use of Huijiao and Sengyou's biographies of Faxian explored in part I, citations to the Chinese edition of Faxian's *Record* use pagination from the SAT Daizōkyō Database edition of the Taishō Canon, which in my reading parallels the Qing edition of the *Record* read by Abel-Rémusat in every line.[1] For easy reference, I mark these with FGZ followed by line number. However, I have found that this digital reproduction of the *Foguo ji* contains occasional erroneous characters, so I have cross-read these against reproductions in Drège (2013) and Deeg (2005) before including passages or proper names as annotations to my translation of the Tibetan and Mongolian *Record* below.[2]

Because of pandemic-related closures and travel restrictions, the actual edition read by Abel-Rémusat and preserved at the Bibliothèque Nationale de France remained unavailable to me. Happily, a digital copy was provided before going to press, but not with enough time for me to change the pagination in the regular references to the Chinese below. Interested readers who, like me, want to see Abel-Rémusat's source will find it in the archives of the BnF.[3] In all, my intention has been to produce a readable (and, I hope, teachable) translation of the Tibetan version of the Mongolian, read against the French and the Chinese, yet unburdened by too much scholarly apparatus. Still, to guide those interested in consulting any of the Chinese, French, Mongolian, and Tibetan primary sources used here, I have included references to pagination in the original. I have included page numbers in the 1917 version of Lubsangdamdin's Tibetan translation (marked below as LD)[4] in parentheses in the body of the English translation precisely when they occur. The Mongolian pagination is based on the Rinchen edition of Dorji Banzarov's text (marked below as DBR). When discussing clarifications in the lightly edited 1970 edition of the Tibetan by Rinchen, I give pagination following LDR. The French, as elsewhere in this book, is based on the first edition of Jean-Pierre Abel-Rémusat's *Foĕ kouĕ ki* (marked below with the author's name or JPAR).

The Emanated Mirror That Completely Illuminates the Source of the Victor's Teachings: The Story of the Great Han-era Monk Faxian's Journey to the Land of Noble Ones

by Zava Damdin Lubsangdamdin (1867–1837)

(Translated into Tibetan from Dorji Banzarov's Mongolian translation of Jean-Pierre Abel-Rémusat's French translation of Faxian's Chinese *Foguo ji*)

Lubsangdamdin's Foreword to the Tibetan Translation

[146] Whosoever simply discusses marvelous life stories
Dispels all types of Māras and the three poisons.
To the infallible objects of refuge, the three precious gems,
Upon the crowns of all sentient beings: Victory!

Concerning this, the fourth of the one thousand guides of this fortunate aeon, the matchless teacher Śākyamuni, was born here in Jambudvīpa as the son of King Śuddhodana[5] in India the land of Noble Ones, when the lifespan of human beings was one hundred years.

[When the emperor of the Zhou dynasty (*Co'u dbang*), fifth in the line of the Te'u kingdom (*Te'u rgyal srid*), was twenty-six years old, an omen appeared on the eighth day of the fourth month of the Wood Male Tiger Year in the form of a great mass of light that arose from the southwest border of China. Seeing this, the emperor conferred with his diviners,[6] who determined that this was a sign that a Great Being[7] would be born in that region. Once a thousand years had passed, what they had perceived came to be in this land. So it has been prophesied. Moreover, this is further established in various writings .][8]

Some one thousand years later, during the reign of Emperor Ming of the great Han dynasty, the precious teachings of the Buddha began to flourish in the easterly kingdom of China.[9] Since that time, roughly three renowned figures [**this master, Xuanzang,**[10]**and the great translator Yijing**][11] have emerged from among the Indian arhats and paṇḍitas and the Chinese monks and translator-scholars.

As for the first of these, the great Han dynasty monk named Faxian, it is recorded in the great translator Güng Gombojab's *History of Buddhism in China* (*Rgya nag chos 'byung*):

The master named Thö-zung [Faxian] went to India in the company of four companions.[12] In Magadha they studied the Indian language and some of the auxiliary fields of knowledge.[13] Enduring many hardships, they journeyed all the way to Siṅghala. Although they saw a direct disciple of the Elder Kāśyapa, they did not have the opportunity to request any Dharma teachings from him.[14] After his companions died, the master [Faxian] was left all alone. In the company of a merchant, he continued along his journey. He produced his own translations (*rang 'gyur*) of many Dharma texts, including of the *Mahāsāṃghika-vinaya*.[15] He greatly benefited sentient beings again and again. When he was eighty-six, he departed for the Pure Lands.

It is clear that this refers to [Faxian].[16] The Dharma histories (*chos 'byung*) of India, China, and so on illuminate how such journeys, full of hardships, were undertaken back and forth between different lands for the sake of the Dharma. Just so, from those pages the names [147] of authentic Chinese monks (*tshad mar gyur pa*) are clearly recorded in the biographical literature of India, Land of Noble Ones.

The biography of such a great being who journeyed to the Land of Noble Ones survives in the Chinese language. It was discovered by a foreigner European who then translated it into his language.[17] The meaning of what was described therein helped verify authentic research already undertaken about India. A Buryat translator-lama translated it into Mongolian. The present work is a Tibetan translation. Consequently, since [this text] has passed through the vernaculars (*skad cha*) of so many regions, specific names for a great many of the environs and beings have become corrupted (*zur chags*). Even so, here I left them unchanged, just as I found them. Please keep in mind that in the future it will be necessary to edit these names by examining other texts and visiting [the sites described herein].

I
Departure from Chang'an; Mount Long; Western Dzi and Southern Liang; Northern Liang and Dunhuang (Thwang Kwang); The Sandy Wilderness

It is thus: long ago, Faxian resided in Chang'an.[18] The Tripiṭika was unknown there and religious scriptures (*glegs bam*) were scarce. Seeing that the way of the Dharma (*chos tshul*) was coming to ruin, his mind was greatly tormented.[19] For that reason, in the second year of the reign of Emperor Hongshi [399 CE][20] he departed in the company of several like-minded companions, such as Huijing, Daozheng, Huiying, and Huiwei.[21] They set out on their journey in order to acquire Indian [works of] Dharma and monastic discipline (*rgya gar yul gyi chos dang chos khrims*).

They departed from Chang'an [**This (city) is very wellknown today as *Shi ti chang ang h+phu*.**] Having traversed the mountain range named "Long,"[22] they arrived in a region governed by Qiangui.[23] [**This is the Lanzhou fortress (*Lan ju mkhar*) on the banks of the Machu River.**][24] They rested a while there to recover from their fatigue. Setting out upon the path once more, they arrived in a region called Noutan.[25] Afterward they crossed a mountain range called Amyé Gangkar (Tib. *A myes gangs dkar*) and happened upon the garrison (*dmag sde*) of Zhangye.[26]

> [**Although this appears to be a region in Amdo (*A mdo*), today it remains unknown, though I am thinking it may refer to a snowy region to the north of Serkhok (*Gser khok*).** [148]]

At that time, a period of warfare (*dus gzir*) had arisen in Zhangye territory. Consequently, they could no longer progress along the path. With a gentle and kind mind toward them, the king of the Zhangye [**though this appears to be in Mongol territory (*hor gyi sa cha*), nowadays it is unclear just where it is located**] provided them with respite and acted as their patron (*sbyin bdag*). During that time, they met Zhiyan, Huijian, Sengshao, Baoyun, Sengjing, and other venerable monks.[27] Seeing that they shared the same goal, they joined [Faxian's party]. Joy and inspiration arose among them for having met on the road, and they dwelt there together.

After this sojourn, they departed together on the path and arrived at Dunhuang.[28] That place is eighty *li* (Tib. *le bar*; Mong. *γaǰar*) wide from east to west, and about forty *li* wide from south to north, and was very strictly fortified. They stayed there for just over one month. Then Faxian along with his companions set out on the path following a courier (*bya ma rta pa*) and parted ways from Baoyun and his other companions.[29]

> [**This was along the borderlands of India and Tibet. [Xuanzang] also journeyed to the Land of Noble Ones along this path. It appears that since [Xuanzang] was a very powerful person, he encountered none of this trouble during his journey.**]

The lord (*mi'i gtso bo*) of Dunhuang was named Li Gao.[30] He provided the necessary supplies so that the Chinese monks could traverse the desert basin (*bye ma'i klung*). Therein are demons (*'dre*), tsan spirits (*btsan*) and a scorching wind that kills whomsoever it blows over. For these reasons, escaping death is impossible. No flying birds appear in the sky nor wandering animals upon the earth. They searched for a suitable path across but found nothing other than a single bone of a dead sentient being marking the path. After journeying seventeen days, they arrived in a land called Shanshan. They had traversed fifteen hundred *li*.

II
The Land Called Shanshan;[31] Qarašahr;[32] Gaochang[33]

As for the region bearing this name (Shanshan), it is mostly mountainous with undulating, arable land.

> **[As for this place, [149] the *Oxhorn Sūtra* says: "In that northerly land known as Shen zha, a statue of the Tathāgatha known as 'Shen zha' surfaced from below the earth to guard the borders." This is the land described in that prophecy.]**

The earth there is without potency or essence [i.e., neither productive nor fertile]. The demeanor and clothing of the local people are promiscuous (*'chal po*). Though similar to the Chinese and other peoples in many ways, they differ in wearing clothing made only of felt and silk. The king of this land upheld the Dharma and all of the nearly four thousand monks dwelling in his domain were practitioners of the Hīnayāna.[34] Though all of the monastics and laity continuously rely upon the Indian Dharma system, there are dissimilarities in the detailed explanations of their practice (*lag len phra rags bshad pa*).

Departing this region and journeying to the west, each successive country along the path was like the one before; they all resembled the territories of the Uighur (*Yu gur gyi yul ljongs*).[35]

> **[This seems similar to a small kingdom called Gaochang (*Ka'u chang*) that was connected by royal succesion to the Uighur, as clearly described in Xuanzang's *Guidebook*.]**

Though each region possessed a distinct local language, the monks read Indian texts and endeavored in particular to study the Indian language [i.e., Sanskrit].

Faxian and companions stayed in this area for more than a month. Heading out onto the path, they once again journeyed to the northwest for about fifteen days before arriving at a land named Yanyi (Qarašahr). This region also had some four thousand saṅgha members, all of whom followed the Hīnayāna. They strictly adhered to the conduct of the vinaya, such that whosoever broke their discipline was severely punished. The practices of the venerable monks arriving from Hétön (*Hwe thon*) were quite dissimilar from those of the local saṅgha.[36]

The travel documents (*dpang rgya'i yi ge*) Faxian carried [150] were sent to the royal court.[37] King Gongsun,[38] who was the sovereign at that time, retained the documents for more than two months. After that, Faxian came together with Baoyun (*Hwe cung*) and their other companions. They all agreed that the people of Yanyi (*U ja[ng]*) did not make effort in the activity of religion and politics, nor did they appropriately respect travelers.[39] For these reasons, Zhiyan, Huijian, and Huiwei immediately reversed course for Gaochang.[40] They realized they would need to beg for whatever provisions the journey required. Faxian and his companions retrieved their travel documents. King Gongsun supplied them with provisions, and so they immediately set out upon the path.

They departed to the southwest. The territory through which they passed was vast wilderness without any owner. Fording the rivers was extremely difficult, and so their journey was exhausting.[40] In general, it is impossible to find an example in our lives that compares with the difficulty they faced. After enduring such travel for a month and five days, they arrived in the land of Khotan.

III
Conditions in Khotan

The region of Khotan[41] is a peaceful, happy, and developed kingdom (*dar zhing rgyap pa'i ljongs*). The locals have an abundance of material possessions. Having relied upon the Dharma, they enjoy a peaceful and happy abode. Most of the several tens of thousands of monastics in this land rely upon the Mahāyāna.[42] They all take their meals together. The people raise their house after observing the stars.[43] Small stūpas[44] are built in front of the doorways of all the homes. The smallest of those is close to two *gyang* high.[45] Inside the temples, which were built in a square [151] shape, monks arriving from foreign lands are venerated and given whatever provisions they require.

The region's king permitted Faxian and companions to stay in the temple called Gomatī,[46] a Mahāyāna monastery.

[It is said in the *Prophecy of the Land of Li Sūtra*:

> **When my beloved place**
> **becomes the land of Li,**
> **at the Dharmarājan Stūpa (*Chos kyi rgyal po'i mchod rten*)**

in that beautiful abode of Gomatī (*'Gu ma ti ra*),
the buddhas of the Fortunate Age
will establish the vinaya.

This [land described by Faxian] is actually the place referred to in the prophecy.]

The three thousand monks of that temple take their meal together upon the sounding of a note.[47] Upon entering the dining hall, with a peaceful, disciplined manner they all perform the feast offering (*mchod ston*) while sitting silently in rows. Not a sound arises from their bowls and utensils. During their meal these pure monks do not call out to one another by name but make signals with their fingers.

Huijing, Daozheng, and Huida set out upon the path and journeyed toward Kāśmīra (Tib. *Ka che'i yul*).[48] Faxian and the other companions planned to witness the procession of the Jowo [image] (*jo bo gling bskor*), so they waited for more than three months. There are fourteen large monasteries in this land. It is impossible to count the small monasteries. Upon the first day of the fourth month, all of the marketplaces in the city are decorated and readied. Large cloth adornments and painted tapestries[49] are spread out before the city gates. All is decorated with whatever is necessary in a beautiful arrangement.

The queen and principally all the beautiful women were carried to this place. [152] Since the saṅgha of Gomatī[50] are practitioners of the Mahāyāna, the king mainly honored and served them. It was also principally he who did the Jowo procession. A four-wheeled chariot was arranged to bring holy objects (*rten rnams*) to a place some three or four *li* from the city. [The chariot] was about three *gyan* high. It was in the shape of a *'khrid thabs* hut adorned with the seven precious jewels and cotton tapestry curtains. The Buddha Śākyamuni [statue] was brought to sit in its brocade-covered center. Two bodhisattvas were on his two sides. All around and to the rear, other statues made of gold and silver were brought. In the intermediate spaces, various kinds of precious stones were strung as ornamentation.

Once the holy objects came within about a hundred paces of the gates, the king, having on a cock-crested hat (*prog zhwa*),[51] wearing clean new clothing, barefoot, with flowers and incense in hand, walked out of the city surrounded by his entourage. Going to meet the holy objects, they then prostrated, scattered flowers, continuously burned fragrant incense, and made offerings. When the holy objects were brought into the city, the wives of the nobility and their young daughters extensively scattered many types of flowers from the upper entrances of the palace, covering all of the chariot.

Different chariots were prepared for different Jowo processions. Holy objects went on procession from all of the monasteries on particular days. Regarding these processions of holy objects:

> **[Concerning this Jowo procession, the *Ox-Horn Sūtra* states:**
>
> > **Moreover, in this land a great statue of my form will be carried about by chariot and installed inside a palace called "Possessing Virtue," where it will become a great object of offering.**
>
> **It is clear that this is what the prophecy references.]**

They began the procession (*bskor*) on the first day of the fourth month and finished on the fourteenth day. After this, the king retreated (*bzhud*) to his palace in the company of his queen [153] and the rest.

In a place seven or eight *gyangdrak*[52] to the south of that city is a monastery called "The New Royal Temple."[53] It took eighty years over the reigns of three kings to build. Twenty-five *gyan* high, its upper reaches are ornamented with gold and silver engravings, and there are a great many holy images. Whatever precious jewels they possessed were spent to erect a stūpa. The inner pillars, wood doors, and the inside of the windows of a temple (*lha khang*) built for a marvelously decorated Jowo Śākyamuni were entirely covered in gold. What's more, elsewhere were houses built for the saṅgha, so excellently arranged and beautifully decorated that it is impossible to describe to others. The kings of some six Mongolian kingdoms (*hor sog gi yul ljongs*) to the east of the mountain range offered whatever valuables they had to this place.[54] Compared with these grand sponsors who offered so much, there are far fewer who serve [the temple regularly].

IV
The Land of Zihe (Dzi'u ho'i yul) and Mount Congling (Tshāung ling ri)[55]

When the Land of Li's[56] fourth-month procession of holy supports (*rte gyi gling bskor*) was complete, Sengshao departed alone toward Jibin[57] in the company of a scholar (*skye bo mkhas pa*). Faxian and his other companions journeyed on toward the country of Zihe,[58] arriving after twenty-five days.

> **[This was the land of the Yeke qoqan (*Yi he khokhan*), a group belonging to the southern Mongols (*Sog po lho sde*). Xuanzang similarly recorded how**

these people greatly served him. It appears most likely that this is the Kardo (*Skar do*) region prophesied in the *Prophecy of the Land of Li Sūtra*.][59]

This country likewise greatly reveres the Buddha's teachings. A Mahāyāna saṅgha of nearly one thousand is in residence there. They stayed for fifteen days, then set off to the south. After a four-day [154] journey, they entered a mountain range called Congling[60] before arriving in the region of Yuhui,[61] where, exhausted, they convalesced. Overcoming their fatigue, they set out once again upon the path. They journeyed for twenty-five days before arriving in Kāśmīra (*Ka che'i yul*). There they were reunited with Huijing (*H+pha zhi king*) and some other of their wayward companions.

V
Conditions in Kāśmīra[62]

The king of Kāśmīra arranged an offering ceremony called "The Quinquennial Assembly Series" (*Lo lnga'i 'du thebs*).[63] When the time comes, saṅgha members from every region are invited. Once they arrive, it is like [the gathering of] a magnificent raincloud. They then convene in order to make offerings. The site where the saṅgha congregate is decorated with cotton tapestry umbrellas (*ras sra rtsi can gyi gdugs*) and canopies. There they arrange a throne covered by gold flowers, silver flowers, water lilies (*me tog ku mud dag*), and silk brocades. The interior is arranged with beautiful adornments. The king and his ministers arrive and make prostrations according to the appropriate Dharma protocols (*chos tshul*). They continue for two or three months. The usual time for this assembly is in the spring.

Once the king has completed this offering celebration (*mchod ston*), he orders his ministers, "Pay homage and make offerings in your respective homes!" They duly accomplish their offering celebrations over the course of one, three, or five days. Once everyone has finished exerting themselves in their devotions (*gus phyag*), the king takes his riding horse (*bzhon pa'i rta*) along with saddle and bridle, and the great ministers of that land and the most prominent of its citizens (*mi drag shos rnams*) take their riding horses, bolts of cotton, valuables, and whatever other necessities, and offer it to the saṅgha. The ministers then vow to purchase all the objects they have offered, such as their riding mounts and so on [155], back from the saṅgha at value (*rin gyis*).

This land is incredibly mountainous and so is intensely cold. Other than grain (*nas*), no seeds can grow there.[64] Soon after the saṅgha receive all their foodstuffs for the year, snow begins falling continuously, even from a clear sky!

Because of this, since long ago there has been a [royal] command (*bsgo ba'i srol ka*) that the saṅgha ought not receive their yearly provisions until the crops have been harvested.

The Buddha's spittle vessel (*ljags mchil gyi snod*) is to be found in this land. It is colored like a begging bowl made of stone. There we find also the Buddha's bejeweled tooth. There is a stūpa that was built by local people upon receiving these relics (*byin rten*). There are more than one thousand saṅgha members there who only practice the Hinayāna.

[Xuanzang's *Guidebook* records: "I came into the presence of a great monastic gathering (*sa gra chen po gcig*) of five thousand saṅgha members **who only practiced the Hīnayāna, as well as the Buddha's tooth, an inch in size (*tshon gang ba*) and white as snow."]**

In the east of those mountains is a region whose people wear summer attire resembling that of the Chinese, but in other seasons wear clothing with a wool-woven blanket (*lwa ba*). Their monks turn the Wheel of the Dharma[65] according to the appropriate manner of practicing. The benefits of turning the Wheel of the Dharma are beyond words.

This land is within the mountain range called Congling [i.e., Pamirs). If one travels to the south of those regions, all of the goods grown from the earth and the varieties of tree fruit (*shing thog*) begin to change. Tree fruit growing in this region, such as fruit-bearing bamboo (*shing thog can gyi smyug ma*), the Akaru tree (*a ka ru'i shing*, i.e., pomegranate), and the Likara tree (*li ka ra'i shing*, i.e., sugarcane), resemble those grown in China.[66]

VI
The Congling Mountains and the Snow Mountain Range; The Tuoli region of Northern India; An Eighty-Cubit Statue of the Bodhisattva [156] Maitreya

Proceeding west from Kāśmīra into Northern India,[67] it took one month to cross the Congling mountains.

[Xuanzang's *Guidebook* calls this place "Tsongla" (*Btsong la*). However, it seems to me that it bears some likeness to what the *History of Buddhism in China* calls "Mount Bikjé" (*'Bigs byed*). Despite this, it is clear from descriptions in the Kangyur and Tengyur that Mount Bikjé refers to a mountain in south India.]

Snow clings to the peaks of these mountains regardless of whether it is summer or winter. Venom-spitting poisonous snakes appear during times of hunger.[68] There are exceptional obstacles en route, including frigid wind, rain, snow, desert wind, and rockslides. For this reason, it is said that if thousands all together traveled along this path, not even one would cross over alive. Locals are known as the "peoples of the snowy mountains."

Crossing that mountain range, one arrives at the northern border of India. There is a small kingdom there called Tuoli[69] with a great many monastic communities adhering to the Hīnayāna. In ancient times, an arhat living in this region had a vision (*zhal mthong*) of the bodhisattva Maitreya.[70] Afterward, he used his magical abilities (*rdzu'phrul*) to transport a human sculptor to Tuṣita Heaven (*Dga' ldan gyi lha gnas*), telling him, "Create a wood statue that looks like (Maitreya)!"

> **[Xuanzang's *Guidebook* records, "I came into the presence of a statue of the Protector Maitreya twenty fathoms (*'dom*) high, fashioned from the "snake's heart sandalwood" (*tsandan sprul snying*) by a student of Ānanda's (*Kun dga' bo*) named Arhat Madhyāntika (*Nyi ma gung pa*)."[71]]**

This sculptor went thrice in this manner [to Tuṣita]. From his visions he built a statue eighty cubits (*khru*) high with eight-cubit foot soles. On holy days (*dus chen rnams*), light radiates from this statue. On such occasions, kings from numerous regions clamber over one another (*hab thob byed*) to make offerings. This statue [157] may still be found in this area.

VII
The River Named "Sindhu"

Once out of the mountains, they traveled along the southwest of the range for fifteen days. This route makes for exceptionally difficult travel. It abounds with colossal obstacles (*bar bcod chen po*) and dreadful precipices. The mountains are eight thousand *gyangdrak* high.[72] There are only precariously narrow footpaths bounded by sheer walls.

> **[From Xuanzang's *Guidebook*: "I arrived at a locale near the Sindhu River with treacherous paths, a very narrow iron bridge, and an extended wooden platform path a thousand *li* long." That is this place.]**

Just coming near this area afflicts the human body, as if by fever (*tshad nad*).[73] If one's feet slide while advancing, there is nothing whatsoever to grasp onto and save oneself.

Below is a river called Sindhu.[74] To open a path, ancient peoples cut a seven-hundred-step staircase into the rocky cliffside.[75] This staircase has since deteriorated. One crosses the river by means of a rope suspension bridge (*thag pa 'dogs pa'i zam pa*). The width of the river ravine is some eighty paces (*gom pa*). Not a single person reached this location in the generation of Zhang Qian[76] and Gan Ying.[77] The translator-ministers of the cabinet of foreign affairs (*phyi rol gyi khrims khang*) wrote about the customs of these peoples.[78]

Local monks asked [Faxian]: "Can you explain to us when the Buddha's teachings began to flourish in the East?" Faxian explained:

> I have put this question to people from this region (i.e., "the East"), and they told me, "According to accounts (*tshig ris*) in our ancient records, after this statue of Maitreya was built, Indian lamas in possession of sūtras [158] and volumes of the vinaya were invited (to China). They forded the Sindhu River and came here." This statue was built three hundred years after the Buddha's nirvāṇa;[79] if we were to calculate the years, this occured during the reign of Emperor Ping of the Zhou dynasty (*Ce'u gur*).[80] Another account is that the holy Dharma started to spread continuously into the East the very moment this [Maitreya] statue was built. Either explanation is acceptable. If not for this great teacher Maitreya, who else could we identify as establishing the tradition of Śākyamuni? As facilitating (*bcug par nus*) the study of the scriptures? As propagating the explanation of the Three Jewels into the extremity of the world? (As illuminating) hidden phenomena[81] and the end of activity (ie. right conduct, [*yang dag pa'i*] *las kyi mtha'*)? As being powerful enough to translate the scriptures and their commentaries to foster excellent understanding and study? Ordinary people hardly have the ability to accomplish such activities at their leisure! This is why Emperor Ming of the Great Han dynasty[82] was beset with such marvelous dreams.

VIII
Odiyāna and Śākyamuni's Footprint

Immediately upon crossing the river, one arrives in a land called Odiyāna.[83] Nowadays, that area is in the northern frontiers of India.[84] It is called Tsa hé (*Tsha he*) in the dialect of the central region; "Central Region' (*yul dbus*) refers to Central

India. Local people don clothing and eat food just as they do in Central (India). They venerate the Buddha's teachings with extraordinary faith. There are temples everywhere monastics reside. There are five hundred monasteries housing only Hīnayāna meditators (*theg pa chung ngubsam gtan pa*). When foreign [159] laymen or monks arrive, they are received with warm hospitality. They are served for three days and then told to find their own private lodging (*gnas tshang zur pa*).

It is told in the Buddha's biography that once, long ago, he was freely wandering about and arrived in a region of northern India. This is the region mentioned there. Our Teacher Śākyamuni impressed his footprint into stone at this place. Depending upon the mind of viewers, that footprint may sometimes appear as longer and sometimes as shorter. It may still be found there today. There is also the stone where the Buddha laid out his upper robe while warming himself in the sun, and also the site where he tamed a poisonous snake. These stones are one *gyan*[85] [*sic*] high. Each of their four corners is two (*do*) *gyan* [high]. One side is flat.

Huijing, Daozheng, and Huida had earlier gone to Nagarahāra,[86] where the Buddha's shadow[87] is located. Faxian and his companions stopped in that place for a while. After a full day, they journeyed on to the district of southern Swāt (*Sho ka tho*).

IX
Swāt District

The Buddha's teachings also flourished extensively in the district of Swāt.[88] Long ago, Indra Lord of Gods (*lha'i dbang po brgya byin*)[89] manifested as a hawk and a pigeon for the sake of testing the Buddha. To save the life of the pigeon, the bodhisattva weighed out his own flesh upon a scale. Later, after the King of Subduers (*thub pa'i dbang po*) had discovered the nectar [i.e., become enlightened], he came to this place with a group of disciples. "Long ago, in order to protect a pigeon," he told his entourage of disciples, "I cut off my flesh and gave it away. This is that place." Later, local peoples recognized this history and built a great stūpa ornamented with gold and silver [160] over the ruins that still exists.

X
Gandhāra (Gandhāvati) District

Descending toward the east from Swāt, one journeys for five days before arriving in a kingdom called Gandhāra.[90] This land is the kingdom once ruled by King Aśoka's son Dharmavivardhana.[91] The Buddha Śākyamuni, when he was a bodhisattva, gave his eyes as *dāna* at this place. Also, a great stūpa ornamented by gold and silver was erected over these ruins. Most people there practice the Hīnayāna.

XI
Takṣaśilā (Taxila) and the Starving Tigers

Seven days' journey eastward from Gandhāra is a country known as Takṣaśilā.[92]

> **[(Muslim) barbarians (*kla klo*) call this place Gandhāra (*ka+nd hā ra*). (It is) the place of Jālandhara (*Dza la n+d+ha ra*).]**

The name of this place means "to cut off the head." Long ago when he was a bodhisattva, the Buddha Śākyamuni gave away his head as a gift here.

> **[Regarding this, it is known as "Bru sha si li." Xuanzang explains that this is the birthplace of Asaṅga and his brother (Vasubandhu), the arhat Dharmatrāta,[93] Rāmaṇa, and others.]**

Because of that, this region bears this name.

From there, they arrived in a land to the east where previously the Buddha gave away his body to a starving tigress.[94] In these two places great stūpas, ornamented by all manner of precious materials, were built. Early in the morning, the king, ministers, and subjects of these lands go one after the other to those stūpas to make prostrations and offerings. They continuously scatter flowers and burn fragrant incense. Local people say that these two stūpas and the two mentioned earlier are together known as the "Four Great Stūpas."

XII
Puruṣa (Peshawar) and the Buddha's Begging Bowl

[161] Traveling four days to the south of the kingdom of Gandhāra,[95] one arrives at the region of Puruṣa (Peshawar).[96] Long ago the Buddha came to this place in the company of a group of disciples. On that occasion, he spoke thus to Ānanda (*Kun dga' bo*): "Following my *parinirvāṇa*, a king named Kaniṣka (*Ka ni ka*) will appear in this region and will build a stūpa here."[97] [Puruṣa] is the prophesied place. King Kaniṣka was later born into this world and once while setting out upon a journey (*lam du chas shing*), traveled through this region. In order to rouse his mind, Śakra [i.e., Indra], the Lord of the Gods,[98] manifested as a youthful cowherd[99] and began building a stūpa alongside the roadway.

[The *Detailed Explanation of the World ('Dzam [gling rgyas] bshad)* records that it was, in fact, the Buddha who manifested in the form of this child.]

The king asked, "Young man, what are you doing?" "I am building the Buddha's stūpa," replied the youthful cowherd. The king greatly praised him and, in addition to the cowherd's stūpa, proceeded to have another built as well. That stūpa is more than forty *gyan* high and is ornamented by many types of jewels. Whoever sees the unrivaled splendor of this stūpa and its temple is struck with tremendous wonder. One hears that this stūpa is superior in its design to all other stūpas of Jambudvīpa.[100] While the king was building that stūpa, he had another, smaller stūpa about three *gyan* high built in front.

The Buddha's begging bowl[101] is to be found in this land.

[Xuanzang's *Guidebook* says that in the land of Jālandhara, (people) ask for blessings from the Bhagavān's begging bowl.]

[162] In ancient times, a king named Yuezhi (*Tsu yu she*)[102] had the idea to raise a powerful army in order to destroy this land and acquire the Buddha's begging bowl. Just so, after his conquest on account of his great devotion to the holy Dharma, King Yuezhi conspired to take the begging bowl and carry it away. To that end, he made preparations for an offering *pūjā* (*mchod pa*). After he had made offerings to the Triple Gem, he brought a beautifully adorned elephant. When he set the begging bowl upon the elephant's back, it fell to the earth and was impossible to move. A four-wheeled chariot was prepared, upon which the begging bowl was set, and then eight elephants were commanded to pull. Though they would take a step forward, they were powerless to make any advance. Seeing this, the king thought: "*Kye ma*! Alas! It will be nearly impossible to transport this begging bowl!" His heart gripped by fear (*yid ches cher skrag*), he ordered a stūpa and temple built at this site. He also set aside a military unit to stand guard and had many types of veneration and service performed there.

Nearly seven hundred saṅgha members reside there. Before mid-day, all of them gather in the temple of the Teacher's begging bowl. Wearing immaculately clean robes, they offer various pūjās to the Teacher's begging bowl and then take their noontime meal.[103] Once evening arrives, they burn sweet-smelling incense before taking their leave. About two *dhu*[104] can fit inside this offering bowl. As for its color, it is multicolored but mostly black. All four sides are beautiful. It is about two palm widths high.[105] It appears glistening and polished. [163] A few poor people have the chance to fill the begging bowl with flowers. The rich also come carrying flowers, and though they might scatter them by the hundreds, thousands, and tens of thousands while exerting great effort, they are unable to fill it.

Baoyun and Sengjin continued on into the presence (*mjal*) of the Buddha's begging bowl, after which they returned. Huijing, Huida, and Daozheng had all set out onto the path earlier. They intended to journey to Nagara[hāra] (*Nang hi*) and enter into the presence of the Buddha's shadow, tooth, and skull (*dbu thod*). Along the path, Huijing fell ill and Daozheng stayed behind to protect him. Huida was the only one among them to return home to the land of Puruṣa (*Phu s+tsā+u sha*). Just after their companions had arrived, Huida, Baoyun, and Sengjing returned home to the kingdom of Mahā Tsina ("Great China"). Huiying had especially strong devotion to the Temple of the Begging Bowl, and so stayed behind there.[106] Alone, Faxian proceeded to that land housing the Buddha's skull bone.

XIII
Nagarahāra and the City of Haḍḍa; The Tathāgatha's Skull Bone, Tooth, Mendicant's Staff, and Monastic Robes; The Teacher's Shadow

From there, journeying sixteen *dpag tshad* to the east, one arrives to the city of Haḍḍa[107] on the frontier of the land of Nagarahāra.[108] Here is the reliquary (*lha khang*) wherein the Buddha's skull bone is kept.[109]

> **[As for the Buddha's skull bone, which remained unburnt by [the funerary] fire and was shaped like a parasol (*gdugs*), the Teacher's mendicant's staff (*'khar gsil*) with iron ring and red sandalwood handle, the Teacher's saffron-colored Dharma robe, and so on, Xuanzang records that he came into their presence at a place called Nāgārāga.[110] It seems probable that the name of this place either has changed or was inaccurate.]**

[164] That reliquary is completely covered in gold and adorned by the seven precious substances. That region's king had roused an exceptionally strong devotion to the Buddha's skull bone. Terrified at the thought that someone might steal it, he selected eight powerful men from among the local nobility and entrusted them each with a stamp (*taṁ thel*) (authorizing them) to close the door of the reliquary (*lha khang*). Early in the morning, those eight powerful men would come and, providing their stamps as credentials (*dpang po bgyis shing*), wash their hands with fragrant water and then open the gates. They would then carry the Buddha's skull bone aloft and set it upon a high throne and cushion laid upon a foundation of a circle of vajras and many

varieties of precious substances. They would then depart the temple. Additionally, underneath is a vajra throne and above is an umbrella of water crystal jewels (*nor bu chu shel*) and a beautiful adornment of pearl and varieties of precious stones.

The skull is yellowish white in color and twenty-four finger widths in circumference. There is a protrusion in the upper portion. Just after sunrise each day, temple residents (*lha khang gi mi*) climb atop a high pavilion (*ldings* [*sic*] *khang mthon po*) and beat drums, blow a conch shell, and sound a gong. Immediately upon hearing this, the king proceeds to the reliquary temple and offers flowers and incense to the skull bone. Then he receives blessings and pays homage.

Following this, all his subjects touch their crowns to the skull bone, receive blessings, and depart. To do this, they enter from a door to the east side and exit from one to the west. So goes every morning [165] for the king, who venerates and pays homage to the skull bone and, when this is done, attends to political affairs. So too is it for the chiefs (*rje dpon*) and ministers, who similarly venerate and pay homage before attending to their affairs. In their daily venerations and homage to the skull bone, there is no difference in the practices of those engaged in governmental affairs and those who are not. Afterward, once others have also finished venerating and paying homage, the skull bone is taken back to the reliquary. As for that (reliquary), it is decorated with all manner of precious substances. One of its doors remains open and the other closed. It is about five feet high and in the shape of a Nirvāṇa Stūpa (*myang 'das mchod rten*).

As for how such activities are sustained, flower and fragrant incense merchants congregate near the entranceway to the temple each morning, from whom those arriving to enter into worshipful contact (*mchod mjal*) may pay the price and acquire whatever requisites they need. There is a tradition whereby kings from regions nearby dispatch envoys to make offerings on their behalf. The area of this temple is some forty paces in circumference. In this land, even if the sky were to fall or the earth were to be pierced (*brdol ba*), it is impossible for this temple to move. Were the sky to crumble or the firmament of the earth to swell in this land, it is impossible this temple would so much as tremble (*g.yo ba*).

Traveling to the north, while passing through an area one *dpag tshad* (away), one arrives at the great capital (*rgyal khab*) of the land of Nagarahāra. Long ago, the Teacher Śākyamuni made an offering of the five types of flowers, which he had purchased with silver coins, to the Buddha Dīmpaṃkara.[111] As for the place where [Dīmpaṃkara] accepted (this offering), it is here. [166] The stūpa containing one of the Buddha's teeth is to be found in this city. The manner of venerating and paying homage here are very similar to the traditions associated with the skull bone.

One *dpag tshad* to the northeast of this city is the city gate,[112] wherein is kept the Buddha's mendicant staff.[113] There, a stūpa was also built and offerings are made continuously according to ancient custom. Also, atop [the staff] is a bull's head (*glang skyes kyi mgo*) made of sandalwood. It is was put inside a wood container six or seven *rgyan* long. Neither a hundred nor even a thousand people could remove it from this [container]. After that, one enters into a valley. Traveling westward, there is a temple containing the Buddha's outer robe (*snam sbyar*).[114] There also, many varieties of offerings are made. In the event that a drought arises in this land, all of the subjects gather together and bring the outer robe outside and pay homage and make offerings. Then the gods make fall a great rain.

Half a *dpag tshad* to the south of Nagarahāra is a westward-facing structure at the foot of a mountain. That is where the Buddha left his shadow.[115]

> **[This stone building still exists today. When you first enter inside, nothing is visible at all. I have heard it said that by prostrating and circumambulating, and if one makes supplications, these impure obscurations are slightly illuminated, though still with some blurriness. If one makes supplications again and again, things become more and more illuminated. This does not appear in Xuanzang's *Guidebook*.]**

If one gazes upon the shadow from ten paces away, it appears gold colored, adorned by the major and minor marks of buddhahood (*mtshan dpes brgyan pa*), [167] and abides emitting rays of light. Seeing (this shadow) is just like gazing upon the actual form of the Buddha. If you approach closer and closer, the shadow becomes smaller and smaller. It is exceedingly similar in its radiance to the (Buddha's) actually existing body. Royally commissioned artists from many kingdoms had been appointed to paint it, but not even one succeeded. Locals say that all of the One Thousand Buddhas leave their shadow there.

When he resided in this world, the Buddha cut his hair and fingernails[116] at a spot nearly one hundred paces from this shadow. Later, he built a stūpa together with a group of disciples and prayed "May this be the prototype (*ma phyi*) for all stūpas that will later be built!" That stūpa still exists today. Nearby is a monastery wherein nearly seven hundred saṅgha members reside. At this site are one thousand stūpas of the arhats and pratyekabuddhas.

XIV
The Small Snowy Mountains and Luoyi; Bho na and the Sindhu River

In the second month of winter, Faxian and his companions[117] journeyed to the south of the small snowy mountains.[118] Snow adheres to the peaks of those mountains in summer just as in winter. An extremely bitter wind (*grang ngad*) [blows] in the south of this region; on account of its strength, there is the possibility (*rkyen*) that beings will freeze there. In those conditions, only Huijing could not endure the intensely savage cold (*grang ba'i ngar rtsub*). Journeying in front [168], his bodily vigor began to decline (*lus stobs ni shor*). Bubbles dribbled from his mouth. He spoke thus to Faxian: "Now there is no way I can survive. You all must quickly move on! There is no reason that we all should die here." With those words he passed away. Though many means were used to console Faxian, he expressed no mournful lamentation. Instead, he deliberated upon the meaning of what occurred: "This is the general karma of sentient beings as well as my own bad karma arising as an obstacle. Though I am sad, there is nothing I can do."[119]

Having strengthened their resolve and collected their physical energy, [Faxian and Daozheng] proceeded once more along the south of the snowy mountain range and arrived in the land of Luoyi.[120] In that place are three thousand monks who are devoted equally to both the Mahāyāna and the Hīnayāna. They stayed there a while, then continued descending toward the south. After ten days they arrived in Baṇṇu.[121] In that region is a monastic community of close to three thousand who are Hīnayāna meditators (*theg pa chung du'i bsam gtan pa*).[122] From there, they journeyed three days eastward and then once again forged the Sindhu River. There the land flattens evenly alongside both banks of the river.

XV
Conditions in Bhiḍa

Upon fording the river is a land called Bhiḍa.[123] The Buddha's Teachings had widely spread there. Followers of the Hīnayāna widely respected followers of the Mahāyāna. Seeing monks arriving from China, the local people showed great tenderness (*shin tu snying brtse*) and amazement. [169] They spoke these words: "*E ma!* Just so. It has come to pass that beings from the easternmost frontiers of the world are ripening their minds and understanding the benefits of the holy Dharma! As such, from far away they have come searching for the Buddhadharma!" They offered whatever provisions the Chinese monks required and served them according to the Dharma.

XVI
Mathurā and the Great Yamunā River

They journeyed some eighty *dpag tshad* from there toward the southeast. Along the path [they] passed near a great many monasteries housing tens of thousands of monks. Having traversed those regions, [one] arrives in the dominion of a king. His kingdom is called Mathurā.[124] In addition, passing along the length of the banks of the Yamunā River,[125] all along the east and west sides are some twenty regional monasteries wherein three thousand monks reside year round. It was only recently that the Buddha's teachings spread and increased here.

After crossing the great sandy desert and passing the rivers of the west, the kings along the borderlands of the country of India, Land of Noble Ones respect the Buddha's Teachings from the depths of their heart. When they prostrate to the saṅgha they remove their crowns (*prog zhu*). From their own residences, these kings along with the princes and ministers each use their own wealth and offer food to the monastics. After, they unfurl a carpet over the ground and sit facing each other upon cushions. They dare not ever sit upon beds in the presence of the saṅgha. This [170] custom of kings offering gifts and hospitality began when the Buddha abided in the world. It has continued up to today.

The kingdoms to the south of this region are famously known as "the Middle Kingdom."[126] In the Middle Kingdom, cold and heat moderate each other so that it remains temperate. There are neither frigid rains nor snow. The people are wealthy and live happily. There are neither a census nor taxes. There are only those who harvest fruits grown in the king's fields. There are also those who serve as guardsmen and messengers (*pho nyar gtong mkhan*) for the king. If a law is broken, the only punishment is to pay some money for the criminal offense; the amount will depend upon the severity of the crime. If it happens that a criminal commits another crime, they cut off his right hand. Other than this, they impose no further punishment.

The king, ministers, and those [officials] posted in ranks to the right and left all [subsist only upon] a salary and gifts.[127] The people of this country kill no animals whatsoever. Those from the untouchable caste are kept separate from the general population. The appelation "untouchable" means "to be despoiled" (*btsog grib pa can*). Even their housing is kept separate from those of other castes. Upon arriving in towns and markets, they announce their presence by beating upon a piece of wood; thereupon, those of other castes may avoid them so as not to make contact with their bodies. Neither pigs nor fowl are raised in this land. Livestock are never sold alive. In the markets [171] there are no abattoirs (*phyugs gsod pa'i sa*) or taverns. When engaged in business, they exchange conch shells. Only those embodied as an untouchable dare hunt or sell flesh.

Ever since the parinirvāṇa of the Buddha, rulers and chieftains (*rje dpon rnams dang mi gtso bo*) have constructed vihāras to benefit monastics.[128] They have also offered them material provisions, arable lands (*zhing sa rnams*), pleasure groves and orchards, farmers and livestock handlers (*bkol spyod kyi phyugs*) to cultivate all these, and so forth. Lists of offerings are memorialized by being engraved upon an iron inscription plate, which no king who comes later may so much as touch. This tradition has continued uninterruptedly to today. Lacking nothing, monastics here are provided every requisite of life, including a dwelling for shelter, bedding for sleeping, food and beverage for eating and drinking, Dharma robes to wear, and so on. It is the same with all of the vihāras.

All monastics exert themselves in virtuous activities and the study of worthwhile topics (*yon tan slob pa*) for the entirety of their lives. What's more, they principally focus upon reading the scriptures and practicing meditation. When a foreign monastic appears, local people go to receive them and accompany them while taking turns carrying their Dharma robes and begging bowls. They then bring water to wash their feet, oil to anoit their body, and beverages if it is an unsuitable time [for a monastic to eat]. After they have rested a while, they are asked which number of offerings and festivities (*ston mo dag*) they wish to perform. Then they are led to their quarters, after which they are provided with necessities according to the internal rules of their tradition.

In the residences [172] of the monastics who permanently reside there are stūpas of Śāriputra (*shā ri bu*), Maudgalyāyana (*mo'u gal gyi bu*), and Ānanda (*kun dga' bo*),[129] as well as temples dedicated to the divisions [i.e., *piṭakas*] of the Abhidharma, the Vinaya, and the Sūtras.[130] After the Chinese monks had recuperated for a month in this region, those wishing to achieve the conditions for a blissful existence requested of them: "Now please accomplish some Dharma practice [on our behalf]!"[131] After taking their food as mentioned before,[132] all the monastics assemble on cushions and read the scriptures aloud. After they were released from the assembly, they made offerings to the Śāriputra stūpa using many varieties of fragrant incense and lit butter lamps for the whole night. Afterward they made offerings to the other [stūpas]. As for he who is named Śāriputra: long ago when he was born as a brāhman he became a monk in the presence of the Teacher Śākyamuni. It was the same with the great Maudgalyāyana and Mahākāśyapa.[133] Most of the nuns (*rab byung ma*) make offerings to the stūpa of Ānanda. The reason for this is that it was Ānanda who had requested the Principal of the World (*'Jig rten gyi gtso bo*) to allow women (*bud med*) to be ordained as monastics. In addition, they continually advise disciples of the Buddha,

"Make progress in your training in moral discipline!"[134] The practitioners of the Abhidharma,[135] the upholders of the Vinaya,[136] and the upholders of the Sūtras make offerings to those baskets (of scriptural collections).[137] Furthermore, they practice in this way every year, each allotted their dedicated day. Those with keen devotion to the Mahāyāna make offerings to Prajñāpāramitā, Lord Mañjuśrī, and Avalokiteśvara.[138]

The monastics collect offerings [173] as the new year approaches. Others, such as the very elderly endowed with virtue, throngs of followers, and brāhmans, prepare arrangements of various monastic robes, other requisite items, and alms for the saṅgha. The saṅgha sit in the place where (the Buddha) offered his body in order to feed the tigress. Regarding the required practices (*'os pa'i phyag bzhes*) and Dharma traditions that the saṅgha perform, these have been maintained continuously without any interruption since the Buddha's parinirvāṇa.

After fording the Sindhu River, one arrives in the lands of southern India. From there to the great Southern Ocean,[139] (one must cross) some four or five thousand *rgyang grags* overland. Regarding that territory, there are neither forbidding mountain ranges nor any great rivers. There is only a vast plain with great and small valleys and minor rivers.

XVII
Sāṃkāśya

After that, if one journeys to the southwest for ten *dpag tshad* there is the kingdom of Sāṃkāśya.[140] **[Regarding this place, Xuanzang's *Guidebook* says that it is the region of Ka bi na.]** It is from this place that the Buddha departed for the realm of the Heaven of the Thirty-Three,[141] where he turned the Wheel of the Dharma for three months in order to repay his mother's kindness. This is where he descended [as well]. The Buddha ascended to the (Heaven) of the Thirty-Three on account of his supernatural power (*rdzu 'phrul*). His disciples did not understand and wept for seven days. While the Buddha displayed his abilities and powers (*nus mthu*) there, Aniruddha (*Ma'gags pa*)[142] could see the Principal of the World from afar because of being endowed with divine vision (*lha'i mig can*). They told all this to the Elder Maudgalyāyana, saying, "Please, may you invite the Principal of the World [to return]!"

Thereupon, [174] Maudgalyāyana went there, prostrated at (the Buddha's) feet, and then, in his presence, passed along their request. The Buddha responded thus: "One week hence I will descend back to the world." Maudgalyāyana then returned. The eight kings of the greater regional kingdoms, as well as the chieftains of the minor districts, all of whom had long desired to see the Buddha, gathered like clouds and awaited the Principal of the World's arrival. At that time, the bhikṣuṇī Utpāla (*dge slong ma ut pā la*)[143] thought: "Today all these kings and crowds of people are awaiting the Buddha in order to make prostrations. Since we are women, there will be no chance for us to see the Teacher first." By the power of the Buddha, she manifested as a Cakravartin king[144] so that she could prostrate to the Buddha before anyone else.

When the time came for the Buddha to descend from the [Heaven] of the Thirty-Three, three bejeweled staircases were manifested. The Buddha descended down the central one, which was ornamented by seven precious substances (*rin chen sna bdun*). Brahmā, King of the Gods, manifested (*gtsugs*) a staircase made of silver to the right. He descended after the Buddha while holding aloft a white whisk in his hand. Indra manifested a staircase of refined gold to the left. He also descended after the Buddha while holding aloft a whisk ornamented by the seven precious substances. An uncountable, inconceivable number of gods also descended after the Buddha. Once they had all alighted, the three ladders sank into the earth, leaving only about seven rungs still visible. [175]

In later times, King Aśoka (*Rgyal po mya ngan med*) desired to see the base of these ladders. He dispatched some of his subjects, ordering, "Dig until you reach the base of these ladders!" Though they dug for a month, they were unable to unearth (*gtugs*) the base. Thereafter, the king's faith and devotion greatly increased. Over the top of these ladders he built a statue six *gyan* high. Behind the gandhola temple, he erected a stone pillar thirty *khru* high with a lion on top.

> **[Xuanzang recorded that this [stone pillar] is forty *'dom* high, its sides are as reflective as a mirror, and that its surfaces can reflect virtue and nonvirtue.]**

Buddha images are engraved into its four sides. Inside and out are unblemished and resplendent as crystalline water. Heretical tīrthika (*mu stegs pa*) paṇḍitas stole this site from the Buddhist monks. The saṅgha conversed and came together in one big assembly, proclaiming: "If we Buddhists have rightful ownership of this site, show them some marvelous sign!" The stone lion atop the pillar immediately sounded an awesome roar. Those heretics were terrified. They then developed sincere respect for the Buddha and received blessings.[145]

During the third month, their bodies emit a heavenly fragrance completely unlike that of ordinary people. There we find a tradition of bathing, with bathhouses built in this region that still stand today. They also built a stūpa at the site where the bhikṣuṇī Utpāla prostrated to the Buddha first. There is also a stūpa marking the site [176] where, during his lifetime, the Buddha cut his hair and nails. They built statuary and stūpas at the sites where the three Buddhas of bygone ages once walked and where they passed away. These remain to this day.

> **[Xuanzang wrote that upon the banks of the Ganges, at Ga nya+dza ku, he came into worshipful encounter (*mjal*) with the stone foundations of the dais of the four Univeral Guides (*rnam 'drin bzhi ka*), stūpas containing hair and tooth relics of the Tathāgata, and so forth.]**

There is also a display (*bkod pa*) marking the site where Brahmā, King of the Gods, and Indra alighted while serving as attendants for the Buddha. At these sites about a thousand bhikṣu and bhikṣuṇi, devotees of the Mahāyāna and the Hīnayāna, intermix and convene to take their food in each other's company.

In the saṅgha's abode they fashioned a (statue) of the White-Eared Nāga (*Klu rna ba dkar po can*).[146] Whenever it is needed that nāga causes a fine rain to fall and purifies all manner of land-afflicting destructive poisons so that each year they grow an exceptional harvest with abundant crops. Because of all this, the monastic assembly lives contentedly. To pay back (that nāga's) kindnesses, they raised a temple for him with a throne, make propitious offerings of clean food, and each day elect three śramaṇas (*dge sbyong*) from the monastic assembly and dispatch them to the Nāga Temple (*klu'i lha khang*) with the command to eat their meal there. After the period of their obligation there has finished, the nāga will emanate as a small snake with white-edged ears. Recognizing him upon his arrival, the monks fill a copper bowl with milk and feed it to him. Elated, [177] the nāga descends from on high to the base of the throne. Contented once more, he circumambulates and then disappears. This happens once each year. This Central Land always has rich harvests and an abundance of crops (*lo tog*) and grasses (*rtsi thog*). Its peoples have copious kin and opulent wealth. Compared to populations in other places, they are uncommonly skilled in craft (*gsor mtho khyad zhugs so*).

In a place fifty *rgyan grags* to the north of that temple is a temple named Fire Border (*me'i mtha'*). It is where the Buddha once led a wicked *yakṣa* demon[147] into the Dharma. Later generations erected a temple and offered it to an arhat. A few drops once fell when the Buddha was washing his hands, which one can still see today at this site. No matter how much you wipe away those drops, they return again and again. It is impossible to completely dry them!

Elsewhere in this place, a faithful god once made the offering of wiping and washing a stūpa of the Buddha such that it always remained clean without ever requiring any human exertion. An evil king once led an enormous army there and said: "If you possess such ability and power (*nus mthu*), are you able to you wash and clean away all of our grime?" That god then drew up a great gust of wind that carried away all of their filth. There are [about] hundred small stūpas at this site, but even [178] if someone counts them all day, their exact number cannot be known with any certainty. If someone were to think (*snyam*) that they wanted to properly know, they might arrange a person at the base of each stūpa and then later count the people. But because some stūpas are quite small, others are quite large, and there a great many of them, it would still be impossible to arrive at an exact count.

There is a temple there that can hold six or seven hundred monastics. It is said here a Solitary Realizer[148] once received alms. The place called "Passing Into Nirvāṇa" looks like a chariot wheel. Though grass grows nearby, here not a blade will sprout. Just so, (grass) does not grow in places where monastic robes were removed (*phrol ba*). The patches of the Dharma robe (*chos gos kyi rnangs brgal dag*) are clearly visible upon the surface of the rock. These traces (*mtshan ma de dag*) exist today just as then.

XVIII
The City of Kanyākubja; The Ganges River; The Öma Garden[149]

Faxian then arrived at the Nāga Temple (Tib. *Klu'i gtsug lag khang*; Mong. *Luus-un süm-a*). After residing there a few days, he journeyed southeast for seven *dpag tshad* before arriving at Kanyākubja city,[150] close to the Ganges River.[151] Two monasteries there are dedicated to the practice of the Hīnayāna. Six or seven *dpag tshad* west of that city is the north shore of the Ganges. There one finds a site where the Buddha taught the Dharma for the benefit of his disciples. According to local oral tradition (*ngan rgyun*), there he pronounced, "The human body is impermanent and [179] its nature is sickness, like river foam," and delivered other Dharma discourses on related subjects. They built a stūpa at that site that still stands today.

Fording the Ganges, if one faces south and then proceeds for three *dpag tshad*, one arrives in a forest (*nags khrod*) called Heli.[152] There the Buddha propounded the Dharma. At this site they have built individual stūpas everywhere the Buddha proceeded, returned, and abided.

XIX
The Kingdom of Sāketa

Journeying ten *dpag tshad* to the southwest, one arrives at a great kingdom called Sāketa.[153] Outside the southern gate of Sāketa City is a place on the left side of the road where the Buddha had once chewed a toothpick (*tshems shing*) and then planted it into the earth. This grew into a tree some seven fathoms high[154] and then never grew any taller or shorter. Heretical brāhmans, beset by jealous and vindictive minds, would fell the tree and dispose of it far away. Whenever they did this, however, the tree would rejuvenate from its remains and grow back to its previous stature. There are about three sites in this land where the Buddha once resided.[155] Stūpas were built at each of them and remain to this day.

XX
The Region of Kośala; Śrāvastī Village; Jetavana Park; Tadwa Village

Journeying eight *dpag tshad* to the south[156] from that land, one arrives in the region of Kośala[157] and the village [180] of Śrāvastī.[158] A great many people live in that village, which numbers two thousand households.[159] This village is where King Prasenajit resided.[160] The locals deeply entrust themselves to the holy Dharma. At sites such as the well wall (*khron pa'i rwa skor dag*) of the householder Anāthapiṇḍada,[161] the place where the harmful god (*gdug pa'i lha*) Imhuwi [i.e., Aṅgulimāla][162] entered into the Dharma, and the site of his cremation, the faithful of later generations from among these households built stūpas.[163] All these still stand today. Heretical brāhmans, their mental continuums disturbed by jealousy, began to destroy these stūpas. As they did so, a dragon's roar came from the sky, lightning flashed, and thunder sounded such that those brāhmans could not bring themselves to destroy the stūpas.

Two hundred paces (*gom*) from the east side of the path that leaves from the village's southern gate is a temple built with the householder Anāthapiṇḍada's permission. Its door is east facing. There are two pavilions (*ldings* [*sic*] *khang*) and two stone columns, the left fashioned with a wheel atop its peak, the right with a bull. Using canals, very pure water is brought and used to fill a pool. The dense forest was grown using trees with thick foliage. Exceedingly beautiful flowers bloom there; just the sight of them is enough to enchant sentient beings. This is the famous Jetavana Park.[164]

[181] When the Buddha had departed for [the Heaven] of the Thirty-Three in order to propound the Dharma over the course of forty-nine days to repay the kindness of his mother, King Prasenajit wanted to see the Buddha and pay homage to him. Therefore, he ordered a skilled craftsman to fashion a statue of the Buddha made from *gośīrṣa-candana* [sandalwood].[165] This was installed in the Buddha's sleeping quarters. As the Buddha descended from the heavenly realm into his sleeping quarters, the sandalwood Buddha statue set off to leave before he arrived. The Buddha commanded: "Return

here and sit! Later, after my parinirvāṇa, you will be a facsimile (*mtshon dpe*) by which the four types of disciples[166] may recollect the Buddha!" The statue duly returned and resided there. This was the very first statue of the Buddha. All others were made by later generations on its example. At that time, the Buddha separated himself from the sleeping quarters of the statue and departed to a small sleeping quarter that had been erected twenty paces (*gom pa*) away.

The gandhola of the Jetavana Park was originally seven stories. All kings and their subjects have been tremendously devoted to this site. From time to time they visit and make offerings.

> **[Xuanzang wrote, "In Śrāvastī's Jetavana Park there are only a few trees, a stone pillar, a statue of the Teacher in the aspect of expounding the Dharma to his mother, and a stone house. There is nothing other than these." I think that over time this site has deteriorated.]**

A "sky umbrella" (*gnam rgyan*) and a canopy were hung at this site, and they scattered flowers and burned fragrant incense. The lights in its butter lamp house [182] were never extinguished, day or night. Once, a rat scurried about with oil (*spra tshil*) from the butter lamps in its mouth and set ablaze the temple's canopy and the hanging coverings (*g.yogs pa rnam*) inside. All its seven stories burned down. Thinking that the sandalwood statue had also burnt in the fire, the king and subjects were stricken with grief and set to wailing. Four or five days later, the door of a small temple on the east side (of the complex) suddenly opened. There stood the actual sandalwood statue. Everyone was delighted and felt tremendous joy and inspiration and newly built the gandhola. Once they had completed the second story, they reinstalled that statue.

Both Faxian and Daozheng visited the Jetavana Park and reflected:

> *E ma*! Just consider that the Principal of the World lived in this place for twenty-five years! *Kyi hyud*! We have wandered to a great many blessed sites (*gnas chen*), and to come into worshipful contact with this place we joined many travel companions upon the path. Among them, some have since returned to their homeland. Others have exhibited the fundamental nature of impermanence of the life span (*tshe'i 'du byed*). Though we two arrived here today, the Buddha Bhagavān no longer abides here!

With unsettled minds, they became despondent. Some other monks asked the two from China, "Where have you come from?" "We have arrived from the easterly kingdom of Great China (*shar phyogs mahā tsi na rgyal khams*)," they replied.

They were asked again and again, and after drawing a deep breath (in wonderment), [the local monastics] said: "*E ma!* How amazing! [183] You have succeeded in coming from the easternmost frontiers of Jambudvīpa to its center in order to search for the holy Dharma!" They said to each other, "We and other bhikṣus and upāsakas have traveled from place to place, but never before have we seen a scholar arriving from somewhere called 'the kingdom of China' (*tsi na'i rgyal khams*)."

Four *rgyang grags* to the northwest of that temple is a medicinal region (*sman ljongs*) known as "The Forest of Restored Vision" (*Mig gsos pa'i nags*). Long ago there were five hundred blind people who, while journeying to visit Jetavana Park, took rest here. The Buddha spoke about the Dharma as medicine for them, and their eyes became unblemished. Those previously blinded people became joyous, planting their walking canes into the ground and paying homage to this area. Later, the roots [of the walking sticks] intertwined with one another and they consequently began to grow and become enormous. Later generations showed respect and never cut this wood. That is the reason it is known as the Forest of Restored Vision. There is a tradition among the saṅgha of the Jetavana Park that after they take their meals, they retire to this wood to settle their minds into single-minded contemplation (*bsam gtan la sems 'jogs pa*).

Six or seven *rgyang grags* to the northeast of Jetavana Park is [a temple] built with the permission of Mṛgāra's[167] mother. This is a place to which the Buddha was later invited and is included within the Jetavana Park.[168] There is an enclosure (*lcags ri*) with doors, one on the north side and one on the east. This is the site of the park, which the householder Anāthapiṇḍada gave permission [184] to build and which he funded with money, gold, and silver. The Buddha resided in the temple there for a long time in order to benefit sentient beings. The site where he expounded the Dharma is in the center of the park. They built gandholas wherever the Buddha had journeyed or resided. All of these sites have their own individual names. This appears to be where Sundarī[169] accused the Buddha of committing murder.

After departing from the eastern gate of the Jetavana Park and heading north, on the right side of the road seventy paces away is where ninety-six heretical teachers and the Buddha competed in magical display (*chos 'phrul 'gran*). Once when regional kings, leaders (*rje dpon rnams*), chiefs (*gtso bo dag*), and their subjects gathered like clouds in the presence of the Buddha to listen to the Dharma, the daughter of a heretical teacher named Ciñcāmāṇa[vikā][170] was afflicted with extreme jealousy. Fastening a bundle of cloth over her stomach, she declared "I've become pregnant!" This cunning proclamation amounted to inconceivable slander against the Buddha. Indra, Lord of the Gods, manifested as a white mouse that bit through the rope holding together the bundle of clothing at her waist. Just as the bundle of clothes fell to the ground, so too did the ground open and that girl tumble into hell while still alive. Devadatta (*Lhas byin*) put poison on his nail and planned on scratching the Buddha's body. Just so, he too fell into hell while still alive.

[Xuanzang wrote that he observed a very deep hole that could never be filled by rainwater at the ruins of where Devadatta fell alive into the Vajra Hell.]

Later generations [185] recognized (*ngos bzung*) those places and used them as [moral] examples (*mtshan ma 'jog par gda'*). A temple was built at the site of the magical contests. That temple is about six *rgyan* in height, and statues of the Buddha were installed inside.

On the left side of the road is a small temple called Covered by Shadow (*grib mas g.yogs pa*), which honors the gods of the heretical tīrthikas. It is directly across from the temple marking the site of the magical contest. These two temples are on either side of the road and compete against each other. The [other] temple is also nearly six *rgyan* high. As for the reason it was given the name Suppressed by Shadow Temple (*grib mas gnon pa'i lha khang*): the Principal of the World's temple is located to the west and casts its shadow over the tīrthikas' temple. When the sun shines from the east, the shadow of the tīrthikas' temple is cast to the north but never over the temple of the Buddha.

The tīrthikas dispatch people to protect their temple, clean it, sprinkle water [to settle the dust], and burn fragrant incense, as well as to read the Vedas (*rig byed*) and burn butter lamps. However, they noticed that all their butter lamps would transfer to the Buddha's temple each night. Consequently, the brāhmaṇas became quite upset and complained to each other, "*Kye ma*! Those bhikṣus [186] take our butter lamps and use them to make offering to Śākyamuni! What reason have we not to regard them as our enemies?" Once night fell, the brāhmaṇas hid and waited. Then offering gods appeared, each in their own bodies, carried off the butter lamps, and set them before Śākyamuni. They then circumambulated the temple three times, prostrated to the Buddha, and disappeared. Then the brāhmaṇas understood that the Buddha was superior in knowledge to their gods. With this recognition, they entered into the Teachings.

According to their oral tradition (*ngag rgyun*), not too long after this situation there were eighty-eight[171] monasteries in the vicinity of Jetavana Park. All of these had dwelling places inhabited by the saṅgha, with the exception of one that remained empty. Today in Central India there are ninety-six kinds of tīrthika who follow (*khas lan*) the Creator of the World.[172] There are a great many disciples who follow other kinds (of teachers). Though they live by begging food, they do not have begging bowls. They also build houses and prepare cushions, food, and drink for those who are homeless or for travelers on the road searching for health and happiness. Buddhist renunciants who are coming and going may stay in them, but it is unsuitable for them to reside there at their leisure. Followers of Devadatta[173] make offerings to the three [187] previous buddhas. They do not only pay homage to the Teacher Śākyamuni.

About four *rgyang grags* to the southeast of the city of Śrāvastī (*Myan yod*) is the territory of the Śākyas,[174] where King Virūḍhaka[175] prepared for battle. A stūpa was built there after the birth of the Principal of the World. Fifty *rgyang grags* to the west of that city is a small village named Tadwa.[176] This is the birthplace of the Buddha Kāśyapa.[177] Stūpas were built where son and father had met and where the Buddha [Kāśyapa] renounced. A reliquary stūpa for Kāśyapa was also built there.

XXI
Nābhika City; The Birthplaces of the Buddhas Krakucchanda and Kanakamuni

If one travels south[178] two *dpag tshad* from Śrāvastī, one arrives at Nābhika city.[179] This is the birthplace of the Buddha Krakucchanda.[180] A monastery stands where father and son met, and a stūpa was built where he renounced. Close to one *dpag tshad* to the north of there is the birthplace of the Buddha Kanakamuni.[181] There too, stūpas were built where son and father met and where he renounced.

["The birthplaces of those two buddhas are located about a half day to the south of the well[182] of the lower part of Kapilavastu," explains Xuanzang's *Guidebook*.]

XXII
Kapilavastu City; The Royal Field; How the Tathāgatha Was Born

Traveling one *dpag tshad* to the east, one arrives in the city of Kapilavastu.[183]

[Xuanzang wrote that the ruins of the city of Kapilavastu are some fifteen li (*le bar*) in circumference. [There] are more than ten empty cities and [188] many dilapidated temples. Nothing remains in the center of the palace, other than a stūpa [commemorating] the [Buddha] entering the womb.]

There is no king in that city. Nor are there any subjects. It is vast and barren land without owner. Only a few monastics and a paltry few of the śūdra servant caste (*dmangs rigs*) are to be found here and there. This is the site of the ruins of King Śuddhodana's palace.[184] Therein is an image of the Buddha manifesting (*rnam rol*) as a great white elephant and inhabiting his mother's womb, as well as an image of the prince [Siddhārtha] and his mother.

A stūpa was built where the prince left the city through the eastern gate, and stūpas have been erected where he turned and returned [to the palace] after seeing a sick man. They also raised temples where Asita observed the prince;[185] where Nanda[186] and his companions tried to injure the elephant; where the arrow shot by [the Buddha] flew thirty *rgyan grags* to the southeast before plunging into the ground, causing a spring to bubble forth where later generations fashioned something like a waterwheel to provide drinking water; at the site from which the arrow was shot; where the Buddha met his father after he had "found the nectar" (*bdud rtsi brnyes*, i.e., became enlightened); where the five hundred sons of the Śākya became monks and prostrated to Upāli;[187] where the earth shook six times; where King Śuddhodana and his subjects were blocked by the Four Heavenly Kings who protected the four doors while the Buddha spoke the Dharma for the benefit of the gods; where Mahāprajāpatī offered [189] Dharma robes to the Buddha when he dwelt facing east near the root of the *nyagrodha* tree,[188] which still exists there; and where all the friends and relatives of the Śākyas, who had long since achieved realizations (equal to) that of the āryas,[189] were killed by King Virūḍhaka.[190] All these temples have remained continuously until today.

Many *rgyang grags* to the northeast of that city is the Royal Field (*rgyal po'i shing*). There, under a tree, the prince witnessed the [farming] laborers (*bsnyen bkur mkhan*).[191] Fifty *rgyang grags* to the east of that city is the royal pleasure garden (*rgyal po'i skyed mos tshal*)

> **[Xuangzang wrote: "About a hundred *li* (*le bar*) to the south from there, the temple of Lumbinī Park (*lu mbi ni'i tshal gyi lha khang*) still exists." That also still survives today. I have seen a reproduction (*'dra ris*) of a painting from inside [that temple] depicting the Buddha's birth from his mother's side.]**

That pleasure garden is named "Lumbinī Park."[192] In order to wash her body, the queen entered into a pool [there]. She emerged at the north embankment and took twenty steps. Holding a tree branch with her hand, she turned her face toward the east and delivered the prince. After the prince descended to the earth, he took seven steps and two nāga kings received him by showering him and picking him up. They soon constructed a water well (*khron pa*) at the site where [the prince] was offered this shower. A monastic community (*dgon gnas*) there draws its drinking water from this well and the pool in which [the prince's] mother bathed.

As for sites famous for being associated with all the buddhas, there are four. First, where they obtained enlightenment. Second, where they turned the Wheel of the Dharma. Third, where they subdued congregations of tīrthikas by means of magical display. Fourth, where they first departed to the Heaven of the Thirty-Three in order to repay the kindness of their mothers by teaching them the Dharma, and then where they descended afterward. Other than these four, places come to be regarded as a holy site because of individual, particular reasons.

Kapilavastu is nowadays a wilderness without owner. [190] Few people use its roadways, as these are unsuitable for travel because of very fearsome white elephants and tigers.

XXIII
Rāmagrāma and the Nāga Lake; The Reason King Aśoka went with the Nāga; The Elephants Who Served the Dharma

If one walks five *dpag tshad* to the east of the Buddha's birthplace, one arrives in a region called Rāma [grāma].[193] The ruler of that land, upon acquiring a portion of the Buddha's relics, built a stūpa called the Rāma Stūpa. Near that stūpa is a pool, wherein a nāga[194] lives who continually protects the stūpa. After King Aśoka freed himself from anger, he opened the eight stūpas and thought, "I will open these eight stūpas and then build 84,000 stūpas [using their contents]!" He had already opened the seven other stūpas, but when he tried to touch this stūpa, the nāga appeared and kidnapped King Aśoka to his own palace. The nāga then showed [Aśoka] items that had already been used in the stūpa and he said, "If you are able to offer better substances than these, than you may destroy this stūpa and I will not cause any obstacles for you." King Aśoka thought, "Incredible! These sorts of offering substances are impossible to acquire within the human world!" He therefore left [that eighth stūpa alone] and departed.

That place has no crops and it appears to have no owner. Nobody sweeps there, nor are there any water spreaders. Even so, a herd of elephants serves the stūpa by continuously collecting water with their trunks, spreading it upon the earth, and offering many kinds of flowers and other fragrant items. In the past, when Bön practitioners[195] came from various regions [191] to do prostrations, they encountered the elephants and were terrified. They escaped to the forests and hid there. From that vantage they saw that the elephants were actually serving the stūpa, even when no humans were. Seeing those elephants do such wonderful activity, those people became devoted and surprised. At that place, Bön people abandoned their root tenets. In order to attend to the stūpa, they brought their own grass and wood, offered service, and kept the site very clean. With effort, those people brought their regional king into the Dharma, who then let them build temples and meditation sites for monks to reside in. Even nowadays, many monks still stay at that place. This occurred not so long ago, and the decorations still are to be seen there. Regional people continuously ordain as monks at this temple.

If one travels three *dpag tshad* to the east of there, one arrives to where the prince [Siddhārtha] abandoned the white horse and returned by chariot. Even there, a temple has been built.

XXIV
The Charcoal Stūpa and Kuśingarī

From there, if you travel to the east for about fourteen *dpag tshad*[196] you arrive in the vicinity of the Charcoal Stūpa.[197] That site, too, has a monastery. A further twelve *dpag tshad* to the east, one arrives at Kuśingarī.[198]

[Xuanzang (wrote):

> **About four *dpag tshad* to the northwest of the ruins of that city is a great jasmine garden[199] some thirty *li* wide. The eastern reaches are at a lower elevation and the center at a higher elevation. [192] Inside this temple is another temple made of bricks. Inside that is a clay statue of a standing Buddha Śākyamuni and beside it a stūpa. On a pillar at that stūpa is an inscription that reads, "The two traditions of dating [when the Buddha] passed beyond are 'The fifteenth day of the second month' and 'The eighth day of the ninth month.'"**

Furthermore, the *Root Tantra of Mañjuśrī* prophesies:

> **I will pass beyond near a river full of gold, surrounded by formidable people (*gyad rnams*) in a forest with two śāla trees.**

When I think about this, tears well up in my eyes!

To the north of the city, the Principal of this World passed beyond suffering between two sāla trees,[200] his head facing north. A stūpa was built where

(Parivrājika) Subhadra[201] became a disciple and where for seven days people came to make offerings to the golden vase that contained the Principal of the World's relics (Tib. *gser gdung gi bum pa*; Mong. *altan šaril-un bumba*) and casket.

[Xuanzang wrote, "The land where the Buddha's body was cremated, to the north of the city, near a river, was originally elevated two *li* all around. Nowadays, there is a big hole six cubits deep. The reason is that so many people have come continuously to remove earth from that site.]

A stūpa was built where Vajrapāṇi[202] dropped his golden vajra[203] to the earth. And at the place where the eight great kings divided the relics (Skt. *śarīra*)[204] a stūpa was built that still exists nowadays. People are very rare and scarce in this city; only monks and those of the servant class reside there.

[Xuanzang wrote: "In the ruins of the city of Kuśa are the ruins of a derelict, empty house."]

From there, if one travels twenty *dpag tshad* to the south, one arrives at the places where the Licchavi people,[205] determined to kill themselves after the Buddha passed away, were denied permission to do so by the Buddha; where the Buddha [193] emanated a very deep, unfordable river; where the Buddha discovered an amazing gift inside his begging bowl; and where he ordered members of his family "You must erect a pillar with an inscription upon its crest!"

XXV
Vaiśālī; Ānanda's Reliquary Stūpa; Āmrapālī's Garden; How the Buddhas Displayed Passing Beyond Sorrow; [The Stūpa of] Laying Down the Bows; Collecting the Words [of the Buddha]

If one travels east from there for five *dpag tshad*, one arrives at Vaiśālī.[206]

[Xuanzang wrote, "For seventy li in the vicinity of Vaiśālī there are only a few houses. I encountered seven stūpas dedicated to arhats. Although many sūtras say that long ago this city possessed wealth equal to the gods, it is well known that nowadays because of the time the many noble families of Magadha (*li tsa byi rnams*) have passed away and their houses have come to ruin."]

There is a small temple in the forest there. That is the place where the Buddha resided. There is a stūpa with Ānanda's[207] relics. Long ago, a woman named

Āmrapālī[208] lived in this city. She built a gandhola and offered it to the Buddha, and the Buddha resided there. That garden is nowadays about three *rgyang grags* to the south of the city, along the right side of the street. When the Buddha was about to pass into nirvāṇa, he left via the western gate of Vaiśālī. He turned to the right and, looking back, gave this prophecy: "The last of my enlightened activity will occur in that place." Later generations built a stūpa there.

From that city [194] to the northeast is a place called The Stūpa Where the Thousand Bows Were Laid Down (*bor ba'i ga nu dag dang stong phrag gi mchod rten*). The reason for that name is as follows. Far from the banks of the Ganges River, a king's younger wife who had been pregnant delivered a heap of meat (*sha'i gong bu*).[209] Because the older queen was jealous of the other queens, she told [the younger queen], "Your delivery is a bad omen!" As a result, that meat heap was put into a wooden box and thrown into the Ganges River and swept away by its current. Later, a king who was frolicking in the water saw the box. Retrieving it, he opened the box and saw a thousand children inside who all looked alike. He removed all the children and raised them. When they grew up, they became heroic and very powerful. Whoever they chose to fight could not defeat them and were conquered.

Once they threatened to destroy the kingdom of their [actual] father, the king. He became terribly worried, about which his younger queen inquired. The king told her, "Such and such country has a very powerful king with a thousand unbeatable sons. They will try to conquer our land. Because of that, I am terribly worried!" The younger queen replied, "Don't worry about this! You should order that a high grass house be built on the east side of the city. Once those enemies arrive, let me abide atop it. I have a method to protect our people." The king acted according to her words.

When their adversaries arrived, the queen spoke the following words to her kingdom's enemies from atop the grass house: [195] "All of you are my children! Why do you despise us so and aspire to destroy us?" The enemies retorted, "Who could believe that you are our mother?" "If all of you don't believe me," the queen replied, "you should open your mouths." From her two breasts she drew forth milk, and from each breast came five hundred drops of milk. All at once, these drops flew into the mouths of her thousand children. Then those enemies understood, "This is our mother!" They then laid down their weapons and armor.

On account of these causes and conditions, both kings attained the enlightenment of a pratyekabuddha (*rang rgyal gyi byang chub*). The stūpas dedicated to these two pratyekabuddhas still stand today. Once, after the Principal of the World had achieved enlightenment, he said, "This is the place where, long ago, I laid down my bow and other weaponry." Because of this, future generations understood why this site was important. They built a stūpa there and gave it this name. The "thousand children" of this tale are in fact the thousand buddhas of this fortunate aeon. When the Buddha Śākyamuni was staying at this site where they had thrown down their armor and weapons, he said to Ānanda, "Three months from now, I will pass into nirvāṇa." Just at that moment, Māra, King of Demons, distracted Ānanda so that he did not take the opportunity to request the Buddha to abide longer in this world.

There is a stūpa to the east of there about three or four *rgyang grags*. Some hundred years after the Buddha's parinirvāṇa, it arose that a monk who lived in the city of Vaiśālī recklessly reinforced the practice of [196] Ten Transgressions[210] that did not appear in any of the Buddha's teachings or in his counsel on the vinaya precepts. As a result, five hundred monks who were very knowledgeable in the five fields of knowledge, who upheld the vinaya, and who were arhats, along with a congregation of seven hundred monastics, gathered the saṅgha in order to further correct any mistakes in the treasury of the Dharma. Later generations built a stūpa at that place, which still exists today.

XXVI
The Confluence of Five Rivers; How Ānanda Passed Into Nirvāṇa

If one travels four *dpag tshad* from that [stūpa], one arrives at the confluence of five rivers.[211] When Ānanda departed for the city of Vaiśālī in the country of Magadha[212] in order to pass into nirvāṇa, the gods (Tib. *lha rnams*; Mong. *tngriner*) alerted King Ajātaśatru.[213] The king departed hastily on horseback to the banks of this river, accompanied by his army. All the Licchavi of Vaiśālī realized that Ānanda would soon arrive. They all gathered near the river to receive him. [Ānanda] grew saddened, thinking: "Should I progress ahead, Ajātaśatru will seize me. Should I retreat, the Licchavi are behind me." By means of the fire of concentration (*bsam gtan gyi me khams*), he self-immolated in the middle of the river and passed into nirvāṇa. His bodily remains then split into two portions. The king and the Licchavi of Vaiśālī each took a portion and each built a stūpa in their homeland.

XXVII
Magadha, the Central Land; The Great City of Pāṭaliputrā; The Mountain Known as Vulture's Peak; The Mountain Built by Yakṣas; The Celebration of the Buddha's Birth; the Footprint of the Buddha and the Inscribed Stone Pillar

If one travels one *dpag tshad* to the south and fords the Ganges, one arrives in the region of Magadha and [197] the great city of Pāṭaliputrā.[214]

[The great city of Pāṭaliputrā and the Benagara fort are all completely destroyed. Only ruins remain. A new city named Trana has since risen there.]

This was the city of King Aśoka. The fence of the king's palace in this city was built using stones brought by yakṣas (*gnod sbyin*). Ornamented bricks (*pa tra*) and so forth adorn the windows. There are so many features of such amazing design that they could never have been constructed by humans alone. All this still exists in the city. King Aśoka's younger brother achieved arhathood and resided contentedly at Vulture's Peak whenever he found time. King Aśoka served him and once asked, "Please stay in my palace and teach the Dharma." His brother replied, "I really enjoy being on the mountain," and, despite the king's invitation, he stayed there. The king told his brother, "If you come here as my guest, I will build a mountain in the middle of the city and offer it to you!" He then prepared food and drink and then the yakṣas came to partake. He [King Aśoka] said to them, "All of you, by the power of my prayers you should return here tomorrow. When you come, if you don't bring any gifts as offerings you may not sit on the throne!" The next day, all the yakṣas each brought a very big stone. Each stone was four or five paces wide. When the area was full of stones, the king commanded, "You should assemble those stones together and build a mountain! Using five large square stones, you must build a house in a gorge on that mountain three *gyan*[215] wide, [198] and the same number of *gyan* high!"

At that time, a Mahāyāna brāhmaṇa named Raivatasvāmin (*Lo ti tsyu wo*) resided in that city. He possessed profound wisdom and was versed in all objects of knowledge. He also upheld very pure moral conduct. The king served him in various ways, respecting him as his personal lama. The king once went to hold counsel with him, but was unable to stay there with him. The king touched the brāhmaṇa's hand to show respect, which the brāhmaṇa immediately washed. For more than fifty years, all people had devotion and trust in this single person. On account of their faith, the Buddha's teaching increased and the heretics could not prevail. The saṅgha community became elevated to a high position in the view of King Aśoka. They mostly established Mahāyāna monasteries, though there were Hīnayāna monasteries as well. There are more than six hundred monks, almost seven hundred monks, who reside in that monastery.

Furthermore, at that time there was a spectacular temple to which people showed enormous respect. Lamas who were very knowledgeable and students who wanted to study the five fields of knowledge gathered together in this temple from the four directions. The brāhmaṇa's students addressed their lama as "Mañjuśrī." In this region, monks with pure moral conduct practiced only the Mahāyāna. From following those [lamas], all these śramaṇas acted according to their instructions. [199] Monks of all different races (*thams cad kyi skye bo*) resided permanently together in these temples. The villages and cities of this region are very vast. People there are very wealthy. Although they love to fight, they behave very honestly and are very compassionate.

Every year, on the eighth day of the first month, they build five bamboo structures for the saṅgha cut using a special spear (*mdung*). They have a chariot that appears to be more than two *gyang* high that looks a stūpa, which they cover with white wool carpet. On top of the carpet and wool cloth they spread out a tangkha painting of the Buddha made with various colors. They decorate this using gold- and silver-colored glass. They hoist a parasol overhead. They build small temples in the four directions, inside of which they fashion statues of the buddhas and bodhisattvas. Their beauty is amazing! On this occasion, they had nearly twenty such chariots. On the appointed day, the market is full of crowds. The people show off their skills, such as wrestling and playing musical cymbals. They also make offerings with flowers of many colors and fragrances. Even brāhmaṇas come to see the Buddha Śākyamuni [image] that day. Accordingly, the Buddha's statue enters the city [in a procession]. Once it is nighttime, people frolic about showing their physical power, sound musical cymbals, and create butter light lanterns. People from many different areas gather together for this special day.

The nobility of this city, in order to open the door to [200] happiness and as the root of virtue, built a medical clinic. Local people who are deaf, blind, and crippled, as well as the very poor, congregate there. It provides whatever will help those people. Doctors carefully examine the ill and give the food, drink, and medicine they require. Whatever they provide is very helpful to those patients. Once they recover, they return to their home region.

When King Aśoka opened the seventh stūpa and built the 84,000 stūpas, the place he chose to build the first is about three *dpag tshad* to the south of that city. In front of the stūpa is the Buddha Śākyamuni's footprint. To the north of the stūpa, a gandhola was built whose door faces the stūpa. To the south of the stūpa is a stone pillar, four or five *gyang* in circumference and three *gyang* high. The letters written on the pillar reads: "King Aśoka offered this area to the saṅgha of the four directions. Furthermore, the king bought this area from the saṅgha with silver, and then paid them the cost three times again."

To the north of that stūpa four or five hundred steps is a city called Niraya,[216] built long ago by King Aśoka. In the city center are remains of a stone pillar some three *gyang* high, on the top of which is a lion. The inscription written [201] on this pillar records the origins of Niraya city and the year, month, and day when the pillar was erected.

XXVIII
Wangpo Cave; The Village of Nāla; The New City of Rājagṛha; The Five Mountains; The Ruins of the Castle of King Bimbisāra

If one travels nine *dpag tshag* to the east until reaching the small mountain of Wangpo Cave,[217] there is a stone house facing the south upon its peak. When the Buddha resided there, in order to make offerings, Śakra (i.e., Indra) had five *deva* goddesses appear from the sky to pluck the lute (*pi wam*) for him. There, Indra made a sign of respect using his fingers upon a stone and then inquired about the two kinds of conduct (*spyod pa*). The imprint of his fingers is still visible there today. There is a monastery at this site.

If one travels one *dpag tshad* to the southwest, one arrives at the town of Nālandā.[218] This is the birthplace of Śāriputra.[219]

[Xuanzang wrote, "Nālanda is located forty *li* to the north of Rājagṛha. It has eight walls and was built by five Indian kings, one from Central India and the others from the four directions. It is wellknown that nowhere in the world is there a larger or more beautifully constructed [building]. Near the door, it is four stories high. The laneway is forty *'dom* wide. The fence is ten *'dom* high. It is beautified by being surrounded by water and flowers. The inner temple has more than four thousand monks. They built a six-story temple around the ruins of the place where the Buddha once taught the Dharma. Its outer and inner design is beautiful, as are the sky and earth decorations. Its principal holy object is a blessed golden Buddha statue about twenty *'dom* high. The paṇḍitas reside in the third to the tenth of these temples, and at that time there were more than three hundred with the title 'paṇḍita.'"

It is mentioned in the *Geography of the World* that although Nālanda was not destroyed by the army of Mahāmati, after [his conquest] the number of students continued to decrease there. I have not heard anything regarding its current status.]

Śāriputra returned to this town in order to pass into nirvāṇa. They built a stūpa at that place, which still exists today.

Traveling one *dpag tshad* to the west, one arrives at the new city of Rājagṛha.[220] [202] That city was built by King Ajātaśatru. Departing from the northern gate and walking three hundred steps, one passes a very high, large, and brilliant stūpa built by King Ajātaśatru when he received his portion of the Buddha's relics. Departing from the south of the city and traveling southward four *rgyan grags*, one arrives in the foothills of the Five Mountains. The Five Mountains surround the old city like an iron fence. At that place is the old city of King Bimbisāra,[221] which from east to west is from five to six *rgyan grags* wide, and from north to south seven to eight *rgyang grags* wide.

[Xuanzang wrote, "The circumference of the ruins of Rājagṛha is 150 *li*. The inner palace is more than 30 *li*." He described coming inside and coming into worshipful contact with many blessed holy objects.]

Also in that area is the place where Śāriputra and Maudgalyāyana first met Aśvajit (*Rta thul*); where Nirgrantha (*Dpal spas*) dug a hole, hid it using fire, and offered poisoned food to the Buddha; where King Ajātaśatru made a black elephant drunk on alcohol in order to kill the Buddha; and where, in the northeast corner of the city, Jīvaka (*Am gho lo*) invited the Buddha and over two thousand of his disciples to receive food offerings in this garden. Previous generations erected a stūpa in that place that still stands. Today, the city surrounding this royal palace is completely empty and desolate, without any owner.

XXIX
Vulture's Peak Mountain; The Demon Who Manifested as a Bird and Terrified Ānanda; The Ruins of the Four Buddhas' Thrones; The Stone That Is Like a Deva; Faxian's Offerings

From there one enters a valley, and after journeying for fifteen *rgyan grags* one reaches a mountain. That is Vulture's Peak.[222]

[Xuanzang wrote, "To the northeast of the ruins of that city is Vulture's Peak, which is higher than any of the surrounding mountains. It has stone steps that are ten cubits wide and six*li* long. At that time, there was a fence on the peak of that mountain that enclosed the site where the Buddha taught the Perfection of Wisdom. Inside that fence was a life-size statue of the Buddha turning the Wheel of the Dharma. The Buddha taught the *White Lotus Sūtra* (*Mdo sde pad dkar*) [203] to the east of there, where there is a big stone that served as the Buddha's throne. To the south, under amazing caves, is a stone house where the Buddha once resided. Surrounding it are the meditation huts of a great many arhats. Behind the stone houses is a very big rock. It bears marks from vultures that were once manifested by demons."

Although Xuangzang described many blessed temples there, pilgrims who visit today report that there are only a few caves, the ruins of some houses, and the stone throne. Other than these, nothing remains.]

Arriving upon the back of the mountain in about three *rgang grags*, on its neck there is a cave facing the south side and a cliff. The Buddha once stayed there and engaged in practice in order to achieve enlightenment.

Thirty steps to the northeast of there is a cave. In this cave, Ānanda once lived and practiced the Dharma. The son of Māra named Pāpīyān (*Pa swan*) manifested as vultures who stood in front of the cave in order to scare Ānanda. The Buddha manifested from another location and he held Ānanda's hand and removed his fears. At that place there are still footprints of the birds and a hole where the Buddha extended his hand. That is why they call it Mountain with the Vulture's Cave (*Bya rgod kyi phug can gyi ri bo*). In front of the cave are the foundations of the thrones of the four buddhas. There is also a cave where all the arhats once resided and meditated. Those caves number a few hundred. The Buddha once traveled to the southeast in front of those caves while Devedatta stayed atop the mountain to the north. [Devadatta] hurled a huge boulder down, causing a small cut on the Buddha's big toe. That boulder exists there still. The building where the Buddha once turned the Wheel of the Dharma [204] is now destroyed. Nowadays, the only remaining items are the foundation of the fence made with bricks. The peak of this mountain becomes very rugged; it is very magnificent and higher than the other five mountains.

Faxian purchased fragrant flowers and ox butter lamps in the New City (*grong khyer so ma*) and paid two resident monks to help transport it all up to the caves of Vulture's Peak. Once there, he offered the sweet-smelling incense and various flowers and afterward lit the remaining ox butter lamp. His mind then became deeply tormented. Tears fell from his eyes and he thought: "*Kye ma*! Long ago the Buddha resided here and taught the Perfection of Wisdom!"[223] Though Faxian had worked his entire life to meet the Buddha, here he saw nothing other than the material ruins of places where the Buddha had once lived. Despite this, he spent the whole night in front of this cave reciting the *Perfection of Wisdom Sūtra*.

Chapter XXX
The Bamboo Grove and the Cool Grove Charnel Ground; The "Pippala" Stone House; The Site of the First Council; Devadatta's Cave; The Stone Bhikṣu

After that, Faxian departed from the old city **[This is known as the old castle in central Magadha]** and went to the New City. **[During King Aśoka's time,**

this city was known as the "City of Lotuses."] Leaving toward the north of the Old City and walking three hundred steps, the Bamboo Grove of Kalandaka[224] is on the right, **[Xuanzang wrote that close to the northern gate of Rājagṛha, in the Bamboo Grove, there are the remains of a brick house]** in the center of which a small temple was built [205] that can still be seen today. Monks still spread water and sweep this temple. To the north of that temple two or three *rgyang grags*, there are the ruins of the Cool Grove charnel ground (*dur khrod*).[225] If one climbs the southern mountain slope three hundred steps, there is a stone house known as Pippala Cave.[226] After the taking of alms, the Buddha would retire here to engage in meditation.

If one travels five or six *dpag tshad* to the west, in the shadow of the mountain upon its northern slope is a stone cave called Caitya (*Dza ti*).

> **[Xuanzang wrote, "Six *li* to the southwest of the Mik Grove (*Smig tshal*) is a stone house where [Mahā] kāśyapa gathered the Abhidharma and Ānanda gathered the sūtras. Additionally, twenty *li* to the west I saw the place where they gathered the vinaya of the Mahāsāṃghika school.]**

This is where the five hundred arhats gathered all of the Buddha's teachings after his parinirvāṇa. Afterward, [the Buddha's] discourse spread across all regions and the three decorated thrones remained, with Śāriputra's to the right and Maudgalyāyana's to the left. Among the five hundred arhats, just one was missing. That was Ānanda. This was because after Mahākāśyapa was enthroned, [Ānanda] was unable to join the assembly and remained outside.[227] That is why there were four hundred and ninety-nine, with one missing. A stūpa was built at this site that still exists today.

On the other side of the mountain are caves where arhats once lived and practiced. There are many of these. If you leave the Old City and walk to the east for about three *rgyang grags*, there is the cave of Devadatta. From there, if you walk five steps there is a large black stone. Some people say that long ago [206] a fully ordained monk visited this area. He thought, "My body will soon become tortured by illness and will be abandoned in a desolate valley." He pulled out a knife and tried to slash his body. Before he could, he thought: "The Lord of the World said that it is unsuitable to cut one's own body!" Further, he thought: "Whatever it takes, from today on I will put in effort to kill the three afflicted emotions!" He then pierced his body, making a fresh wound. By this, he achieved the state of a stream enterer (*rgyun du zhugs pa*). He then pierced the other side of his body and, as a result, achieved the state of "never returner" (*phyir mi 'ong*). After he had sliced up his entire body, he achieved arhathood and passed into nirvāṇa.

XXXI
(Bodhi) gayā; Where the Buddha Endured Hardship; Where the Buddha Achieved Enlightenment; Where the Buddha Tamed Māra; The Famous Holy Sites; The Four Stūpas

Journeying about four *dpag tshad* to the west, one arrives in the city of (Bodhi) gayā.[228]

[Xuanzang wrote that Gāya city is located near the Niryagana River [where the Buddha meditated for six years]. About six *li* from there is Kayagori City, where in there is a stone stūpa ten *'dom* high.]

That city is now empty. From there, if you travel south about twenty *rgyang grags*, you will arrive where the bodhisattva practiced austerities (*dka' spyad*) for six years. A tree grows there. If one travels three *rgyang grags* to the west, one arrives at the place where the bodhisattva entered the water in order to wash his body. At the time, when the bodhisattva emerged from the pool the gods used tree branches as a canopy. From there, if one travels two *rgyang grags* [207] to the north, one will arrive at where the Buddha received the offering of the essence of milk from two girls at the village where the Mekā (*U tshas*) dwelt.[229] About two *rgyangs grags* from there is where the Buddha sat facing east while eating the milk porridge upon a stone lying atop tree roots. This tree and stone still exist today. The stone is six cubits (*khru*) wide and about two cubits (*khru*) high. Because Central India is neither too hot nor too cold, you can find trees that are a few thousand or even ten thousand years old.

About half a *dpag tshad* from there, one arrives at a cave where the bodhisattva stayed facing the north in the vajra posture thinking, "Here I wish to see some sign of whether I will achieve enlightenment or not." Just then, the shadow of the Buddha's body appeared on the round stone, three cubits high and very clear to see. It appears radiant continuously day and night, pervading the sky. At that time, the gods sang him this song: "This is not the place where the buddhas of the past and future will achieve enlightenment. If you go just a little more than one *dpag tshad* to the north, near the Bodhi tree, that is where the buddhas of the past achieved enlightenment and where the buddhas of the future will achieve enlightenment!" Then they showed him the route to the tree. Then the bodhisattva stood up in that place and took some thirty steps. A god offered him auspicious grass. Then again the bodhisattva [208] took fifteen steps before five hundred cuckoo birds circumambulated him three times and then flew away. The bodhisattva approached the tree and prepared a seat to the east side with the kusha grass. Then, in order to destroy [the Buddha], Māra, King of Demons, sent three beautiful girls from the north and came himself with the same motivation. The bodhisattva then touched his finger to the ground, and the demons dispersed. Then he turned the three beautiful demon daughters into old women. At the place where the bodhisattva engaged in six years of hardship, later generations built a stūpa and made a statue. Those still exist today.

[This type of statue is nowadays very popular.]

Where the Buddha found the nectar [of enlightenment] and stayed for seven days looking at the Bodhi tree (*Byang chub kyi shing*) and then found permanent happiness and joy; where for seven days he traveled from the west to the east of the Bodhi tree; where the gods built a seven-jeweled terrace and made offerings to the Buddha for seven days; where the blind gold-colored nāga coiled around the Buddha for seven days; where there is a square stone on top of the roots of the *nyagrodha* tree, upon which the Buddha sat facing east and where the great god Indra came to pay homage; where the Four Worldly Protectors offered the begging bowl; where [Mahā]kāśyapa, his relatives, and some one thousand of his students entered into the Dharma: they built stūpas in all those places.

The place where the Buddha achieved enlightenment [209] has three gandholas.

[Xuanzang wrote, "From the southwest corner of the Kala stūpa surrounding Bodhgayā, if one takes 100 steps there is the Mahābodhi Temple. In front of this is the Bodhi Tree that stands 10 fathoms high. Surrounding this is a brick fence 500 fathoms long. Facing the Niryagana [River] is a temple connected to this temple. The Mahābodhi Temple has six inner-monks' quarters (*grwa tshang*) and a three-story monastery administration house (*gzhung khar*). There is a fence about eight fathoms high. There are more than one thousand saṅgha members. They are of the Sthavira school, yet practice the conduct of the Mahāyāna. The bone relic there appears to be of a fingerjoint. The flesh relics appear to be pure. I received blessings from these."

After a while, all those were destroyed and burnt down by the Turks (*Tur u shka*) and vanished. Nowadays, Europeans (*phe ring*) have built a temple, and Buddhist and non-Buddhist people continually travel there.]

Near that, there is a temple where many saṅgha members reside. Because [lay] people are very devoted to them, they want for nothing and receive all they need from donations. Everyone there strongly follows the Dharma system. Their behavior while walking, sitting, or coming into the presence of others is very peaceful. In order to remember the Buddha's kind activities for the benefit of sentient beings when he was in this world, they built four great stūpas. Those stūpas have remained without being damaged from the time of the Buddha's parinirvāṇa to today. Those four great stūpas mark the site where [the Buddha] was born, where he achieved enlightenment, where he turned the Wheel of the Dharma, and where he passed into nirvāṇa.

XXXII
How Aśoka, the Iron Cakravartin King, Became Sovereign of the World; When He Put Priminals Into Hell; How a Monk Tamed Him and Brought Him Into the Dharma

Once, in a previous life, King Aśoka[230] had been a boy playing with a wheel. Śāriputra happened by, begging for alms, and they met.[231] As a game, he offered a handful of soil. Before departing on his way, Śāriputra accepted the offering and threw it over some mud so that he could more easily cross. [210] As a result, [in a later life] that boy became [Aśoka] the Iron Wheel-Possessing King[232] with sovereignty over the world. Once, while atop his Iron Wheel and surveying (*myul ba*) the breadth of Jambudvīpa, [Aśoka] saw a hell situated between two mountains inside an iron enclosure imprisoning many wicked beings (*sdig pa can*). He asked his ministers, "What is this place?" They replied, "This is where Yama, Lord of Death,[233] punishes the wicked." The king reflected, "The Lord of Death has the power to punish the wicked in hell. I am the king of humans, so why can't I create a hell wherein I may punish criminals (*nyes can*)?" He asked his ministers "Who is capable of building a hell wherein to punish criminals?" The ministers told him, "Only an exceptionally cruel person (*zhe gnag pa*) would be capable of this."

The king ordered his ministers to different regions to find such a cruel person. The ministers saw a large young man upon the bank of a river with a black complexion, yellowish teeth, red eyes, with live fish beneath his feet, who could draw any bird or large animal to him with a shrill whistle (*so sgras po*), and from whose arrows nothing could escape. The ministers returned to the king and reported who they had found. The king discreetly summoned this man and told him, "Build upon the earth an enclosure with high walls on all sides. Fill the inside with many types of flowers and fruit and also fashion a very beautiful ground so that it possesses a spectacular appearance such that people desire to go there. Also, make a water pool such that people will be shocked to know that this is the gateway to a prison. [211] There you should install the prison door. Whoever enters should be seized and considered a criminal. No one should escape, and you should punish them! I will also consider anyone who enters that door to be a criminal. I appoint you King of Hell!" That man acted accordingly.

At some later time, a monk searching for alms entered the doorway and the gatekeeper duly considered him a criminal. The gatekeeper thought: "If we consider him a criminal, we should torture him!" That monk was terrified and tried to postpone until he'd finished his noontime meal. In the meantime, another person walked through the doorway. The gatekeeper put that person inside a pestle and beat him until he became like a red bubble. Seeing this, the monk thought: "*Kye ma!* These aggregates are impermanent and in their nature suffering, just like a water bubble." With this realization, he became an arhat. When the prison guard put him in the pestle, the monk sat down happily. The prison guard then tried to boil him in water, but the monk appeared sitting upon a lotus flower. One of the prison guards was particularly amazed and went to file a report with the king. He said, "O King, you should physically come and see all this for yourself!" The king said, "I cannot go, as I have important matters to attend to here." The prison guard replied, "This is no small matter! O King, you should understand the meaning of this for yourself. It is important that you come." [212]

The prison guard escorted the king to the prison. As soon as the monk taught him the Dharma, the king entered into the holy Dharma and dismantled the Hell [i.e., prison]. He also profoundly regretted his previous negative actions. The king immediately took refuge in the Triple Gem. He visited the roots of the Bodhi tree and regretted what he had done such that pain arose in his body. He did the eight branches of confession practice. The queen inquired of a minister, "Where does the king usually go?" The minister responded, "The king always goes to the Bodhi Tree." In order to stop the king from going there, she asked some servants to chop the Bodhi tree down and take it away. When the king next went there and saw what had happened, he became very sad and deeply grieved and, falling to the ground, he fainted. The minister threw water upon his face, and after a long time he was roused. The king then had his servants build a very high fence around the roots of this tree. He poured a hundred buckets of cow's milk upon the roots and caused it to grow again. The king laid upon the ground and promised, "If this tree will no longer grow, I will never stand up!" Just then, the roots of the tree began to grow once more. From then until today, it has grown at least ten *rgyang* high.

XXXIII
Sublime Mount Kukkuṭapāda, Where Mahākāśyapa Once Lived; How Numerous Arhats Live Upon This Mountain

Traveling three *rgyang grags* to the south, one arrives at Mount Kukkuṭapāda.[234]

[Xuanzang wrote: "100 *li* to the east of Bodhigayā is Mount Kukkuṭapāda. On its peak there is a stūpa containing relics. At auspicious times, these

produce light. Surrounding this mountain is thick forest. [213] **Because there are so many dangerous animals about, it has been years since the path was cleared. We requested the king's permission to visit on pilgrimage, which he granted. The king sent some three hundred guards armed with spears and knives to accompany us. In the company of some ten thousand devotees, we visited there. Since [the mountain] is very difficult to climb, only about three thousand of us could reach the summit. There we did prostrations and made offerings."]**

Mahākāśyapa's body remains there to this day. He lived inside the cave below the mountain and would bar others from entering. Peering in from the mouth of the cave, deep inside you can see Mahākāśyapa's entire body. Outside the entrance is soil that Kāśyapa used to wash his hands. Locals who suffer headaches visit and, rubbing that earth upon their brow, are cured.

The residences of the arhats lie upon the western slope of this mountain. Scholars and Bön practitioners from every country come here to prostrate to Kāśyapa. People with uncertainty about the meaning of the scriptures come each evening to hold discussions with the arhats. Once their doubts are removed, those [arhats] disappear. You can still see this! Dense brush covers this mountain, and so many lions, tigers, and coyotes (*ce spyad*) live there. You cannot visit without being struck with terror.

XXXIV
Returning to Pāṭaliputrā; A Temple Named The Great Solitary Place; The City of Kāśī; Deer Park, Where the Buddha Taught the Dharma to the Five Disciples; The Region of Kauśāmbī

After that, Faxian returned to the city of Pāṭaliputrā. Journeying against the current of the Ganges River, he traveled west ten *dpag tshad* and arrived at the temple called "Great Solitary Place" (*Dben pa chen po*). [214] The Buddha had once visited and inhabited this abode. Saṅgha live there today. Faxian traveled twelve *dpag tshad* to the west of the upper Ganges. There he arrived at Vārāṇasī city[235] in the kingdom of Kāśī.[236]

[Nowadays, this is called Kāśī Saher. That city has many houses. There are so many human beings there that they can compete with specks of dust in a sunbeam. Most houses there are built from stone and have three or four floors. Lining all the laneways they have fashioned holes three or four fathoms wide as a conduit for water covered with flat stone. The people of that city are very wealthy, and there you can

buy many varieties of things. Inside the city is an amazing copper statue of the Buddha in the posture of teaching the Dharma. There is also a statue of the Powerful Lord of the World [Īśvara] made of stone and white *jati* nearly eight cubits high.

In short, between the Temple of the Teacher Buddha to the flesh eaters of the charnel ground, the people of Kāśī say that there are thirty-three million different statues and temples! I have heard it claimed that nowadays these remain!

Even nowadays, the king of that region is known as the Hindu Mahārajā and is very famous around the world.]

Ten *rgyang grags* northeast from that city is the garden of Sārnāth (*Drang srong lhun ba*), in the center of which they built a gandhola.

[Xuanzang wrote:

> **"From there, if you travel to the northeast across the Vārana River for ten *li* you will arrive at Sārnāth's Deer Park (*Drang srong lhung ba ri dwags gyi nags*). That place has a great monastery decorated by flower petals and built up over many stories. It is beautifully decorated and has close to two thousand monks. Its principal inner holy supports are the Buddha in teaching posture and the five hundred stūpas of pratyekabuddhas. I visited and saw all of these."**

After that, long ago barbarians destroyed this site. I have heard that nowadays you can see the foundations of the stūpas and the remains of two or three houses. Other than that, nothing remains.]

A pratyekabuddha already dwelt there, alongside many deer living peacefully. When the Principal Being of the World had almost achieved enlightenment, *devas* sang from the sky: "The son of King Śuddhodana has become a renunciant [215] and has become knowledgeable in all dharmas. He will become enlightened in some seven days!" Hearing this song, the pratyekabuddha passed into nirvāṇa. For these reasons, this place became known as Deer Park.[237] After the Principal of the World achieved enlightenment, he first turned the Wheel of the Dharma here.[238] Later generations built a small gandhola upon the site.

The Buddha had the thought that among the five disciples, he would first bring Kauṇḍinya (*Kō di nāya*) into the Dharma. The five disciples said to one another: "For six years, the śrāmaṇa Gautama practiced hardships and ate whatever he received, such as seeds. Still he did not achieve enlightenment. In paricular, he mixed with those with undisciplined body, speech, and mind. If we now accompany this man, how will we achieve enlightenment? Now that man approaches us. We should not speak to him!" When the Buddha arrived, all five stood up and showed respect. About sixty steps to the north of there is where the Buddha faced the east and turned the Wheel of the Dharma and brought Kauṇḍinya and the others into the Dharma. Some twenty steps to the north of there is where the Buddha explained his personal lifestory to Maitreya. From there, about fifty steps to the south is where the nāga Elāpattra (*E la'i 'dab*) asked the Buddha when he escaped from having the body of a nāga. In each of these places they have built a stūpa, and there are saṅgha members living in each.

From the center of Deer Park to the northeast [216] about thirteen *dpag tshad* is an area called Kauśāmbī.[239]

[Xuanzang wrote: At Kauśāmbī, I saw a snake-essence sandalwood statue of the Buddha made by the tirthika king Chergyé (*Cher rgyas*) used as a substitute for the Sandalwood Jowo.]

The name of the temple there is Koṣila Forest.[240] The Buddha visited and resided at this place. Most of the saṅgha are of the Hīnayāna. To the east of there about nine *dpag tshad* is where, long ago, the Buddha brought a yakṣa into the Dharma. Also, there is the place where the Buddha performed such activities as arising, departing, and abiding. In all of those places, they have built stūpas. More than a hundred monks reside in each of those temples.

XXXV
The District of Dakṣiṇā; Pārāvata Monastery

Traveling about two hundred *dpag tshad* to the south, there is a region called Dakṣiṇā.[241]

[Xuanzang wrote: "To the east of Nālandā about four thousand *li*, you arrive in the region of Saladana. From there, two hundred li to the southwest is the region of Dakṣiṇā. At that place are imprints of the buddha reposing (*bzhugs rjes*) and of his footprint, as well as a statue of the Fourth Buddha made from black jade some eight cubits (*khru*) high. Also, there are three monasteries of Devadatta's tradition wherein they do not eat meat, milk, or *ghi*. These I saw.]

In that place is a temple dedicated to Kāśyapa, the buddha of the previous age. To build it, they demolished (*gshegs pa*) a large rocky mountain. Moreover, it has five stories: the lowest is shaped like an elephant with five hundred [217] stone monk's cells; the second is shaped like a lion with four hundred cells; the third is shaped like a horse with three hundred cells; the fourth is shaped like a bull with two hundred monk's cells; and the top story is shaped like a pigeon with a hundred monk cells. There are water fountains upon its peak. Water flows from the rock and descends encircling all the cells until the bottom. In all these cells, they have fashioned small holes so that the inside is illuminated. In the four corners of this temple are caves and also stairs to access the upper stories. Long ago, a person impressed his footprints upon them. Nowadays, people bring a small footstool to be able to step over that section. That gandhola is called "Pārāvata,"[242] meaning "pigeon." There are arhats who reside in that temple, which lies in vast, empty mountainous land without owner.

Far away from that demolished rocky mountain [218] are savage peoples who know nothing of the way of the true Dharma. Local devotees of perverse dharma systems (*gzhan log pa'i chos lugs can*),[243] including śramaṇas (*sa rma wa*) and brāhmaṇas as well as other locals, continually witness visitors flying through the air to visit this temple from other lands. When knowledgeable people from other regions say that they want to visit and practice the Dharma, local people say "Why don't you come here by flying? We have seen lamas visit by flying before!" They respond, "We have not yet grown our feathers!" The path to Dakṣiṇā is very difficult to cross and not easy to find. People who are interested to go there make monetary offerings to the local king, who will then send guides who know the path to show you the way. If you wish to enter inside, they will take you one by one. Faxian said that he was unable to go to that place, but that he heard this story from the local people.

XXXVI
Faxian's Search and Discovery of the Buddha's Word; The Monastic Discipline of the Sautrāntikas; The Discourses Collected [219] by Arhats; The Abhidharma-piṭaka

From Vārāṇasī, [Faxian] traveled to the east and returned to the region of Pāṭaliputrā. Faxian had searched and searched for the word of the Buddha across Northern India. There, masters expounded orally upon the Dharma and monastic discipline, but he had not found even a single volume of the Buddha's discourses. For that reason, he journeyed still further and arrived in Central India.

There, in a Mahāyāna monastery, he discovered a compendium of the Buddha's discourses.[244] This was a collection of teachings assembled by arhats.[245] After the Buddha's parinirvāṇa, the arhats predominantly relied upon these instructions. Furthermore, those texts given to Faxian had come originally from the temple at Jetavana.

Moreover, regarding the teaching collections of the eighteen schools: their principle original [scriptural] reference (*khungs gtugs*). For the most part, there are only small differences between them. You can understand these small differences by investigating the volumes found by Faxian. These details, however, are very vast and detailed. There is a single volume in seven thousand verses that gathers together all the historical narratives (Tib. *rtogs brjod,* ie. Skt. *avadāna)* and textual meaning. That was collected by Sawoto. All the lamas of China (*Tsi na'i yul)* rely upon this text . Long ago, the teachings of those texts were passed from master to master, and were never written down. In addition, [Faxian] collected one volume of the Abhidharma in [220] six thousand verses. He also acquired a sūtra in two thousand five hundred verses, one volume showing the method to achieve liberation in five thousand verses, and also an Abhidharma text assembled by the arhats.

Faxian stayed there for three years. In that time, he learned Sanskrit and studied the Tripitiḳa. He also copied down all these texts. Daozheng journeyed to Central India and visited any lamas he found interesting and also received Dharma teachings from them. He saw amazing Indian lamas teach profound, vast, and detailed commentaries. He let out a long sigh, saying, "*Kyé ma!* The borderland (of China) is beyond the rules of vinaya and their behavior contradicts the Dharma rules. If in the future I achieve enlightenment, may I never be reborn in a borderland!" Deciding to remain in Central India, he never returned to his homeland. Faxian thought, "If I am to fulfill my wish, no matter what, I will spread these texts in China (*Tsi na*)!" He then returned to his homeland alone.

[Xuanzang wrote: "The ruins of Nāgārjuna's monastery is three hundred *li* south of the palace of the king of Krisnarā. Farther south seven thousand *li* is the border of Jambudvīpa's southern continent called Marukutha. Four thousand *li* to the northwest is the region of Mahāratha and Bhabarā. Xuanzang passed through all these places and then returned again to Nālandā. In these ways, he extensively benefited sentient beings. Soon afterward he returned to his homeland. He traveled there gradually while visiting all the holy sites across the east of the kingdom of India [221], and then he passed through the western Chinese region called K'an ti'u and arrived safely back in his homeland in great China.]

XXXVII
Campā; The Regions of Tāmralipti; Faxian's Time Upon a Great Vessel; Sea Journey to Siṃhala Island

Following the flow of the Ganges River for eighteen *dpag tshad* to the west, the great kingdom called Campā[246] is located on the southern bank. Along the path one sees a few clusters of Buddhist temples and stūpas built in the four places where the Buddha traveled,[247] wherein it appears that communities of saṅgha permanently reside. Some fifty *dpag tshad* to the east is a place called Tāmralipti,[248] which is positioned just above the shoreline of the outer ocean (*phyi'i rgya mtsho*). There are twenty-five monasteries in that area. Saṅgha reside therein, and the Buddha's teachings have spread widely there. Faxian resided there for two years, during which time he penned volumes of scripture and commissioned paintings of the Buddha.[249]

After that, Faxian joined a group of merchants and set out to sea upon a great vessel, sailing toward the southwest. They set out at the start of winter, [when] along their route a leading wind (*drongs pa'i rlung*) was stirring (*ldangs pa*). After nine days and nine nights of ocean travel,[250] they arrived at the island of Siṃhala.[251] Locals in Tāmralipti claim that it is seven hundred *dpag tshad* from their homeland to this island. The breadth of this land rests above the ocean shore.[252] It is fifty *dpag tshad* wide from east to west and thirty *dpag tshad* from south to north. Along its east and west flanks are a hundred small inlets (*chus ngogs phran bu*). As for where these are [222] in relation to the great shoreline: some are ten *rgyang grags*, others twenty *rgyang grags*, and still others two hundred *rgyang grags*, while all of them are subject to the great tides. Within those [bodies of water], you can discover very valuable jewels and pearls. One area ten *rgyangs grags* wide contains a stone named *maṇi*."[253] The king ordered a person there to protect them. When you gather up these stones, for every ten you collect, he will take one.

XXXVIII
The Origins of the Siṃhala Kingdom (Ceylon), the Buddha's Footprint, the Temple at Fearless Mountain, the Bodhi Tree, the Buddha's Tooth, and the Manner of Offering to All These; The Bodhi Temple; The Venerable Dharmakīrti

This island did not at first have any human beings.

[I have directly heard from many Tibetans and Mongolians who have gone on pilgrimage to Siṃhala. They tell me that the power and wealth

of Siṃhala Island, its temples, their three supports, the manner in which the saṅgha study and practice, and the old demon fort (*sngon gyi srin mo'i rdzong*) all remain the same today.]

Although the sentient beings who continually remained there were demons (*bdud*), yakṣas (*gnod sbyin*), and nāgas (*klu dag*), people from other regions traded their merchandise with them. When selling and buying, those demons, yakṣas, and nāgas would not appear in their bodies, but would display their jeweled wares. They would leave a sign giving the cost of everything. If interested, a merchant would leave what was owed and collect the jewels. Merchants would travel from afar and stay in this area, and so people from other places began to hear about the beauty of this island. They then began to move there, [223] and it eventually became a country.

This country possesses a great variety of material goods. People there know no difference between summer and winter. The grass and trees ever remain green. One may plant whatever one desires; there is no unsuitable season wherein to plant crops. The Buddha went to this place in order to tame the wrathful Poisonous Nāga (*Klu gdug pa can*) and bring him into the Dharma. By the "power of the feet of miraculous concentration" (*rdza 'phrul gyi rkang pa'i stobs*), he impressed a footprint on the north side of the king's city. Another footprint can be found on top of the mountain. It is fifteen *dpag tshad* between the two footprints. On top of the footprint to the north of the city, they built a stūpa that is forty stories high, decorated with silver, and made from various expensive substances. On top they built a monastery called Temple of the Fearless Mountain.[254]

[From among the eighteen schools of the Vaibhāṣikas (*Bye brag smra ba*), one is called "the 'Remain at Fearless Mountain' school" (*'Jigs med kyi ri la gnas pa sde pa*). I think that this is the same group described here.]

That place has a community of five thousand saṅgha members. They built a great temple for the Buddha and decorated it with cast metal (*blugs ma*), gold, and silver. Inside, they display various offering substances made form jewels. In the center is a two-story-high statue of the Buddha made from blue jati (*g.yan ti*). The whole body is [decorated with] with the seven precious jewels [224]; when light strikes it there is a radiance that is difficult to describe. Its right hand holds precious pearl jewels.

Faxian came to this Land of Noble Ones and resided there for many years. His companions were all from other countries. He directly experienced all of its amazing mountains, rivers, grasses, trees, and so on. In particular, from among all of his travel companions, some quickly returned to their home country, some stayed in India, and some died on their journey. If one were to think about those memories, that would cause such sadness in one's heart and one would dwell endlessly upon it. Suddenly one day, [Faxian] saw a merchant offering a whisk made from Chinese cloth in front of the Jati (*g. yang ṭi*) Statue. His mind was moved, and his eyes brimmed with tears.

Long ago, a king from that region sent people to India in order to find the seed of the Bodhi tree. They procured such seeds and planted them in front of the principal Buddha temple. Those seeds grew into a tree about twenty stories high and tilting slightly to the southwest. The king worried that it would fall over, so he had eight or nine pillars erected as supports. These pillars became a kind of fence. [225] In the center of that tree a branch grew that winds around the pillar, goes back into the earth, and then became a root that shoots up new branches. It is almost four stories high. The pillars are as high as the door of the temple, and people have never removed them. They built a temple at the roots of this tree, and inside they fashioned casted statues. There is a tradition there for a scholar to always make offerings to those statues.

The tooth of the Teacher Buddha is within the city, for which they built a temple.

[Xuanzang wrote: "Although I did not go to Siṃhala Island, I heard that the region of Ode is seven hundred *dpag tshad* to the southwest from the Dakṣiṇā region. To the east, upon the shore of the ocean is Siṃhala Island. It has a stūpa that contains the Buddha's relics. The jewel of the peak of that stūpa shines light, even at night. It can be seen from a great distance away."

People say that even nowadays you can see this from Kalikata [Calcutta], which is part of the Bangala region. I once even held a picture of this amazing gandhola temple in my hands.]

It is made from the seven precious jewels.

[Long ago, a Buryat Khenpo named Chödzin (*Chos 'dzin*) went by boat to this island. He met [226] **Paṇḍita Sumangala. This Khenpo explained the-approach of his Dharmato [the paṇḍita]. Then the paṇḍita asked, "Who do you believe created this universe?" He answered, "We believe that the many different types of worlds are created by karma." Happy, [the**

pandita] asked, "Has the Buddha's teaching spread into your region?" He answered, "Yes, it has spread, but it has spread more into Tibet." He responded, "Even nowadays, the Buddha's teaching is spreading into many regions, but in terms of maintaining the Dharma discipline (*vinaya*), this is the only place where it is carefully followed." He continued, saying, "Although I have heard that the Buddha's teaching has spread to the north, there it is mixed with many Buddhist and non-Buddhist [traditions]."

Then [Chödzin] requested the local saṅgha to do an auspicious upoṣadha (*gso sbyong*) [confession and purification ritual]. He offered them a handful of silver thamka coins, but no monks would accept it. He was shocked, and when laypeople came they took it. He was so embarrassed. This last teaching of that paṇḍita had a very profound meaning and exposed our shameful secret (*mtshang thog tu'ang babs 'dug*). I think based on all this that when people say "The Mahāyāna teachings do not exist in Siṃhala," this is just uninformed babble!]

That king kept his body very clean, but otherwise he avoided the Dharma tradition of the brāhmaṇas. The city dwellers are very honest, use honorable language, and have a stable sort of wisdom. Since that country was established, there has never been any suffering from a shortage of food or from fighting.

In the treasury of the saṅgha, there are priceless jewels and many other kinds of jewels. The king entered the saṅgha's treasury and saw a certain jewel, which he stole. After three days [227] he returned to the temple to confess his sinful action. He invited members of the saṅgha, and in front of them he regretfully confessed what he had done. After that, with an open mind the king asked the saṅgha, "Any future king who does not perform the forty ways of offering like a monk will not be not allowed to enter your treasury. If they do [that offering], they are allowed to enter. I would like to make this kind of tradition, are you interested?" The monks remained silent.

Many older masters, captains, and merchants lived in the city. The houses are nice and beautiful. In general, the designs on all these are decorated with beautiful jewels. The markets where people gather to do business are very orderly and level. Along the roads and intersections, they have built houses wherein the Dharma is taught.

[I heard that these old traditions, such as studying the Dharma during auspicious times, continue today.]

On the 8th, 14th, and 15th day of every month, they display the higher throne, and the four races of beings gather together to listen to the Dharma. The people of that region say that fifteen to sixteen thousand monks gather here and eat together at the same time. In the city, they have a separate four to five thousand monks who receive food from the king. [228] When it comes time for the noon meal, they proceed holding aloft (*thogs*) their begging bowls (*lhung bzed*) and seek out (*'tshol*) alms (*bsod snyoms*). Once their begging bowls become filled, they do not accept any excess (*lhag po*). Immediately upon being satiated, they return. In the middle of the third month, they display the Buddha's tooth relic to the public. Ten days before that, the king will choose an excellent elephant to bring. The king gives his own clothes to those who will teach the Dharma. He puts them on the elephant and lets them go forth teaching the following words:

> The bodhisattva undertook challenging practices for three countless eons without any concern for his body or mind. He gave up his own queen. He gave his eyes to somebody. The bodhisattva saved the life of a peacock by cutting his flesh hundreds of times. He even gave his own head. He had no attachment to his jewels and let the hungry tigress eat his body without any hesitation. He engaged in challenging practices (*dka' sbyad ba*) such as these. He achieved enlightenment for the benefit of all sentient beings in this manner of putting his body through great hardships. He lived in this world until he was eighty years old, teaching the Dharma and leading many people into the Dharma. He transformed those without stable devotion to having stable devotion. Those beings without a Dharma system were made to know a system of Dharma. In these ways, countless beings found liberation from saṃsāra into nirvāṇa. Then he passed to nirvāṇa. Since he passed to nirvāṇa [229], 1,467 years have passed.[255] When the Eyes of the World were closed, all sentient beings were profoundly grieved.

After ten days have passed, the Buddha's tooth is brought to the Temple of Fearless Mountain (Abhayagiri). Those who wish to remove their darkness through the light of the Dharma and who want to increase the root of their virtues make the path very smooth and decorate the entire path with beautiful flowers and fragrant incense.

At that time, after the king finishes his performance, many different paintings of the bodhisattva's five hundred previous forms (*skyes rabs*) are displayed on either side of the road, such as when the Buddha was previously born as a *ruru* deer (*ri dwags ruru*), as a Shingtamo bird (*bya shing rta mo*), as the elephant king, and as a Sharbharu beast (*rid wags shar bha ru*).[256] Rendered in various colors, they appear as if alive; they are prepared with incredible effort. Later, the Buddha's tooth is retrieved and brought through the center of the thoroughfare. Wherever it passes, people make prostrations. Then it is taken to the Temple of Fearless Mountain and installed in the gandhola. At that time, they burn excellent incense and the cloud of smoke gathers like a cloud in the sky. They continually light butter lamps. People continually do Dharma practice, day and night, for sixteen days. After that, the precious tooth is returned to the city temple. That temple is very beautiful. During the daytime, they open the doors and people do Dharma practice.

About forty *rgyang grags* to the east of the Temple of Fearless Mountain is a mountain. On that mountain they have a temple [230] called Bhadri.[257] Two thousand monks live there. Among them is a śramaṇa with more merit named Dharmagupta,[258] whom local people more strongly respect and serve. He resided inside a stone cell for close to forty years while engaged in continuous Dharma practice. Because of him, snakes and rats would abide in peace together in his house.

XXXIX
How They Cremated the Arhat's Body; The Story of the Buddha's Begging Bowl[259]

To the south of the city about seven *rgyang grags* is a temple called Mahāvihāra.[260] Some three thousand monks reside there. Among them is a monk with great merit who strictly follows the Dharma and is exceptionally pure. Local people consider him to be an arhat. Soon before he passed away, the king went to be in his presence (*mjal*). [The king] asked the assembled monks: "It is said this monk has achieved enlightenment. Is it so?" The monks replied, "Yes, there is no doubt that he has perfectly achieved arhathood!" After he passed away, after consulting the protocals of both the Dharma tradition and the system of [monastic] regulations (*khrims srol*),[261] the king led [the funeral] for the monk's body in a manner appropriate for one who has achieved arhathood.

Four or five *rgyang grags* to the east of the temple, they piled firewood three stories high. Atop this sweet-smelling wood, such as sandalwood and *aga* wood, they built a square platform, over the top of which they draped a white cloth. There was no roof (*luang gyu*) overhead. They fashioned a chariot that was similar to the ones used [to transport] the dead. When the body [231] was laid in the chariot, four of the king's queens from that region gathered and threw flowers and [offered] sweet fragrances. When the time came to burn the chariot, the king himself offered flowers and sweet fragrances.

After those offerings were made, that chariot was put on the aforementioned platform and set ablaze. While it burned, many people with strong respect and devotion covered themselves with an upper garment, and in order to help incinerate the body, threw bird feathers upon the pyre. After they cremated the body, the picked out whatever bones were left, and then built a stūpa on the site.

While Faxian visited this place, he did not meet the arhat while he was still living. He was, however, able to attend the cremation. This king had a strong, stable devotion to the Buddha's teachings. He desired to build a new temple for the monks. After making offerings and after finishing their meal, they chose two excellent oxen. Both horns were covered with gold and silver and then decorated with jewels. Then a beautiful plow (*thong gshol*) was commissioned, and then the king himself plowed four sides of a field. Afterward, these were abandoned. The people of that region gave each other houses. That kind of offering tradition has endured for generation after generation, with fathers passing it along to sons. On a stone pillar, a message was carved that forbade anyone from ever ruining this tradition.

While Faxian resided in this region, Indian [232] paṇḍitas sat upon a high throne. During a discourse delivered upon the sūtras, Faxian heard: "The Buddha's begging bowl was [first] kept at Vaiśālī (*Wa tsi sa la*). Then, for twelve hundred years, it was kept at Gandhāra (*Him tu bar*)." **[Faxian said that while he stayed in that region, people were reading and saying the exact years, but later he came to forget.]**[262] After that, [the begging bowl] returned to the western territory of the Yuezhi (*Yus thya*), where it stayed for a hundred or perhaps a thousand years. Then it was taken to Khotan (*Ho tan*), where it stayed for hundreds of thousands of years. It was then taken to Kāśmīra (*Kha che*), where it stayed for hundreds of thousands of years. From there it came to the emperor's sovereign land [i.e., China],[263] where it was kept for hundreds of thousands of years. It was then taken to the Siṃhala region, where it was kept for hundreds of thousands of years. It will one day return to Central India. From there, it will fly off to the heavenly realm of Tuṣita.

When the bodhisattva Maitreya sees it, he will let out a long sigh and say, "*Kye ma*! It is sad to see that the Buddha Śākyamuni's begging bowl has come here." Then, together with all his godly disciples, they will make flower and incense offerings to it for one week. That begging bowl will then return to the world once more. The king of the ocean nāgas will bring it to his palace. When the Buddha Maitreya comes [to earth] in order to achieve enlightenment, the begging bowl will manifest into four begging bowls and each will go to one of the four slopes of Mount Sumeru. The four guardian kings will pray to come and offer (four begging bowls) after Maitreya achieves enlightenment, just as they did for the buddhas of previous ages. All thousand buddhas of this Fortunate Eon (*Bskal pa bzang po*) will eat from this begging bowl. When this begging bowl disappears from the world, the Buddha's teachings will begin to diminish and then vanish from the world. The life expectancy of humans [233] will dramatically decrease until they live for just ten years. Grain and butter will be exhausted. People will experience great mental suffering. Bearing knives and weapons, they will kill and beat each other.

Whoever survives will retreat to the mountains, and then the period of "Hidden Fortune" (*Sbas pa'i skal pa*) will begin. After evildoers have perished, those [in the mountains] will descend into the city and join together with others. They will say to one another, "Long ago, people lived a very long time. Because we engaged in so many kinds of nonvirtuous actions and did not practice the Dharma correctly, our lifespan became just ten years! With regret, now is the time to engage in virtuous activity and be more compassionate toward one another." They will trust each other and act truthfully, and then their lives will become longer, increasing to eighty thousand years. So it is said.

After the Buddha Maitreya[264] finds the nectar [of enlightenment] and turns the Wheel of the Dharma, those who followed the Buddha Śākyamuni and those who became monks and received the three and five vows and who followed the Triple Gem will become his first group of [Maitreya's] disciples. The second and the third group of disciples will be those who were protected by the Buddha Śākyamuni's kindness.

At that time, [Faxian] went to make a copy of the texts [that record this story]. He was told, [234] "This story is not to be found in texts. We learned it from the oral tradition."

XL, The Final Chapter
Departing Siṃhala Upon a Boat; Yavadvīpa [Java] and Mount Lao; Arriving Safely in Guangzhou

Faxian remained on that island for two years, during which time he discovered [a text] called *E he ma*. After much searching, he also found volumes on [monastic] discipline (*bca' khrims gyi glegs bam*). He had not previously heard of the *Ehema*, but then he found it. Also, he found various other teachings. Furthermore, he found all the texts that had not yet arrived in the kingdom of China (*ci na'i rgyal khams*).[265] Faxian found those volumes written in Sanskrit (*legs sbyar gyi skad*).

He loaded them onto a ship that carried two hundred merchants. A small ship was tied to the main vessel in case of emergency. After they had set out to sea, a great squall arose. They were able to continue sailing eastward for two days.

They then encountered a great red wind (*rlung dmar chen po*). The passengers in the main vessel said they wanted abandon ship and board the small boat, but those in the small ship said that if something bad were to happen with too many people, they should cut the ropes holding luggage at night. Then the merchants were scared they would drown, so they took all the large luggage and threw it into the sea. Faxian continued to sail on with the others. They then threw whatever [baggage] was left over into the sea. Faxian began to worry [235] that the merchants would next pitch his scriptures and holy images. He prayed single-mindedly to his root guru and to Avalokiteśvara for safe passage to China: "*Ema*! I have traveled such a far distance in search of the holy Dharma. Buddhas of the Ten Directions, please consider my activity and please kindly protect me!" For thirty nights and thirty days, the storm raged incessantly. They sailed near a shoreline where the waves somewhat quieted. They carefully examined [the boat] to see where the water was entering. They plugged all the holes and then set out to sea once more.

There were many enemies and robbers (*chak pa*) upon the sea. Should one encounter them, no one would escape alive. The ocean is immeasurably vast. Travel proceeds only by knowing the direction of east and west by reading the sun, the moon, and the stars. When it becomes very dark, when a strong wind rises, or when it becomes foggy, one has no choice but to go with the wind. In the nighttime, when great darkness descends, merchants worry that their boats will collide with [other ships], about the arrival of a great wave, about light the color of fire, about great ocean creatures like turtles or sea monsters, and so on. What's more, when they see amazing or sometimes terrifying things [they know to reset their course]; but when they cannot see a thing, the merchants know not where to go and thus suffer from terrible fear. The ocean is bottomless, so should they consider resting there is not even a stone [236] to be found. When the sky is clear, one may not know how to travel eastward and head off instead to the south. When there is an accident upon the ocean, there is no way to escape with your life!

They traveled in this way for ninety days and then arrived at Yavadvīpa [i.e., Java].[266] That island is inhabited by many heretical brāhmaṇas (*mu stegs pa'i bram ze*) and there was no opportunity to announce the Buddha's teaching. Faxian stayed for five months. Then he once again boarded a merchant vessel along with two hundred other passengers. On the sixteenth day of the fourth month, they once again set sail. Faxian stayed on this great ship as it made a mostly pleasant passage northward. Crossing towards the northeast, they headed toward the city of Guangzhou.[267] One night, after a month had passed, a great rain and terrifying wind arose. The merchants and everyone else became terrified. At that time, Faxian prayed very strongly to the lamas and saṅgha of China as well as to Avalokiteśvara for protection from fear and so the sky would clear and the wind dissipate. The wind then died down.

In light of all this, the brāhmaṇas spoke to one another, saying: "We are experiencing such obstacles because this monk has boarded the ship. We should pitch him over the side of the boat! We don't have a tradition of saving a single life if it means putting everyone else in danger!" Then one virtuous man spoke up: "If you want to kick this monk off this boat, you should kick me off as well! If you expel this Chinese monk, when we arrive in China, I will report everything to the Emperor. [237] The Chinese Emperor strongly respects the Buddha's teachings. He also serves and respects the Buddhist lamas and monks." The brāhmaṇas became fearful and could not pitch [Faxian] overboard.

At that time, the sky became very dark. The crew captains looked at one another in surprise and didn't know what to do. They traveled onward for more than seventy days and nights, exhausting their water and food reserves. They used brackish water from the ocean to cook the food. They apportioned drinking water, giving each person only one glass of tea. Even so, their water was exhausted. Then those merchants discussed among themselves: "It takes fifty days to sail to Guangzhou, but by now many more days have passed. We no longer have anything to eat. We must sail to the north and try to find the shoreline." After twelve days and nights, they arrived at a place called Changguang (*Chāng hwas gūng*) at the base of a mountain called Lao.[268] There they found good water and *abikha* [vegetables]. After so many days of terrifying passage, they finally arrived in this northerly place. They saw *yihatsa* being grown [as a crop],[269] and so understood that they had arrived in China, but they could not spot even the footprint of a human being. They had no idea just where they had arrived. Some claimed they had not yet arrived at Guangzhou, saying, "We have already passed it!" Nobody knew exactly where they were.

After that, [238] they searched for inhabitants who could tell them where they were. They came across two hunters sitting on a small boat who were returning to their house. Faxian translated. Everyone was very happy, and they asked, "What kind of person are you?" They said, "We are followers of the Buddha!" "What did you search for in the mountain?" They lied: "Tomorrow is the fifteenth day of the seventh month, so we went to the mountains in search for something to offer the gods." "Who does this region belong to?" they asked. "This is [the prefecture] of Qing (*Chang ha*)," they replied, "on the border of the Changguang (*Chang hus*) district, under the power of the district commander (*yul gyi tā dpon*) of the Liao."[270]

The merchants were overjoyed when they heard this. They unloaded the boat. One person was sent to Changguan (*Chwang hus gu'ang*). The prefect of that city was named Li yi (*Li īng*).[271] He was a follower of the Buddha's teaching and heard that a monk had arrived from India bringing with him texts and images. He came as far as the shoreline, and then sent envoys ahead in small wooden boats. They invited the texts, statues, and Faxian into the city. The merchants sailed on to Yangzhou (*Dzāng cha'u*). A merchant named Mang-nwa who was a tobacco seller invited Faxian [into his home]. He stayed there the entire winter. Although Faxian deeply wanted to [239] return quickly to Chang'an (*Zheng an*), his homeland, that person [the tobacco seller] had only one intention, which was for Faxian to stay in southern China and copy all the scriptures and śastras he had acquired.

[Lubsangdamdin's Postscript]

Regarding all this, it was six years between Faxian's departure from Chang'an[272] and his arrival in Central India. He stayed in Central India a further six years. After his departure, it was more than three years until his arrival in Qingzhou (*Dzāng cha'u*). The large kingdoms he encountered numbered thirty, counting those he visited intentionally and those he happened upon. In the westerly direction of the setting sun, he passed through many desert mountainous passes and valleys in Mongol territories (*Hor yul*) in order to reach India.[273] In the Land of Noble Ones, the monks strictly followed the vinaya and made great effort to hear teachings, which he found extraordinary. It is impossible to explain all this in any detail here. In these pages I have described just the rough idea and some scattered events. This small depiction is difficult enough for us to believe, never mind the detailed story! Furthermore, he experienced profound difficulties while crossing the vast ocean but eventually joyfully arrived in his homeland. [Then] the sentient beings of the three realms received their share of the Dharma.[274] Though he encountered so many perils, he arrived home happily and in good health. He wrote down all that he had seen and heard on bamboo in order to share with scholars.

Later, after the *jiaying* year (414 CE),[275] in the twelfth reign year (416 CE) of the Yixi emperor (*Wā ye*)[276] of the great Han dynasty (*chen po hān gur*),[277] abiding in the Canopus [240] star (*O rto lig gi skar ma*), envoys were sent to personally welcome the Dharma traveler (*chos kyi 'grul pa*) Faxian. After he arrived during the summer festival (*dbyar ston*), a large thanksgiving celebration was thrown in his honor.

> [Interlocutor:] While conversing with him,
> [I] inquired about the nature of [his] travels.

Whoever is interested in the truth about [what he saw upon his] journey,
you should investigate for yourself and you will develop confidence.
This text clearly provides information
that you and I never before knew.
[Faxian:] From beginning to end, whatever I have described
comes from thoroughly recalling what I have seen and said.
I have not added anything from my imagination.
My aim when I left as a traveler for distant lands,
though I left with a healthy body,
I did not know whether I would return healthy or alive.
In those unknown places, I decided the Dharma was more valuable
than my body or my life.
I am a courageous son of China who decided that,
whatever the reasons that led me to travel,
no matter what, I would achieve my goals.

In general, even though people have heard this kind of story before, they themselves do not act accordingly. Even if such people see with their own eyes, their mind will not believe it! Many people are saying to one another that those who sacrifice their body for the Dharma are very rare. Not only that, in order to search for the Buddha's teaching, Faxian completely forgot about his own body and life. That had never happened before. [241]

We should understand that true actions come from the power of truth.
Or, that the kindness of fulfilling human desires
is difficult for ordinary people to understand.
If we do not remember to pay back the kindness of such beings,
nothing whatsoever will be successful.
If you think someone has been kind and supportive,
you should never forget about it!
It is funny: we sometimes forget those who have been kind
and remember those who have been cruel.

So it is said.

[The actual Chinese text finishes here. That text is found in the catalogues of the canon of the Buddha's word and the [Indian] commentaries,

which has it clearly indexed under the title *The Biography of the Great Translator Faxian*.]

[Lubsangdamdin's Afterword]

In ancient times, Chinese and Indian translators and paṇḍitas traveled to each other's lands. Their biographies clearly prove that the Dharma arrived in Mongolia (*hor yul*) prior to arriving in China or Tibet. I am inadequate and unqualified to bear even the name of a translator. Because the Chinese text chronicles many local dialects, I cannot correctly discern even the names of people and places. Still, in the above I think I have correctly translated the meaning.

By this virtue, in the future may we not hesitate to sacrifice our bodies or lives for the sake of the Dharma! May I be able to teach the correct meaning of the Dharma to the varieties of sentient beings in their own language!

As for *The Emanated Mirror That Completely Illuminates the Source of the Victor's Teachings: The Story of the Great Han-era Monk Faxian's Journey to the Land of Noble Ones*; it was translated, edited, and finalized by the bhikṣu Aśvaghoṣa [i.e., Zava Damdin Lubsangdamdin] in the great land of Mongolia in the north of the world, at that great monastery prophesied by the Buddha in the center of the Glorious Yeke-yin Küriy-e (*Tā khurel*), when according to trustworthy Chinese texts 2,943 years had passed since the Buddha was born in India. Nowadays, based on the inscriptions of Aśoka's pillars, Europeans claim that more than 2,500 years have passed since the Buddha's birth. According to the Puk system (*Phugs lugs*), 2,300 [years after have passed]. According to the New Astrology of Genden (*Dge ldan rtsis gsar*), [2,]200 years have passed, and according to the Golden astrological system (*Gser rtsis*), more than [2,]400 years have passed. Since the jewel of the Buddha's Teachings spread into the land of Mahā China, more than 1,900 years have passed. Since the venerable Faxian of the Great Han dynasty traveled to Central India, 1,500 years have passed. According to the Kālacakra system, [this translation was completed] during Pingala, the fifty-second year of the fifteenth rapjung (1917), in the virtuous waxing moon period of the tenth month known as mindruk (*smin drug*).

By all this, may the door of the precious teachings of scripture and realization of the King of Subduers, the Supramundane Victor, spread everywhere in the ten directions, and may it increase for a very long time to come! *Dzayantu*!

It is said in *The History of Buddhism in China*:

I have not seen any extensive travel guides (*lam yig*) composed by Tibetan translators. It is very difficult to trust the embellishments and descriptions of gold and musk sellers!

[There] are several [Chinese] works about coming into the presence of holy sites (*gnas mjal skor*). There is Xuanzang's abbreviated edition in two sections (*bam po*) and the extensive edition in ten sections. I have abridged the meaning of the latter and presented it in these pages. Furthermore, regarding both India and China, the erudite monk Faxian (*Hwa shang yan tsung*) prepared a narrative geography in ten chapters about the Land of Noble Ones. If one studies this tenth chapter (*le'u*) and the tenth section (*bam po*) of Xuanzang's work describing the geography of India, you are left feeling that you have yourself traveled to the Land of Noble Ones!

O Knowledgeable One, in addition to these two great texts [by Faxian and Xuanzang], please allow to ripen within the sphere of your wisdom mind that you should search for the work of the great translator Yijing (*Yi kying*), who traveled across India for twenty-five years. Should you find it, translate it into Tibetan!

Notes

Introduction

1. As reported in Jean-Pierre Abel-Rémusat, "Mémoire Sur Un Voyage Dans l'Asie Centrale, Dans Le Pays Des Afghans et Des Beloutches, et Dans l'Inde, Exécuté à La Fin Du IVe Siècle de Notre Ère Par Plusieurs Samanéens de La Chine," *Mémoires de l'Institut de France* 13, no. 2 (1838): 345–412.
2. Zhitang Drocourt, "Abel-Rémusat et Sa Pensée Linguistique Sur Le Chinois," in *Le XIXe Siècle et Ses Langues*, ed. Sarga Moussa, Actes En Ligne Du Ve Congrès de La Société Des Études Romantiques et Dix-Neuvièmistes, 2013, 1.
3. This was decades before the splitting of the sciences from the humanities, the invention of World Religions, the professionalization of the human sciences, or the impact of Darwinism on scholarly taxonomies of human difference. A clearer field history of Orientalism (and the study of Buddhism specifically) in the pre- and post-Darwinian moment is needed. For key surveys that provide a framework, see: David Cahan, *From Natural Philosophy to the Sciences: Writing the History of Nineteenth-Century Science* (Chicago: University of Chicago Press, 2003); Henry M. Cowles, *The Scientific Method: An Evaluation of Thinking from Darwin to Dewey* (Cambridge, Mass.: Harvard University Press, 2020).
4. For example: Jean-Pierre Abel-Rémusat, *Élémens de La Grammaire Chinoise, Ou, Principes Généraux Du Kou-Wen Ou Style Antique: Et Du Kouan-Hoa c'est-à-Dire, de La Langue Commune Généralement Usitée Dans l'Empire Chinois* (Paris: Imprimerie Royale, 1822); Jean-Pierre Abel-Rémusat, *Recherche Sur Les Langues Tartares, Ou Mémoires Sur Différens Points de La Grammaire et de La Littérature Des Mandchous, Des Mongols, Des Ouigours et Des Tibetains* (Paris: Imprimerie Royale, 1820).
5. For surveys beyond what I can summarize here, see: Michael G. Chang, *A Court on Horseback: Imperial Touringand the Construction of Qing Rule, 1680–1785* (Cambridge, Mass.: Harvard University Asia Center, 2020); Pamela Kyle Crossley, *A Translucent Mirror: History and Identity in Qing Imperial Ideology* (Berkeley: University of California Press, 1999); Patricia Ann Berger,

Empire of Emptiness: Buddhist Art and Political Authority in Qing China (Honolulu: University of Hawai'i Press, 2003); Johan Elverskog, "Mongol Time Enters a Qing World," in *Time, Temporality, and Imperial Transition: East Asia from Ming to Qing*, ed. Lynn A. Struve (Honolulu: Association for Asian Studies and University of Hawai'i Press, 2005); Johan Elverskog, *Our Great Qing: The Mongols, Buddhism and the State in Late Imperial China* (Honolulu: University of Hawai'i Press, 2006); Nicola Di Cosmo, "Qing Colonial Administration in Inner Asia," *The International History Review* 20, no. 2 (June 1998): 287–309; Mark C. Elliott, *The Manchu Way: The Eight Banners and Ethnic Identity in Late Imperial China* (Stanford, CA: Stanford University Press, 2001).

6. Michel de Certeau, *The Practice of Everyday Life: Vol. 1* (Berkeley: University of California Press, 1988), 174.
7. As we shall see in chapter 2, Abel-Rémusat was less admired for his armchair textual study and his foregoing of Sanskrit and Pāli for the polluted texts of Tartary by some prominent amateur Orientalist working in the British colonial administration, such as Brian Houghton Hodgson.
8. Roger-Pol Droit, *The Cult of Nothingness: The Philosophers and the Buddha*, trans. David Streight and Pamela Vohnson (Chapel Hill; London: University of North Carolina Press, 2003).
9. Jean Rousseau et al., *Lettres édifiantes et curieuses sur la langue chinoise: un débat philosophico-grammatical entre Wilhelm von Humboldt et Jean-Pierre Abel-Rémusat (1821–1831)*, ed. Denis Thouard and Jean Rousseau (Villeneuve-d'Ascq: Presses universitaires du Septentrion, 1999); Jean-Pierre Abel-Rémusat, "Compte Rendu de 'Sur La Naissance Des Formed Grammaticales de Humboldt,'" *Journal Asiatique*, no. V (1824): 51–61; Jean-Pierre Abel-Rémusat, "Observations Sur Quelques Passages de La Lettre Précédente," in *Lettres Édifiantes et Curieuses Sur La Langue Chinoise: Un Débat Philosophico-Grammatical Entre Wilhelm von Humboldt et Jean-Pierre Abel-Rémusat (1821–1831)*, ed. Denis Thouard and Jean Rousseau (Villeneuve-d'Ascq: Presses universitaires du Septentrion, 1999), 181–96; Wilhelm von Humboldt and Jean-Pierre Abel-Rémusat, *Brief an M. [Monsieur] Abel-Rémusat über die Natur grammatischer Formen im allgemeinen und über den Geist der chinesischen Sprache im besonderen* (Stuttgart: Bad Cannstatt Frommann, 1979); Wilhelm von Humboldt, Jean-Pierre Abel-Rémusat, and Wilhelm Humboldt von Freiherr, *De l'origine des formes grammaticales* (Bordeaux: Ducros., 1969); Abel-Rémusat, "Observations Sur Quelques Passages de La Lettre Précédente."
10. Summarized from the following record of events: Abel-Rémusat, "Mémoire Sur Un Voyage Dans l'Asie Centrale, Dans Le Pays Des Afghans et Des Beloutches, et Dans l'Inde, Exécuté à La Fin Du IVe Siècle de Notre Ère Par Plusieurs Samanéens de La Chine."
11. The concept of the "Silk Road," or *Seidenstraße*, which encompasses much of Faxian's journey, was unknown to Abel-Rémusat and his audience, and I have not used it in this book. It was coined in 1877 by the German geographer Ferdinand von Richtofen (Ferdinand von Richtofen, "Über Die Zentralasiatischen Seidenstrassen Bis Zum 2. Jh. n. Chr," *Verhandlungen Der Gesellschaft Für Erdkunde Zu Berlin* 4 [1877]: 96–122).
12. Included in the early twentieth-century Taishō Canon as: Faxian 法顯, "The Biography of the Eminent Monk Faxian (Gaoseng Faxian Zhuan 高僧法顯傳)," vol. 51, 2085 (Tokyo: Taishō Shinshū Daizōkyō Kankōkai, 1988).
13. Abel-Rémusat, "Mémoire Sur Un Voyage Dans l'Asie Centrale, Dans Le Pays Des Afghans et Des Beloutches, et Dans l'Inde, Exécuté à La Fin Du IVe Siècle de Notre Ère Par Plusieurs Samanéens de La Chine," 347.
14. This is not to say that the Buddha's biographical narrative was then unknown to Europe. Abel-Rémusat's colleague Julius von Klaproth, for example, had published a translation of a

Mongolian biographical account in 1824. Even Marco Polo had provided key elements in the thirteenth century (a source regularly referenced by these Parisian scholars, and by Abel-Rémusat himself in deciphering certain chapters of the *Record*). But Abel-Rémusat's breakthrough with the *Record* mapped these partial biographical narratives to particular places and epochs. "For the European view of the life of the Buddha," notes Donald Lopez in one of the few passages about Abel-Rémusat in field histories of Buddhist studies, "[Abel-Rémusat's translation] was the first concerted attempt to identify the places of the Buddha's biography with actual locations in India." Donald S. Lopez, *From Stone to Flesh: A Short History of the Buddha* (Chicago: University of Chicago Press, 2016), 180.

15. Abel-Rémusat, "Mémoire Sur Un Voyage Dans l'Asie Centrale, Dans Le Pays Des Afghans et Des Beloutches, et Dans l'Inde, Exécuté à La Fin Du IVe Siècle de Notre Ère Par Plusieurs Samanéens de La Chine," 349.
16. Abel-Rémusat, 349.
17. Abel-Rémusat, 347.
18. Abel-Rémusat, 347.
19. See Charles E. Rosenberg, *The Cholera Years. The United States in 1832, 1849, and 1866* (Chicago: University of Chicago Press, 1962).
20. "Extrait du Registre des actes de décès du 2. arrond. de Paris, pour l'année 1832," in *Le Curieux, Deuxième volume, N. 35, Décembre 1886* (Le Curieux, 1888), 176.
21. Faxian and Jean-Pierre Abel-Rémusat, *Foĕ Kouĕ Ki, Ou, Relation Des Royaumes Bouddhiques: Voyage Dans La Tartarie, Dans l'Afghanistan et Dans l'Inde, Exécuté à La Fin Du IVe Siècle*, ed. Julius von Klaproth and Ernest Augustin Xavier Clerc de Landresse (Paris: Imprimerie Royale, 1836). For some of the best known English retranslations of the *Record*, see: J. W. Laidley, *The Pilgrimage of Fa Hian; From the French Edition of the Foe Koue Ki of MM. Remusat, Klaproth, and Landresse with Additional Notes and Illustrations* (Calcutta: J. Thomas, Baptist Mission Press, 1848); James Legge, *A Record of Buddhistic Kingdoms: Being an Account by the Chinese Monk Fa-Hien of His Travels in India and Ceylon (A.D. 399–414) in Search of the Buddhist Books of Discipline, Translated and Annotated with a Corean Recension of the Chinese Text* (Oxford: Oxford University Press, 1886); M. Remusat and H. H. Wilson, "Account of the Foe Kúe Ki, or Travels of Fa Hian in India, Translated by M. Remusat [Read 9th March and 7th April, 1838]," *The Journal of the Royal Asiatic Society* 5, no. 1 (1839): 108–40; Fa-hsien and Herbert Allen Giles, *Record of the Buddhistic Kingdoms. Translated from the Chinese by H.A. Giles* (London: Trübner & Co., 1877).
22. For example: Jean-Jacques Ampère, "De La Chine et Des Travaux de M. Abel-Rémusat," *Revue Des Deux Mondes* III (November 15, 1832): 249–75, 361–95; E. Jacquet, "Examen de La Traduction Du Fo Koue Ki, Ouvrage Posthume de M. Abel-Rémusat, Complété Par MM. J. Klaproth et C. Landresse," *Journal Asiatique* 3, no. 4 (Aout 1837): 141–79; Ernest-Augustin Clerc de Landresse, "Notice Sur La Vie et Les Travaux de M. Abel-Rémusat, Lue à La Séance Générale Annuelle de La Société Asiatique, Le 28 Avril 1834," *Journal Asiatique* 14, no. 2 (1834): 205–31, 296–316; Neumann Karl, "Review of Foe Koue Ki Ou Relation Des Royaumes Bouddhiques: Voyage Dans La Tartarie, Dans l'Afghanistan et Dans l'Inde, Execute à La Fin Du IVe Siècle, Par Chy Fa Hian. Traduit Du Chinois et Commenté Par M. Abel Rémusat Ouvrage Posthume, Rev., Complété, et Augm. d'éclaircissements Nouveaux Par MM. Klaproth et Landresse," *Zeitschrift Für Die Kunde Des Morgenlandes* 3 (1840): 105–51; Eugène Burnouf, "Foĕ Kouĕ Ki, Ou Relation Des Royaumes Bouddhiques; Voyages Dans La Tartarie, Dans l'Afghanistan et Dans l'Inde, Exécuté, à La Fin Du IV Siècle, Par Chy Fa Hian. Traduit Du Chinois et Commenté Par M. Abel Rémusat; Ouvrage Posthume, Revu, Complété et Augmenté d'éclaircissements Nouveaux, Oar MM.

Klaproth et Landresse. Paris, Impr. Royale, 1836. Un Vol. Gr. in-4; LXVI et 424 Pag., Avec 3 Cartes et 2 Pl. Premier Article," *Journal Des Savants*, March 1837, 160–76; Antoine-Isaac Silvestre de Sacy, "Notice historique sur la vie et les ouvrages de M. Abel Rémusat," *Mémoires de l'Institut national de France* 12, no. 1 (1839): 375–400.

23. For example: Philip C. Almond, *The British Discovery of Buddhism* (Cambridge: Cambridge University Press, 2007); Donald S. Lopez, *Curators of the Buddha: The Study of BuddhismUnder Colonialism* (Chicago: University of Chicago Press, 1995); Donald S. Lopez, *Prisoners of Shangri-La: Tibetan Buddhism and the West* (Chicago: University of Chicago Press, 1998); Erik Braun, *The Birth of Insight: Meditation, Modern Buddhism, and the Burmese Monk Ledi Sayadaw* (Chicago: University Of Chicago Press, 2015).
24. See "What is an Author?" and "Nietzsche, Genealogy, History" in Michel Foucault, Donald F. Bouchard, and Sherry Simon, *Language, Counter-Memory, Practice: Selected Essays and Interviews* (Ithaca, N.Y.: Cornell University Press, 2006).
25. Prasenjit Duara, *The Crisis of Global Modernity: Asian Traditions and a Sustainable Future* (Cambridge; New York: Cambridge University Press, 2015).
26. Duara, 54.
27. Duara, 54.
28. Michel de Certeau, *Heterologies: Discourse on the Other*, trans. Brian Massumi (Minneapolis: University of Minnesota Press, 2010), 8.
29. Catherine Chin, "Marvelous Things Heard: On Finding Historical Radiance," *The Massachusetts Review* 58, no. 3 (2017): 478–91.
30. Several works that name and think outside of humanist reproduction of fundamental orientations to place, time, agency, and society—always tied inextricably to "the rise of the West" and its modernist staging as site and source of the universal—have been important in organizing this book, but because of space I cannot individually explore them here: Wael B. Hallaq, *Restating Orientalism: A Critique of Modern Knowledge* (New York: Columbia University Press, 2018); Amy Allen, *The End of Progress: Decolonizing the Normative Foundations of Critical Theory* (New York: Columbia University Press, 2016); Webb Keane, "Secularism as a Moral Narrative of Modernity,"*Transit: Europäische Revue*, Verlag Neue Kritik, no. 43 (2013): 159–70; Gayatri Chakravorty Spivak, *A Critique of Postcolonial Reason: Toward a History of the Vanishing Present* (Cambridge, Mass.: Harvard University Press, 1999); Dipesh Chakrabarty, *Provincializing Europe: Postcolonial Thought and Historical Difference* (Princeton, N.J.: Princeton University Press, 2009); Timothy Mitchell, *Questions of Modernity* (Minneapolis; London: University of Minnesota Press, 2000); Prasenjit Duara, *Rescuing History from the Nation: Questioning Narratives of Modern China* (Chicago: University of Chicago Press, 1996); Robert Young, *White Mythologies: Writing History and the West* (London; New York: Routledge, 1990); Cedric J. Robinson, *Black Marxism: The Making of the Black Radical Tradition* (Chapel Hill: University of North Carolina Press, 1983); Ranajit Guha, *History at the Limit of World-History* (New York: Columbia University Press, 2002); Susan M. Hill, *The Clay We Are Made Of: Haudenosaunee Land Tenure on the Grand River* (Winnipeg, Manitoba: University of Manitoba Press, 2017); Engseng Ho, "Inter-Asian Concepts for Mobile Societies," *The Journal of Asian Studies* 76, no. 4 (2017): 907–28.
31. Lisa Lowe, "The Intimacies of the Four Continents," in *Haunted by Empire: Geographies of Intimacy in North American History*, ed. Ann Laura Stoler (Durham, N.C.: Duke University Press, 2006), 191–212.
32. Lisa Lowe, *The Intimacies of Four Continents* (Durham, N.C.: Duke University Press, 2015).

33. Kuan-Hsing Chen, *Asia as Method: Toward Deimperialization* (Durham, N.C.: Duke University Press, 2010).
34. Blo bzang rta mgrin, "Chen Po Hān Gur Gyi Btsun Pa Phā Hyin Gyis 'phags Pa'i Yul Du 'Grims Pa'i Rnam Thar Rgyal Bstan 'Byung Khungs Kun Gsal 'Phrul Gyi Me Long," in *Rje Btsun Blo Bzang Rta Dbyangs Kyi Gsung 'bum*, vol. 1 (New Delhi: Mongolian Lama Guru Deva, 1975), 182.
35. Blo bzang rta mgrin, 182–83.
36. Gilles Deleuze and Félix Guattari, *A Thousand Plateaus*, trans. Brian Massumi (Minneapolis; London: University of Minnesota Press, 2005).
37. Deleuze and Guattari, *A Thousand Plateaus*, 23.
38. Hartman, "Venus in Two Acts," 12.
39. John Muir, *My First Summer in the Sierra: With Illustrations from Drawings Made by the Author in 1869 and from Photographs by Herbert W. Gleason* (Boston: Houghton Mifflin, 1911), 248.

1. Chang'an to India

1. What is today the city of Nanjing 南京, Jiangsu province 江蘇省. One of the four great ancient capitals of China (along with Beijing, Chang'an, and Luoyang).
2. David R. Knechtges and Taiping Chang, eds., "Sengyou 僧祐 (445–518)," in *Ancient and Early Medieval Chinese Literature: A Reference Guide*, vol. 2 (Leiden; Boston: Brill, 2014), 804.
3. Sengyou 僧祐, "Collection of Notes on the Translation of the Tripiṭaka (Chusanzang Jiji 出三藏記集)," in *Taishō Shinshū Daizōkyō* 大正新脩大藏經, ed. Takakusu Junjiro, vol. 55, 2145 (Tokyo: Taishō Shinshū Daizōkyō Kankōkai, 1988), 0111b27–0112b27. In addition to cataloguing for posterity a vast spectrum of literary endeavor, Sengyou laid the groundwork for a genre of Chinese Buddhist literature known as *jinglu* 經錄.
4. In contemporary Zhejiang province 浙江省. Huijiao 慧皎, "Biographies of Eminent Monks (Gaoseng Zhuan 高僧傳)," in *Taishō Shinshū Daizōkyō* 大正新脩大藏經, ed. Takakusu Junjiro, vol. 50, 2059 (Tokyo: Taishō Shinshū Daizōkyō Kankōkai, 1988), 0337b19–0338b25.
5. Between the year 67, the tenth reign year of Emperor Ming (明, r. 58–75) of the Later Han dynasty (後漢, 25–220), and the eighteenth reign year of Sengyou's admirer, Emperor Wu of the Liang (519). These many lives are organized by Huijiao into ten categories: thirty-six translators (*yijing* 譯經), such as Dharmarakṣa, Kumārajīva, and Faxian's collaborator Buddhabhadra; one hundred and one exegetes ("expounders of righteousness," *yijie* 義解); twenty monks of extraordinary spirit (*shenyi* 神異); twenty-one meditators (*xichan* 習禪); thirteen vinaya specialists (*minglu* 明律); eleven self-immolators (*yishen* 遺身); twenty-one reciters of scripture (*songjing* 誦經); fourteen promoters of virtuous acts (*xingfu* 興福); eleven masters of scripture (*jingshi* 經師); and ten chant masters (*changdao* 唱導). Shih seems to have reversed categories nine and ten, giving "Biographies de onze chanteurs-compositeurs d'hymnes" for 經師 and "Biographies de dix intructeurs religieux" for 唱導. Robert Shih, *Biographies Des Moines Éminents (Kao Seng Tchouan) de Houei-Kiao*, Bibliothèque Du Muséon 54 (Louvain: Institut Orientaliste, Bibliothèque de Université de Louvain, 1968), viii.
6. The *Lives of Famous Monks* (Mingseng zhuan 名僧傳抄) had been written just a decade earlier, in 519, by Baochang (寶唱, c. 466–c. 534). It is now lost, but some extracts are preserved in the *Mingseng zhuanchao* 名僧傳抄, examined by Yuan-ju Liu, Max Deeg, and others.
7. For studies and select translations from these biographical collections, see: John Kieschnick, *The Eminent Monk: Buddhist Ideals in Medieval Chinese Hagiography* (Honolulu:

University of Hawai'i Press, 1997); Erik Zürcher, *The Buddhist Conquest of China: The Spread and Adaptation of Buddhism in Early Medieval China* (Leiden: Brill, 2007); James A. Benn, *Burning for the Buddha: Self-Immolation in Chinese Buddhism* (Honolulu: University of Hawai'i Press Kuroda Institute, 2007); Yuan-ju Liu, "Stories Written and Rewritten: The Story of Faxian's Search for the Dharma in Its Historical, Anecdotal, and Biographical Contexts," trans. Jack W. Chen, *Early Medieval China* 22 (2016): 1–25; Arthur F. Wright, "Biography and Hagiography: Hui-Chiao's Lives of Eminent Monks," in *Studies in Chinese Buddhism*, ed. Robert M. Somers (New Haven, Conn.: Yale University Press, 1990); Tom De Rauw, "Baochang: Sixth-Century Biographer of Buddhist Monks . . . and Nuns?," *Journal of the American Oriental Society* 125, no. 2 (2005): 203–18; Shih, *Biographies Des Moines Éminents (Kao Seng Tchouan) de Houei-Kiao.*

8. Liu, "Stories Written and Rewritten," 5.
9. Sengyou 僧祐, "Collection of Notes on the Translation of the Tripiṭaka (Chusanzang Jiji 出三藏記集)," 0111b27.
10. Huijiao 慧皎, "Biographies of Eminent Monks (Gaoseng Zhuan 高僧傳)," 0337b19.
11. Sengyou 僧祐, "Collection of Notes on the Translation of the Tripiṭaka (Chusanzang Jiji 出三藏記集)," 0111b28–b29.
12. Sengyou gives the convalescence period at the temple as two nights.
13. *chujia* 出家: "going forth" into homelessness (Skt. *pravrajita*; Tib. *Rab tu byung ba*). Leaving behind householder life, this is the first act of joining the ordained Buddhist saṅgha (Ch. *zhongseng* 叔父; Tib. *dge'dun*; Mong. *bursang, sangga*). "Going forth" refers specifically to ordination as a novice monk (Skt. *śrāmeṇera*; Ch. *shami* 沙彌; Tib. *dge tshul*; Mong. *gečül*) or nun (Skt. *śrāmaṇerikā*; Ch. *shamani* 沙彌尼; Tib. *dge tshul ma*; Mong. *gečülma*).
14. Huijiao 慧皎, "Biographies of Eminent Monks (Gaoseng Zhuan 高僧傳)," 0337b27; Shih, *Biographies Des Moines Éminents (Kao Seng Tchouan) de Houei-Kiao*, 108.
15. Zürcher guesses that this event took place during or soon after the Later Zhao (*The Buddhist Conquest of China*, 85); Liu, "Stories Written and Rewritten," 19.
16. Huijiao 慧皎, "Biographies of Eminent Monks (Gaoseng Zhuan 高僧傳)," 0337b29–c02; Shih, *Biographies Des Moines Éminents (Kao Seng Tchouan) de Houei-Kiao*, 108–9.
17. Ch. *dajie* 大戒 = Skt. *upasaṃpadā*; or *shoujie* 受戒; Tib. *gnyen par rdzogs pa*. Refers to the monastic ceremony whereby a male novice (*śrāmaṇera*) becomes a fully ordained monk, or *bhikṣu* (or, for a female novice, *śikṣamāṇā*, the ceremony whereby she becomes a *bhikṣuṇī*). Huijiao 慧皎, "Biographies of Eminent Monks (Gaoseng Zhuan 高僧傳)," 0337c03–c04.
18. See Yifa, *The Origins of Buddhist Monastic Codes in China: An Annotated Translation and Study of the Chanyuan Qinggui* (Honolulu: University of Hawaii Press, 2002).
19. Kieschnick, *The Eminent Monk*.
20. Rongxi Li, "The Journey of the Eminent Monk Faxian: Translated from the Chinese of Faxian (Taishō Volume 51, Number 2085)," in *Lives of Great Monks and Nuns*, ed. Sengaku Mayeda and et al., Numata English Tripiṭaka Project (Berkeley, CA: Numata Center for Buddhist Translation and Research, 2002), 157.
21. See, for example: Jan Nattier, *A Guide to the Earliest Chinese Buddhist Translations: Texts from the Eastern Han [Dong Han] and Three Kingdoms [San Guo] Periods*, Bibliotheca Philologica et Philosophica Buddhica (Tokyo: International Research Institute for Advanced Buddhology, Soka University, 2008); Zürcher, *The Buddhist Conquest of China*; Kenneth K. S Ch'en, *Buddhism in China: A Historical Survey* (Princeton, N .: Princeton University Press, 1973); Kieschnick, *The Eminent Monk*; Yifa, *The Originsof Buddhist Monastic Codesin China: An Annotated Translationand*

Studyofthe Chanyuan Qinggui (Honolulu: University of Hawai'i Press, n.d.); Max Deeg, "Chinese Buddhists in Search of Authenticity in the Dharma," *The Eastern Buddhist* 45, no. 1 & 2 (2014): 11–22; Max Deeg and Faxian, *Das Gaoseng-Faxian-Zhuan Als Religionsgeschichtliche Quelle: Der Älteste Bericht Eines Chinesischen Buddhistischen Pilgermönchs Über Seine Reise Nach Indien Mit Übersetzung Des Textes* (Wiesbaden, Germany: Harrassowitz, 2005).

22. In the the *Record*, Faxian writes that the lacuna of text that most concerned him was the *vinaya*, or *lü* 律. In 1968, Robert Shih hazarded a reasonable guess that Huijiao and Sengyou speculated retrospectively in this way about Faxian's motivation, since, as we shall see, he had washed ashore in China after his long journey with both Sanskrit vinayas and sūtras under his arms, and since he devoted some of his remaining years to translating both genres of canonical literature with Buddhabhadra (*Biographies Des Moines Éminents (Kao Seng Tchouan) de Houei-Kiao*, 109 n. 2).
23. Dao'an's *Comprehensive Catalogue of Sūtras* is now lost but was partly incorporated into Sengyou's *Compilation of Notices*, the sixth-century work that gives us our first biography of Faxian .
24. Of consequence to the world of translation inhabited most directly by Faxian, it was upon Dao'an's urging that Fujian invited the Central Asian master translator Kumārajīva (鳩摩羅什 344–409/413) to China. Dao'an also inaugurated a tradition of Chinese monastics substituting their family names for *Shi* 釋, a transcription of the Buddha's Śākya clan, thus symbolically bringing monks into the Buddha's lineage. It is for this reason that Faxian is called Shi Faxian, and not Gong Faxian, in the *Record* and in Abel-Rémusat's writing (Robert E. Buswell and Donald S. Lopez, *The Princeton Dictionary of Buddhism* [Princeton, N.J.: Princeton University Press, 2013], 213).
25. This was a treatment soon taken up by imperial authorities that, as Kyoko Tokuno and Max Deeg have argued, bureaucratized Chinese analytics about authentic scripture while decentering the authority of the saṅgha in China to make such determinations independently. Deeg, "Chinese Buddhists in Search of Authenticity in the Dharma," 15; Kyoko Tokuno, "The Evaluation of Indigenous Scriptures in Chinese Buddhist Bibliographical Catalogues," in *Chinese Buddhist Apocrypha*, ed. Robert E Buswell (Honolulu: University of Hawai'i Press, 1990), 31–74.
26. Buswell and Lopez, *The Princeton Dictionary of Buddhism*, 794.
27. Translation from Deeg, "Chinese Buddhists in Search of Authenticity in the Dharma," 14.
28. Jacques Gernet, *Die chinesische Welt: die Geschichte Chinas von den Anfängen bis zur Jetztzeit* (Frankfurt am Main, Germany: Suhrkamp, 1988), 191. Quoted in Deeg and Faxian, *Das Gaoseng-Faxian-Zhuan Als Religionsgeschichtliche Quelle: Der Älteste Bericht Eines Chinesischen Buddhistischen Pilgermönchs Über Seine Reise Nach Indien Mit Übersetzung Des Textes*, 54 n. 203.
29. As with the dates of Faxian's birth and death, there are discrepancies in the dating of his long journey. Huijiao and Sengyou wrote that Faxian and company set out from Chang'an in the third reign year of Long'an 隆安 (397–401 CE) of the Jin dynasty, or 400 CE (Huijiao 慧皎, "Biographies of Eminent Monks [Gaoseng Zhuan 高僧傳]," 0337c05; Sengyou 僧祐, "Collection of Notes on the Translation of the Tripiṭaka [Chusanzang Jiji 出三藏記集]," 0111c12). Faxian's *Record*, however, has the departure "in the second year of Hongshi, the cyclical year of Jihai," which is a nonsensical date (second year of Hongshi is not the cyclical year of Jihai). As in any scribal culture, there were many mistakes made in copying, many intentional edits and elongations of the narrative, and thus many variant readings of what passed as Faxian's work. Indeed, such inconsistencies were noted by the likes of Hu Zhenheng, an editor and

interpreter of the *Record* during the late Ming dynasty (1368–1644) (Li, "The Journey of the Eminent Monk Faxian: Translated from the Chinese of Faxian [Taishō Volume 51, Number 2085]," 160). Though a standard scholarly dating of Faxian's birth is 337, Max Deeg hazards that Faxian was most likely born sometime between 336/340 and 341/345. This makes him, in Deeg's view, possibly as young as fifty-four years old, not the more conventional sixty-two, when he departed westward from Chang'an (Deeg and Faxian, *Das Gaoseng-Faxian-Zhuan Als Religionsgeschichtliche Quelle: Der Älteste Bericht Eines Chinesischen Buddhistischen Pilgermönchs Über Seine Reise Nach Indien Mit Übersetzung Des Textes*, 22–30).

30. Skt. *varsā/varṣa*; Ch. *anju* 安居, though in these sources it is *xia zuo* 夏坐. A rains retreat is generally a three-month period in which Buddhist monastics are required to stay in one place. According to the various vinayas, this tradition grew from the Buddha's requirement that monks stop their wandering during the monsoon period (generally from July to October) so as to protect the lives of insects. This grew into a tradition of gathering the saṅgha together at this time in *varṣāvāsa*, or "rains abode," still preserved in the Tibetan *yarné* (*dbyar gnas*). The tradition of the rains retreat likely led, in time, to the establishment of permanent monasteries (Skt. *vihara*) as yearlong housing for the Buddhist saṅgha.
31. Huijiao 慧皎, "Biographies of Eminent Monks (Gaoseng Zhuan 高僧傳)," 0337c06; Sengyou 僧祐, "Collection of Notes on the Translation of the Tripiṭaka (Chusanzang Jiji 出三藏記集)," 0111c13–c14.
32. "Beasts" (*zoushou* 走獸) might be better translated as "quadruped," as Shih has it (*Biographies Des Moines Éminents (Kao Seng Tchouan) de Houei-Kiao*, 109).
33. Huijiao 慧皎, "Biographies of Eminent Monks (Gaoseng Zhuan 高僧傳)," 03337c06–7; Shih, *Biographies Des Moines Éminents (Kao Seng Tchouan) de Houei-Kiao*, 109; Sengyou 僧祐, "Collection of Notes on the Translation of the Tripiṭaka (Chusanzang Jiji 出三藏記集)," 0111c14.
34. According to Buddhist sources, Aśoka was the quintessential Dharmic king of ancient India, who greatly promoted the Buddha's teachings, instituted just laws based on the latter's ethical teachings, sent missionary monks southward and northward from India, and marked many important sites associated with the Buddha's life with pillars and temples visited by Faxian. On *pañcavārṣika*, see: Jinhua Chen, "Pañcavārṣika Assemblies in Liang Wudi's Buddhist Palace Chapel," *Harvard Journal of Asiatic Studies* 66, no. 1 (2006): 43; Max Deeg, "Origins and Development of the Buddhist Pañcavārṣika—Part I: India and Central Asia" (Ph.D. diss., University of Nagoya, 1995); Andrew Chittick, *The Jiankang Empire in Chinese and World History* (Oxford; New York: Oxford University Press, 2020), 306.
35. Huijiao 慧皎, "Biographies of Eminent Monks (Gaoseng Zhuan 高僧傳)," 0337b19. Shih gives *jen* for this unit, not *ren*. He says this Chinese unit is "équivaut à huit pieds" (*Biographies Des Moines Éminents (Kao Seng Tchouan) de Houei-Kiao*, 109 n. 3).
36. As Shih notes (p. 109 n. 4), here Huijiao seems to misrepresent Faxian's *Record*, since the latter wrote of these rocky ascents that he and his companions crossed not "in seven hundred places" (七百餘所) but in one place, with seven hundred steps.
37. Huijiao 慧皎, "Biographies of Eminent Monks (Gaoseng Zhuan 高僧傳)," 03337c10–c13.
38. Huijiao 慧皎, 03337c14–c16.
39. Huijiao used the term "India" (Tianzhu 天竺); Sengyou more precisely calls it "Northern India" (Bei tianzhu 北天竺). Sengyou 僧祐, "Collection of Notes on the Translation of the Tripiṭaka (Chusanzang Jiji 出三藏記集)," 0111c24.
40. Skt. *Gṛdhrakūṭaparvata*; Tib. *Bya rgod phung po'i ri.*

41. "Perfection of Wisdom": Skt. *prajñāpāramitā*; Ch. *bore boluomiduo* 般若波羅蜜多; Tib. *shes rab kyi pha rol tu phyin pa*; Mong. *belge bilig-ünčinadu kiǰaɣar-a kürügsen;šerčin.*
42. For example: the *Lotus Sūtra* (Skt. *Saddharmapuṇḍarīkasūtra*; Ch. *Miaofa lianhua* 妙法蓮華經; Tib. *Dam pa'i chos padma dkar po'i mdo*); the *Heart Sūtra* (Skt. *Prajñāpāramitāhṛdayasūtra*; Ch. *Bore boluomiduo xin jing* 般若波羅蜜多心經; Tib. *Shes rab kyi pha rol tu phyin pa'i sny ing po'i mdo*); the *Diamond Sūtra* (Skt. *Vajracchedikāprajñāpāramitāsūtra*; Ch. *Jingang jing* 金剛經; Tib. *Rdo rje gcod pa shes rab kyi pha rol tu phyin pa'i mdo*); and the *Perfection of Wisdom Sūtras,* in 100,000, 25,000, and 8,000 verses. For helpful introductions in English to the Perfection of Wisdom literature, see: Edward Conze, *The Prajñāpāramitā Literature* (Tokyo: Reiyukai, 1978), 93–120; Ryūshō Hikata, *Suvikrāntavikrāmi-paripṛcchā prajñāpāramitā-sūtra* (Kyoto: Rinsen, 1983); Hajime Nakamura, *Indian Buddhism: A Survey with Bibliographical Notes* (Hirakata: KUFS Publ. Kansai University of Foreign Studies, 1980), 159–65; Donald S. Lopez, *Elaborations on Emptiness: Uses of "The Heart Sutra"* (Princeton, N.J.: Princeton University Press, 1998); Donald S. Lopez and Jacqueline Stone, *Two Buddhas Seated Side by Side: A Guide to the Lotus Sūtra* (Princeton, N.J.: Princeton University Press, 2019); Donald Sewell Lopez, *The Lotus Sūtra: A Biography* (Princeton, N.J.: Princeton University Press, 2016).
43. Abel-Rémusat's junior colleague, Eugène Burnouf, first translated a Perfection fo Wisdom sūtra, the *Lotus Sūtra* (Skt. *Saddharmapuṇḍarīka-sūtra*), into a European language in 1852 (*Le lotus de la bonne loi* [Paris: Imprimerie nationale, 1852]).
44. In Sengyou's version, it is not the abbot but the saṅgha of their host monastery who caution them against leaving for Vulture's Peak.
45. Huijiao 慧皎, "Biographies of Eminent Monks (Gaoseng Zhuan 高僧傳)," 0337c21–c23; Shih, *Biographies Des Moines Éminents (Kao Seng Tchouan) de Houei-Kiao*, 110.
46. Sengyou 僧祐, "Collection of Notes on the Translation of the Tripiṭaka (Chusanzang Jiji 出三藏記集)," 0112a02; Huijiao 慧皎, "Biographies of Eminent Monks (Gaoseng Zhuan 高僧傳)," 0338a01.
47. Huijiao 慧皎, "Biographies of Eminent Monks (Gaoseng Zhuan 高僧傳)," 0338a01–a05.
48. Huijiao 慧皎, 0338a09. Sengyou gives "It was Dhūta, the disciple Mahākāśyapa" 頭陀弟子大迦葉也 ("Collection of Notes on the Translation of the Tripiṭaka [Chusanzang Jiji 出三藏記集]," 0112a11).
49. Huijiao 慧皎, "Biographies of Eminent Monks (Gaoseng Zhuan 高僧傳)," 0338a10–a11; Shih, *Biographies Des Moines Éminents (Kao Seng Tchouan) de Houei-Kiao*, 111.
50. Huijiao 慧皎, "Biographies of Eminent Monks (Gaoseng Zhuan 高僧傳)," 0338a17; Sengyou 僧祐, "Collection of Notes on the Translation of the Tripiṭaka (Chusanzang Jiji 出三藏記集)," 0112a18.
51. It seems that Pātaliputrā is better known in Chinese sources as Huashi cheng 華氏城, but Huijiao gives 波連弗 and Sengyou 巴連弗. Huijiao 慧皎, "Biographies of Eminent Monks (Gaoseng Zhuan 高僧傳)," 0338a17; Shih, *Biographies Des Moines Éminents (Kao Seng Tchouan) de Houei-Kiao*, 112; Sengyou 僧祐, "Collection of Notes on the Translation of the Tripiṭaka (Chusanzang Jiji 出三藏記集)," 0112a19.
52. Skt. *Vaipulyaparinirvāṇa-sūtra*; Ch. *Fangdeng niepan jing* 方等泥洹經. Huijiao 慧皎, "Biographies of Eminent Monks (Gaoseng Zhuan 高僧傳)," 0338a18. Concerning the Sarvāstivāda, Ann Heirman reminds us that Faxian mentions that their vinaya was the primary monastic code used by Chinese monastics at the time, but it existed only orally (Ann Heirman, "Vinaya: From India to China," in *The Spread of Buddhism*, ed. Ann Heirman and Stephan Peter Bumbacher [Leiden: Brill, 2007], 174).

53. For example, the early fourth-century author Dharmatāra's *Saṃyuktābhidharmasāra*, Ch. *Za apitanxinyan jing* 雜阿毘曇心緃經. Huijiao 慧皎, "Biographies of Eminent Monks (Gaoseng Zhuan 高僧傳)," 0338a19; Sengyou 僧祐, "Collection of Notes on the Translation of the Tripiṭaka (Chusanzang Jiji 出三藏記集)," 0112a20–a21.
54. Huijiao 慧皎, "Biographies of Eminent Monks (Gaoseng Zhuan 高僧傳)," 0338a19; Shih, *Biographies Des Moines Éminents (Kao Seng Tchouan) de Houei-Kiao*, 112; Sengyou 僧祐, "Collection of Notes on the Translation of the Tripiṭaka (Chusanzang Jiji 出三藏記集)," 0112a21.
55. Huijiao 慧皎, "Biographies of Eminent Monks (Gaoseng Zhuan 高僧傳)," 0338a20; Sengyou 僧祐, "Collection of Notes on the Translation of the Tripiṭaka (Chusanzang Jiji 出三藏記集)," 0112a21.
56. Shih gives "shadow" for *ying* 影, though I suppose this could also be translated as "reflection" or "image."
57. Shih, *Biographies Des Moines Éminents (Kao Seng Tchouan) de Houei-Kiao*, 112; Huijiao 慧皎, "Biographies of Eminent Monks (Gaoseng Zhuan 高僧傳)," 0338a22–a24; Sengyou 僧祐, "Collection of Notes on the Translation of the Tripiṭaka (Chusanzang Jiji 出三藏記集)," 0112a23–a25.
58. According to Deeg's dating, Faxian may have been a decade younger.
59. Huijiao 慧皎, "Biographies of Eminent Monks (Gaoseng Zhuan 高僧傳)," 0338a24; Sengyou 僧祐, "Collection of Notes on the Translation of the Tripiṭaka (Chusanzang Jiji 出三藏記集)," 0112a25. A more conventional appellation is Huadi bu lü 化地部律 (see Buswell and Lopez, *The Princeton Dictionary of Buddhism*, 516).
60. Zhang ahan 長阿含 (Skt. Dīrgha āgama). For this and the Saṃyukta Āgama, Huijiao gives only 長雜 ("Biographies of Eminent Monks [Gaoseng Zhuan 高僧傳]," 0338a24). Thankfully, Sengyou provides the full text names for at least the two *āgamas* (Sengyou 僧祐, "Collection of Notes on the Translation of the Tripiṭaka (Chusanzang Jiji 出三藏記集)," 0112a25–a26.
61. Za ahan 雜阿含 (Skt. Saṃyukta āgama).
62. Foshuo zazang jing 佛說雜藏經. Huijiao 慧皎, "Biographies of Eminent Monks (Gaoseng Zhuan 高僧傳)," 0338a24–a25; Sengyou 僧祐, "Collection of Notes on the Translation of the Tripiṭaka (Chusanzang Jiji 出三藏記集)," 0112a26.
63. Huijiao 慧皎, "Biographies of Eminent Monks (Gaoseng Zhuan 高僧傳)," 0338a28; Sengyou 僧祐, "Collection of Notes on the Translation of the Tripiṭaka (Chusanzang Jiji 出三藏記集)," 0112a29.
64. Huijiao 慧皎, "Biographies of Eminent Monks (Gaoseng Zhuan 高僧傳)," 0338b02–b03; Sengyou 僧祐, "Collection of Notes on the Translation of the Tripiṭaka (Chusanzang Jiji 出三藏記集)," 0112b05–b06.
65. In contemporary Shandong. Huijiao 慧皎, "Biographies of Eminent Monks (Gaoseng Zhuan 高僧傳)," 0338b13–b14; Sengyou 僧祐, "Collection of Notes on the Translation of the Tripiṭaka (Chusanzang Jiji 出三藏記集)," 0112b13.
66. Many other fragmentary vinayas and texts related to precepts (Skt. *prātimokṣa*) and procedures (*karmavācanās*) were later translated into Chinese, in addition to these four complete vinayas. See, for example: Akira Yayuma, *Systematische Übersicht Über Die Buddhistische Sanskrit-Literatur, Vinaya Texte, Erster Teil* (Wiesbaden: Franz Steiner, 1979); Heirman, "Vinaya: From India to China," 175 n. 50.
67. It is unclear whether Faxian spent this time in Jingkou 京口 or Pengcheng 彭城. Liu, "Stories Written and Rewritten," 5–6.
68. It is unclear whether Faxian spent this time in Jingkou 京口 or Pengcheng 彭城. Liu, "Stories Written and Rewritten," 5–6, 9.

69. For the broader context, influence, and motives bearing upon the composition of the *Record*, quite beyond what I have space to summarize here, see Deeg and Faxian, *Das Gaoseng-Faxian-Zhuan Als Religionsgeschichtliche Quelle: Der Älteste Bericht Eines Chinesischen Buddhistischen Pilgermönchs Über Seine Reise Nach Indien Mit Übersetzung Des Textes*, 35–43.
70. Mohesengqi lü 摩訶僧祇律 (T. 1425) and Mohesengqi biqiuni jieben 摩訶僧祇比丘尼戒本 (T. 1427).
71. Da banniepan jing 大般泥洹經 (T. 0376).
72. Da banniepan jing 大般涅槃經 (T. 0007).
73. Fangdeng nihuan jing 方等泥洹經 (T. 0378).
74. Za'apitanxinyan jing 雜阿毘曇心綖經 (T. 1552).
75. Za zang jing 雜藏經 (T. 0745).
76. Mishasaibu wu fen lü 彌沙塞部和醯五分律 (T. 1421).
77. Za ahan jing 雜阿含經 (T. 0099).
78. Liu, "Stories Written and Rewritten," 13.
79. In this regard, Faxian's *Record* stands quite apart from comparable, contemporaneous descriptions of foreign travel in biographies of monks like Zhu Fawei 竺法維 (fl. 397–439) and Sengbiao 僧表 (fl. 397–439).
80. Huijiao and Sengyou each note obliquely "other than those sūtras and vinayas, the remainder are not yet translated." Indeed, as I mention above, there was no need to translate them; they were already set in Chinese letters by the time Faxian washed ashore.
81. To be specific, Faxian's influence here was a negative one: he and Buddhabhadra's translation of the *Mahāparinirvāṇa Sūtra* ran against certain philosophical propositions of the powerful Chan'an monk Daosheng 道生 (355–434), a disciple of several eminent monk scholars, such as Lushan Huiyuan 盧山慧遠, an early proponent of Pure Land practices and, later, Kumārajīva. Daosheng took issue with Faxian's translation since it included a passage denying buddha nature (and, thus, the possibility of enlightenment) to "incorrigibles" (Skt. *icchantika*; Ch. *yichanti* 一闡提; Tib. *'dod chen*), a class of sentient beings beholden to desire who deny the fundamental causal laws of karma and hence, possess no ethical or soteriological impulse. A newer Chinese translation of the *Mahāparinirvāṇa Sūtra* appeared in Chang'an just four years after Faxian's which omitted this passage and thus confirmed Daosheng's powerful position on buddha nature and much of the later Nirvāṇa exegetical school.
82. Huijiao 慧皎, "Biographies of Eminent Monks (Gaoseng Zhuan 高僧傳)," 0338b18; Sengyou 僧祐, "Collection of Notes on the Translation of the Tripiṭaka (Chusanzang Jiji 出三藏記集)," 0112b21.
83. Liu, "Stories Written and Rewritten," 15–16.
84. Faxian was born in 337, and so he died at eighty-six (not eighty-five) by Chinese reckoning, which includes the "year" in the womb.
85. For an interesting study on this very topic, unfortunately beyond the scope of the present chapter to explore, see Haiyan Hu-von Hüber, "Faxian's (法顯 342–423) Perception of India—Some New Interpretations of His Foguoji 佛國記," in *Annual Report of The International Research Institute for Advanced Buddhology at Soka University for the Academic Year 2010 XI*, 2011, 223–47.
86. Antonino Forte, "Hui-Chih (Fl. 676–703 A.D.), a Brahmin Born in China,"*Annali Dell'Istituto Orientale Di Napoli* 45 (1985): 105–34; Janine Nicol, "Outsiders: Medieval Chinese Buddhists and the 'Borderland Complex': An Exploration of the Eight Difficulties,"*The SOAS Jounral of Postgraduate Research* 6 (2014): 27.
87. Deeg, "Chinese Buddhists in Search of Authenticity in the Dharma," 14.
88. Deeg, 19.

2. Beijing to Paris

1. Mark C. Elliott, "Abel-Rémusat, La Langue Mandchoue et La Sinologie,"*Comptes Rendus Des Séances de l'AIBL* 2 (2014): 973–93.
2. Pierre-Augustin Guys, *Marseille ancienne et moderne, par M. Guys*, 1786, 91. Referenced in: Une société de gens de lettres et de savants, *Biographies Des Hommes Vivants, Ou Histoire Par Ordre Alphabétique de La View Publique de Tous Les Hommes Qui Se Sont Fait Remarquer Par Leurs Actions Ou Leurs Écrits*, vol. 5 (Paris: L. G. Michaud, 1819), 172.
3. Antoine-Isaac Silvestre de Sacy, "Notice historique sur la vie et les ouvrages de M. Abel Rémusat,"*Mémoires de l'Institut national de France* 12, no. 1 (1839): 377.
4. Sacy, 377.
5. The Quai des Tuileries, next to the Jardin des Tuileries, runs between the Louvre and the Place de la Concorde.
6. Ernest-Augustin Clerc de Landresse, "Notice Sur La Vie et Les Travaux de M. Abel-Rémusat, Lue à La Séance Générale Annuelle de La Société Asiatique, Le 28 Avril 1834,"*Journal Asiatique* 14, no. 2 (1834): 207.
7. Landresse, 209.
8. Sacy, "Notice historique sur la vie et les ouvrages de M. Abel Rémusat," 377.
9. Landresse, "Notice Sur La Vie et Les Travaux de M. Abel-Rémusat, Lue à La Séance Générale Annuelle de La Société Asiatique, Le 28 Avril 1834," 207, 210.
10. Landresse, 211.
11. Landresse, 211.
12. Landresse, 214.
13. Landresse, 213.
14. For a useful survey of Silvestre de Sacy's contributions to systematizing Orientalist disciplinary knowledge during this complex moment in French intellectual life, see Michel Espagne, Nora Lafi, and Pascale Rabault-Feuerhahn, *Silvestre de Sacy: le projet européen d'une science orientaliste* (Paris: Éditions du Cerf, 2014). Silvestre de Sacy was also a major object of Edward Said's *Orientalism* (New York: Vintage, 1979), 76; Alexander Lyon Macfie, *Orientalism* (Oxford; New York: Routledge, 2014), 31–36, 62.
15. For a useful survey, see Desmond Hosford and Chong J. Wojtkowski, *French Orientalism: Culture, Politics, and the Imagined Other* (Cambridge; New York: Cambridge Scholars Publishing, 2010).
16. Matthew W. Mosca, "Comprehending the Qing Empire: Building Multilingual Competence in an Age of Imperial Rivalry, 1792–1820,"*The International History Review* 41, no. 5 (2019): 1057.
17. Mosca, 1057.
18. Two seminal works in Egyptology produced in this constellation of invasion and research were Dominique-Vivant's 1802 *Voyage dans la Basse et la Haute Egypte Pendant les Campagnes du Général Bonaporte* and the French Commission on the Sciences and Arts's twenty-four-volume *Déscription de l'Egypte* (1809–29). For criticism of Said's claim that Napoleon's invasion of Egypt was inextricable from the growth of Orientalism see: Daniel Martin Varisco, *Reading Orientalism Said and the Unsaid: With a New Preface by the Author* (Seattle: University of Washington Press, 2017), 123–26.
19. Said, 76.
20. Anyone researching the quickly expanding fields of science in turn-of-the-nineteenth-century Paris—whether paleontology (a word coined in Paris in 1822), ancient Egyptian

astronomy, or comparative anatomy—will frequently encounter references to "L'Abbé de Tersan" and his curiosity cabinet. For a survey of the life of the Abbé Campion de Tersan, see Françoise Arquié-Bruley, "L'omnisicient Abbé de Tersan (Charles-Philippe Campion de Tersan, 1737–1819),"*Bulletin de Société Nationale Des Antiquaires de France*, 2002, 114–34.

21. Landresse, "Notice Sur La Vie et Les Travaux de M. Abel-Rémusat, Lue à La Séance Générale Annuelle de La Société Asiatique, Le 28 Avril 1834," 217–18.
22. Jean-François Champollion (1790–1832), Abel-Rémusat's contemporary and another prodigy of Silvestre de Sacy, is a well-known example. Like Jean-Pierre, Champollion was first brought to the abbé's collection and then went on to decipher the Rosetta Stone and render Egyptian hieroglyphics legible to European readers (Une société de gens de lettres et de savants, *Biographie Universelle, Ancienne et Moderne*, vol. 66 [Paris: L. G. Michaud, 1839], 6 (CHA). Champollion's decipherment was not without controversy, involving characters we will meet below, including Alexandre and Wilhelm von Humboldt and one of Abel-Rémusat's colleagues who saw his Faxian study to print, Julius von Klaproth. See Jean-François Champollion, *Précis du système hiéroglyphique des anciens Egyptiens* (Paris: Treuttel et Würtz, 1824); Jean Lacouture, *Champollion: une vie de lumières* (Paris: Grasset, 1988); Hermine Hartleben, *Champollion: sein Leben und sein Werk* (Berlin: Weidmann, 1906).
23. Three decades later, Silvestre de Sacy memorialized the epochal transition represented by this gift in much loftier terms: "It is most often, gentlemen, a fortuitous circumstance which leads a man of genius to the most important discoveries in the study of nature . . . It is also, for most men who hold high rank in letters, a kind of chance that reveals to them the secret of the career in which they must distinguish themselves" ("Notice historique sur la vie et les ouvrages de M. Abel Rémusat," 379).
24. Sacy, "Notice historique sur la vie et les ouvrages de M. Abel Rémusat."
25. David B. Honey, *Incense at the Altar: Pioneering Sinologists and the Development of Classical Chinese Philology* (New Haven, Conn.: American Oriental Society, 2001), 25.
26. Dominique Da Fano and Michel Ange Andre Le Roux Deshauterayes, *Vocabulaire thibetan-latin*, 1773; Michel Ange Andre Le Roux Deshauterayes, *Doutes sur la dissertation de M de Guignes, qui a pour titre, Mémoire dans lequel on prouve, que les chinois sont une colonie égyptienne* (Paris: Praulx, Duchesne, 1759); Michel Ange Andre Le Roux Deshauterayes, *Doutes sur la dissertation de M de Guignes, qui a pour titre, Mémoire dans lequel on prouve, que les chinois sont une colonie égyptienne* (Paris: Praulx, Duchesne, 1759); Michel Ange Andre Le Roux Deshauterayes, "Alphabet Des Tartare Mouantcheoux," in *Recueil de Planches Sur Les Sciences, Les Arts Libéraux, et Les Arts Méchaniques Avec Leur Explication. Seconde Livraison, En Deux Parties. Troisieme Édition*, ed. Denis Diderot, 2 vols. (Livourne: L'imprimerie des éditeurs, 1772), 1:122, plate XXIII; Michel Ange Andre Le Roux Deshauterayes, *Histoire général de la chine: ou annales de cet empire* (Paris: Clousier, 1783). For a short summary, see "Une société de gens de lettres et de savants,"*Biographie Universelle, Ancienne et Moderne*, 66:158–59.
27. On Fourmont, see: Henri Cordier, *Notes Pour Servir à l'histoire Des Études Chinoises En Europe, Jusqu'à l'époque de Fourmont l'aîné* (Leiden: Brill, 1895); Cécile Leung, *Etienne Fourmont (1683–1745): Oriental and Chinese Languages in Eighteenth-Century France* (Leuven: Leuven University Press, 2002); Urs App, "Fourmont's Dirty Little Secret," in *The Birth of Orientalism* (Philadelphia: University of Pennsylvania Press, 2010), 191–97; and "Learned Laity" in David B. Honey and American Oriental Society, *Incense at the Altar: Pioneering Sinologists and the Development of Classical Chinese Philology* (New Haven, Conn.: American Oriental Society, 2001).

28. For a summary of Arcadio Hoang's life and afterlife in the context of Chinese scholarship in France during the eighteenth century, see: Danielle Elisseeff, *Moi Arcade: interprète chinois du Roi-Soleil* (Paris: Arthaud, 1985).
29. See: Elisseeff, *Moi, Arcade*; Jonathan D. Spence, "The Paris Years of Arcadio Huang," in *Chinese Roundabout: Essays in History and Culture* (New York: Norton, 1993), 11–24.
30. Arcadio Hoang was preceded in Paris by Michael Alphonsius (Shen Fuzong 沈福宗, 1657–1691), a Christian convert from Nanjing who arrived, via Portuguese Macao, to the court of Louis XIV in 1684. He lectured on Chinese customs and demonstrated Chinese character writing to French high society before leaving for England, where he met King James II and, at Oxford, Thomas Hyde in 1685 (D. E. Mungello, *Curious Land: Jesuit Accommodation and the Origins of Sinology* [Honolulu: University of Hawai'i Press, 1988], 255).
31. An organizational structure for dictionaries and other reference works, based on a standardized list of 214 Chinese characters organized by radical and stroke number. Though invented prior to the Qing period, the system was implemented under the Kangxi emperor.
32. Leung, *Etienne Fourmont (1683–1745)*, 146–49. Fourmont's paltry dictionary was eclipsed in rigor and influence by the *Notitia linguae sinicae* of the French Jesuit Joseph Henri-Marie de Prémare (1666–1736), completed in 1700 but not published until 1831. In addition to some other technical pieces on Chinese grammar, Prémare published a very popular 1735 French translation of the Yuan drama *Zhao shi gu er* (趙氏孤兒), or *Orphan of Zhao* (Harriet Thelma Zurndorfer, *China Bibliography: A Research Guide to Reference Works About China Past and Present* [Leiden: Brill, 1995], 9, no. 18). This work not only was quickly translated from French into English, German, and Dutch, but also came to influence new dramatical and literary forms across Europe, including a 1753 work by Voltaire (*L'Orphelin de la Chine*) and a 1756 work by the Irish playwright Arthur Murphy (*Orphan of China*) (Adrian Hsia, "'The Orphan of the House of Zhao' in French, English, German, and Hong Kong Literature," *Comparative Literature Studies* 25, no. 4 [1988]: 335–51).
33. Jean-Pierre Abel-Rémusat, *Mélanges Asiatiques, Ou Choix de Morceaux de Critique et de Mémoires Relatifs Aux Religions, Aux Sciences, Aux Coutumes, à l'Histoire et à La Géographie Des Nations Orientales* (Paris: Librarie Orientale de Dondey-Dupré Père et Fils, 1826), 2:109. For a biography of Fourmont by Abel-Rémusat that includes a detailed exposition of the former's duplicity, see Jean-Pierre Abel-Rémusat, "Étienne Fourmont: Savant Français," in *Nouveaux Mélanges Asiatiques, Ou Recueil de Morceaux de Critique et de Mémoires*, 2 :291–304.
34. The result of Deguignes's effort was published in 1813, entitled *Dictionnaire Chinois, Francoise, et Latin, publie d'apres l'ordre de Sa Majeste l'empereur et roi Napoleon le Grand.* Abel-Rémusat did not even once, to my knowledge, deign to open this dictionary or reference its contents in any of his published works over the next twenty years. See Isabelle Landry-Deron, "Le Dictionnaire Chinois, Français et Latin de 1813," *T'oung Pao* 101, 4-5 (2015): 407–40.
35. Jean-Pierre Abel-Rémusat, *Essai sur la langue et la littérature chinoises: avec cinq planches, contenant des textes chinois, accompagnés de traductions, de remarques et d'un commentaire littéraire et grammatical, suivi de notes et d'une table alphabétique des mots chinois.* (Paris: Treuttel et Wurtz, 1811), viii–ix. As he recalled bitterly in a report to the *Journal Asiatique* in 1824: "Those who first approached this field of study kept everything to themselves because they possessed so little" ("Lettre Au Rédacteur Du Journal Asiatique, Sur l'état et Les Progrès de La Littérature Chinoise En Europe," *Journal Asiatique* 1, no. 1 [1822]: 26).
36. Zurndorfer, *China Bibliography*, 8.

37. *Catalogue Des Livres, Imprimés et Manuscrits, Composant La Bibliothèque de Feu M. Abel-Rémusat* (Paris, n.d.), p. ex. nos. 1584, 1596, 1606, 1608, 1615, 1616, 1617, 1618, 1619, 1620, 1621, 1623, 1624, 1633, etc.
38. Sheldon I. Pollock, Benjamin A. Elman, and Ku-ming K. Chang, eds., *World Philology* (Cambridge, Mass.: Harvard University Press, 2015).
39. Saarela Mårten Söderblom, *The Early Modern Travels of Manchu: A Script and Its Study in East Asia and Europe* (Philadelphia: University of Pennsylvania Press, 2020).
40. For an exploration of this broader trend toward polylingual fluency in Europe in relation to the Qing, see Matthew W. Mosca, "Comprehending the Qing Empire: Building Multilingual Competence in an Age of Imperial Rivalry, 1792–1820," *The International History Review* 41, no. 5 (2019): 1057–75.
41. Abel-Rémusat, *Essai sur la langue et la littérature chinoises*, ix.
42. Landresse, "Notice Sur La Vie et Les Travaux de M. Abel-Rémusat, Lue à La Séance Générale Annuelle de La Société Asiatique, Le 28 Avril 1834," 304.
43. Landresse, 304.
44. Beginning with the 1811 *Essai* and then in the 1813 Latin study (Jean-Pierre Abel-Rémusat, "Utrum Lingua Sinica Sit Vere Monosyllabica,"*Fundgraben Des Orients* 3 [1813]: 279–88). Abel-Rémusat proved: "the Chinese language cannot be qualified as monosyllabic, since in fact it combines several syllables to express the same word. This leads him to show us how the written language, rich in expressions and formed according to learned principles, came to the aid of the spoken language, so poor, so imperfect" (Landresse, "Notice Sur La Vie et Les Travaux de M. Abel-Rémusat, Lue à La Séance Générale Annuelle de La Société Asiatique, Le 28 Avril 1834," 311). The issue most explicitly addressed was the old European presumption that Chinese was monosyllabic. This idea had been weaponized by generations of Orientalist scholars to other and diminish not simply the literary but also the intellectual heritage of China and continued, despite Abel-Rémusat's pioneering work, well into the twentieth century (George A. Kennedy, "The Monosyllabic Myth," *Journal of the American Oriental Society* 71, no. 3 [1951]: 165; Honey, *Incense at the Altar*, 26).
45. In 1813, Abel-Rémusat completed his medical training and produced a short dissertation in Latin on Chinese methods of diagnosing disease using tongue scrutiny, based on the *materia medica* gifted by the abbé. It was published separately in 1816 as *Recherches historiques sur la médecine des Chinois.*
46. To see the difference in rigor, we can compare Abel-Rémusat's work in the original Chinese of the *materia medica* to a parallel thesis on Chinese medicine completed at the same time. This is François-Albin Lepage's *Recherches Historiques Sur La Médecine Des Chinois*, a thesis defended at the Faculté de Médecine in Paris in August 1813 (François-Albin Lepage, *Recherches Historiques Sur La Médecine Des Chinois; Thèse Présentée et Soutenue à La Faculté de Médecine de Paris, Le 31 Aout 1813* [Paris: Didot jeune, Imprimeur de la Faculté de Médecine, 1813]). We see a microcosm of the stark methodological departure of Abel-Rémusat, who worked laboriously in primary source and text criticism, from the fray of eighteenth-century French scholarship very much reproduced in Lepage's study. For example, the latter first approaches the study of Chinese medicine by reference to existing European studies about Persian and Indian medicine; the Orient is here without particularity in form or scholarly approach. Neither does Lepage include any sustained study of an actual Chinese medical text. In his sources and method, he relies only on comparing the impressions of travelers to the Orient, such as those of Chardin in Persia and Sonnerat in East India, or

else such works as Kaempfer's *Amaenitates exotica*. Lepage's study is in three parts: an "exposition" of Chinese medical doctrine and practice; therapeutic practices and *materia medica*; and finally, general observations about the lifestyle and climate of the Chinese in relation to the maladies from which they most suffer.

47. Sacy, "Notice historique sur la vie et les ouvrages de M. Abel Rémusat," 382; Abel-Rémusat, *Essai sur la langue et la littérature chinoises*, x.
48. Abel-Rémusat, *Essai sur la langue et la littérature chinoises*, i.
49. Abel-Rémusat, *Essai sur la langue et la littérature chinoises*, i. An example is the *Zhengzitong* (正字通), a Chinese dictionary Abel-Rémusat made abundant use of in these early years. Originally published in 1627 by Zhang Zilie (張自烈) as the *Zihui bian* (字彙辯), this dictionary was written as a supplement to the Ming-era *Zihui* (字彙). It was later purchased, retitled *Zhengzitong*, and republished by the Qing scholar Liao Wenying (廖文英) in 1671. This work became a major reference for the dictionary compiled and published on the order of emperor Kangxi in 1710, the *Kangxi Zidian* (康熙字典), the largest of all character dictionaries. Kangxi's *Zhengzitong* provided much of the structure for Abel-Rémusat's momentous *Essai*, such as the *fanqie* method for indicating pronunciation of a monosyllabic character by using two other characters, alternative graphs using character headwords, and citations from classical texts. See Renaud Gagné, Simon Goldhill, and Geoffrey Lloyd, eds., *Regimes of Comparatism: Comparatism: Frameworks of Comparison in History, Religion and Anthropology* (Leiden; Boston: Brill, 2018), 211ff.
50. Une société de gens de lettres et de savants, *Biographies Des Hommes Vivants, Ou Histoire Par Ordre Alphabétique de La View Publique de Tous Les Hommes Qui Se Sont Fait Remarquer Par Leurs Actions Ou Leurs Écrits*, 5:173.
51. Sacy, "Notice historique sur la vie et les ouvrages de M. Abel Rémusat," 381.
52. Denis Thouard, "Humboldt, Abel-Rémusat et Le Chinois: La Recherche de La Correspondence," in *Lettres Édifiantes et Curieuses Sur La Langue Chinoise: Un Débat Philosophico-Grammatical Entre Wilhelm von Humboldt et Jean-Pierre Abel-Rémusat (1821–1831)*, ed. Jean Rousseau and Denis Thouard (Villeneuve-d'Ascq: Presses universitaires du Septentrion, 1999), 14.
53. Honey, *Incense at the Altar*, 18.
54. Une société de gens de lettres et de savants, *Biographies Des Hommes Vivants, Ou Histoire Par Ordre Alphabétique de La View Publique de Tous Les Hommes Qui Se Sont Fait Remarquer Par Leurs Actions Ou Leurs Écrits*, 5:173.
55. Ernest Augustin Xavier Clerc de Landresse and Jean-Pierre Abel-Rémusat, "Introduction," in *Foĕ Kouĕ Ki, Ou, Relation Des Royaumes Bouddhiques: Voyage Dans La Tartarie, Dans l'Afghanistan et Dans l'Inde, Exécuté à La Fin Du IVe Siècle* (Paris: Imprimerie Royale, 1836), xvi.
56. A version of this inaugural lecture was published in 1826 in Abel-Rémusat's *Mélanges Asiatiques*, volume 2. "Review of the Mélanges Asiatique, Ou Choix de Morçeaux de Critique et de Mémoirs Relatifs Aux Religions, Aux Sciences, Aux Coutumes, à l'Histoire et à La Géographie Des Nations Orientales. Par M. Abel Rémusat. Tom. II. Paris, 1826. 8vo. Pp. 428,"*Asiatic Society* 22 (1826): 191.
57. Jean-Pierre Abel-Rémusat, "Discours à l'ouverture Du Cours de Langue et Littérature Chinoises, Au Collège Royal, Le 16 Janvier, Sur l'origine, Les Progrès et l'utilité de l'étude Du Chinois En Europe," in *Mélanges Asiatiques, Ou Choix Morceaux de Critique et de Mémoirs Relatifs Aux Religions, Aux Sciences, Aux Coutumes, a l'histoire et a La Géographie Des Nations Orientales* (Paris: Librarie Orientale de Dondey-Dupré Père et Fils, 1826), 2:2–3.
58. Zurndorfer, *China Bibliography*, 13.

59. Jean-Pierre Abel-Rémusat, *Mélanges Asiatiques, Ou Choix de Morceaux de Critique et de Mémoires Relatifs Aux Religions, Aux Sciences, Aux Coutumes, à l'Histoire et à La Géographie Des Nations Orientales* (Paris: Librarie Orientale de Dondey-Dupré Père et Fils, 1825), 1:6.
60. Edward W. Said, *Orientalism* (New York: Vintage, 1979), 124.
61. Sacy, "Notice historique sur la vie et les ouvrages de M. Abel Rémusat," 386.
62. For example: Jean-Pierre Abel-Rémusat, *Observations Sur Histoire Des Mongols Orientaux de Ssanang-Ssetsen* (Paris: Imprimerie Royale, 1832); Abel-Rémusat, "Uranographia Mongolica Sive Nomenclatura Siderum, Quae Ab Astronomis Mongolis Agnoscuntur et Describuntur," *Les Mines de l'Orient* 3 (1811); Abel-Rémusat, *Observations Sur Histoire Des Mongols Orientaux de Ssanang-Ssetsen*; Abel-Rémusat, *Mémoires Sur Les Relations Politiques Des Princes Chrétiens, et Particulièrement Des Rois de France Avec Les Premiers Empereurs Mongols* (Paris: Imprimerie Nationale, 1824); Jean-Pierre Abel-Rémusat, "Aperçu d'un Mémoire Intitulé: Recherches Chronologiques Sur l'origine de La Hiérarchie Lamaique," *Journal Asiatique* 4 (1824): 257–74.
63. For example, Abel-Rémusat, *Recherche Sur Les Langues Tartares, Ou Mémoires Sur Différens Points de La Grammaire et de La Littérature Des Mandchous, Des Mongols, Des Ouigours et Des Tibetains.*
64. Abel Rémusat, *De l'Étude des Langues Étrangères che les Chinois* (Paris: Extrait du Magasin Encyclopédique, 1811).
65. Sacy, "Notice historique sur la vie et les ouvrages de M. Abel Rémusat," 384.
66. Elliott, "Abel-Rémusat, La Langue Mandchoue et La Sinologie." On "inter-Asia," see Ho, "Inter-Asian Concepts for Mobile Societies," *The Journal of Asian Studies* 76, no. 4 (2017): 907–28.
67. Landresse and Abel-Rémusat, "Introduction," 4.
68. Dorinda Outram, *The Enlightenment* (Cambridge: Cambridge University Press, 1995), 48–49.
69. Jacquet, "Examen de La Traduction Du Fo Koue Ki, Ouvrage Posthume de M. Abel-Rémusat, Complété Par MM.J. Klaproth et C. Landresse," 142. On elements of Jacquet's fascinating work, see Jérôme Petit, "Eugène Jacquet and His Pioneering Study of Indian Numerical Notations," *Ganita Bharati: Journal of the Indian Society for History of Mathematics* 31, no. 1–2 (2009): 23–33.
70. "Sur l'origine, les progrès et l'utilité de l'étude du chinois en Europe, Discours à l'ouverture du cours de langue et littérature chinoises, au Collège royal, le 16 janvier, 1815." Sacy, "Notice historique sur la vie et les ouvrages de M. Abel Rémusat," 383.
71. For a useful survey, see Philip C. Almond, *The British Discovery of Buddhism* (Cambridge: Cambridge University Press, 2007); Donald S. Lopez, *The Scientific Buddha: His Short and Happy Life* (New Haven, Conn.: Yale University Press, 2012); Donald S. Lopez, *Strange Tales of an Oriental Idol: An Anthology of Early European Portrayals of the Buddha* (Chicago: University of Chicago Press, 2016); Lopez, *Curators of the Buddha: The Study of BuddhismUnder Colonialism* (Chicago: University of Chicago Press, 1995), Robert H. Sharf, "Buddhist Modernism and the Rhetoric of Meditative Experience,"*Numen* 42, no. 3 (1995): 228–83; Gregory Schopen, "Archaeology and Protestant Presuppositions in the Study of Indian Buddhism,"*History of Religions* 31, no. 1 (1991): 1–23.
72. Michel Ange Andre Le Roux Deshauterayes, "Recherches Sur La Religion de Fo, Professée Par Le Bonzes Ho-Chang de La Chine,"*Journal Asiatique* I, no. VII (1825): 150–51. Translation from Martino Dibeltulo Concu, "Buddhism, Philosophy, History. On Eugène Burnouf's Simple Sūtras," *Journal of Indian Philosophy* 45, no. 3 (2017): 4.
73. Landresse and Abel-Rémusat, "Introduction," v–vi.
74. In the opinion of his colleagues, Abel-Rémusat's work centered instead on "a rational set of ideas opposed almost in every way to the systematic *nihilism* that we had recognized at first" (Landresse and Abel-Rémusat, "Introduction," iv–v).

75. Urs App, "Schopenhauer and the Orient," in *The Oxford Handbook of Schopenhauer* (New York; Oxford: Oxford University Press, 2020), 88–107; Urs App, *Richard Wagner and Buddhism* (Rorschach, Kyoto: UniversityMedia, 2011); Roger-Pol Droit, *The Cult of Nothingness: The Philosophers and the Buddha*, trans. David Streight and Pamela Vohnson (Chapel Hill; London: University of North Carolina Press, 2003); Freny Mistry, *Nietzsche and Buddhism* (Berlin; New York: Walter de Gruyter, 1981); Benjamin A Elman, "Nietzsche and Buddhism," *Journal of the History of Ideas* 44, no. 4 (n.d.): 671–86; Antoine Panaïoti, *Nietzsche and Buddhist Philosophy* (Cambridge: Cambridge University Press, 2013); Martino Dibeltulo Concu, "Buddhism, Philosophy, History. On Eugène Burnouf's Simple Sūtras,"*Journal of Indian Philosophy* 45, no. 3 (2017): 473–511.
76. Jean-Pierre Abel-Rémusat, "Sur L'Asie Polyglotte de M. Klaproth," in *Mélanges Asiatiques*, 2 vols. (Paris: Librairie orientale de Dondey-Dupré, n.d.), 1:267–309.
77. Abel-Rémusat, "Sur L'Asie Polyglotte de M. Klaproth," 1:267. At the turn of the 18th century, Leibniz was also deeply curious about Qing imperial dictionary and encyclopdia projects, much like the ones that Abel-Rémusat would find so useful a century later. For a fascinating account, see : Söderblom, Saarela Mårten. *The Early Modern Travels of Manchu: A Script and Its Study in East Asia and Europe*. Philadelphia: University of Pennsylvania Press, 2020, 121-144.
78. Abel-Rémusat, "Sur L'Asie Polyglotte de M. Klaproth," 1:267.
79. Abel-Rémusat, "Sur L'Asie Polyglotte de M. Klaproth," 1:267.
80. Abel-Rémusat, "Sur L'Asie Polyglotte de M. Klaproth," 1:267.
81. Abel-Rémusat, "Sur L'Asie Polyglotte de M. Klaproth," 1:267.
82. I am very grateful to my colleague Prof. Adam Harmer for helping me understand what of Leibniz's work Abel-Rémusat may have been specifically reading and referencing. It seems most likely to have been ideas explored in paragraphs 60–61 of the *Monadology* (1714), for example, or such works as *A Specimen of the Universal Calculus* (1679–86?). See Gottfried Wilhelm Leibniz, "The Principles of Philosophy, or, the Monadology," in *G.W. Leibniz: Philosphical Essays*, ed. Roger Ariew and Daniel Garber (Indianapolis and Cambridge: Hackett, 1989), 213–25; Gottfried Wilhelm Leibniz, "A Specimen of the Universal Calculus," in *Leibniz: Logical Papers: A Selection Translated and Edited with an Introduction*, ed. George Henry Radcliffe Parkinson (Oxford: Oxford Univeristy Press, 1966), 33–39.
83. Jean-Pierre Abel-Rémusat, "Ouvrage Sur Le Bouddhisme,"*Journal Asiatique* 7 (1831): xxxv–xxxvi.
84. Abel-Rémusat, "Ouvrage Sur Le Bouddhisme," xxxv–xxxvi.
85. Roger-Pol Droit, *The Cult of Nothingness: The Philosophers and the Buddha*, trans. David Streight and Pamela Vohnson (Chapel Hill; London: University of North Carolina Press, 2003), 29.
86. George Stanley Faber, *The Origin of Pagan Idolatry Ascertained from Historical Testimony and Circumstantial Evidence . . . Three Volumes . . .* (London: A. J. Valpy, 1816), 1:131.
87. Michel Jean François Ozeray, *Recherches sur Buddou ou Bouddou: instituteur religieux de l'Asie orientale: précédées de considérations générales sur les premiers hommages rendus au Créateur: sur la corruption de la religion, l'établissement des cultes du soleil, de la lune, des planètes, du ciel, de la terre, des montagnes, des eaux, des forêts, des hommes et des animaux* (Paris: Chez Brunot-Labbe, 1817).
88. Jean-Pierre Abel-Rémusat, "Note Sur Quelques Épithètes Descriptives Du Bouddha,"*Journal Des Savants*, 1819, 625.
89. See Camille de Rochemonteix, *Joseph Amiot et les derniers survivants de la mission française à Pekin (1750–1795)* (Paris: A. Picard et fils., 1915). Amiot was also a musical mediator,

performing European music for the Qing court and sending dispatches of studies and instruments from the court to rapt audiences in Europe. See Joseph Marie Amiot and Pierre-Joseph Roussier, *Mémoire sur la musique des Chinois: tant anciens que modernes* (Paris: Nyon l'ainé, 1779). For an example of his work to share Qing literature in France—a translation of Qianlong's eulogy to Mukden owned by Abel-Rémusat—see Joseph-Marie Amiot et al., *Éloge de la ville de Moukden et de ses environs; poeme composé par Kien-Long, empereur de la Chine & de la Tartarie, actuellement régnant. Accompagné de notes curieuses sur la géographie, sur l'histoire naturelle de la Tartarie orientale, & sur les anciens usages des Chinois; composées par les editeurs chinois & tartares. On y a joint une piece de vers sur le thé, composé par le même empereur. Traduit en françois par le P. Amiot, missionnaire à Péking; et publié par M. Deguignes.* (A Paris, chez N. M. Tilliard, libraire, quai des Augustins, à S. Benoît. M. DCC. LXX, 1770).

90. Jean-Pierre Abel-Rémusat, "Sur Un Vocabulaire Philosophique En Cinq Langues, Imprimé a Peking," in *Mélanges Asiatiques*, 1:154.
91. Abel-Rémusat, "Sur Un Vocabulaire Philosophique En Cinq Langues, Imprimé a Peking," 1:154.
92. Abel-Rémusat, "Sur Un Vocabulaire Philosophique En Cinq Langues, Imprimé a Peking," 1:157. See also Jean-Pierre Abel-Rémusat, "Note Sur La Partie Samskrits Du Vocabulaire Philosophique En Cinq Langues," in *Mélanges Asiatiques*,1:452–54.
93. Abel-Rémusat, "Sur Un Vocabulaire Philosophique En Cinq Langues, Imprimé a Peking," 1:158.
94. Jean-Pierre Abel-Rémusat, "Sur Quelques Épithètes Descriptives de Bouddha, Qui Font Voir Que Bouddha n'appartenait Pas a La Race Nègre," in *Mélanges Asiatiques*,1:110.
95. Lopez, *Strange Tales of an Oriental Idol*, 225. In another work, *From Stone to Flesh*, Lopez provides a translation of a few paragraphs from *Relations des Royaumes Bouddhique*, stating in a short introductory note that reproduces the above quote that "Until 1844 [the publication date of Burnouf's *Introduction à l'Histoire de Bouddhisme Indien*], the *Foe koue ki* was the most detailed study of Buddhism to be produced in Europe" (180).
96. Max Deeg and Faxian, *Das Gaoseng-Faxian-Zhuan Als Religionsgeschichtliche Quelle: Der Älteste Bericht Eines Chinesischen Buddhistischen Pilgermönchs Über Seine Reise Nach Indien Mit Übersetzung Des Textes* (Wiesbaden, Germany: Harrassowitz, 2005), 18.
97. Fr. *Khian-loung*. Emperor Qianlong 乾隆 ruled from 1735 to 1796 .
98. Abel-Rémusat, "Mémoire Sur Un Voyage Dans l'Asie Centrale, Dans Le Pays Des Afghans et Des Beloutches, et Dans l'Inde, Exécuté à La Fin Du IVe Siècle de Notre Ère Par Plusieurs Samanéens de La Chine," 346.
99. Abel-Rémusat, 346. This version of the *Foguo ji*, he says, came in forty-four pages and was compiled in the tenth volume of the collection. The citation provided in this 1838 version of Abel-Rémusat's lecture is "*Tsin taï pi choou*, Catal. De Fourmont, n° CCCIV."
100. This same collection is still available in Paris, now in the holdings of the Bibliothèque Nationale de France and catalogued as a late Ming-era collection published between 1628 and 1643 under the auspices of Mao Jin (毛晉, 1599–1659). The *Record* that Abel-Rémusat consulted is found in volume 17 of that collection. See Mao Jin (毛晉), *Jin Dai Mi Shu/(Ming) Mao Jin Jiao Kan*;津逮秘書/毛晉校刊; *Tsin Tai Pi Chou/Mao Tsin Kiao k'an*, 25 vols. (汲古閣刊本, 1628). FRBNF44591130.
101. Faxian and Jean-Pierre Abel-Rémusat, *Foĕ Kouĕ Ki, Ou, Relation Des Royaumes Bouddhiques: Voyage Dans La Tartarie, Dans l'Afghanistan et Dans l'Inde, Exécuté à La Fin Du IVe Siècle*, ed. Julius von

Klaproth and Ernest Augustin Xavier Clerc de Landresse (Paris: Imprimerie Royale, 1836), 110–11 n. 26.

102. I.e., Mao Jin 毛晉 (1599–1659) and Hu Zhenheng 胡震亨.
103. Abel-Rémusat, "Mémoire Sur Un Voyage Dans l'Asie Centrale, Dans Le Pays Des Afghans et Des Beloutches, et Dans l'Inde, Exécuté à La Fin Du IVe Siècle de Notre Ère Par Plusieurs Samanéens de La Chine," 347.
104. Abel-Rémusat, "Mémoire Sur Un Voyage Dans l'Asie Centrale, Dans Le Pays Des Afghans et Des Beloutches, et Dans l'Inde, Exécuté à La Fin Du IVe Siècle de Notre Ère Par Plusieurs Samanéens de La Chine," 349–50.
105. Landresse and Abel-Rémusat, "Introduction," lii.
106. "Société Asiatique (Séance Du 7 Février 1831),"*Journal Asiatique* 7 (1831): 239.
107. "Société Asiatique (Séance Du 7 Février 1831)," 240.
108. *Catalogue Des Livres, Composant La Bibliothèque de Feu M. J.P. Abel-Rémusat, Professeur de Langue et de Littérature Chinoise et Tartare Mandchoue Au Collége Royal de France, Membre de l'Académie Des Inscriptions et Belles-Lettres, Président de La Société Asiatique de Paris, Etc. Dont La Vente Se Fera, Le Lundi, 27 Mai 1833 et Jours Suivans, 6 Heures de Relevé, Maison Silvestre, Rue Des Bons-Enfans, n. 30* (Paris: Imprimerie de Mme. Huzard [Née Vallat la Chapelle], rue de l'Éperon, n. 7, 1833).
109. David Jasper, "The Translation of China in England: Two 19th-Century English Translations of the Travels of Fa-Hsien (399–414 A.D.),"*Literature & Theology* 28, no. 2 (2014): 190.
110. "To introduce in the notes which belong to him these bizarre and difficult pronunciations, more Russian than French, which do not appear to be the result neither of a regular system, nor of invariable principles" (Landresse and Abel-Rémusat, "Introduction," lxiv).
111. Landresse and Abel-Rémusat, xlii–xliii.
112. Eugène Burnouf, *Introduction à l'histoire du bouddhisme Indien* (Paris: Imprimerie Royale, 1844), 162.
113. M. Remusat and H. H. Wilson, "Account of the Foe Kúe Ki, or Travels of Fa Hian in India, Translated by M. Remusat [Read 9th March and 7th April, 1838],"*The Journal of the Royal Asiatic Society* 5, no. 1 (1839): 139.
114. Remusat and Wilson, 139.
115. As translated in Max Deeg, "The Historical Turn: How Chinese Buddhist Travelogues Changed Western Perception of Buddhism,"*Hualin International Journal of Buddhist Studies* 1, no. 1 (2019): 56.
116. Burnouf, *Introduction à l'histoire du bouddhisme Indien*, 161.
117. Donald Lopez does mention "the Sinologist" Abel-Rémusat in passing in several of his popular field histories, including in two instances *Relation des royaumes bouddhiques* (quoted elsewhere in this book), though never in a comprehensive overview of the latter's scholarship or with any discussion of his methodological innovation and impact (*From Stone to Flesh*, 180;*Strange Tales of an Oriental Idol*, 224–27;*Critical Terms for the Study of Buddhism* [Chicago; London: University of Chicago Press, 2005], 21).
118. Specifically, Abel-Rémusat makes regular reference to B. H. Hodgson, *Sketch of Buddhism; Derived from the Bauddha Scriptures of Nipal.* (London: J. L. Cox, 1828).
119. For example: Brian Houghton Hodgson, *Essays on the Languages, Literature, and Religion of Nepál and Tibet: Together with Further Papers on the Geography, Ethnology, and Commerce of Those Countries* (London: Trübner & Co., 1874), 103.

120. For more on the complex milieu of the early Société Asiatique, see Douglas McGetchin, "Wilting Florists: The Turbulent Early Decades of the Société Asiatique, 1822-1860,"*Journal of the History of Ideas* 64, no. 4 (2003): 565–80.
121. Burnouf, *Introduction à l'histoire du bouddhisme Indien*, 28.
122. Prasenjit Duara, "Afterword: The Chinese World Order as a Language Game—David Kang's East Asia before the West and Its Commentaries,"*Harvard Journal of Asiatic Studies Harvard Journal of Asiatic Studies* 77, no. 1 (2017): 123–29.
123. A characteristic example is Honey, *Incense at the Altar.*

3. Buddhist Asia to Jambudvīpa

1. Claude Lévi-Strauss, *The Savage Mind* (Chicago: University of Chicago Press, 1966), 261.
2. Several longer biographical sources on Banzarov are available in various languages, especially Russian. Nykolay Tsyrempilov provides a catalogue entry for an incomplete Mongolian manuscript biography and genealogy of Banzarov at the Siberian Branch of Russian Academy of Sciences: *Jegün sibiri-yin bayiyul dalai emen-e morin čereg-ün böged mongyul buriyad nigedüger qosiyun-u tabunuyud uringqai ijayur-un bangjar burqun-u köbegün bangjar-un dorji kemegči domuy bölüge* (Nikolay Tsyrempilov, *Catalogue of the Collection of Mongolian Manuscripts and Xylographs MII* [2006], 205).
3. Robert A. Rupen, "The Buriat Intelligentsia," *The Far Eastern Quarterly* 15, no. 3 (1956): 395.
4. D. Ulymzhiev, "Dorzhi Banzarov—the First Buryat Scholar,"*Mongol Studies* 16 (1993): 55.
5. Ulymzhiev, 55.
6. This study was republished near the close of the nineteenth century. See Dorzhi Banzarov, *Chernaya Vera Ili Shamanastvo u Mongolov i Drugiya Stat'i D. Banzarova [The Black Faith or Shamanism Among the Mongols, and Other Articles by D. Banzarov]*, ed. G. N. Potanin (St. Petersburg, 1891).
7. Ulymzhiev, "Dorzhi Banzarov—the First Buryat Scholar," 56.
8. Ulymzhiev, 56.
9. Byambyn Rinchen, *Travels of Fa Hsian Translated by Dordĵi Bansaroff*, Corpus Scriptorum Mongolorum Instituti Linguae Litterarum Academiae Scientiarum Reipublicae Populi Mongolici 5 (Ulaanbaatar: Mongol Ulsîn Shinjlekh Ukhaani Akademi, 1970), 3.
10. Nikolay Tsyrempilov, "From the Faith of Lamas to Global Buddhism: The Construction of Buddhist Tradition in Russian Trans-Baikal from the Eighteenth to the Early Twentieth Century," *Entangled Religions—Interdisciplinary Journal for the Study of Religious Contact and Transfer* 8 (2019).
11. Rupen, "The Buriat Intelligentsia."
12. Rupen, 396.
13. He is widely remembered as the first professional scholar of Buryatia, not only by postsocialist nationalists today but also in odes written by several Soviet-era historians including F. Kudryavtsev, L. Petrov, and D. Ulymzhiev.
14. In 1947, the Buryat Pedagogical Institute in Ulan Ude was named in his honor. As recently as 2010, statues of Banzarov were being erected to commemorate the seventy-fifth anniversary of Dzhidinsky district, dedicated to this "outstanding son of the Buryat people, the first Buryat scientist." "Доржи Банзаров—Первый Бурятский Учёный.,"*ДжидинскийРайон* (blog), accessed September 26, 2017, http://dzhida.ru/dorzhi-banzarov-pervyj-buryatskij-uchyonyj/.

15. Christopher P. Atwood, "Buddhism and Popular Ritual in Mongolian Religion: A Reexamination of the Fire Cult,"*History of Religions* 36, no. 2 (1996): 113.
16. Rinchen, *Travels of Fa Hsian Translated by Dordji Bansaroff*, 3.
17. Rinchen, 10. This Banzarov copy seems to have circulated alongside another copy, which the great Russian linguist Nicholas Poppe discovered in Alair Province and which he planned to reproduce—though World War II and his subsequent exile to the United States and a professorship at the University of Washington intervened.
18. Rinchen, 9.
19. This would make the composition date of Banzarov's translation between 1835 and 1842. See Rinchen, 9.
20. Matthew W. King, *Ocean of Milk, Ocean of Blood. A Mongolian Monk in the Ruins of the Qing Empire* (New York: Columbia University Press, 2019).
21. Rinchen, *Travels of Fa Hsian Translated by Dordji Bansaroff*, 4.
22. Rinchen, 8.
23. Mgon po skyabs, *Rgya Nag Gi Yul Du Dam Pa'i Chos Dar Tshul Gtso Bor Bshad Pa Blo Gsal Kun Tu Dga' Ba'i Rna Rgyan* (Sde dge: Sde dge par khang, unknown).
24. 'Gos lo tsa ba gzhon nu dpal, *Deb Ther Sngon Po* (Kun bde gling bla brang gi par khang: International Academy of Indian Culture, 1974).
25. Extensive analysis of his socialist-era ouevre can be found in King, Matthew W. *Ocean of Milk, Ocean of Blood.*
26. See King, *Ocean of Milk, Ocean of Blood.*
27. Kurtis Schaeffer, "New Scholarship in Tibet, 1650–1700," in *Forms of Knowledge in Early Modern Asia: Explorations in the Intellectual History of India and Tibet, 1500–1800*, ed. Sheldon Pollock (Durham, N.C.: Duke University Press, 2011), 291–310; International Association for Tibetan Studies, *Power, Politics, and the Reinvention of Tradition: Tibet in the Seventeenth and Eighteenth Centuries: PIATS 2003: Tibetan Studies: Proceedings of the Tenth Seminar of the International Association for Tibetan Studies, Oxford, 2003*, ed. Bryan J. Cuevas and Kurtis R. Schaeffer (Leiden; Boston: Brill, 2006); Kurtis Schaeffer, "Tibetan Biography: Growth and Criticism," in *Editions, Éditions: L'Écrit Au Tibet, Évolution et Devenir* (München: Indus Verlag, 2010); Janet Gyatso, *Being Human in a Buddhist World: An Intellectual History of Medicine in Early Modern Tibet* (New York: Columbia University Press, 2015); Janet Gyatso, "Experience, Empiricism, and the Fortunes of Authority: Tibetan Medicine and Buddhism on the Eve of Modernity," in *Forms of Knowledge in Early Modern Asia*, 311–35; Matthew Kapstein, "Just Where on Jambudvīpa Are We? New Geographical Knowledge and Old Cosmological Schemes in Eighteenth-Century Tibet," in *Forms of Knowledge in Early Modern Asia*, 336–64; Matthew Kapstein, *Buddhism Between Tibet and China* (Boston: Wisdom, 2009).
28. For a fuller introduction to the life and works of Güng Gombojab than is possible to make here, see: Shagdaryn Bira, "Indo-Tibetan and Mongolian Historiographical Mutual Contacts,"*Acta Orientalia Academiae Scientiarum Hungaricae* 43, no. 2/3 (1989): 177–84; Shagdaryn Bira and John Richard Krueger, *Mongolian Historical Writing from 1200 to 1700: Shagdaryn Bira; Translated from the Original Russian by John R. Krueger and Revised and Updated by the Author* (Bellingham, Wash.: Center for East Asian Studies, Western Washington University, 2002); Gonpo Kyab, *The Buddhist Canon of Iconometry (Zaoxiang Liangdu Jing): With Supplement. A Tibetan-Chinese Translation from about 1742. Translated and Annotated from This Chinese Translation Into Modern English*, trans. Michael Henss (Ulm: Fabri Verlag, 2006); Guilaine Mala, "A Mahayanist Rewriting of the History of China by Mgon Po Skyabs in the Rgya Nag Chos

'byung," in *Power, Politics, and the Reinvention of Tradition*, ed. Bryan J Cuevas and Kurtis R. Schaeffer (Leiden: Brill, 2006), 145–70; Vladimir Uspensky, "Ancient History of the Mongols According to Gombojab, an Eighteenth-Century Mongolian Historian,"*Rocznik Orientalistyczny.* 58, no. 1 (2005): 236–41; Vladimir Uspensky, "Gombojab: A Tibetan Buddhist in the Capital of the Qing Empire," in *Biographies of Eminent Mongol Buddhists*, ed. Johan Elverskog (Halle: International Institute for Tibetan and Buddhist Studies, 2008), 59–70; Fan Zhang, "Reorienting the Sacred and Accommodating the Secular: The History of Buddhism in China (RGya Nag Chos 'byung),"*Revue d'Etudes Tibétaines* 37 (2016): 569–91; Mufei He, "Gonbujab མགོན་པོ་སྐྱབས་," in *The Treasury of Lives*, July 2020, https://treasuryoflives.org/biographies/view/mgon-po-skyabs/7473.

29. Isaak Jakob Schmidt, "Über Den Ursprung Der Tibetischen Schrift,"*Mémoires de l'Academie Impériale Des Sciences de St. Pétersbourg* 6, no. 1 (1832): 41–54; Isaak Jakob Schmidt, *Grammatik Der Tibetischen Sprache* (St. Petersburg, 1839); Isaak Jakob Schmidt, *Mongolisch-Deutsch-Russisches Wörterbuch: Nebst Einem Deutschen Und Einem Russischen Wortregister* (St. Petersburg, 1835); Isaak Jakob Schmidt, "Ursprung Des Namens Mandschu,"*St. Petersburgische Zeitung* 253 (1834).
30. Schmidt himself was an interlocutor of Klaproth and Abel-Rémusat, and their correspondences, often contentious, were regularly published in the pages of *Journal Asiatique* during the 1820s and early 1830s. For oft-cited work by Schmidt among the Parisian milieu of Abel-Rémusat, see: Ssanang Ssetsen and Isaak Jakob Schmidt, *Geschichte der Ost-Mongolen und ihres Fürstenhauses; aus dem Mongolischen übersetzt und mit dem Originaltexte, nebst Anmerkungen, Erläuterungen und Citaten aus andern unedirten Originalwerken herausgegeben* (St. Petersburg; Leipzeg: Gedruckt bei N. Gretsch, 1829); Jean-Pierre Abel-Rémusat, *Observations Sur Histoire Des Mongols Orientaux de Ssanang-Ssetsen* (Paris: Imprimerie Royale, 1832); Isaak Jakob Schmidt, "Extrait d'une Lettre de M. Schmidt, de St. Pétersbourg, Addressée à M. Klaproth, En Réponse à l'Examen Des Extraits d'une Histoire Des Khans Mongols,"*Journal Asiatique* 3 (1823): 107–13; Isaak Jakob Schmidt, "Extrait d'une Lettre de M. Schmidt, à M., Sur Quelques Sujets Relatifs à l'histoire et à La Littérature Mongoles, 10/22 Octobre 1820, St.-Pétersbourg, Dec. 1822," *Journal Asiatique* 1 (1822): 320–34; Isaak Jakob Schmidt, *Philologisch-Kritische Zugabe Zu Den von Herrn Abel-Rémusat Bekannt Gemachten, in Den Königlich-Französischen Archiven Befindlichen Zwei Mongolischen Original-Briefen Der Könige von Persien Argun Und Öldshaitu an Philipp Den Schönen* (St. Petersburg, 1824); Isaak Jakob Schmidt, "Über Einige Grundlehren Des Buddhaismus," *Mémoires de l'Academie Impériale Des Sciences de St. Pétersbourg* 6, no. 1 (1832): 89–120; Isaak Jakob Schmidt, *Über Die Verwandtschaft Der Gnostisch-Theosophischen Lehren Mit Den Religions-Systemen Des Orients, Vorzüglich Des Buddhaismus* (Leipzig, 1828); Isaak Jakob Schmidt, *Forschungen Im Gebiete Der Älteren Religiösen, Politischen Und Literärischen Bildungsgeschichte Der Völker Mittel-Asiens, Vorzüglich Der Mongolen Und Tibeter* (St. Petersburg; Leipzig, 1824).
31. Uspensky, "Ancient History of the Mongols According to Gombojab, an Eighteenth-Century Mongolian Historian"; Johan Elverskog, "Mongol Time Enters a Qing World," in *Time, Temporality, and Imperial Transition: East Asia from Ming to Qing*, ed. Lynn A. Struve (Honolulu: Association for Asian Studies and University of Hawai'i Press, 2005).
32. Mgon po skyabs, *Chen Po Thang Gur Dus Kyi Rgya Gar Zhing Gi Bkod Pa'i Dkar Chag* (Beijing: Krung go'i bod rig pa dpe skrun khang, 2006). I am taking a little liberty here in translating *zhing gi bkod pa* as "geography," especially as the nineteenth century saw the rise of a dedicated genre of global geography and cartography among these frontier Géluk

scholastic communities, influenced by mapping projects directed by the Qing court, the influence of new geographic knowledge from Jesuit and other traditions, and the new participation in Tibetan letters by Mongols and eastern Tibetans. An example is the 1865 *Oceanic Book:A Clear Description of the Manner in Which the Precious Buddha's Teachings SpreadInto the Land of Amdo* (Tib. *Yul mdo smad kyi ljongs su thub bstan rin po che ji ltar dar ba'i tshul gsal bar brjod pa deb ther rgya mtsho*), written from the 1830s to 1865 by Drakgön Zhapdrung Konchok Tenpé Rapgyé (Tib. Brag dgon zhabs drung Dkon mchog bstan pa rab rgyas, 1800/1–1869) (Brag dgon zhabs drung dkon mchog bstan pa rab rgyas, *Yul Mdo Smad Kyi Ljongs Su Thub Bstan Rin Po Che Ji Ltar Dar Ba'i Tshul Gsal Bar Brjod Pa Deb Ther Rgya Mtsho*, 3 vols., Satapitaka Series [New Delhi: Sharada Rani, 1975]). The first edition of *The Oceanic Book* was completed in 1833, expanded in 1849, and supplemented in 1865. See Gray Tuttle, "Challenging Central Tibet's Dominance of History: The Oceanic Book, a Nineteenth-Century Politico-Religious-Geographic History," in *Mapping the Modern in Tibet. PIATS 2006: Proceedings of the Eleventh Seminar of the International Association for Tibetan Studies. Königswinter 2006*, ed. Gray Tuttle ([Andiast, Switzerland]: IITBS, International Institute for Tibetan and Buddhist Studies GmbH, 2011), 135–72.

33. Blo bzang rta mgrin, "Chen Po Hān Gur Gyi Btsun Pa Phā Hyin Gyis 'phags Pa'i Yul Du 'Grims Pa'i Rnam Thar Rgyal Bstan 'Byung Khungs Kun Gsal 'Phrul Gyi Me Long," in *Rje Btsun Blo Bzang Rta Dbyangs Kyi Gsung 'bum* (New Delhi: Mongolian Lama Guru Deva, 1975), 1:241.
34. Tib. *Rgyal po zas gtsang.*
35. Skt. *mahātma*; Tib. *bdag nyid chen po.*
36. Blo bzang rta mgrin (1975, 146) has this last sentence as *de yang yig tshang du bzhag'dug*, while Rinchen (*Travels of Fa Hsian Translated by Dordji Bansaroff*, 42) has it nonsensically as *de yang yig tshang du zhag bdun'dug.*
37. Tib. *Hān gur gyi ming dhi rgyal po.* This would be Emperor Ming Di (明帝, 28–75 CE) of the Han Dynasty (漢朝, 202 BCE–9CE, 25–220CE).
38. Tib. *Thang zing bla ma.*
39. Tib. *I kying.*
40. Tib. *Thos bzung.*
41. Tib. *rig gnas.*
42. Tib. *Gnas brtan'od srung.*
43. Tib. *Phal chen sde'i'dul ba.*
44. *Zhes gsungs pa de nyid yin par snang.* This line is only in Rinchen (*Travels of Fa Hsian Translated by Dordji Bansaroff*, 42/2r3)
45. Tib. *rgya ser phe ling.*
46. Blo bzang rta mgrin, "Chen Po Hān Gur Gyi Btsun Pa Phā Hyin Gyis 'phags Pa'i Yul Du 'Grims Pa'i Rnam Thar Rgyal Bstan 'Byung Khungs Kun Gsal 'Phrul Gyi Me Long," 146–47.
47. José Ignacio Cabezón, *Buddhism and Language: A Study of Indo-Tibetan Scholasticism*, SUNY Series, toward a Comparative Philosophy of Religions (Albany: State University of New York Press, 1994).
48. A. Amar, *Monggol-Un Tobci Teüke [A Brief History of Mongolia]*, vol. 9, The Mongolia Society Papers (Bloomington, Ind.: The Mongolia Society, 1986).
49. Tib. *rgya ser phe ling.*
50. Tib. *bla ma lo tsā ba*, i.e., a religious adept (*lama*) translator (*lotsawa*).

51. Blo bzang rta mgrin, "Chen Po Hān Gur Gyi Btsun Pa Phā Hyin Gyis 'phags Pa'i Yul Du 'Grims Pa'i Rnam Thar Rgyal Bstan 'Byung Khungs Kun Gsal 'Phrul Gyi Me Long," 147.
52. Throughout this book I refer to the version of this Tibetan translation found in Lubsangdamdin's *Collected Works,* though in part II I note small editorial differences between this version and the one published by Rinchen. Blo bzang rta mgrin, "Chen Po Hān Gur Gyi Btsun Pa Phā Hyin Gyis 'phags Pa'i Yul Du 'Grims Pa'i Rnam Thar Rgyal Bstan 'Byung Khungs Kun Gsal 'Phrul Gyi Me Long."
53. Blo bzang rta mgrin, 241.
54. Michel-Rolph Trouillot, "Culture on the Margins: Caribbean Creolization in Historical Context," in *From the Margins: Historical Anthropology and Its Futures*, ed. Brian Keith Axel (Durham, N.C. and London: Duke University Press, 2002), 147.

4. Jambudvīpa to Science

1. For a fascinating survey, see Roger-Pol Droit, *The Cult of Nothingness: The Philosophers and the Buddha.* Trans. David Streight and Pamela Vohnson (Chapel Hill; London: University of North Carolina Press, 2003).
2. Georg Wilhelm Friedrich Hegel, *Lectures on the Philosophy of Religion*, trans. Peter Crafts Hodgson (Berkeley: University of California Press, 1988), 253.
3. J. B. Du Halde, *Description geographique historique, chronologique, politique, et physique de l'empire de la Chine et de la Tartarie chinoise: enrichie des cartes generales et particulieres de ces pays, de la carte générale & des cartes particulieres du Thibet, & de la Corée & ornée d'un grand nombre de figures et de vignettes gravées en taille-douce*, vol. 3 (Paris: P. G. Lemercier, 1735), 50–51.
4. Ernest Augustin Xavier Clerc de Landresse and Jean-Pierre Abel-Rémusat, "Introduction," in *Foĕ Kouĕ Ki, Ou, Relation Des Royaumes Bouddhiques: Voyage Dans La Tartarie, Dans l'Afghanistan et Dans l'Inde, Exécuté à La Fin Du IVe Siècle* (Paris: Imprimerie Royale, 1836), liii.
5. Landresse and Abel-Rémusat, liii.
6. Landresse and Abel-Rémusat, li.
7. Jean-Pierre Abel-Rémusat, "Mémoire Sur Un Voyage Dans l'Asie Centrale, Dans Le Pays Des Afghans et Des Beloutches, et Dans l'Inde, Exécuté à La Fin Du IVe Siècle de Notre Ère Par Plusieurs Samanéens de La Chine,"*Mémoires de l'Institut de France* 13, no. 2 (1838): 350.
8. Abel-Rémusat, 350.
9. Abel-Rémusat, 350–52.
10. Abel-Rémusat, 350–52.
11. Abel-Rémusat, 352.
12. Landresse and Abel-Rémusat, iv.
13. Abel-Rémusat, ix.
14. For more on Qianlong's evaluation of Khotan in relation to Buddhist history, including references to Faxian's *Record,* see Françoise Wang-Toutain, "Le royaume de Khotan ne fut jamais bouddhiste: L'historiographie selon l'empereur mandchou Qianlong (r. 1736–1796),"*Journal Asiatique* 302, no. 2 (2014): 531–50.
15. "Da Qing Yi Tong Zhi 大清一統志," 1735, Chinese Rare Book Collection (Library of Congress); Jean-Pierre Abel-Rémusat, *Histoire de La Ville de Khotan: Tirée Des Annales de La Chine et Traduite Du Chinois; Suivie de Recherches Sur La Substance Minérale Appelée Par Les Chinois Pierre de Iu, et Sur Le Jaspe Des Anciens* (Paris: L'imprimerie de doublet, 1820), xiii. Such resources, though

consulted on his behalf by no less than the great British missionary and translator to the Qing, Rev. William Morisson (1782–1834), were frustratingly unavailable in Paris for Abel-Rémusat to explore directly.

16. Landresse and Abel-Rémusat, "Introduction," xvi.
17. Landresse and Abel-Rémusat, "Introduction," xvii.
18. Faxian and Jean-Pierre Abel-Rémusat, *Foĕ Kouĕ Ki, Ou, Relation Des Royaumes Bouddhiques: Voyage Dans La Tartarie, Dans l'Afghanistan et Dans l'Inde, Exécuté à La Fin Du IVe Siècle*, ed. Julius von Klaproth and Ernest Augustin Xavier Clerc de Landresse (Paris: Imprimerie Royale, 1836), 18 n. 1.
19. I.e., Mong. *Balγasu(n).*
20. Faxian and Abel-Rémusat, *Foĕ Kouĕ Ki, Ou, Relation Des Royaumes Bouddhiques: Voyage Dans La Tartarie, Dans l'Afghanistan et Dans l'Inde, Exécuté à La Fin Du IVe Siècle*, 18 n. 1, a.
21. For the wider place of relics and reliquaries in Buddhist Asia and in European scholarship about it, see John S. Strong, *Relics of the Buddha* (Princeton, N.J.: Princeton University Press, 2004).
22. Michel-Rolph Trouillot, *Silencing the Past: Power and the Production of History* (Boston: Beacon, 2015).
23. B. H. Hodgson, *Sketch of Buddhism; Derived from the Bauddha Scriptures of Nipal* (London: J. L. Cox, 1828).
24. Faxian and Abel-Rémusat, *Foĕ Kouĕ Ki, Ou, Relation Des Royaumes Bouddhiques: Voyage Dans La Tartarie, Dans l'Afghanistan et Dans l'Inde, Exécuté à La Fin Du IVe Siècle*, 19 n. 3.
25. Skt. *Mahāyāna*; Ch. *Dasheng* 大乘; Tib. *Theg pa chen po*; Mong. *Yeke kölgen*. Skt. *Hinayāna*; Ch. *Xiaosheng* 小乘; Tib. *Theg pa dman pa*; Mong. *Baγa kölgen*.
26. Faxian and Abel-Rémusat, *Foĕ Kouĕ Ki, Ou, Relation Des Royaumes Bouddhiques: Voyage Dans La Tartarie, Dans l'Afghanistan et Dans l'Inde, Exécuté à La Fin Du IVe Siècle*, 7.
27. Faxian and Abel-Rémusat, 9 n. 4.
28. Faxian and Abel-Rémusat, 9, n.4.
29. Isaac Jac Schmidt, *Forschungen im Gebiete der älteren religiösen, politischen u. literarischen Bildungsgeschichte der Völker Mittelasiens, vorz. der Mongolen und Tibeter* (St. Petersburg, 1824), 254.
30. Faxian and Abel-Rémusat, *Foĕ Kouĕ Ki, Ou, Relation Des Royaumes Bouddhiques: Voyage Dans La Tartarie, Dans l'Afghanistan et Dans l'Inde, Exécuté à La Fin Du IVe Siècle*, 9 n. 4.
31. Faxian and Abel-Rémusat, 10 n. 4.
32. Faxian and Abel-Rémusat, 10 n. 4.
33. Faxian and Abel-Rémusat, 10 n. 4.
34. Landresse and Abel-Rémusat, "Introduction," 11 n. 4.
35. Landresse and Abel-Rémusat, 11 n. 4.
36. Faxian and Abel-Rémusat, *Foĕ Kouĕ Ki, Ou, Relation Des Royaumes Bouddhiques: Voyage Dans La Tartarie, Dans l'Afghanistan et Dans l'Inde, Exécuté à La Fin Du IVe Siècle*, 12 n. 4.
37. Faxian and Abel-Rémusat, 12 , n. 4.
38. Faxian and Abel-Rémusat, 12 , n. 4.
39. Skt. *Maitreya*; Ch. *Mile* 彌勒; Tib. *Byams pa*; *Maidari*.
40. Zhang Qian 張騫 (d. c. 114 BCE, Fr. *Tchang khian*; Mong. *Ĵang kin;* Tib. *Chāng ke yāng*) was a famous envoy of Emperor Wu of the Han dynasty. Gan Ying 甘英 (Mong. *Gan ying*; Tib. *Ge yāng*) was sent by the Chinese general Bao Chao as an envoy to the Roman Empire in 97 CE, though the former only made it as far as "the western sea" (the Mediterranean, the Persian Gulf, or perhaps the Black Sea). Nonetheless, Gan Ying did provide China with its first descriptions of Roman

territories, customs, and political economy. See Ying-shih Yü, "Han Foreign Relations," in *The Cambridge History of China: The Ch'in and Han Empires, 221 B.C.–A.D. 220*, trans. Denis Twitchett and John K. Fairbank, vol. 1 (Cambridge: Cambridge University Press, 1986), 377–462.

41. Faxian and Abel-Rémusat, *Foĕ Kouĕ Ki, Ou, Relation Des Royaumes Bouddhiques: Voyage Dans La Tartarie, Dans l'Afghanistan et Dans l'Inde, Exécuté à La Fin Du IVe Siècle*, 33 n. 8.
42. Faxian and Abel-Rémusat, 33 n. 8.
43. Abel-Rémusat, "Mémoire Sur Un Voyage Dans l'Asie Centrale, Dans Le Pays Des Afghans et Des Beloutches, et Dans l'Inde, Exécuté à La Fin Du IVe Siècle de Notre Ère Par Plusieurs Samanéens de La Chine," 360.
44. Abel-Rémusat, "Mémoire Sur Un Voyage Dans l'Asie Centrale, Dans Le Pays Des Afghans et Des Beloutches, et Dans l'Inde, Exécuté à La Fin Du IVe Siècle de Notre Ère Par Plusieurs Samanéens de La Chine," 360.
45. Joseph De Guignes, *Histoire générale des Huns, des Turcs, des Mongols, et des autres Tartares occidentaux, etc. Avant et depuis Jesus-Christ jusqu' a present; précédée d'une introduction contenant des tables chronologique et historiques des princes qui ont regné dans l'Asie. Ouorage tiré des livres chinois, et des manuscrits orientaux de la bibliotheque du roi* (Paris: Chez Desaint: Saillant, 1756), 1:17; 2:48.
46. Faxian and Abel-Rémusat, *Foĕ Kouĕ Ki, Ou, Relation Des Royaumes Bouddhiques: Voyage Dans La Tartarie, Dans l'Afghanistan et Dans l'Inde, Exécuté à La Fin Du IVe Siècle*, 37 n. 3.
47. Jean-Pierre Abel-Rémusat, *De l'Étude des Langues Étrangères chez les Chinois* (Paris: Extrait du Magasin Encyclopédique, 1811); Abel-Rémusat, *Histoire de La Ville de Khotan.*
48. Faxian and Abel-Rémusat, *Foĕ Kouĕ Ki, Ou, Relation Des Royaumes Bouddhiques: Voyage Dans La Tartarie, Dans l'Afghanistan et Dans l'Inde, Exécuté à La Fin Du IVe Siècle*, 41 n. 5.
49. Faxian and Abel-Rémusat, 44 n. 7.
50. Faxian and Abel-Rémusat, 44 n. 7.
51. Faxian and Abel-Rémusat, 44 n. 7.
52. Faxian and Abel-Rémusat, 44 n. 7.
53. Faxian and Abel-Rémusat, 41 n. 5.
54. Faxian and Abel-Rémusat, 41 n. 5.
55. Abel-Rémusat's source here is Thsian ban chou's *Vie de Wou ti.*
56. Faxian and Abel-Rémusat, *Foĕ Kouĕ Ki, Ou, Relation Des Royaumes Bouddhiques: Voyage Dans La Tartarie, Dans l'Afghanistan et Dans l'Inde, Exécuté à La Fin Du IVe Siècle*, 41 n. 5.
57. Faxian and Abel-Rémusat, 42 n. 5.
58. Not before Abel-Rémusat's scholarship between 1819 and 1832, that is. He had given this timeline already in: Abel-Rémusat, *Mélanges Asiatiques, Ou Choix de Morceaux de Critique et de Mémoires Relatifs Aux Religions, Aux Sciences, Aux Coutumes, à l'Histoire et à La Géographie Des Nations Orientales*, vol. 1 (Paris: Librarie Orientale de Dondey-Dupré Père et Fils, 1825), 115, 117.
59. Faxian and Abel-Rémusat, *Foĕ Kouĕ Ki, Ou, Relation Des Royaumes Bouddhiques: Voyage Dans La Tartarie, Dans l'Afghanistan et Dans l'Inde, Exécuté à La Fin Du IVe Siècle*, 42 n. 5.
60. For a summary of contemporary European views, including Abel-Rémusat's at the time, see "On the Eras of the Buddhas,"*Asiatic Journal* 23 (June 1827): 782–86.
61. Landresse and Abel-Rémusat, "Introduction," xxx.
62. Landresse and Abel-Rémusat, xxx.
63. Landresse and Abel-Rémusat, xxx.
64. Jean-Pierre Abel-Rémusat, "Essai Sur la Cosmographie et la Cosmogonie des Bouddhistes," in *Mélanges posthumes d'histoire et littérature orientales* (Paris: Imprimerie Royale, 1843), 65–131.
65. Landresse and Abel-Rémusat, "Introduction," xxxi.

66. Landresse and Abel-Rémusat, xxxii.
67. Landresse and Abel-Rémusat, xxxii.
68. Landresse and Abel-Rémusat, xxxii–xxxiii.
69. Landresse and Abel-Rémusat, xxxiii.
70. Abel-Rémusat, "Mémoire Sur Un Voyage Dans l'Asie Centrale, Dans Le Pays Des Afghans et Des Beloutches, et Dans l'Inde, Exécuté à La Fin Du IVe Siècle de Notre Ère Par Plusieurs Samanéens de La Chine," 579.
71. Abel-Rémusat, 579.
72. De Guignes, *Histoire générale des Huns, des Turcs, des Mongols, et des autres Tartares occidentaux, etc. Avant et depuis Jesus-Christ jusqu' a present; précédée d'une introduction contenant des tables chronologique et historiques des princes qui ont regné dans l'Asie. Ouorage tiré des livres chinois, et des manuscrits orientaux de la bibliotheque du roi*, 4 vols. (Paris: Chez Desaint: Saillant, 1756), II:223.
73. Abel-Rémusat, "Mémoire Sur Un Voyage Dans l'Asie Centrale, Dans Le Pays Des Afghans et Des Beloutches, et Dans l'Inde, Exécuté à La Fin Du IVe Siècle de Notre Ère Par Plusieurs Samanéens de La Chine," 380.
74. Here Abel-Rémusat cites Abdalla Beidavaeus, Andreas Mullerus Greiffenhagius, and Abraham Müller, *Abdallæ Beidavæi Historia Sinensis: Percice e gemino Manuscripto edita, Latine quoque reddita ab Andrea Mullero Greiffenhagio Berolini, Typis Christophori Rungii, Anno MDCLXXVII expressa, nuc vero una cum additamentis edita ab Autoris filio, Quodvultdeo Abraham Mullero* (Jenae: Bielkius, 1689), 29.
75. Abel-Rémusat, *Mélanges Asiatiques, Ou Choix de Morceaux de Critique et de Mémoires Relatifs Aux Religions, Aux Sciences, Aux Coutumes, à l'Histoire et à La Géographie Des Nations Orientales*, 1:122.
76. Horace H. Wilson, *A Dictionary, Sanscrit and English: Translated, Amended and Enlarged, from an Original Compilation Prepared by Learned Natives for the College of Fort William* (Calcutta: Printed by Philip Pereira, at the Hindoostanee Press, 1819).
77. Abel-Rémusat, "Mémoire Sur Un Voyage Dans l'Asie Centrale, Dans Le Pays Des Afghans et Des Beloutches, et Dans l'Inde, Exécuté à La Fin Du IVe Siècle de Notre Ère Par Plusieurs Samanéens de La Chine," 381.
78. Abel-Rémusat, 380.
79. Abel-Rémusat, 382.
80. Abel-Rémusat, 383.
81. The major contribution here was Abel-Rémusat's widely read, field-defining 1831 article in *Journal Asiatique*: "Observations Upon a Few Points of the Samanéen Doctrine, and in Particular, Upon the Names of the Supreme Triade Among Different Buddhist Peoples" (Jean-Pierre Abel-Rémusat, "Observations Sur Quelque Points de La Doctrine Samanéene et En Particulaire Sur Les Noms de La Triade Suprème Chez Les Différens Peuples Bouddhistes"), *Journal Asiatique*, 1831, 3–67.
82. Abel-Rémusat.
83. Antonio Agostino Giorgi, *Alphabetum Tibetanum Missionum Apostolicarum Commodo Editum. Praemissa Est Disquisitio Qua De Vario Litterarum Ac Regionis Nomine, Gentis Origine Moribus, Superstitione, Ac Manichaeismo Fuse Disseritur: Beausobrii Calumniae In Sanctum Augustinum, Aliosque Ecclesiae Patres Refutantur* (Romae: Sacra Congregatio de Propaganda Fide, 1762), 212, 245.
84. "*Thseng I A han king*, cited in the *Yuan kian louï han*, book CCCXVII, p. 24" (Faxian and Abel-Rémusat, *Foĕ Kouĕ Ki, Ou, Relation Des Royaumes Bouddhiques: Voyage Dans La Tartarie, Dans l'Afghanistan et Dans l'Inde, Exécuté à La Fin Du IVe Siècle*, 60 n. 5, b).
85. "*Thseng I A han king*, cited in the *Yuan kian louï han*, book CCCXVII, p. 24" (Faxian and Abel-Rémusat, 60 n.5, b).

86. Von Klaproth provided scholarly Europe with another early biographical picture of the Buddha, drawn primarily from Mongolian sources, a decade earlier: "Vie de Bouddha, d'Après Les Livres Mongols,"*Journal Asiatique* 4, no. 1 (1824).
87. Faxian and Abel-Rémusat, *Foĕ Kouĕ Ki, Ou, Relation Des Royaumes Bouddhiques: Voyage Dans La Tartarie, Dans l'Afghanistan et Dans l'Inde, Exécuté à La Fin Du IVe Siècle*, 67 n. 4.
88. Faxian and Abel-Rémusat, 73 n. 4.
89. Faxian and Abel-Rémusat, 67 n. 4.
90. Faxian and Abel-Rémusat, *Foĕ Kouĕ Ki, Ou, Relation Des Royaumes Bouddhiques: Voyage Dans La Tartarie, Dans l'Afghanistan et Dans l'Inde, Exécuté à La Fin Du IVe Siècle*, 80 n. 4.
91. Ch. *Da banniepan jing* 大般涅槃經; Tib. *Yongs su mya ngan las 'das pa chen po'i mdo.*
92. "On the Eras of the Buddhas."
93. Padma dkar po, *History of Buddhism. Written by Kunkhyen Pema Karpo (1527–1592) (Chos 'byung Bstan Pa'i Pad+ma Rgyas Pa'i Nyin Byed)*, ed. Lokesh Chandra, vol. 75, Śata-Piṭaka Series (Indo-Tibetan Literatures) (Delhi: International Academy of Indian Culture, 1968).
94. "On the Eras of the Buddhas," 782.
95. "On the Eras of the Buddhas," 782.
96. I.e., Abu'l-Fazl ibn Mubarak, 1551–1602.
97. Abdul Fazl-I-Allámí, *The Ain I Akbari*, trans. H. S. Jarrett, vol. 3 (Calcutta: The Asiatic Society of Bengal [Baptist Mission Press], 1894), 212.
98. "On the Eras of the Buddhas," 783.
99. Faxian and Abel-Rémusat, *Foĕ Kouĕ Ki, Ou, Relation Des Royaumes Bouddhiques: Voyage Dans La Tartarie, Dans l'Afghanistan et Dans l'Inde, Exécuté à La Fin Du IVe Siècle*, 257–58.
100. Stanislas Julien, *Histoire de la vie de Hioun-thsang et de ses voyages dans l'Inde, depuis l'an 629 jusqu'en 645* (Paris: Imprimerie Impériale, 1853).
101. Faxian and Abel-Rémusat, *Foĕ Kouĕ Ki, Ou, Relation Des Royaumes Bouddhiques: Voyage Dans La Tartarie, Dans l'Afghanistan et Dans l'Inde, Exécuté à La Fin Du IVe Siècle*, 237 n. 6.
102. Faxian and Abel-Rémusat, 237 n. 6.
103. Faxian and Abel-Rémusat, 237 n. 6.
104. Abel-Rémusat, "Mémoire Sur Un Voyage Dans l'Asie Centrale, Dans Le Pays Des Afghans et Des Beloutches, et Dans l'Inde, Exécuté à La Fin Du IVe Siècle de Notre Ère Par Plusieurs Samanéens de La Chine."
105. Klaproth mistakenly says that the Mongolian was a translation of the Sanskrit, but it in fact came from the Tibetan. His source, as usual, was his sometime nemesis in matters of Mongolian linguistics and literature, Isaak Jacob Schmidt. This Mongolian source was also referenced by Eugène Burnouf in his much fêted *Introduction à l'histoire du bouddhisme indien.* Isaak Jacob Schmidt, *Ueber die sogenannte dritte Welt der Buddhaisten: als Fortsetzung der Abhandlungen ueber die Lehren des Buddhaismus ; gelesen den 21 December 1831* (St. Petersburg, 1834), 17; Burnouf, *Introduction à l'histoire du bouddhisme Indien* (Paris: Imprimerie Royale, 1844), 142.
106. Landresse and Abel-Rémusat, "Introduction," xlii–xliii.

5. Science to History of the Dharma

1. Benno Weiner, *The Chinese Revolution on the Tibetan Frontier* (Ithaca, N.Y.; London: Cornell University Press, 2020); Jianglin Li and Susan Wilf, *Tibet in Agony: Lhasa 1959* (Cambridge, Mass.: Harvard University Press, 2016).

2. In 1973, Mysore was renamed the state of Karnataka.
3. For some useful surveys of the history and experience of Tibetan refugees in India, see: A. S. Bentz, "Being a Tibetan Refugee in India,"*Refugee Survey Quarterly* 31, no. 1 (2012): 80–107; Imogen Rose Clark, "Is Home Where the Heart Is?: Landscape, Materiality and Aesthetics in Tibetan Exile" (thesis, Oxford University, 2015); Bibhu Prasad Routray, "Tibetan Refugees in India: Religious Identity and the Forces of Modernity,"*Refugee Survey Quarterly* 26, no. 2 (January 1, 2007): 79–90.
4. Shagdariin Sandag, Harry H. Kendall, and Frederic E. Wakeman, *Poisoned Arrows: The Stalin-Choibalsan Mongolian Massacres, 1921–1941* (Boulder, Colo.: Westview Press, 2000); Christopher Kaplonski, *The Lama Question: Violence, Sovereignty, and Exception in Early Socialist Mongolia* (Honolulu: University of Hawai'i Press, 2014); Thomas E. Ewing, *Between the Hammer and the Anvil?: Chinese and Russian Policies in Outer Mongolia, 1911–1921* (Bloomington: Research Institute for Inner Asian Studies, Indiana University, 1980); Melissa Andrea Cakars, "Being Buryat: Sovietization in Siberia" (Ph.D. diss., Indiana University, 2008); S. Purevzhav, *BNMAU-D sum khiid, lam naryn asuudlyg shiidverlesen ní: 1921–1940 on* (Ulaanbaatar: Ulsyn khevleliin khereg erkhlekh khoroo, 1965); William A. Brown, Urgunge Onon, and B Shirėndėv, *History of the Mongolian People's Republic* (Cambridge, Mass.: East Asian Research Center, Harvard University: Distributed by Harvard University Press, 1976); Robert Arthur Rupen, *How Mongolia Is Really Ruled: A Political History of the Mongolian People's Republic, 1900–1978* (Stanford, Calif.: Hoover Institution Press, Stanford University, 1979); Danzanhorloogiin Dashpurev and S. K. Soni, *Reign of Terror in Mongolia: 1920–1990* (New Delhi: South Asian Publ. [u.a.], 1992); Irina Y. Morozova, "Socialist Revolutions in Asia: The Social History of Mongolia in the Twentieth Century" (London: Routledge, 2009); George G. S. Murphy, *Soviet Mongolia; a Study of the Oldest Political Satellite* (Berkeley: University of California Press, 1966); Irina Y. Morozova, *The Comintern and Revolution in Mongolia* (Cambridge: White Horse Press for the Mongolia and Inner Asia Studies Unit, University of Cambridge, 2002).
5. To borrow Sebastian Conrad's provocative formulation in his study of Japan ("What Time Is Japan?: Problems of Comparative [Intercultural] Historiography," *History and Theory* 38, no. 1 [1999]: 67–83.)
6. Myriam Revault d'Allonnes, *La crise sans fin: essai sur l'expérience moderne du temps* (Paris: Seuil, 2012).
7. Among exiled Tibetans to this day, the Lhasa resistance is solemnly celebrated on March 10th as "Tibetan Uprising Day," while its suppression on March 28 is celebrated in China-controlled Tibetan regions as "The Day of Emancipation of Tibet's One Million Serfs" (Xizang bai wan nongnu jiefang jinian ri 西藏百萬農奴解放紀念日).
8. For a short introduction to Ngakwang Nyima's life and a longer excerpt from his *Lamp of Scripture and Reasoning,* see: Matthew W. King, "Agvaannyam: 'The Origin of Human Beings and the Holy Dharma Kings and Ministers in Mongol Lands,' from the History of the Dharma, The Lamp of Scriptures and Reasoning," in *Sources of Mongolian Tradition*, ed. Vesna A Wallace (Oxford; New York: Oxford University Press, 2020), 453–75.
9. Ngag dbang nyi ma, *Chos 'byung Lung Rigs Sgron Me* (Varanasi, India: n.p., 1965).
10. Tib. *Lam yig*, or "travel guide," here referring to Faxian's *Record.*
11. Skt. *munindra*; Tib. *thub dbang.*
12. Tib. *Nam mkha'i snying po.* A bodhisattva usually considered to be a form of Akṣobhya. His position is in the north.

13. Tib. Mar pa to tsā ba chos kyi blo gros, 1012–1097. His deceased son was named Darmadodé (Dar ma mdo sde). "Marpa the Translator" transmitted many vital teaching and practice lineages from India in the southern Tibet region of Trowolung (Bro bo lung) and was famously the guru of Tibet's great yogi Milarepa (Mi la ras pa, c. 1028–1111).
14. Faxian and Jean-Pierre Abel-Rémusat, *Foĕ Kouĕ Ki, Ou, Relation Des Royaumes Bouddhiques: Voyage Dans La Tartarie, Dans l'Afghanistan et Dans l'Inde, Exécuté à La Fin Du IVe Siècle*, ed. Julius von Klaproth and Ernest Augustin Xavier Clerc de Landresse (Paris: Imprimerie Royale, 1836), 95.
15. For important studies of the tradition of Inner Asian *nam-thar*, or "liberated life story," that contextualize Lubsangdamdin's approach to Faxian's *Record* beyond what is possible to say here , see: Janet Gyatso, *Apparitions of the Self: The Secret Autobiographies of a Tibetan Visionary: A Translation and Study of Jigme Lingpa's Dancing Moon in the Water andḌākki's Grand Secret-Talk* (Princeton, N.J.: Princeton University Press, 1998); Andrew Quintman, *The Yogin and the Madman: Reading the Biographical Corpus of Tibet's Great Saint Milarepa* (New York: Columbia University Press, 2013); Andrew Quintman, "Between History and Biography: Notes on Zhi Byed Ri Pa's 'Illuminating Lamp of Sun and Moon Beams,' a Fourteenth-Century Biographical State of the Field," *Revue d'Etudes Tibétaines* 23 (Avril 2012): 5–41; Sarah Jacoby, *Love and Liberation: Autobiographical Writings of the Tibetan Buddhist Visionary Sera Khandro* (New York: Columbia University Press, 2014); Kurtis Schaeffer, "Tibetan Biography: Growth and Criticism," in *Editions, Éditions: L'Écrit Au Tibet, Évolution et Devenir* (München: Indus Verlag, 2010).
16. Blo bzang rta mgrin [Agvan Dorjiev], "Chen Po Hān Gur Gyi Btsun Pa Phā Hyin Gyis 'phags Pa'i Yul Du 'Grims Pa'i Rnam Thar Rgyal Bstan 'Byung Khungs Kun Gsal 'Phrul Gyi Me Long," in *Rje Btsun Blo Bzang Rta Dbyangs Kyi Gsung 'bum* (New Delhi: Mongolian Lama Guru Deva, 1975), 1:167–68.
17. For details, see chapter 2 in King, *Ocean of Milk, Ocean of Blood: A Mongolian Monk in the Ruins of the Qing Empire* (New York: Columbia University Press, 2019).
18. Blo bzang rta mgrin, "Chen Po Hān Gur Gyi Btsun Pa Phā Hyin Gyis 'phags Pa'i Yul Du 'Grims Pa'i Rnam Thar Rgyal Bstan 'Byung Khungs Kun Gsal 'Phrul Gyi Me Long," 151.
19. Blo bzang rta mgrin, 152.
20. Tib. *Dzu ho ci'i yul khams*; Mong. *Tsi hi orun* (15); Fr. *le royaume de Tsen hŏ* (22); Ch. *Zihe guo* 子合國 (0857c03).
21. Lubsangdamdin has this line: *thang zing la'ang bdag rkyen dpe med mdzad 'dug cing*, while Rinchen's edited version from 1970 provides a correction to *mdzad*: *thang zing la'ang bdag rkyen dpe med brjod 'dug cing*. I have followed Rinchen's useful correction in the translation above.
22. Not all contemporary readers of Lubsangdamdin's historiography were convinced by his identification of Khotan as the Land of Li, and thus all the historical implications this entailed. For a remarkable example, see Agvan Dorjiev's pointed challenges and Lubsangdamdin's response in: Matthew W. King, "Agwan Dorjiev's Questions about the Past and Future of Mongolian Buddhism," in *Sources of Mongolian Buddhism*, ed. Vesna A. Wallace (Oxford; New York: Oxford University Press, 2020), 416–37.
23. Faxian 法顯, "The Biography of the Eminent Monk Faxian (Gaoseng Faxian Zhuan 高僧法顯傳)," Vol. 51, 2085 (Tokyo: Taishō Shinshū Daizōkyō Kankōkai, 1988), 0857a09.
24. Faxian and Abel-Rémusat, *Foĕ Kouĕ Ki, Ou, Relation Des Royaumes Bouddhiques: Voyage Dans La Tartarie, Dans l'Afghanistan et Dans l'Inde, Exécuté à La Fin Du IVe Siècle*, 5 n. 10.
25. Blo bzang rta mgrin, "Chen Po Hān Gur Gyi Btsun Pa Phā Hyin Gyis 'phags Pa'i Yul Du 'Grims Pa'i Rnam Thar Rgyal Bstan 'Byung Khungs Kun Gsal 'Phrul Gyi Me Long," 147.

26. Serkhok—also known as Tsenpo Monastery (*Btsan po dgon*; Ch. *Guanghui Si* 广惠寺)—was founded in 1649 and is directly related to the circulatory history of Faxian's *Record* explored in this book. Serkhok Monastery was famously destroyed in 1724 by Qing forces, but was later rebuilt and eventually flourished until the events of the mid-twentieth century. In today's administrative units, it is located in Datong Autonomous County of Qinghai province, to the north of Xining. Tsenpo Monastery was the seat of the Mindröl incarnation lineage (*Smin grol sku phreng*, alias the Tsenpo Nominhan lineage), a series of vital intermediaries between Tibetan, Mongol, Manchu, Chinese, and European knowledge traditions and sovereignty. Though if this was what Lubsangdamdin had in mind, his geography was a little askew, as Serkhok Monastery is east of Lake Kokonor, well northeast of Amyé Machen.
27. Faxian 法顯, "The Biography of the Eminent Monk Faxian (Gaoseng Faxian Zhuan 高僧法顯傳)," 0857a23.
28. Faxian and Abel-Rémusat, *Foĕ Kouĕ Ki, Ou, Relation Des Royaumes Bouddhiques: Voyage Dans La Tartarie, Dans l'Afghanistan et Dans l'Inde, Exécuté à La Fin Du IVe Siècle*, 7.
29. J. W. Laidley, *The Pilgrimage of Fa Hian; From the French Edition of the Foe Koue Ki of MM. Remusat, Klaproth, and Landresse with Additional Notes and Illustrations* (Calcutta: J. Thomas, Baptist Mission Press, 1848), 14 n. 8.
30. Blo bzang rta mgrin, "Chen Po Hān Gur Gyi Btsun Pa Phā Hyin Gyis 'phags Pa'i Yul Du 'Grims Pa'i Rnam Thar Rgyal Bstan 'Byung Khungs Kun Gsal 'Phrul Gyi Me Long," 149.
31. Jean-Pierre Drège and Faxian, *Memoire Sur Les Pays Bouddhiques* (Paris: Les Belles Lettres, 2013), 5 n. 32.
32. Abel-Rémusat explains his reading of the characters in a footnote: Faxian and Abel-Rémusat, *Foĕ Kouĕ Ki, Ou, Relation Des Royaumes Bouddhiques: Voyage Dans La Tartarie, Dans l'Afghanistan et Dans l'Inde, Exécuté à La Fin Du IVe Siècle*, 15 n. 10.
33. Faxian and Abel-Rémusat, 15 n. 10.
34. Faxian and Abel-Rémusat, 15 n. 10.
35. Dorji Banzarov, "Burqan-u Nom Delgeregsen Ulus-Nuγud-Tur J̌ iγulčilγsan Bičig," in *Travels of Fa Hsian Translated by Dordji Bansaroff*, ed. Byambyn Rinchen, Corpus Scriptorum Mongolorum Instituti Linguae Litterarum Academiae Scientiarum Reipublicae Populi Mongolici 5 (Ulanbator: Mongol Ulsîn Shinjlekh Ukhaani Akademi, 1970), 13.
36. For a broad discussion of this vast vision in the broader historiography of Lubsangdamdin, which drew on not only Qing sources but also newly available Orientalist texts, see chapter 2, "Felt," in King, *Ocean of Milk, Ocean of Blood*.
37. Faxian and Abel-Rémusat, *Foĕ Kouĕ Ki, Ou, Relation Des Royaumes Bouddhiques: Voyage Dans La Tartarie, Dans l'Afghanistan et Dans l'Inde, Exécuté à La Fin Du IVe Siècle*, 5–6 n. 12.
38. Blo bzang rta mgrin, "Chen Po Hān Gur Gyi Btsun Pa Phā Hyin Gyis 'phags Pa'i Yul Du 'Grims Pa'i Rnam Thar Rgyal Bstan 'Byung Khungs Kun Gsal 'Phrul Gyi Me Long," 148.
39. Faxian 法顯, "The Biography of the Eminent Monk Faxian (Gaoseng Faxian Zhuan 高僧法顯傳)," 0866b19.
40. Faxian and Abel-Rémusat, *Foĕ Kouĕ Ki, Ou, Relation Des Royaumes Bouddhiques: Voyage Dans La Tartarie, Dans l'Afghanistan et Dans l'Inde, Exécuté à La Fin Du IVe Siècle*, 362.
41. Banzarov, "Burqan-u Nom Delgeregsen Ulus-Nuγud-Tur J̌ iγulčilγsan Bičig," 40.
42. Blo bzang rta mgrin, "Chen Po Hān Gur Gyi Btsun Pa Phā Hyin Gyis 'phags Pa'i Yul Du 'Grims Pa'i Rnam Thar Rgyal Bstan 'Byung Khungs Kun Gsal 'Phrul Gyi Me Long," 239.
43. Faxian 法顯, "The Biography of the Eminent Monk Faxian (Gaoseng Faxian Zhuan 高僧法顯傳)," 0857c01.

44. Faxian and Abel-Rémusat, *Foĕ Kouĕ Ki, Ou, Relation Des Royaumes Bouddhiques: Voyage Dans La Tartarie, Dans l'Afghanistan et Dans l'Inde, Exécuté à La Fin Du IVe Siècle*, 18.
45. Banzarov, "Burqan-u Nom Delgeregsen Ulus-Nuyud-Tur J̌ iyulčilysan Bičig," 14.
46. Blo bzang rta mgrin, "Chen Po Hān Gur Gyi Btsun Pa Phā Hyin Gyis 'phags Pa'i Yul Du 'Grims Pa'i Rnam Thar Rgyal Bstan 'Byung Khungs Kun Gsal 'Phrul Gyi Me Long," 153.
47. Blo bzang rta mgrin, 153.
48. Faxian and Abel-Rémusat, *Foĕ Kouĕ Ki, Ou, Relation Des Royaumes Bouddhiques: Voyage Dans La Tartarie, Dans l'Afghanistan et Dans l'Inde, Exécuté à La Fin Du IVe Siècle*, 36.
49. Blo bzang rta mgrin, "Chen Po Hān Gur Gyi Btsun Pa Phā Hyin Gyis 'phags Pa'i Yul Du 'Grims Pa'i Rnam Thar Rgyal Bstan 'Byung Khungs Kun Gsal 'Phrul Gyi Me Long," 158.
50. Blo bzang rta mgrin, 493.
51. Blo bzang rta mgrin, 493.
52. Faxian and Abel-Rémusat, *Foĕ Kouĕ Ki, Ou, Relation Des Royaumes Bouddhiques: Voyage Dans La Tartarie, Dans l'Afghanistan et Dans l'Inde, Exécuté à La Fin Du IVe Siècle*, 227.
53. Faxian and Abel-Rémusat, 250 n. 6.
54. Faxian and Abel-Rémusat, 250 n. 6.
55. For some quite relevant introductions to Bön in relation to Tibetan historical traditions, see: Samten G. Karmey, *A General Introduction to the History and Doctrines of Bon* (Tokyo: Toyo Bunko, 1975); Zeff Bjerken, "The Mirrorwork of Tibetan Religious Historians: A Comparison of Buddhist and Bon Historiography" (Ph.D. diss., University of Michigan, 2001). For an important scaling of Bön in relation to competing philosophical "views" across Inner and East Asia by a Géluk scholastic working in the Qing frame (one widely referenced by Lubsangdamdin in his broader historiography), see Thuken Losang Chökyi Nyima, *The Crystal Mirror of Philosophical Systems: A Tibetan Study of Asian Religious Thought*, trans. Geshé Lundub Sopa, vol. 25, The Library of Tibetan Classics (Boston: Wisdom, 2009), 321–30.
56. For related discussions, see: Jacob Paul Dalton, *The Taming of the Demons: Violence and Liberation in Tibetan Buddhism* (New Haven, Conn.: Yale University Press, 2011); Janet Gyatso, "Down with the Demoness: Reflections on a Feminine Ground in Tibet," in *Feminine Ground: Essays on Women and Tibet*, ed. Janice Dean Willis (Ithaca, N.Y.: Snow Lion, 1995), 33–51; Martin A. Mills, "Ritual as History in Tibetan Divine Kingship: Notes on the Myth of the Khotanese Monks,"*History of Religions History of Religions* 51, no. 3 (2012): 219–20; Charlene Makley, "Gendered Boundaries in Motion: Space and Identity on the Sino-Tibetan Frontier,"*American Ethnologist: The Journal of the American Ethnological Society* 30, no. 4 (2003): 597–619.
57. Dorzhi Banzarov, *Chernaya Vera Ili Shamanastvo u Mongolov i Drugiya Stat'i D. Banzarova [The Black Faith, or Shamanism Among the Mongols, and Other Articles by D. Banzarov]*, ed. G. N. Potanin (St. Petersburg, 1891).
58. Not only has Klaproth misread and mistranscribed *dao ren* 道人, he comes up with a translation for 士道 that is unreferenced and seems uncorroborated. Faxian and Abel-Rémusat, *Foĕ Kouĕ Ki, Ou, Relation Des Royaumes Bouddhiques: Voyage Dans La Tartarie, Dans l'Afghanistan et Dans l'Inde, Exécuté à La Fin Du IVe Siècle*, 251 n. 6.
59. I.e., *Bonbo-nar-yin nom*. Here Klaproth is referring to the putative founder of the Bön tradition, Tönpa Shénrap Miwoché (*Ston pa gshen rabs mi wo che*), a founding figure unknown in any Tibetan source prior to the tenth century who is said to have lived many tens of thousands of years ago, thus long predating the life of the Buddha Śākyamuni. Faxian and Abel-Rémusat, 251 n. 6.

60. Sandor Csoma de Körös, *Essay Towards a Dictionary Tibetan and English. Prepared with the Assis Tance of Bande Sangs-Rgyas Phun-Tshogs* (Calcutta: Baptist Mission Press, 1834).
61. Ssanang Ssetsen and Isaak Jakob Schmidt, *Geschichte der Ost-Mongolen und ihres Fürstenhauses; aus dem Mongolischen übersetzt und mit dem Originaltexte, nebst Anmerkungen, Erläuterungen und Citaten aus andern unedirten Originalwerken herausgegeben* (St. Petersburg; Leipzeg: Gedruckt bei N. Gretsch, 1829), 23.
62. Blo bzang rta mgrin, "Chen Po Hān Gur Gyi Btsun Pa Phā Hyin Gyis 'phags Pa'i Yul Du 'Grims Pa'i Rnam Thar Rgyal Bstan 'Byung Khungs Kun Gsal 'Phrul Gyi Me Long," 213.
63. Faxian 法顯, "The Biography of the Eminent Monk Faxian (Gaoseng Faxian Zhuan 高僧法顯傳)," 0864a02–03.
64. Faxian and Jean-Pierre Abel-Rémusat, *Foĕ Kouĕ Ki, Ou, Relation Des Royaumes Bouddhiques: Voyage Dans La Tartarie, Dans l'Afghanistan et Dans l'Inde, Exécuté à La Fin Du IVe Siècle*, 302.
65. Blo bzang rta mgrin, "Chen Po Hān Gur Gyi Btsun Pa Phā Hyin Gyis 'phags Pa'i Yul Du 'Grims Pa'i Rnam Thar Rgyal Bstan 'Byung Khungs Kun Gsal 'Phrul Gyi Me Long," 231. And then in Rinchen's 1970 published version of Banzarov's Mongolian we find an editorial insertion, most likely by Rinchen based on Lubsangdamdin's creative translation from a half century earlier, that makes "scholarly Bön practitioner" into Mong. *ulus nuɣud-un [merged] bumbu-ner.* Banzarov, "Burqan-u Nom Delgeregsen Ulus-Nuɣud-Tur J̌ iɣulčilɣsan Bičig," 33.
66. Tib. *Phugs lugs, Dge ldan rtsis gsar*, and *Gser rtsis*, respectively. For a magisterial series of studies on Tibetan calendrical and mathematical systems (in their wider astrological context), see Dieter Schuh, *Studien zur Geschichte der Mathematik und Astronomie in Tibet*, Zentralasiatische Studien des Seminars für Sprach und Kulturwissenschaft Zentralasiens der Universität Bonn 4, 1970.
67. Blo bzang rta mgrin [Agvan Dorjiev], "Mtshan Zhabs Mkhan Chen Gyis Chos 'Byung Las Brtsams Te Bka' 'dri Gnang Ba'i Chab Shog," in *Rje Btsun Blo Bzang Rta Dbyangs Kyi Gsung 'bum*, 17 vols. (New Delhi: Mongolian Lama Guru Deva, 1975), 2:551–54.
68. "Valid cognition based on scripture" (Skt. *agamapramāṇa*; Tib. *lung gi tshad ma*). This is considered a species of valid knowledge (Skt. *pramāṇa*) for only some Tibetan scholastic traditions, and then only in conjunction with other kinds of *pramāna*.
69. Tib. *Phug.* This is one of the major Buddhist astrological/astronomical reckoning systems (*skar rtsis*) in Inner Asia, also referenced in Lubsangdamdin's colophon to his translation of Faxian's *Record.*
70. Tib. *Dga' ldan rtsis gsar.* Another major astrological/astronomical reckoning system (*skar rtsis*) from Inner Asia, which like the *Phug* system cited above was referenced in Lubsangdamdin's colophon to his translation of Faxian's *Record.*
71. This comes from Candrakīrti's *Entrance to the Middle Way* (Skt. *Madhyamakāvatāra*, Tib. *Dbu ma la'jug pa*).
72. The reference is to the Jétsun Rendawa Zhonnu Lodrös (Rje btsun red mda' ba gzhon nu blo gros, 1349–1412). Rendawa was a great scholar of the Sakya (Sa skya pa) tradition and one of the primary teachers of the founder of the Géluk school, Jé Tsongkhapa Lozang Drakpa (Rje tsong kha pa blo bzang grags pa, 1357–1419). In addition to his particular lineage of Madhyamaka teachings, Rendawa is most remembered by Géluk historians for channeling Mañjuśrī so that Tsongkhapa could make inquiries on philosophical and meditative subjects. See Bhikṣuṇī Jampa Tsedroen, *Red Mda' Ba: Buddhist Yogi-Scholar of the Fourteenth Century: The Forgotten Reviver of Madhyamaka Philosophy in Tibet* (Wiesbaden: L. Reichert, 2009).

73. Blo bzang rta mgrin, "Mtshan Zhabs Mkhan Chen Gyi Dogs Lan Tshangs Pa'i Drang Thig," 2:561–72.
74. Blo bzang rta mgrin, "Chen Po Hān Gur Gyi Btsun Pa Phā Hyin Gyis 'phags Pa'i Yul Du 'Grims Pa'i Rnam Thar Rgyal Bstan 'Byung Khungs Kun Gsal 'Phrul Gyi Me Long," 241.
75. Faxian 法顯, "The Biography of the Eminent Monk Faxian (Gaoseng Faxian Zhuan 高僧法顯傳)," 0865a26–27; Faxian and Abel-Rémusat, *Foĕ Kouĕ Ki, Ou, Relation Des Royaumes Bouddhiques: Voyage Dans La Tartarie, Dans l'Afghanistan et Dans l'Inde, Exécuté à La Fin Du IVe Siècle*, 346.
76. Blo bzang rta mgrin, "Chen Po Hān Gur Gyi Btsun Pa Phā Hyin Gyis 'phags Pa'i Yul Du 'Grims Pa'i Rnam Thar Rgyal Bstan 'Byung Khungs Kun Gsal 'Phrul Gyi Me Long," 228–29.
77. On the eyewitnessing of Sumpa Khenpo in relationship to the historicity of Ling Gésar, and its long interpretative legacy in late- and postimperial Mongolia and the Soviet Union, see Matthew W. King, "Knowing King Gésar Between Buddhist Monastery and Socialist Academy, Or the Practices of Secularism in Inner Asia,"*Himalaya: The Journal of the Association for Nepal and Himalayan Studies* 36, no. 10 (2016): 44–55.
78. Blo bzang rta mgrin, "Bka' Drin Gsum Ldan Rtsa Ba'i Bla Ma Rdo Rje 'chang Mkhan Chen Sangs Rgyas Mtshan Can Gyi Rnam Thar Gsol 'Debs Dad Ldan Yid Kyi Mdzas Rgyan," in *Rje Btsun Blo Bzang Rta Dbyangs Kyi Gsung 'bum*, 17 vols. (New Delhi: Mongolian Lama Guru Deva, 1975), 1:7–19. For a translation, see Matthew W. King, "Zava Damdin's 'Beautifying Ornament for the Mind of the Faithful: A Praise-Biography of My Root Lama Vajradhara, He Who Possesses the Three Types of Kindess, the Great Mahāpaṇḍita Endowed with Excellent Discipline and Learning Named 'Sanjaa,'" in *Sources of Mongolian Buddhism*, ed. Vesna A. Wallace (Oxford; New York: Oxford Univeristy Press, 2020), 99–122.
79. Blo bzang rta mgrin, "Chen Po Hān Gur Gyi Btsun Pa Phā Hyin Gyis 'phags Pa'i Yul Du 'Grims Pa'i Rnam Thar Rgyal Bstan 'Byung Khungs Kun Gsal 'Phrul Gyi Me Long," 202.
80. Blo bzang rta mgrin, 214.
81. Blo bzang rta mgrin, 222.
82. Blo bzang rta mgrin, 225.
83. Blo bzang rta mgrin, 226.

Conclusion

1. "Société Asiatique (Séance Du 7 Février 1831)," 237.
2. "Société Asiatique (Séance Du 7 Avril, 1831)," 405.
3. Bernard S. Cohn, *An Anthropologist Among the Historians and Other Essays* (Delhi: Oxford University Press, 1987); Michel-Rolph Trouillot, *Silencing the Past: Power and the Production of History* (Boston: Beacon, 2015).
4. Wael B. Hallaq, *Restating Orientalism: A Critique of Modern Knowledge* (New York: Columbia University Press, 2018).
5. Rens Bod, *A New History of the Humanities: The Search for Principles and Patterns from Antiquity to the Present* (London; New York: Oxford University Press, 2016), 5.
6. Zeynep Çelik, *Europe Knows Nothing About the Orient: A Critical Discourse (1872–1932)*, trans. Gregory Key and Aron Aji (Chicago: University of Chicago Press, 2021).
7. Braun, *The Birth of Insight*; David L. McMahan, *The Making of Buddhist Modernism* (New York: Oxford University Press, 2008); Robert H. Sharf, "Buddhist Modernism and the Rhetoric of Meditative Experience," *Numen* 42, no. 3 (1995): 228–83.

8. Sudipta Kaviraj, "Said and the History of Ideas," in *Cosmopolitan Thought Zones: South Asia and the Global Circulation of Ideas*, ed. Sugata Bose and Kris Manjapra (New York: Palgrave Macmillan, 2010), 75–76.
9. For example: E. Natalie Rothman, *Brokering Empire Trans-Imperial Subjects Between Venice and Istanbul* (Ithaca, N.Y.; London: Cornell University Press, 2012); Natalie Zemon Davis, "Decentering History: Local Stories and Cultural Crossings in a Global World,"*History and Theory* 50, no. 2 (2011); Natalie Zemon Davis, *Trickster Travels: A Sixteenth-Century MuslimBetween Worlds* (London: Faber and Faber, 2007); Danielle Elisseeff, *Moi, Arcade: interprète chinois du Roi-Soleil* (Paris: Arthaud, 1985).
10. Davis, *Trickster Travels*, 11.
11. Engseng Ho's fascinating study of the Hadrami Yemeni spread across empires ringing the Indian Ocean is a standout example (Engseng Ho, *The Graves of Tarim: Genealogy and Mobility across the Indian Ocean* [Berkeley: University of California Press, 2010]).
12. Bernard S. Cohn, *Colonialism and Its Forms of Knowledge: The British in India* (Princeton, N.J.: Princeton University Press, 1996); Homi K. Bhabha, *The Location of Culture* (London; New York: Routledge Classics, 1994); Michel-Rolph Trouillot, *Silencing the Past: Power and the Production of History* (Boston: Beacon Press, 2015); Michel-Rolph Trouillot, "Culture on the Margins: Caribbean Creolization in Historical Context," in *From the Margins: Historical Anthropology and Its Futures*, ed. Brian Keith Axel (Durham and London: Duke University Press, 2002), 189–210.
13. Natalie Zemon Davis, *Women on the Margins: Three Seventeenth-Century Lives*, rev. ed. (Cambridge, Mass: Belknap Press: An Imprint of Harvard University Press, 1997); Richard White, *The Middle Ground: Indians, Empires, and Republics in the Great Lakes Region, 1650–1815* (Cambridge; New York: Cambridge University Press, 1991); Paul Gilroy, *The Black Atlantic: Modernity and Double Consciousness* (London: Verso, 1993).
14. Brian Keith Axel, ed., *From the Margins: Historical Anthropology and Its Futures* (Durham; London: Duke University Press, 2002), 28.
15. Saidiya Hartman, "Venus in Two Acts,"*Small Axe: A Journal of Criticism* 26 (2008): 11; Fred Moten, *In the Break: The Aesthetics of the Black Radical Tradition* (Minneapolis: University of Minnesota Press, 2003), 14.
16. Johan Östling, "Circulation, Arenas, and the Quest for Public Knowledge: Historiographical Currents and Analytical Frameworks,"*History and Theory* 58 (2020): 120.
17. Alejandro A. Vallega and Indiana University, *Latin American Philosophy: From Identity to Radical Exteriority* (Bloomington: Indiana University Press, 2014).
18. Walter D. Mignolo, "Epistemic Disobedience, Independent Thought and De-Colonial Freedom,"*Theory, Culture, and Society* 26, no. 7–8 (2009): 1–23.
19. Arjun Appadurai, *Fear of Small Numbers: An Essay on the Geography of Anger* (Durham, N.C.: Duke University Press, 2006).
20. João Biehl and Peter Locke, *Unfinished: The Anthropology of Becoming* (Durham, N.C.: Duke University Press, 2017).
21. Tomoko Masuzawa, *The Invention of World Religions, or, How European Universalism Was Preserved in the Language of Pluralism* (Chicago: University of Chicago Press, 2005); Donald S. Lopez, *Curators of the Buddha: The Study of BuddhismUnder Colonialism* (Chicago: University of Chicago Press, 1995); Lopez, *Prisoners of Shangri-La: Tibetan Buddhism and the West* (Chicago: University of Chicago Press, 1998); Philip C. Almond, *The British Discovery of Buddhism* (Cambridge: Cambridge University Press, 2007); Gregory Schopen, "Archaeology and Protestant Presuppositions in the Study of Indian Buddhism,"*History of Religions* 31, no. 1 (1991):

1–23; David L. McMahan, *The Making of Buddhist Modernism* (New York: Oxford University Press, 2008); Thierry Dodin and Heinz Räther, *Imagining Tibet: Perceptions, Projections, and Fantasies* (Boston: Wisdom, 2001).

22. Ann Laura Stoler and Brian Keith Axel, "Developing Historical Negatives: Race and the [Modernist] Visions of a Colonial State," in *From the Margins: Historical Anthropology and Its Futures* (Durham, N.C. and London: Duke University Press, 2002), 157.
23. Gilles Deleuze and Félix Guattari, *A Thousand Plateaus*, trans. Brian Massumi (Minneapolis; London: University of Minnesota Press, 2005), 7.
24. Jeremy Ahearne, *Michel de Certeau: Interpretation and Its Other* (Stanford, Calif.: Stanford University Press, 1995), 24.

Appendix. The Inner Asian *Record*

1. Shi Faxian 釋法顯, "Fo Guo Ji: 1 Juan/(Song) Shi Fa Xian Zhuan 佛國記: 1卷/(宋) 釋法顯撰," in *Jin Dai Mi Shu* 津逮秘書, vol. 17, 200 vols., Anc. Fourmont 304 (Zhong guo 中國: Ji gu ge cang 汲古閣藏, 1628), Feuillet 25 ms. Because of the pandemic, I could not visit Paris as I planned to make a copy of this manuscript and use it as the basis for pagination here. In my reading, happily, there are no divergences from T 2085 in the Parisian edition, and so hopefully the cross-referencing I provide will still be of use.
2. Faxian 法顯, "The Biography of the Eminent Monk Faxian (Gaoseng Faxian Zhuan 高僧法顯傳)" Vol. 51. 2085 (Tokyo: Taishō Shinshū Daizōkyō Kankōkai, 1988); Jean-Pierre Drège and Faxian, *Memoire Sur Les Pays Bouddhiques* (Paris: Les Belles Lettres, 2013); Max Deeg and Faxian, *Das Gaoseng-Faxian-Zhuan Als Religionsgeschichtliche Quelle: Der Älteste Bericht Eines Chinesischen Buddhistischen Pilgermönchs Über Seine Reise Nach Indien Mit Übersetzung Des Textes* (Wiesbaden, Germany: Harrassowitz, 2005).
3. Volume 17 of Mao Jin (毛晉), *Jin Dai Mi Shu/(Ming) Mao Jin Jiao Kan;*津逮秘書/毛晉校刊*; Tsin Tai Pi Chou/Mao Tsin Kiao k'an*, 25 vols. (汲古閣刊本, 1628). FRBNF44591130.
4. Blo bzang rta mgrin, "Chen Po Hān Gur Gyi Btsun Pa Phā Hyin Gyis 'phags Pa'i Yul Du 'Grims Pa'i Rnam Thar Rgyal Bstan 'Byung Khungs Kun Gsal 'Phrul Gyi Me Long," in *Rje Btsun Blo Bzang Rta Dbyangs Kyi Gsung 'bum* (New Delhi: Mongolian Lama Guru Deva, 1975), 1:145–244.
5. Tib. *Rgyal po zas gtsang.*
6. Tib. *ltas mkhan rnams.*
7. Skt. *mahātma*; Tib. *bdag nyid chen po.*
8. Blo bzang rta mgrin (1975, 146) has this last sentence as *de yang yig tshang du bzhag'dug*, while LDR (42) has it nonsensically as *de yang yig tshang du zhag bdun'dug.*
9. Tib. *Hān gur gyi ming dhi rgyal po.* This would be Emperor Ming Di (明帝, 28–75 CE) of the Han dynasty (漢朝, 202 BCE–9 CE, 25–220 CE).
10. Tib. *Thang zing bla ma*. Xuanzang 玄奘 (c. 600–665) was the author of the *Records of the Western Regions of the Great Tang Dynasty* (*Da tang xiyu ji* 大唐西域記).
11. Tib. *I kying*, i.e., Yijing 義淨 (635–713 CE), Tang-era traveler who visited Central Asia, India, and Indonesia, composed *Record of Buddhist Practices Sent Home from the Southern Sea* (*Nanhai jigui neifa zhuan* 南海寄歸內法傳).
12. Tib. *Thos bzung.*
13. Tib. *rig gnas.*
14. Tib. *Gnas brtan'od srung.*

15. Tib. *Phal chen sde'i'dul ba.*
16. *Zhes gsungs pa de nyid yin par snang.* This line is only in LDR (42/2r3).
17. Tib. *rgya ser phe ling,* i.e., Jean-Pierre Abel-Rémusat.
18. Tib. *Chang ang*; Mong. *Čang-an* (13); Fr. *Tchhang'an* (1); Ch. 長安 (0857a08).
19. Banzarov writes that the elderly monk departed Chang'an "in order to increase the Dharma (*nom*) and religious rites (*toγtaγal-nuγud*)" (Dorji Banzarov, "Burqan-u Nom Delgeregsen Ulus-Nuγud-Tur J̌ iγulčilγsan Bičig," In *Travels of Fa HsianTrans. Dordǰi Bansaroff*, ed. Byambyn Rinchen. Corpus Scriptorum Mongolorum Instituti Linguae Litterarum Academiae Scientiarum Reipublicae Populi Mongolici 5 [Ulanbator: Mongol Ulsîn Shinjlekh Ukhaani Akademi, 1970], 13).
20. Tib. *H+phang zhi*; Mong. *Qung-ši qaγaan*; Fr. *Houng chi*; Ch. 弘始.
21. Tib. *H+pha zhi kin, Dha'u chang, H+pha zhi ing,* and *H+pha zhi wyi*; Mong. *Qui-king, Dau-J̌ing, Qui-ying,* and *Qui-u*; Fr. *Hoeï king, Tao tching, Hoeī ing,* and *Hoeï weï*; Ch. 慧景, 道整, 慧應, and 慧嵬.
22. Tib. *Lu'ang zhes pa'i ri rgyud*; Mong. *Lüng aγula*; Fr. *(mont) Loung*; Ch. *Long (shan)* 隴(山).
23. Tib. *Hyin ju sho*; Mong. *Čiyan-qui*; Fr. *Khian koueï*; Ch . Qiangui 乾歸.
24. The Machu (*Rma chu*) is better known outside of Tibetan-speaking (or reading) societies as the Yellow River (黄河 *Huang he*), one of Asia's major river systems and the second longest in China. The settlement where Faxian and his companions rested, near what became known as Lanzhou only in the seventeenth century, had been an important commercial, military, and cultural hub along the northern Silk Route since at least the first millennium BCE. Around the time of Faxian, it was incorporated into the independent Liang state (320–376 CE, one of the Sixteen Kingdoms during the Jin Dynasty, 265–420 CE). Later it was absorbed by the Northern Wei dynasty (386–534 CE). It was conquered by the Tibetan empire in 763 CE, by the Tang dynasty in 843 CE, and by the ever-expanding Mongol Empire in 1235.
25. Tib. *Ni'i tha*; Mong. *Niu tan*; Fr. *Neou than*; Ch. *Noutan guo* 耨檀國.
26. Tib. *Khyo'u wa*; Mong. *J̌ang-ye*; Fr. *Tchang ỹ*; Ch. *Zhangye* 張掖.
27. Tib. *Cha'i yāng, H+pha zhi hyen, Se wang sho'o, Pha lu cung,* and *Sāng kāng*; Mong. *J̌ i yang*; *Küi yin*; *Seng šyu*; *Buu yün*; and *Seng ging*; Fr. *Tchi yan, Hoeï kian, Seng chao, Pao yun, Seng king*; Ch. Zhiyan 智嚴, Huijian 慧簡, Sengshao 僧紹, Baoyun 寶雲, and Sengjing 僧景.
28. Tib. *Tun ha'ang*; Mong. *düng-huwang*; Fr. *Thun houang*; Ch. *Dunhuang* 燉煌. Lubsangdamdin's transcription of Dunhuang here (*Tun ha'ang*) is completely different than the subtitle heading he provides for this chapter (*Thwang kwang*) just a folio earlier.
29. Strangely, instead of translating Baoyun 寶雲 into Tibetan as Pha lu cung (from Mongolian Buu yün), as he does just a few lines above, here and later in this chapter, Lubsangdamdin gives Hwe cun: "Hwe cun dang grogs gzhan dag las gyes so" (Blo bzang rta mgrin, "Chen Po Hān Gur Gyi Btsun Pa Phā Hyin Gyis 'phags Pa'i Yul Du 'Grims Pa'i Rnam Thar Rgyal Bstan 'Byung Khungs Kun Gsal 'Phrul Gyi Me Long," 148).
30. Tib. *Li ke'u*; Mong. *Li hiu*; Fr. *Li hao*; Ch. *Li Gao* 李暠.
31. Tib. *She na zhang*; Mong. *Šin šin* (13); Fr. *Chen chen* (7); Ch. *Shan shan guo* 鄯鄯國 (0857a19).
32. Tib. *U ja* (though just below, as is common in LD, this is spelled differently: *U jang*); Mong. *U i*; Fr. *Ou i*; Ch. *Yanyi guo* 焉夷國. Drège identifies Yanyi as Qarašahr, an "oasis that became Chinese sixty years BCE, then retaken by the Xiongnu, then passed again under Chinese domination in 94 CE" (Drège and Faxian, *Memoire Sur Les Pays Bouddhiques*, 5 n. 32).
33. Tib. *Ka'u chang*; Mong. *Γaučang* (13); Fr. *Kao tchhang*; Ch. *Gaochang* 高昌.
34. Tib. *Theg pa chung ngu*; Mong. *Baγ-a kölgen.*

35. Reading the Uighurs into the *Record* came from Abel-Rémusat's reflections in a footnote, which were then written into the body of the text by Banzarov, and then elaborated upon extensively by Lubsangdamdin in light of his late Qing scholastic historical tradition. See chapter 4 for some details.
36. The reference in the Chinese is to "monks from Qin" (秦土沙門 0857a26). The Qin "references the Former Qin (351–395), Western [Qin] (385–431), and Later [Qin] (384–417), but also, more generally, China as a whole" (Robert E. Buswell and Donald S. Lopez, *The Princeton Dictionary of Buddhism* [Princeton, N. J.: Princeton University Press, 2013], 253).
37. Abel-Rémusat and Faxian's later European translators all struggled with translating *zhingdang* 行當. Abel-Rémusat has "Fă hian, qui était muni d'une patente, se rendit au campement où *Koung sun.*" (JPAR 7). Drège clarifies that the word *zhingdang* 行當 should in fact be *zhingtang* 行堂, referring to rights of passage reserved for monks, which is quite in line with Lubsangdamdin's interpretation of Banzarov above (Drège and Faxian, *Memoire Sur Les Pays Bouddhiques*, 5, n. 34).
38. Tib. *Hung tsun*; Mong. *Küng sün*; Fr. *Koung sun*; Ch. *Gongsun* 公孫.
39. This sentence, a radical departure from previous translations, is an important illumination of the creative liberties and politicization of Faxian's *Record* in Tibetan translation for the twentieth century. See chapter 5 for more details.
40. Here Lubsangdamdin writes Ka'u chāng, whereas just above he writes unmarked Ka'u chang.
41. "Fording the rivers was extremely difficult" (Tib. *chu klung dag ni brgal bar shin tu dka' bas*). In the Chinese it is "crossing [the sand] was difficult" 涉行艱難 (0857b02), which Abel-Rémusat mistranslated as "On a une peine extreme pour passer les rivières" (JPAR 8), apparently focusing on the meaning of *she* 涉 as "to ford (a body of water)."
42. Tib. *Ho thon yul gru*; Mong. *Kotung* (14); Fr. *Royaume d'Yu thian* (15); Ch. *Yutian (guo)* 于闐(國) (0857b03–04).
43. Tib. *Theg pa chen po*; Mong. *Yeke kölgen.*
44. The original Chinese reads something like "The houses of those countrymen (are as vast as the) stars 彼國人 民星居" (GFZ 0857b05–06). Abel-Rémusat has instead "Les gens du pays fixent leur demeure d'apres les étoiles" (JPAR 16). Banzarov followed the French, and later Lubsangdamdin followed Banzarov's Mongolian as above (though in the Tibetan it appears that *'bub* is misspelled and should be *'bubs*: "raise," "pitch," or "put up").
45. Tib. *mchod rten*; Mong. *suburγan.*
46. I.e., "two *zhang* 丈," or as Abel-Rémusat has it, "deux toises": about twenty feet, or 4.62 meters.
47. Tib. *Go ma tri*; Mong. *Γomati*; Fr. *Kiu ma ti*; Ch. *Qumodi* 瞿摩帝. According to Sengyou's *Chu sanzang*, this monastery was the site where the early Chinese translator Anyang Hou met the Indian monk Buddhasena (see Drège and Faxian, *Memoire Sur Les Pays Bouddhiques*, 6 n. 42).
48. *rda*: i.e., the sounding of a gong, etc. Deeg gives the Sanskrit *gaṇḍī* for a monastic bell (Deeg and Faxian, *Das Gaoseng-Faxian-Zhuan Als Religionsgeschichtliche Quelle: Der Älteste Bericht Eines Chinesischen Buddhistischen Pilgermönchs Über Seine Reise Nach Indien Mit Übersetzung Des Textes*, 512).
49. The Chinese reads *Jiecha guo* 竭叉國 (0857b12).
50. *grum tse chen po dang ras sra rtsi can.* The Tibetan is a little convoluted to me. Abel-Rémusat has "large tapestries and hangings" (*grande tapisseries et des tentures*), Drège has "a large wall hanging and curtains" (*une grande tenture et des rideaux*), and Deeg has "a large single-layered cloth" (*einlagiges Tuch*), all to translate 其城門上張 大幃幕" (0857b14–15).
51. As almost always in Lubsangdamdin's translation, the transcription of foreign names is wildly divergent, even in the space of a paragraph or two, or between the chapter headings

and bodies. Here our author gives *Go ma thye* for Gomatrī, whereas just above we have *Go ma tri* (all based, as far as I can tell, on Banzarov's *Γomati*).

52. LD has *brog zhwa.*
53. *rgyang grags.* The unit of measurement in FGZ is *li* 里, which is also given by Abel-Rémusat.
54. *Rgyal po'i gtsug lag khang so ma*; i.e., Wangxin si 王新寺 (FGZ 0857b26).
55. Here we have a rather radical change to the *Record* by Lubsangdamdin, whose insertion of "Mongol princes" into the text is quite at odds with the Chinese. For more details, see chapter 5.
56. LD and LDR both exclude the third subtitle from the Tibetan translation, which Abel-Rémusat gives as *Royaume de Yu hoeï*, faithfully translated by Banzarov as *Iu qui orun* (15).
57. As part of his much larger historiographic project, and as part of his work to Mongolize Faxian's *Record*, here Lubsangdamdin switches from using Khotan (*Ho thon*) to "the Land of Li" (*Li yul*), which helps bring Faxian's witnessing into the tantric-inflected, prophecy-fueled late imperial historical imagination of the Sino-Tibetan-Mongolia-Russian frontiers. See chapter 5 for more.
58. Tib. *Phi ka*; Mong. *Ki ping* (15); Fr. *Ki pin* (22); Ch. *Jibin* 罽賓 (0857c03). Summarizing the secondary literature, Deeg provides that "Jibin" may have been a Han transcription of a Prākṛit rendering of Kāśmīra; which, unlike Lubsangdamdin in the Tibetan, is how Deeg translates "Jibin" in his German translation of Faxian's *Record.* Drège adds that, by the Tang dynasty, "Jibin" came to designate "à la region de Kaboul et de la Kapiśa" (Deeg and Faxian, *Das Gaoseng-Faxian-Zhuan Als Religionsgeschichtliche Quelle: Der Älteste Bericht Eines Chinesischen Buddhistischen Pilgermönchs Über Seine Reise Nach Indien Mit Übersetzung Des Textes*, 514 n. 2310; Drège and Faxian, *Memoire Sur Les Pays Bouddhiques*, 9 n. 55).
59. Tib. *Dzu ho ci'i yul khams*; Mong. *Tsi hi orun* (15); Fr. *le royaume de Tsen hŏ* (22); Ch. *Zihe guo* 子合國 (0857c03).
60. LD has this line: *thang zing la'ang bdag rkyen dpe med mdzad 'dug cing,* while LDR provides a correction to *mdzad: thang zing la'ang bdag rkyen dpe med brjod 'dug cing.* I have followed Rinchen's useful correction in the translation above.
61. Tib. *Tshung ling* (though spelled *Tshāung Ling* in chapter headings in both LD and LDR); Mong. *Tsüng ling*; Fr. *les monts Tsoung ling* (22); Ch. *Congling shan* 葱嶺山 (0857c05).
62. Tib. *U ho iu 'u'i yul*; Mong. *Iu qui orun*; Fr. *royaume de Yu hoeï* (22); Ch. *Yuhui guo* 於麾國 (0857c06).
63. Tib. *Kha tshe'i yul*; Mong. *Kiǰyi ša orun* (15); Fr. *Royaume de Kĕ tchha* (26); Ch. *Jiecha guo* 竭叉國 (0857c06–07).
64. Mong. *Tabunǰil-ün yekečiγulγen* (*Ban ši yüyi si*); Fr. *Grande assemblée quinquennale* (*Pan tche yuĕ sse*); Ch. *Banzhe yueshi* 般遮越師. In Sanskrit: *pañcavārṣika.* A quinquennial assembly convened first by King Aśoka and widely replicated in ancient Buddhist Central Asia. Monastics would gather and publicly perfom rituals and processions for royalty and throngs of laity every five years, all while being honored with offerings and other forms of patronage.
65. *nas* can also be more specifically "barley," but JPAR has "grain" (*blé*).
66. Tib. *chos kyi'khor lo*; Mong. *Nom-un kürdün.*
67. "Bamboo" *zhu* 竹; "pomegranate" *anshiliu* 安石榴; and "sugarcane" *ganzhe* 甘蔗 (FGZ 0857c23–24).
68. I.e., *Bei Tianzhu* 北天竺 (0857c25).
69. Literally: "In the time of (an) empty stomach, there are venom-spitting poisonous snakes (*lto stongs kyi tshe na dug gtong ba'i dug sprul yod cing*)." Like me, JPAR has trouble with this sentence, translating it cautiously and rather creatively as "Il y aussi des dragons venimeux qui vomissent leur venin, s'ils viennent à manquer leur proie" (30). His discussion of

ambiguities in the Chinese root text for this passage is in JPAR 31 n. 1. Drège offers a much clearer translation of this passage from the Chinese (FGZ 0857c26–27), mostly mirrored in Deeg: "There are also venomous dragons who, if they are lost (Fr. *égarés,* Deeg gives "if they are irritated" Ger. *gereizt*), spit poisoned wind, rain, or snow, flying sand or gravel. Of those who encounter these obstacles, not one out of ten thousand would escape 又有毒龍若失其意則吐毒 風雨雪飛沙礫石遇此難者萬無一全" (Drège and Faxian, *Memoire Sur Les Pays Bouddhiques,* 11; Deeg and Faxian, *Das Gaoseng-Faxian-Zhuan Als Religionsgeschichtliche Quelle: Der Älteste Bericht Eines Chinesischen Buddhistischen Pilgermönchs Über Seine Reise Nach Indien Mit Übersetzung Des Textes,* 517).

70. Tib. *Tu li rgyal khams*; Mong. *Tho li*; Fr. *Tho lỳ*; Ch. *Tuoli* 陀歷.
71. Tib. *Byams pa*; Mong. *Maidari bodisadu-a*; Fr. *Mi lě phou sa*; Ch. *Mile pusa* 彌勒菩薩. See chapter 5 for more on Maitreya.
72. LDR (44) completely miscopies the name of Madhyāntika in this interlinear note, writing "*dgra bcom pa zhig byung bas*" instead of "*dgra bcom pa nyi ma gung pa*" as we find in LD (156).
73. *Ri bo 'di dag ni rgyang grags stong phrag brgyad du mtho.* The Chinese reads "rock faces one thousand *ren* high 石壁立千仞" (FGZ 0858a06), which using Drège's reckoning would be somewhere between four thousand and eight thousand feet high (Drège and Faxian, *Memoire Sur Les Pays Bouddhiques*, 12 n. 79). Abel-Rémusat apparent misread this passage and gives "des murailles de rochers qui ont huit mille pieds d'élévation" (JPAR 55), followed by Banzarov and, above, Lubsangdamdin.
74. FGZ (0858a06) and JPAR (55) speak instead of one's vision becoming blurry in these mountains.
75. Tib. *si+ndhu chu klung*; Mong. *Sind mören*; Fr. *le fleuveSin theou*; Ch. *Xintou he* 新頭河.
76. *Them skas* can also be ladder, and indeed this is what JPAR provides (*échelles*) (35), apparently playing off the ambiguity of *ti* 梯 (FGZ 0858a08) as either "stairs" or "ladder." It is difficult to imagine a "ladder" chiseled "across" (*phrad du*) a cliff face that would not be better described as stairs.
77. Tib. *Chāng ke yāng*; Mong. *J̌ang kin*; Fr. *Tchang khian.* Zhang Qian 張騫 (died c. 114 BCE) was a famous envoy of Emperor Wu of the Han dynasty. See chapter 5 for more.
78. Tib. *Ge yāng;* Mong. *Gan ying.* Gan Ying 甘英 was famously sent by the Chinese general Bao Chao as an envoy to the Roman Empire in 97 CE, though the former only made it as far as "the western sea" (the Mediterranean, the Persian Gulf, or perhaps the Black Sea). Nonetheless, Gan Ying did provide China with its first descriptions of Roman territories, customs, and political economy.
79. This is rather different than FGZ or JPAR. The latter has: "*Tchang khian* et *Kan yng*, sous la dynastie des Han, dans leurs voyages, dont les secrétaries interprètes du cabinet des affaires étrangères ont donné la relation, ne sont, ni l'un ni la'autre, parvenus jusqu'a ce point" (35). The former specifies that this perilous passage had "interrupted the 'Nine Translations' (*jiu yi* 九譯, FGZ 0858a09)." This all refers to passages from Zhang Qian's biography (see Drège and Faxian, *Memoire Sur Les Pays Bouddhiques*, 13 n. 83; Deeg and Faxian, *Das Gaoseng-Faxian-Zhuan Als Religionsgeschichtliche Quelle: Der Älteste Bericht Eines Chinesischen Buddhistischen Pilgermönchs Über Seine Reise Nach Indien Mit Übersetzung Des Textes*, 519 n. 2335).
80. Tib. *sangs rgyas mya ngan las 'das (pa)*; Mong. *Burqan-u nirvan.* Here referring to the Buddha Śākyamuni's death, or "final nirvāṇa" (Skt. *parinirvāṇa*), which occurred, as it does, according to the Mahāyāna, for all buddhas of this fortunate eon, at Kuśinagarī. This is described famously in the *Mahāparinirvāṇa Sūtra*, which as we shall soon see, Faxian first brought to

Chinese letters and audiences in a 416 CE translation completed after his journey with Buddhabhadra.

81. Emperor Ping 平王 (r. 770–720 BCE) = Tib. *H+phang nāng rgyal po*; Mong. *Phang qaγan*; Fr. *Phing wang*. "Zhou dynasty" (actually, in Chinese and French, "Family of Zhou") = Tib. *Ce'u gur*; Mong. *J̌iu ulus*; Fr. *la familie de Tcheou*; Ch. *Zhou shi* 周氏. Drège notes that by this reckoning, the Buddha would have passed into nirvāṇa eight hundred years before the Common Era (Drège and Faxian, *Memoire Sur Les Pays Bouddhiques*, 13 n. 86). For Abel-Rémusat, this response by Faxian to the curious monks of north India provided occasion for a truly historic footnote on the life and dating of the life the Buddha Śākyamuni, a paradigmatic statement in the nascent science of Buddhist Asia and the first scholarly statement on the topic to European readers. See chapter 5 for more details.
82. See chapter 5 for more details.
83. Tib. *Chen po hān gyi ming dhī'i rgyal po*; Mong. *Ming-di qaγan*; Fr. *Ming ti de la dynasties des Han*; Ch. *Han Ming Di* 漢明帝. See chapter 5 for more on this important story and the reception of East Asian and European knowledge in late imperial Inner Asian scholasticism.
84. Tib. *U khyāng yul gru*; Mong. *Uǰang-un orun*; Fr. *Ou tchang*; Ch. *Wuzhan guo* 烏長國 (0858a18).
85. It seems that there was a misreading between "precisely" and "presently" here, since Abel-Rémusat reads "This kingdom of Odiyāna precisely makes up the northern section of India" (*Ce royaume d'Ou tchang forme précisément la partie septentrionale de l'Inde*, 45). Banzarov apparently misread "présentement" instead of "précisément," translating this sentence *edüke* ("at present," p. 16), which is followed faithfully by Lubsangdamdin (as *da lta*, "presently") and forever after in the Tibetan.
86. Should be *gyang* (i.e., one wall's height).
87. Tib. *Na he ye*; Mong *Nakei-a he-a*; Fr. *Na kiĕ* (45); Ch. *Najie guo* 那竭國 (0858a27). Deeg and Drège each note that "Najie guo" could refer to either Nagara or Nagarahāra (Drège and Faxian, *Memoire Sur Les Pays Bouddhiques*, 14; Deeg and Faxian, *Das Gaoseng-Faxian-Zhuan Als Religionsgeschichtliche Quelle: Der Älteste Bericht Eines Chinesischen Buddhistischen Pilgermönchs Über Seine Reise Nach Indien Mit Übersetzung Des Textes*, 521).
88. Tib. *Sang rgyas kyi grib ma*; Mong. *Burqan-u següder*. As we shall see, Faxian will visit the Buddha's shadow and give a fascinating "eyewitness" account that offered much fodder for the purificatory treatments of Abel-Rémusat and, especially, his friend and editor Klaproth.
89. Tib. *Sho ka tho yi yul gru*; Mong *Su hi tu orun*; Fr. *Sŭ ho to*; Ch. *Suheduo guo* 宿呵多國 (0858a28).
90. The Chinese sentence refers to Indra by an epithet, Śakra (Tian Di Shi 天帝釋).
91. Tib. *Kanda wa ye* (though, as usual, spelled differently in the chapter heading as *Kanda wye*); Fr. *Kian tho weï*; Ch. *Jiantuowei guo* 揵陀衛國. Interestingtly, in his rendering of Abel-Rémusat's subtitle Banzarov gives both a transcription of Abel-Rémusat's title (Mong. *Kiyan to yei*) and also its reference (*Gandar-a*).
92. Tib. *Wa ye*; Fr. *Fă i*; Ch. Fayi 法益. Interestingly, Banzarov skips transcribing the French and, clearly from reading Abel-Rémusat's identification of Fayi's Sanskrit name in a footnote (67 n. 2), gives: Mong. *Dharmavarddhan-a*.
93. Tib. *Bru sha si li yul*; Mong. *J̌uča ši lo orun* (17); Fr. *Royaume de Tchŭ cha chi lo* (76);*Zhushashiluo* 竺剎尸羅 (0858b06–07). Takṣaśilā, or *Taxila* in Greek, was the capital of Gandhāra (located in Punjab province of today's Pakistan).
94. Tib. *Chos skyob*. "Dharmatrāta (fl. c. 100–150, alias Bhadanta Dharmatrāta or Dharmatrāta I), was a Dārṣṭāntika from northwest India. This Dharmatrāta, along with Vasumitra, Ghoṣa, and Buddhadeva, was one of the four great Abhidharmakas whom Xuanzang says

participated in the Buddhist Council (Saṃgīti) convened by the Kushan king Kaniṣka (r. c. 144–178 CE) and headed by Parśva" (Buswell and Lopez, *The Princeton Dictionary of Buddhism*, 253).

95. Here the reference is to the *Jātaka* tales about the Buddha's spiritual heroism over his many previous lives as a bodhisattva, a favorite literary and visual genre in much of the Buddhist world. For a discussion of how Abel-Rémusat understood and explained the Buddha's previous lives to his European audience (using, among other sources, the Mongolian history *Altan Gerel*), see chapter 4.
96. Lubsangdamdin (or his scribe) here spells "the country of Gandhāra" differently again: *Ki n+to wye ljongs.*
97. Tib. *Phu'i tsa'u sha'i yul,* though spelled differently in the subtitle as *Bha ro si ka*; Mong. *Burušayin orun* (17); Fr. *Foĕ leou cha* (76); Ch. *Fulousha* 弗樓沙國 (0858b12).
98. Mong. *Kanika qaγan*; Fr. *le roi Ki ni kia*; Ch. *Jinijia wang* 罽膩伽王. Kaniṣka (c. 127–151 CE) was a famous king of the Greek-inflected Kushan kingdom of northwest India, a very influential patron of Buddhism (particularly of what became known as the Mahāyāna), and, according to legend, the convenor of the Fourth Buddhist Council. Much of the institutional, ritual, and scriptural world he patronized moved to China and helped create embryonic Buddhist communities there. The envoys of Emperor Ming of the Han dynasty, led by Zhang Qian (whom Faxian has mentioned just above), procured China's first (apocryphal) Buddhist scripture in Kusha: the *Sütra in Forty-Two Sections* (*Sishi'er zhang jing* 四十二章). Even so, as Buswell and Lopez note, recent scholarship suggests that Chinese Buddhism's debt may be owed less to Kaniṣka's Kushans than to "their Indo-Scythian predecessors in the region, the Saka (Skt. Śaka) tribe" (Buswell and Lopez, *The Princeton Dictionary of Buddhism*, 457).
99. Mong. *Tngri-yin qaγan qurmusta.*
100. The first two examples of "cowherd" in Lubsangdamdin are given as *glang rdzi,* which could also be "elephant herder." On the third iteration, we read *phyugs rdzi,* which is more unambiguously "cowherd" (which JPAR gives for each, *bouvier*).
101. Tib.*'Dzam bug ling;* Mong. *Čambudibu*; Ch. *Yanfuti* 閻浮提.
102. Tib. *sangs rgyas kyi lhung bzed*; Mong. *burqan-u badir ayaγ-a* (18); Fr. *pot de Foĕ* (76); Ch. *fo ding* 佛鉢 (0858b21).
103. Here Lubsangdamdin mistakes "a king of the Yuezhi" for "a king named Yuezhi." The Yuzhi region (Fr. *Youeï chi*; Ch. ???) covers Indo-Scythia and Kusha. As is common in this text, Lubsangdamdin or his scribe gives *Tsu yu she rgyal po* as the the name of this king in this sentence, and then just below gives *Tsu yi she* rgyal po.
104. In Lubsangdamdin but not Rinchen, this sentence and the one before are marked with what appear to be two European-style footnotes, with a small number 2) and 3) appearing. There are no corresponding footnotes or endnotes, however. Though Rinchen does not include them, he does insert a missing *ston pa'i lhung bze* to complete "[the Teacher's begging bowl] temple" that is incomplete in LD (LDR 45).
105. Abel-Rémusat translates this as *boisseaux,* explaining in a footnote: "Le teou ou boisseau contient diz livres de riz, ou cent quatre-vingts onces de notres poids commun" (84 n. 13).
106. Tib. *dpungs su mtho do tsam yod.* Inexplicably (to me, at least), *dpungs* and *mtho* are marked by small circles in Lubsangdamdin's text, as we often see in poetic verses playing off of the syllables of a revered lama or deity in Tibetan-language literature. Translating the FGZ, Dège gives for this passage: "if the rich wanted to make offerings of many flowers, should they

begin with a hundred, a thousand, or ten thousand *hu* (1 *hu* = 10 bushels [*boisseaux*]), by the end they would still not have filled it" (Drège and Faxian, *Memoire Sur Les Pays Bouddhiques*, 17).

107. Abel-Rémusat, Banzarov, and Lubsangdamdin all have Huiying staying behind in Puruṣa's temple of the Buddha's begging bowl out of jubilance or devotion. Drège and Deeg, however, point out that here the Chinese expression *wuchang* 無常 is a euphemism for "passing on," or dying. The Chinese thus seems to read that Huiying died at the temple, and that a grief-stricken Faxian moved on alone (Deeg and Faxian, *Das Gaoseng-Faxian-Zhuan Als Religionsgeschichtliche Quelle: Der Älteste Bericht Eines Chinesischen Buddhistischen Pilgermönchs Über Seine Reise Nach Indien Mit Übersetzung Des Textes*, 524 n. 2354; Drège and Faxian, *Memoire Sur Les Pays Bouddhiques*, 18 n. 113). As we saw in chapter 2, this reading was shared by Huijiao and Sengyou in their sixth-century biographies of Faxian.
108. Tib. *Ha lo'i grong*; Mong. *Hi lo balγasun* (18); Fr. *ville de Hi lo* (85); Ch. *Xiluo cheng* 醯羅城 (0858c09).
109. Tib. *Nang hi'i yul*; Mong. *Nagarahar-a, Na kijyieorun*; Fr. *le royaume de Na kiĕ*; Ch. *Najie guo* 那竭國.
110. Tib. *Sangs rgyas dbu thod*; Mong. *Burqan-u Gabala*; Fr. *os du crane de Foĕ*; Ch. *Foding gu* 佛頂骨.
111. Lubsangdamdin gives *Nā gā rā ga*, LDR gives *Nā gā dzā ga*.
112. Tib. *Mar me mdzad*; Mong. *J̌ula-yinǰokiyaγči*; Fr. *Ting kouang Foĕ*; Ch. *Dingguang fo* 定光佛. The Buddha Dīmpaṃkara was the previous buddha of this universal age, preceding the historical Buddha Śākyamuni. According to Mahāyāna accounts especially, all the one thousand buddhas of this eon will perform certain key acts (such as their renunciation, enlightenment, and death) in the same sites, through which Faxian walked.
113. Rather than "city gate" (*grong khyer du'jug pa*), JPAR gives "entrance to a valley" (*l'entrée d'une vallée*, 86).
114. Tib. *Sangs rgyas kyi'gar ba;* Mong. *Burqan-un tayaγ*; Fr. *baton de Foĕ*; Ch. *Fo xizhang* 佛錫杖.
115. Tib. *Sangs rgyas kyi snam sbyar*; Mong. *Burqan-u nomtu debel*; Fr. *Monteau de Foĕ*; Ch. *Fo sengjiali* 佛僧伽梨.
116. "The Buddha's shadow": Tib. *sangs rgyas kyi grib ma*; Mong. *Burqan-u següder*; Fr. *ombre de Foĕ*; Ch. *Fo ying* 佛影.
117. For "fingernails," both Lubsangdamdin and LDR give *bsen mo* in Tibetan , which usually refers to a worldly class of demoness associated with desire and distraction from contemplative pursuit, instead of the more usual spelling *sen mo*.
118. Abel-Rémusat has Faxian traveling with three companions in this sentence, which Banzarov dropped for the more generic "companions" (*nöqüün*), though still, like Abel-Rémusat, allowing that Faxian and friends set out in "the second month of winter (*gool-un qoyar sar-a tor*)." The Taishō Canon Chinese reads straightforwardly: "After resting there for three months during winter, Faxian and his two companions (lit. Faxian etc., three people) traveled to the south of the small snowy mountains" 住此冬三月法顯等三人南度小雪山 (0859a11–12).
119. These mountains are commonly identified as the Safed range to the south of Jalālābād, on the border of contemporary Aghanistan and Pakistan (ex. Drège and Faxian, *Memoire Sur Les Pays Bouddhiques*, 21 n. 132).
120. For more on the very different translations of this passage in French and Tibetan, and the very different characterizations of Faxian that result, see chapter 5.
121. Tib. *Lo ya'i yul*; Mong. *Lo i-yin orun* (18); Fr. *le royaume deLo i* (96); *Luoyi guo* 羅夷國 (0859a16). Like Abel-Rémusat, Deeg gives *Loyi* instead of *Luoyi*, though apparently while looking at the same character 羅 (Deeg and Faxian, *Das Gaoseng-Faxian-Zhuan Als Religionsgeschichtliche Quelle: Der Älteste Bericht Eines Chinesischen Buddhistischen Pilgermönchs Über Seine Reise Nach Indien Mit Übersetzung Des Textes*, 527). For a literature review on the possible location of Luoyi (as

somewhere along the Afghanistan-Pakistan border regions), see Drège and Faxian, *Memoire Sur Les Pays Bouddhiques*, 22 n. 133.

122. Tib. *Bhona'i yul*; Mong. *Bo na-yin orun*; Fr. *le royaume dePo na* (96); Ch. *Bana guo* 跋那國. Drège offers persuasive evidence that the reference here is to historic Baṇṇu (Drège and Faxian, *Memoire Sur Les Pays Bouddhiques*, 22 n. 134).
123. It is interesting that occasionally Banzarov and Lubsangdamdin describe local monks as being either Mahāyāna or Hīnayāna contemplatives, whereas JPAR does not, as in this passage: "Dans ce royaume, il ya aussi trois mille religieux environ, tous appurtenant à la *petite translation*."
124. Tib. *Bha tsa* in chapter title, *Bhi tsa* in paragraph body; Mong. *Bhi ta* (*Bi ta*); Fr. *Pi tchha* (98); Ch. *Pitu* 毘荼. Though often misread by nineteenth- and twentieth-century scholars, Pitu is "Bhiḍa or Bhera upon the Jhelum River, a tributary of the Indus," Drège and Faxian, *Memoire Sur Les Pays Bouddhiques*, 22 n. 135.
125. Tib. *Ma thu ra yi yul gru*; Mong. *Madur-a orun* (19); Fr. *le royaume de Mo theou lo* (99); Ch. *Motouluo guo* 摩頭羅國 (0859a24).
126. Tib. *chu klung ya ma nu* in chapter title, *chu bo ya mu na* in paragraph body; Mong. *Yamun-a mören*; Fr. *rivière de Pou na*; Ch. *Puna he* 蒱那河.
127. I.e., Skt. *Madhyadeśa*; Tib. *Dbus yul*; Mong. *Dumdadu orun* (20); Fr. *royaume de Milieu* (99); Ch. *Zhong guo* 中國 (0859b01).
128. *tshang ma la phogs dang gsol ras yod*. I.e., they are not paid from taxes.
129. In LD this line reads nonsensically as: *sa tu byung ba rnams kyi ched du* (171) but must be a scribal error for *rab tu byung ba rnams kyi ched du*, which I have translated above.
130. Mong. "saribudari-yin suburγ-a mudγalyani-yin suburγ-a ba ananda-yin suburγ-a" (20); Fr. "le tour de *Che li foĕ*, les tours de *Moŭ lian* et d'*A nan*" (101); Ch. "shelifu ta mulian anan ta . . . 舍利弗塔目連阿難塔" (0859b18–19).
131. In the Chinese, these are stūpas (*ta* 塔), not temples, dedicated to the Abhidharma, Vinaya, and Sūtras.
132. Here is a major deviation in tense and gaze to third-person description of Faxian and companions, which deviates markedly from JPAR, which has in a general sense: "Après qu'ils y eurent goûté le repos pendant un mois, tous les gens qui espèrent le bonheur les exhortèrent à reprendre leurs exercices pieux" (101).
133. I.e., at the inappropriate time (*dus ma yin par ni btung ba khyer*). On the strangeness of this detail in his Chinese sources (why would monastic assemblies require eating at the wrong time?), see JPAR 110–11 n. 26.
134. Tib. *mo'u gal gyi bu chen po dang/'od srung chen po*; Mong. *yeke mudγalyani ba yeke γasyaba* (20).
135. This line in FGZ reads "all the śrāmernera make many offerings to Rāhula (*zhu shami duo gongyangluoyun* 諸沙彌多供養羅云)" (0859b25). Abel-Rémusat did not catch the meaning and translated this sentence without any reference to Rāhula, the Buddha's son—"Il ya a aussi un ordre dans lequel les *Cha mi* remplissent leurs devoirs religieux" (101)—leading via Banzarov to Lubsangdamdin's version above.
136. Tib. *chos mngon pa*; Mong. *abhidharm-a-yin baγsi*; Fr. *maître d'A pi than*; Ch. *apitan shi* 阿毘曇師.
137. Tib. *'dul ba 'dzin pa*; Mong. *vinai-yin baγsi*; Fr. *maître en fait de préceptes*; Ch. *lü shi* 律師.
138. This last clause describing "upholders of the Sūtras" who make offerings to the Sūtrapitaka has been added by Lubsangdamdin. It is not found in the Mongolian (20), French (101), or Chinese 阿毘曇師者供養阿毘曇律師者供養律 (0859b25–26).

139. Tib. *Shes rab kyi pha rol tu phyin pa, Mgon po'jam dpal dbyangs, Spyan ras gzigs dbang phyug*; Mong. *Bilig barimid, Manǰusiri, Qongsim bodisadu-a*; Fr. *Phan jo pho lo mi, Wen tchu sse li, Kouan chi*; Ch. *Boreboluomi* 般若波羅蜜, *Wenshushili* 文殊師利, *Quanshiyin* 觀世音.
140. I.e., *Nanhai* 南海, "the South China Sea."
141. Tib. *Se wang ka ya she* in chapter title, *Sa wam ka ya shi* in paragraph body; Mong. *Sam ka siy-a, Samkasiy-a* (21); Fr. *Seng kia chi* (124); Ch. *Sengjiashi* 僧迦施 (0859c05). A village in the state of Uttar Pradesh, contemporary India. Considered one of the "Eight Great Holy Sites."
142. Skt. *Trāyastriṃśa*; Tib. *Sum rtsa gsum (gyi gnas)*; Mong. *Tüsida* (Banzarov apparently interpreted the French transcription of the Chinese as referring to Tuṣita, a mistake that Lubsangdamdin, no doubt more familiar with the details of the Buddha's hagiography, corrected in his Tibetan); Fr. *au ciel de Tao li*; Ch. *Daolitian* 忉利天. A saṃsāric realm understood in Buddhist and other South Asian-inflected cosmologies to be situated upon the peak of the *axis mundi*, Mount Sumeru, and governed by Indra and another thirty-two gods.
143. The Buddha's first cousin, who became one of the former's ten great disciples.
144. Utpāla (i.e., Utpalavarṇā) was an arhat and important nun disciple of the Buddha, in many canonical sources for her meditative accomplishments and supernormal abilities (such as we see in this story from Sāṃkāśya of gender and body transformation). Though an arhat, she was eventually beaten to death by the Buddha's malicious cousin Devadatta. In longer versions of the story recounted here by Faxian, it is Utpālavarṇā (as Cakravartin) and Śāriputra who welcome the Buddha as he descends the ladders from the Heaven of the Thirty-Three at Sāṃkāśya.
145. Tib.*'Khor los bsgyur ba'i rgyal po*; Mong. *Kürdün ergügülügci*; Fr. *saint roi faisant tourner la roue*; Ch. *zhuanlun wang*; i.e., "a wheel-turning king" who is often represented in Buddhist sources and societies as an all-powerful, enlightened, eminently ethical and beneficient sovereign who establishes the social, economic, and political circumstances for the Buddhadharma (and the saṅgha communities) to flourish. Aśoka is the paradigmatic example, though according to the nineteenth-to-twentieth- century monastic chronicles of the Inner Asian interpreters of Faxian's *Record*, the Dharma kings of imperial Tibet as well as Chinggis Khan and his descendents, especially Khubilai, were understood as Cakravartins.
146. On Abel-Rémusat's turn to Mongolian sources to elucidate this line in the *Record*, see chapter 4.
147. Recall this episode for its prominent place in Sengou and Huijiao's biographies of Faxian summarized in chapter 1.
148. *gnod sbyin gdug pa can*. JPAR gives "malevolent genie" (*un mauvais génie*, 126–27).
149. Skt. *pratyekabuddha*; Tib. *rang sangs rgyas*; Mong. *Öber-iyen ilausan*.
150. Tib.*'Od ma'i tshal* (though Lubsangdamdin does not return to *'od ma'i tshal* anywhere in the body of the chapter).
151. Tib. *Ka nya ku p+dza*; Mong. *Ka na u yi* (22); Fr. *ville de Ki jao i* (167); Ch. *Jiraoyi cheng* 罽饒夷城 (0860a28). Drège identifies this place with Kanauj, located between Farrukhābad and Kanpur (Drège and Faxian, *Memoire Sur Les Pays Bouddhiques*, 51 and 52 n. 178).
152. I.e., Skt. *Gaṅgānadī*; Tib. *Gang ga'i klung*; Mong. *Gangga mören*; Fr. *Rivière Heng*; Ch. *Heng shui* 恒水.
153. Abel-Rémusat apparently misread *cun* 村 ("village") as *lin* 林 ("forest"). On that basis, Heli was understood as "forest" in the Inner Asian versions (Tib. *nags khrod*; Mong. *ui*). Tib. *Ko wo li nags khrod*; Mong. *E lo ui*; Fr. *forêt de Ho li*; Ch. *Heli* 呵梨. According to both Deeg and Drège, *Heli* remains unidentified and may also be read as *Hari* (Deeg and Faxian, *Das*

Gaoseng-Faxian-Zhuan Als Religionsgeschichtliche Quelle: Der Älteste Bericht Eines Chinesischen Buddhistischen Pilgermönchs Über Seine Reise Nach Indien Mit Übersetzung Des Textes, 535; Drège and Faxian, *Memoire Sur Les Pays Bouddhiques*, 31).

154. Tib. *Se tshes rgyal khams* in chapter title, *Se tshya rgyal khams* in paragraph body; Mong. *Šači-yin qan orun* (22); Fr. *Grand royaume de Cha tchi* (170); Ch. *Shaqi daguo* 沙祇大國 (0860b04).

155. Lubsangdamdin has "seven *pha cwo*," which has been changed in LDR to "seven *'dom*," or fathoms.

156. Abel-Rémusat mistranslated this passage. It reads in Chinese as "At that place, where the four buddhas [of this universal age] sat in meditation or resided . . . 亦有四佛經行坐處 (0860b07–08). However, in French it became "There are also four locations related to the Buddha in that country" (*Il ya aussi dans ce pays quatre stations de Foĕ*, 170), which led eventually to the Tibetan interpretation above.

157. Both Drège and Deeg, in their contemporary translations of the FGZ into French and German, have Faxian and Daozheng journeying *north* to Kośala. In the Chinese reproduced in Drège, it does indeed read north (*bei* 北, 32). However, the Chinese in the Taishō Canon reads 從此南行八由延 (0860b08) and thus has the direction of their travel as "south" (*nan* 南). It was *nan* also in the Bibliothèque Royale source of Abel-Rémusat, who has the monks walking to Kośala *vers le midi* (171). And, on that basis, southward it remained for the Inner Asian interpreters: Banzarov gave *emün* in Mongolian (23) and Lubsangdamdin *lho phyogs* in Tibetan (179).

158. Tib. *Ko sā la'i yul*; Mong. *Könselen-yin orun* (23); Fr. *royaume de Kiu sa lo* (171); Ch. *Jusaluo guo* 拘薩羅國 (0860b09).

159. Tib. *Mnyan yod kyi grong khyer*; Mong. *Siravasti balyasun*; Fr. *ville de Che 'wei*; Ch. *Shewei cheng* 舍衛城.

160. *Grong khyer'di na skye bo grangs shin tu mang zhing/mi khyim stong phrag nyis rgyar bgrangs.* This is completely opposite to JPAR, which has "There are very few people in this village, and we counted not more than two hundred families (or houses) there" (*La population de cette ville est très-peu considérable, et l'on n'y compte qu'environ deux cents familles (ou maisons)*, 171), which closely follows the Chinese 城內人民希曠都有二 百餘家 (0860b09–10).

161. Tib. *Rgyal po gsal*; Mong. *Ilayuqči qayan*; Fr. *le roiPho sse no*; Ch. *Bosini wang* 波斯匿王. On Abel-Rémusat's use of Mongolian chronicles to introduce European readers to King Prasenajit, see chapter 5.

162. Anāthapiṇḍada, alias Sudatta: Tib. *Mgon med zas sbyin*; Mong. *Sudadda*; Fr. *Siu thă*; Ch. *Xuda zhangzhe* 須達長者. Anāthapiṇḍada is widely recorded in the sūtras as a famous householder (Tib. *khyim bdag*; Mong. *ger-ün ejen*) disciple of the Buddha who used his merchant wealth to patronize the saṅgha. Anāthapiṇḍada offered many dwellings, parks (including, most famously, the Jetavana Park described just below), and other requisites for the monastic community in the vicinity of Śrāvastī.

163. Aṅgulimāla: Tib. *Im hu wi*; Mong. *Ing qüei* (23); Fr. *Ying kiuĕ* (171); Ch. *Yangjuemo* 鴦掘魔 (0860b11).

164. Missing in the French, then Mongolian, and then Tibetan translations of Faxian's list of notable stūpas of Śrāvastī is a clause describing a stūpa marking the monastery of Mahāprajāpatī (Gautamī) (*Da'aidao* 大愛道). Mahāprajāpatī was the Buddha's aunt and caregiver, and, later, a prominent nun who lead the newly established nuns' order.

165. Tib. *Dze ta'i tshal*; Mong. *J̌itavan-a-yin süm-a* (23); Fr. *le temple de Tchi houan* (171); Ch. *Qihuan jingshe* 祇洹精舍 (0860b18).

166. Tib. *tsandan go+O shir+Sha.* Abel-Rémusat translated the Chinese (*niu touzhantan* 牛頭栴檀) literally, and thus confusedly, as: "he accordingly sculpted an ox head of sandal (wood), in the manner of presenting an image of the Buddha" (*il fit en consequence scilpter une tête de boeuf en bois de santal, de manière à représenter une image de Foĕ,* 172). This was followed by Banzarov's Mongolian "[a] sandalwood called 'ox-head'" (*üker-üntoluγai neretučandan,* 23).
167. Tib.*'khor rnam pa bzhi*; Mong. *dörben anggida tonilaγui sanvar* (20); Fr. *les quartre classes* (172); Ch. *sib bu zhong* 四部眾. On Abel-Rémusat's introduction of the saṅgha, see chapter 5.
168. Tib. *Ri dwags'dzin gyi ma*; Mong. *Bi si yin eke, Visaga* (24); Fr. *la mère dePi che khiu*; Ch. *Pishequ mu* 毘舍佉母. Mṛgāra's mother was Viśākhā, one of the Buddha's preeminent female lay disciples.
169. This famous site is known more commonly as the "Hall of Mṛgāra's Mother" (Skt. *Mṛgāram ātṛprāsāda*; Tib. *Ri dwags 'dzin gyi ma'i khang bzang*).
170. Tib. *Sud dhu li*; Mong. *Sündari:Sun to li*; Fr. *Sun to li*; Ch. *Suntuoli* 孫陀利.
171. Tib. *Tshi tshya mu*; Mong. *Činči mön, Činčiman-a* (24); Fr. *Tchen tche mo na* (174); Ch. *Zhanzhemona* 旃遮摩那 (0860c20–21).
172. JPAR gives this number as *quatre-vingt-dix-huit* (175).
173. I.e., Śiva; Tib. *'Jig rten nyid.* Abel-Rémusat gives instead "In the kingdom of Central India, there are ninety-six kinds of sectarians that all known the current existing world (*monde actuel*)" (175), which he clarifies in a footnote refers to proponents of non-Buddhist sects that deny past and future lives, the mechanics of karma, and so on; who, in other words, accept only the worlds known by the senses in this present life. This is a gloss of the FGZ, "each (heretical sect) knows this life and the next" 皆知今世後世 (0861a09).
174. Tib. *lhas byin*; Mong. *Divadad*; Fr. *Thiao thă*; Ch. *Tiaoda* 調達.
175. Mong. *Sagiy-a-yin orun*; Fr. *le royaume de Che i*; Ch. *Sheyi* 舍夷 .
176. Tib. *Rgyal po'phags skyes po*; Mong. *Liu li qaγan, Virudhaga qaγan*; Fr. *le roi Lieou li*; Ch. *Liuli wang* 琉璃王.
177. Tib. *Thu'o Wa* in chapter title, *Dhu wa ye* in text; Mong. *Du vie*; Fr. *le bourgade Tou wei*; Ch. *Duwei* 都維.
178. Tib. *Sangs rgyas'od srung*; Mong. *Kasiaba burqan*; Fr. *Foĕ Kia* chĕ; Ch. *Jiaye* 迦葉.
179. Following the FGZ correctly (*dongnan* 東南), Abel-Rémusat has their direction of travel as to the southeast, but Banzarov has only south (*emün-eǰüg*) in the Mongolian, which was followed by Lubsangdamdin (*lho byogs su*) in Tibetan as above.
180. Tib. *Ka ya'i grong khyer* in chapter title, *E wi ka ya grong khyer* in paragraph body; Mong. *Ni pi ya balγasun* (25); Fr. *ville de Na pi kia* (192); Ch. *Napijia* 那毘伽 (0861a18).
181. Tib. *Sangs rgyas'khor ba'jig*; Mong. *Krakuččanda burqan*; Fr. *Keou leou thsin foĕ*; Ch. *Julouqin fo* 拘樓秦佛. The fourth of the six buddhas to precede the Buddha Śākyamuni, according to the well-known "seven buddhas [of the past]" list (Skt. *saptatathāgata*; Tib. *sang rgyas rabs bdun*; Ch. *qifo* 七佛).
182. *Sangs rgyas gser 'grub.* I believe this is a misspelling of *Sangs rgyas gser thub.* In one tradition, Buddha Kanakamuni is the fifth of the six buddhas who preceded Śākyamuni (see previous note).
183. *Khron pa* could also be referring to a water "spring." However, LDR gives *khrom pa*, meaning "market" (51).
184. Tib. *Gser skya'i grong khyer*; Mong. *Kapilavastubalγasun* (25); Fr. *la ville de Kia 'weï lo 'weï* (198); Ch. *Jiaweiluowei* 迦維羅衛 (0861a22).

185. Śuddhodana was the Buddha's father, leader of the Śākyas. Tib. *Rgyal po zas gtsang*; Mong. *Idekedu qaγan*; Fr. *le roiPĕ tsing*; Ch. *Baijing wang* 白淨王.

186. Tib. *Nyon mongs med*; Mong. *A si ta*; Fr. *A i*; Ch. *Eyi* 阿夷. Asita was the brāhmaṇa who examined the infant Siddhārtha Gautama, the future Buddha, and witnessed the thirty-two marks of a "great being" (Skt. *mahāpuruṣa*; Tib. *skyes by chen po*; Ch. *daren* 大人).

187. Tib. *Gcung dga' bo*; Mong. *Ananda*; Fr. *Nan tho*; Ch. *Nantuo* 難陀.

188. Tib. *Nye bar'khor*; Mong. *Ubali*; Fr. *Yeou pho li*; Ch. *Youboli* 優波離.

189. I.e., a kind of banyan tree. Tib. *Na+ya gro dha*; Mong. *Ni-e grüündha modun*; Fr. *arbre Ni keou liŭ*; Ch. *Nijulüshu* 尼拘律樹.

190. I.e., the realization of a stream-enterer (Skt. *srotāpanna*): the preliminary realization of one who glimpses the nature of reality and, hence, of nirvāṇa, and who thus enters the current of "the stream to liberation." The first of four stages towards arhathood, stream-enterers will never again be reborn in the lower realms.

191. Tib. *Rgyal po'phags skyes po*; Mong. *Lei qu li qaγan, Virudhaja raaja*; Fr. *le roi Lieou li*; Ch. *Liuli wang* 瑠璃王.

192. In both Lubsangdamdin and LDR, each syllable of *bsnyen bkur mkhan* is marked with a dot that is often used to identify syllables of personal names (of lamas or deities, for example) that are made into the basis of devotional poetry. The meaning here, however, is unclear (LDR 51, 25v).

193. Tib. *Lum+bi ni'i tshal*; Mong. *Lümbini-yinčečeglig*; Fr. *Lun ming*; Ch. *Lunmin* 論民.

194. Tib. *La mo*; Mong. *Lan mo-yin orun, Ramagram-a* (26); Fr. *royaume de Lam mŏ* (228); Ch. *Lanmo* 藍莫 (0861b15).

195. Tib. *klu*; Mong. *luu*; Fr. *dragon;long* 龍.

196. Tib. *bon po rnams*; Mong. *bombu nar*; Fr. *Tao sse*; Ch. *Daoren* 道人.

197. The distance Lubsangdamdin gives (fourteen *yojana*, *dpag tshad bchu bzhi*) follows a note inserted by Banzarov ([*arban*] *dürben ber-e*), which departs from the French (*quatreyeou yan*) and Chinese (*si youyan* 四由延), or "four yojana."

198. Tib. *Sol ba'i mchod rten*; Mong. *Negüresün-ü suburγan* (26); Fr. *Tour des Charbons* (235); Ch. *Tan ta* 炭塔 (0861c02).

199. Tib. *Rtsā mchod grong*; Mong. *Küsinagar-a balγasun* here, *Küši balγasun* in chapter header; Fr. *ville de Kiu i na kiĕ*; Ch. *Juyinajie cheng* 拘夷那竭城.

200. *sna ma'i tshal chen chen po.* According to Das, the "nama" (*sna ma*) plant refers to a kind of blossoming jasmine whose Latin name might be either *Cissampelos hexandra* or *Jasminum grandiflorum* (Sarat Chandra Das, Graham Sandberg, and William A. Heyde, *A Tibetan-English dictionary with Sanskrit synonyms* [Calcutta: The Bengal Secretariat Book Depôt, 1902], 766).

201. Tib. *shing sā la*; Mong. *salan morun*; Fr. "deux arbres appelés *So lo* en chinois, et en sanscrit *S'âl* (Shorea robusta)" (236 n. 5): Ch. "two trees," *shuang shu* 雙樹.

202. Tib. *Kun tu rgyu rab bzang*; Mong. *Subhadar-a*; Fr. *Siu pŏ*; Ch. *Shuba* 須跋. Shortly before his *parinirvāṇa* in Kuśingarī, Parivrājika Subhadra was the last person whom the Buddha ordained as a *śramaṇa*.

203. Tib. *Phyag na rdo rje*; Mong. *Vaǰirbani*; Fr. *Jingang lishi* 金剛力士.

204. Tib. *rdo rje*; Mong. *vaǰir*; Fr. *le héros qui porte le sceptre de diamant*; Ch. *jinchu* 金杵.

205. Tib. *ring bsrel*; Mong. *šaril*; Fr. *che li*; Ch. *sheli* 舍利.

206. Tib. *Li tsa wa'i rnams*; Mong. *Ličabi-ner;* Fr. *Li tchhe*; Ch. *Liche* 梨車.

207. Tib. *Yangs pa can gyi grong khyer*; Mong. *Vayisali balγasun* (27); Fr. *Phi che li* (242); Ch. *Pisheli cheng* 毘舍離城 (0861c12).
208. Tib. *Kun dga' bo*; Mong. *Ananda*; Fr. *A nan*; Ch. *Anan* 阿難.
209. Tib. *Ni bho lo* in text, *Na wo la* in chapter heading; Mong. *An bo lo,* and in brackets, *Amrabali*; Fr. *An pho lo*; Ch. *Anpoluo* 菴婆羅.
210. In other words, what appeared at first not to be a living baby. Something like a miscarriage.
211. *Rung ba ma yin pa'i gzhi bcu*. The ten precepts at issue in this famous episode were: 1) exclamations of "Alas!"; 2) celebrating the arhats; 3) engaging intentionally in agriculture; 4) sipping medicine from a pot of ale; 5) misusing sacred stored salt; 6) eating while traveling on the road; 7) desecration of offerings with two fingers; 8) stirring curd and milk together as a beverage after the noontime meal; 9) using a new mat without an old patch; 10) and begging for alms of gold or silver.
212. Tib. *chu bo rnam pa lnga'i 'dres sa*; Mong. *tabunγoul-un belčir* (28); Fr. *réunion des cinq rivières* (250); Ch. *Wu he hekou* 五河合口(0862a13–14).
213. Tib. *ma ga dha'i yul*; Mong. *Magada-yin orun* (though, in just below in the first sentence of chapter 27, *Magadha orun*); Fr. *royaume de Mo kiĕ*; Ch. *Mojie guo* 摩竭國.
214. Tib. *Rgyal po ma skyes dgra*; Mong. *Ačadasaduru qaγan*; Fr. *A tche chi*; Ch. *Asheshi wang* 阿闍世王.
215. Tib. *Pa ta li pu tra'i grong khyer* in text, *Skyar na bu* in chapter header; Mong. *Ba ta li butar-a balγasun* (28); Fr. *la ville de Pa lian foŭ* (253); Ch. *Balianfu yi* 巴連弗邑 (0862a21).
216. Apparently, a misspelling of *rgyang*.
217. Tib. *Na li grong khyer*; Mong. *Ni li balγasun*; Fr. *la ville de Ni li*; Ch. *Nili cheng* 泥梨城.
218. Tib. *Dbang po'i brag phug*; Mong. *Onča qabčaγai-yin aγula* (29); Fr. *Montaigne du Rocher isolé* (262); Ch. *yi xiao gu shi shan* 一小孤石山 (0862c04). While the Mongolian, French, and Chinese all more or less read as "a solitary, rocky mountain," Lubsangdamdin independently names the mountain "Wangpo," apparently after the Tibetan name for Śakra (alias Indra)—Lhé Wangpo Gyajin (*Lha'i dbang po brgya byin*)—whose devotional encounter with the Buddha there is retold above.
219. Tib. *Na lenda'i grong brdal*; Mong. *Na lo tosun* ([*sic*] *tosqun*); Fr. *hameaux de Nalo*; Ch. *Naluo juluo* 那羅聚落.
220. Tib. *Shā ri bu*; Mong. *Šaributara*; Fr. *Che li foĕ*; Ch. *Shelifu* 舍利弗.
221. Tib. *Rgyal po'i gzhugs gnas*; Mong. *Qaγan-u sin-a saγurin*; Fr. *nouvelle ville de la residence royale*; Ch. *Wangshe xincheng* 王舍新城.
222. Tib. *Rgyal po gzugs can snying po*; Mong. *Bimbasar-a*; Fr. *le roi Ping cha*; Ch. *Pinsha wang* 蓱沙王.
223. I.e., Skt. *Gṛdhrakūṭa*. Tib. *Bya rgod phung po*; Mong. *Gridhakuda aγula*, and in brackets, *Qajirčoγčas-un aγula* (30); Fr. *Khi tche, pic de Vautour* (269); Ch. *Qishejue shan* 耆闍崛山 (0862c20).
224. The Chinese reads that Faxian's tears fell while he lamented that the Buddha had taught the *Śūraṃgama* [*Sūtra*] (*Shou Leng Yan* 首楞嚴) upon this site, which is followed in the French (*Cheou leng yan*, 270) and Banzarov's Mongolian (*Suranggam-a sudur*, 30).
225. I.e., Skt. *Kalandakanivāpa*. Tib.*'Od ma'i tshal*; Mong. *Qalandavinün-a-yin qulusun-u oi*, in brackets *Ka lang du* (30); Fr. *le Jardin des bambous de Kia lan tho* (272); Ch. *Zhuyuan jingshe* 竹園精舍 (0863a06).
226. I.e., Skt. *Śitavana*; Tib. *Sil ba'i tshal*; Mong. *Ši-mo-ši-na*; Fr. *Chi mo che na*; Ch. *Shimoshena* 尸磨賒那. Missing in the Tibetan is the clarificatory line of the FGZ "'Shimoshena' refers to the field of tombs wherein the dead are abandoned 尸磨賒那者漢言棄死人墓田" (0863a07–08). This sentence is in Abel-Rémusat's French and Banzarov's Mongolian but absent in Lubsangdamdin's Tibetan.
227. Tib. *Pha cu lo'i phug*; Mong. *Či-tučilaγun ger*; Fr. *la grotte de Pin pho lo*; Ch. *Binboluo ku* 賓波羅窟.

228. The reason being, of course, that Ānanda had spend much of his life serving as the Buddha's attendant and had not yet achieved nirvāṇa. As the story goes, that evening, just as he laid his head down to sleep, he realized ultimate truth and became an arhat.
229. Tib. *Ka ya'i grong khyer*; Mong. *Ka-ya banγasun* ([*sic*] *balγasun*) (31); Fr. *la ville de Kia ye* (275); Ch. *Jiaye cheng* 伽耶城 (0863a22).
230. *U tshas sdod pa'i khyim grong du bu mo gnyis.* Strange, since the usual story, and the Chinese and French, describe a single girl.
231. Tib. *Rgyal po mya ngan med*; Mong. *Γasalang-ugei qaγan* (32); Fr. *le roi A yŭ* (293); Ch. *Ayu wang* 阿育王 (0863b23).
232. Here there is confusion across the different translations. The Chinese reads that it was the previous buddha of this age, Kāśyapa, whom Aśoka met in the road as a boy during his past life (當道戲過迦葉佛行乞食, 0863b24). Abel-Rémusat, with Klaproth's help (or harm?), has in the French that it was Śākyamuni Buddha whom the boy encountered ("il rencontra *Ch'y kia foĕ* qui marchait en mendiant sa nourriture," 293). (This is followed in the modern German translation of Deeg (556) and the French of Drège [59]). In Mongolian, Banzarov goes another route entirely and has the boy meet Śāriputra (*Šaribudari*, 32) upon the road, which Lubsangdamin keeps in the Tibetan as translated above.
233. I.e., Skt. *Āyasa Cakravrtin*; Tib. *Lcags kyi'khor lo can gyi rgyal po*; Mong. *Temur kurdu-taiqaγan*; Fr. *roi de la roue de fer*; Ch. *Tielun wang* 鐵輪王. In general, a Cakravartin, or "wheel-turning emperor," is a figure in Indic cosmology who appears periodically to claim sovereignty over the world and who, like the buddhas who similarly periodically appear, possesses a body endowed with the thirty-two marks of a great being. A Cakravartin wields his power from a great wheel that rolls over the earth and subjects its population to his sovereignty. According to Abhidharma, different Cakravartin kings (gold, silver, iron, etc.) each have different powers (such as having others submit without fighting, just by obeying his commands). The Iron Cakravartin King does have to actually fight.
234. Tib. *Gshin rje rgyal po*; Mong. *Erlig qaγan*; Fr. *le roi des demons, Yan lo*; Ch. *Yanluo wang* 閻羅王.
235. I.e., Mount "Cock's Foot." Tib. *Ri bo bya rkang can*; Mong. *Takiǰan köl-tu aγula* (33); Fr. *montagne Pied de coq* (302); Ch. Jizu wang 雞足山 (0863c27).
236. Tib. *Wa ra nā si'i grong khyer*; Mong. *Varanasi balγasun* (33); Fr. *la ville de Pho lo naï* (304); Ch. *Boluonai cheng* 波羅奈城 (0864a08).
237. Tib. *Ka shi'i yul*; Mong. *Ka si-yin ulus*; Fr. *le royaume de Kia chi*; Ch. *Jiashi guo* 迦尸國.
238. Tib. *Ri dwags gi nags*; Mong. *Arsi-yin kürügesün-ü süm-a*; Fr. *le Parc de cerfs de l'Immortel* (apparently a misreading by Abel-Rémusat, without any clarificatory footnotes from Klaproth); Ch. *Luyeyuan* 鹿野苑.
239. The first turning of the Wheel of the Dharma was, of course, on the "Four Truths Known by Noble Ones" (Skt. *Catvāryāryasatyāni*; Ch. *Si shengdi* 四聖諦; Tib. *'Phags pa'i bden pa bzhi*), or, as it is usually poorly rendered into English in most undergraduate world religion textbooks, the "Four Noble Truths."
240. Tib. *Ke'u shamb+hi'i yul* in the chapter heading, *Kō shamb+hi'i yul* in the paragraph body; Mong. *Kosambi orun*; Fr. *royaume Keou than mi*; Ch. *Jushanmi guo* 拘睒彌國.
241. Tib. *Ko sā la'i nags*; Mong. *Kosai-a-yin ui*; Fr. *Jardin de Kiu sse lo*; Ch. *Qushiluo yuan* 瞿師羅園.
242. Tib. *Daksan na yi yul gru* in chapter heading, spelled *Dakshi na* in paragraph body; Mong. *Daγšin orun* (34); Fr. *royaume de Tă thsen* (314); Ch. *Dachen guo* 達嚫國 (0864a26).
243. Tib. *Pā ra wa ta'i gtsug lag khang* in chapter header, *Wo lo wa* in text body; Mong. *Barvadi-yin kei*; Fr. *Pho lo yuĕ*; Ch. *Boluoyue* 波羅越.

244. I.e., those holding "wrong views" (Skt. *Mithyādṛṣṭi*; Tib. *Log par lta ba*; Mong. *Mayu üǰel*), as it says more explicitly in the Chinese original of this passage (*xiejian* 邪見, 0864b09), which Abel-Rémusat glossed as "gens perverse" (314).
245. Instead of identifying this as the Mahāsāṃghika school, Banzarov apparently relied upon Klaproth's notes, which identify the reference vaguely as to arhats tasked with assembling the Buddha's teachings after his parinirvāṇa. And so it was known in Banzarov and Lubsangdamdin.
246. The Chinese reference is to the vinaya of the Mahāsāṃghika school (*Mohesengji zhong lü* 摩訶僧祇眾律, 0864b19–20), though as Deeg notes, a reference made using a redundant and slightly opaque construction (Deeg and Faxian, *Das Gaoseng-Faxian-Zhuan Als Religionsgeschichtliche Quelle: Der Älteste Bericht Eines Chinesischen Buddhistischen Pilgermönchs Über Seine Reise Nach Indien Mit Übersetzung Des Textes*, 561 n. 2455).
247. Tib. *Tsham+pa rgyal khams chen po*; Mong. *Čamba yeke qan orun* (35); Fr. *le grand royaume de Tchen pho* (328); Ch. *Zhanbo daguo* 瞻波大國 (0864c05).
248. Abel-Rémusat seems to have confused the Chinese here, which reads "Buddhist temples and sites where [Śākyamuni] visited and where the four buddhas visited (佛精舍經行處及四佛坐處, 0864c05). In the French, we have "In Buddhist temples upon our route, and in four sites where the Buddha sat, they built stūpas" (*Dans les chappelles de Foĕ sur nortre route, et dans quatre endroits où Foĕ s'est assis, on a élevé des tours*, 328). The French was followed in Banzarov's Mongolian and Lubsangdamdin's Tibetan, as above.
249. Tib. *Tā mra li+pta*; Mong. *Tamralipdi*; Fr. *To mo li ti*; Ch. *Duomolidi guo* 到摩梨帝國.
250. As we have seen already in Sengyou and Huijiao's biographies, Faxian's time here was spent copying volumes of scripture, not composing original treatises (as we might think with Lubsangdamdin's use of the verb "to write" [*'bri ba*]).
251. The Chinese and French have Faxian journeying for fourteen nights and days.
252. I.e., Ceylon (Skt. *Siṃhaladvīpa*). Tib. *Sing+ga la'i gling*; Ch. *Shizi guo* 師子國.
253. *Yul'di ni ngos yangs la chu bo zhig gi ngogs steng na yod do.* It is, in other words, an island.
254. Tib. *ma nwa rdo.* Both Deeg and Drège maintain that the Chinese *moni zhu* 摩尼珠 (0864c14) transcribes Sanskrit *maṇi*, meaning precious stone or jewel (Drège and Faxian, *Memoire Sur Les Pays Bouddhiques*, 67 n. 342; Deeg and Faxian, *Das Gaoseng-Faxian-Zhuan Als Religionsgeschichtliche Quelle: Der Älteste Bericht Eines Chinesischen Buddhistischen Pilgermönchs Über Seine Reise Nach Indien Mit Übersetzung Des Textes*, 563 n. 2468). This seems not to have been apparent to Lubsangdamdin, however, which is strange, since the Mongolian is so clear (*mani erdeni*). One imagines Lubsangdamdin would surely have written this well-known word as in the ubiquitous mantra *Oṁ maṇi padme hūṁ*, in which he would lead tens of thousands of Mongolians in mass recitation during the escalation of the socialist violence that came within years of this translation of the *Record* (see Matthew W. King, *Ocean of Milk, Ocean of Blood. A Mongolian Monk in the Ruins of the Qing Empire.* [New York: Columbia University Press, 2019], 90–146).
255. I.e., Skt. *Abhayagiri*; Tib.*'Jigs med kyi ri bo'i gtsug lag khang*; Mong. *Aǰul ügei ayula-yin keid* (35); Fr. *Monastère de la Montagne sans crainte* (332); Ch. *Wuwei shan* 無畏山 (0865a28).
256. Lubsangdamdin's count differs from the FGZ: "one thousand four hundred and ninety-seven years have passed since [the Buddha's] parinirvāṇa 泥洹已來一千四百九十七歲" (0865a26–27), which Abel-Rémusat follows faithfully.
257. The references to the Buddha's previous lives in the Tibetan, well known from jātaka (*skyes rabs*) literature, mostly depart from what is in the Chinese. There, the depictions Faxian describes are of the Buddha's previous births as Sudāna (*Xudana* 須大拏), Śyāma (*Shan* 睒), the

elephant king (*Xiang wang* 象王), and then both a deer (*lu* 鹿) and a horse (*ma* 馬) (0865b03; for commentary on the Chinese references, see Drège and Faxian, *Memoire Sur Les Pays Bouddhiques*, 72 nn. 361–65

258. Tib. *Po ta'i gtsug lag khang*; Mong. *Bodi süm-a*; Fr. *chapelle Po thi*; Ch. *Bati jingshe* 跋提精舍. Deeg gives Skt. *Bhadrika* as the full name (Deeg and Faxian, *Das Gaoseng-Faxian-Zhuan Als Religionsgeschichtliche Quelle: Der Älteste Bericht Eines Chinesischen Buddhistischen Pilgermönchs Über Seine Reise Nach Indien Mit Übersetzung Des Textes*, 567).
259. Tib. *Ke mo gupta*; Mong. *Dharmagubta,* though either Banzarov or Rinchen thinks this is in error and gives *Dharmagudi* as well, both in chapter heading (in brackets) and then here; Fr. *Thă mo kiu ti*; Ch. *Damojudi* 達摩瞿諦.
260. Missing in Lubsangdamdin is a reference to the Mahāvihāra in the chapter heading, which we see in both the Mongolian (*Maha jiqer-e kemeku süm-a*, 37) and French (*Chapelle Mo ho pi ho lo*, 350).
261. Tib. *Mo ho lo'i gtsug lag khang*; Mongolian and French as in footnote above; Ch. *Mohe jingshe* 摩訶精舍 (0865b12–13).
262. I.e., the sūtras and the vinaya disciplinary protocols, as is clear in the Chinese ("The king promptly inspected the sūtras and vinaya" 王即按經律, 0865b16), but not in Abel-Rémusat's French translation: "le roi ayant consulté les rituels et les livres sacrés" (350).
263. This aside is the only one not added by Lubsangdamdin. It is found in the original Chinese (0865c03), added by some unknown later hand in one of the editions of the *Record* collated into the more modern versions explored herein.
264. The Tibetan reads, rather imprecisely, as "*rgyal po'i gnas su byon.*" The Chinese and French, by contrast, state plainly that the Buddha's bowl was kept in China ("the territory of the Han . . . *laidao Han di* 來到漢地") before arriving in Siṃhala. It was Banzarov who muddied the reference, translating the French "le Pays de Han" into Mongolian as "emperor/king's sovereign land (*qaγan-u orun*)" (38).
265. Mong. *Maidari burqan.*
266. Quite unlike the Tibetan translated above, the Chinese paragraph in the FGZ is very clear about what texts Faxian aquired in Ceylon (Siṃhala): "Faxian stayed in this kingdom for two years. During that time he sought a complete edition of the collection of the Mahīśāsaka vinaya (*Mishasai lü zang* 彌沙塞律藏). He aquired [copies] of the *Dīrghāgama* (*Chang ahan* 長阿含), the *Saṃyuktāgama* (*Za ahan* 雜阿含), and an edition of the *Kṣudraka* [*sūtra*] (*Za zang* 雜藏)" (0865c24–0865c25). Abel-Rémusat's French follows closely enough: "Fă hian stayed in this kingdom for two years. He inquired and then obtained the precepts of *Mi cha sě.* He aquired the long *Ahan* and the miscellaneous *Ahan*; in the end, he aquired a collection of different *Tsang* [i.e., *zang* 藏, meaning 'collection/basket,' Skt. *piṭaka*]" (359). Unlike in most of the rest of this complicated text, Banzarov loses Abel-Rémusat's rather clear and pointed meaning in his generally lucid Mongolian translation, especially in reference to the names of the texts Faxian aquired in Ceylon. *Mi cha sě* in French [i.e., *Mishasai lü zang* 彌沙塞律藏] is reduced to *E ke ma* (38), though here and in the other glosses, Rinchen has inserted the Mongolian for the correct transcription of two of the Sanskrit texts missed by Banzarov: 1) Skt. *Dīrghāgama* = Dirgham-a; 2) Skt. *Saṃyuktā-āgama* =*Samyuqtagam-a*. These clarifications came decades after Lubsangdamdin's reading of Banzarov, of course, and so he was left with what we see above.
267. Tib. *Dzi wa'i gling*; Mong. *Java dviba* (38); Fr. *royaume de Ye pho ti* (360); Ch. *Yepoti guo* 耶婆提國 (0866a13-14).
268. As we have seen throughout Lubsangdamdin's translation, the city of Guangzhou (廣州) is transcribed differently in each appearance in the Tibetan: *Grong khyer chāng khyo'u zhin gāng*

in the chapter heading, *Ko wa nyan cu* here in the paragraph body, and then *Gu'ang cha'u* in the hushed, terrified exchange of the lost merchant sailors that follows. And then again a few other ways as Faxian and shipmates make land and realize they have found China.

269. Tib. *Ri bo lo'ung* in chapter heading, *Ri bo lo'u* here; Mong. *Lao aγula*; Fr. *Montagne de Lao*; Ch. *Lao shan* 牢山.
270. In other words, crops native to China, which in FGZ are stated explicitly as "pigweed" (*li* 藜), "purple giant hyssop" (*huo* 藿), and "vegetables" (*zai* 菜) (0866b03). The specific reference, as we see above, was lost over the course of the French to Mongolian to Tibetan translations.
271. Tib. *Li ya'u'i*; Mong. *Li qaočoi.* Abel-Rémusat gives "la famille des *Lieou*" (362). However, the edition of the FGZ available to me, Deeg, and Drège read not the family of Liao but "the family of Jin" (*Jin jia* 晉家) (Deeg and Faxian, *Das Gaoseng-Faxian-Zhuan Als Religionsgeschichtliche Quelle: Der Älteste Bericht Eines Chinesischen Buddhistischen Pilgermönchs Über Seine Reise Nach Indien Mit Übersetzung Des Textes*, 575; Drège and Faxian, *Memoire Sur Les Pays Bouddhiques*, 80).
272. Deeg, following the historical work of several Japanese scholars, correct Liyi here to Lini.
273. We will recall that Chang'an (Mong. *Čang an*; Fr. *Tchhang 'an*; Ch. *Chang'an* 長安) was the city from which Faxian and companions departed. At the start of Lubsangdamdin's translation of the *Record*, he faithfully transcribed *Chang ang*, but here he slips in transcribing Tibetan *Zheng an* apparently for Xian 西安, as Chang'an was by Lubsangdamdin's time known (as it is today).
274. *Nyi ma nub phyogs su hor yul gyi bye ma'i la lung mang po brgal ba'i rjes su rgya gar du slebs po.* Here again, Banzarov and Lubsangdamdin infuse the *Record* with late- and postimperial Inner Asian meaning in ways that would radically expand Tibeto-Mongolian historical thinking during the erasure and displacements of the twentieth century.
275. The strange line in the Tibetan is the outcome of a rather circuitous chain of translation. In the original Chinese the reference is rather plainly to refuge in the Triple Gem ("he fortunately benefited from the power of the Three Honorables" 幸蒙三尊威靈, 0866b21–22), which was then muddied in Abel-Rémusat's French without any clarificatory footnotes from Klaproth ("he also happily received three high and noble favors" (*trois hautes et nobles faveurs,* 362). This was followed in Banzarov's Mongolian "he also received three great favors" (*tereber basaγörban yekeγečer-tor kürgegui kesig*, 40), interpreted above in Lubsangdamdin's Tibetan with even less clarity (*sa gsum'gro la'gyer pa'i chos kyi skyes thob gyur*).
276. *Jiayin* 甲寅, the fifty-first year of the sixty-year cycle. This is the end of the text and the beginning of the postscript in FGZ, and Drège offers an interesting argument that the date "the Jiayin year" ought to be considered the last line of the text, separated from the dating that comes at the start of the postscript. This, he says, helps solve controversies of dating Faxian's life and works that I summarize in chapter 2 (Drège and Faxian, *Memoire Sur Les Pays Bouddhiques*, 81 n. 400). I believe he is right, since in the rather convoluted Tibetan translation, which does not use reign years or astronomical measures familiar to Lubsangdamdin, the year of Faxian's invitation is both 414 CE and 416 CE. I've tried to keep the spirit of the Tibetan while also gently clarifying that Faxian set brush strokes to bamboo two years prior to being welcomed in the capital. For details on that period from current scholarship, see chapter 2.
277. The Yixi 義熙 period was 405–418 CE, ruled by Emperor An of the Eastern Jin (Yuming Luo, *A Concise History of Chinese Literature*, vol. 1 [Leiden; Boston: Brill, 2011], 182 n. 15).
278. As mentioned in the note above, and as it says in FGZ itself, Yixi was not emperor of the Han but of the Jin 晉.

Bibliography

Abel-Rémusat, Jean-Pierre. "Aperçu d'un Mémoire Intitulé: Recherches Chronologiques Sur l'origine de La Hiérarchie Lamaique."*Journal Asiatique* 4 (1824): 257–74.

——. "Compte Rendu de 'Sur La Naissance Des Formed Grammaticales de Humboldt.'" *Journal Asiatique* V (1824): 51–61.

——. *De l'Étude des Langues Étrangères chez les Chinois.* Paris: Extrait du Magasin Encyclopédique, 1811.

——. "Discours à l'ouverture Du Cours de Langue et Littérature Chinoises, Au Collège Royal, Le 16 Janvier, Sur l'origine, Les Progrès et l'utilité de l'étude Du Chinois En Europe." In *Mélange Asiatique, Ou Choix Morceaux de Critique et de Mémoirs Relatifs Aux Religions, Aux Sciences, Aux Coutumes, a l'histoire et a La Géographie Des Nations Orientales*, 2:1–18. Paris: Librarie Orientale de Dondey-Dupré Père et Fils, 1826.

——. *Élémens de La Grammaire Chinoise, Ou, Principes Généraux Du Kou-Wen Ou Style Antique: Et Du Kouan-Hoa c'est-à-Dire, de La Langue Commune Généralement Usitée Dans l'Empire Chinois.* Paris: Imprimerie Royale, 1822.

——. "Essai Sur la Cosmographie et la Cosmogonie des Bouddhistes." In *Mélanges posthumes d'histoire et littérature orientales*, 65–131. Paris: Imprimerie Royale, 1843.

——. *Essai sur la langue et la littérature chinoises: avec cinq planches, contenant des textes chinois, accompagnés de traductions, de remarques et d'un commentaire littéraire et grammatical, suivi de notes et d'une table alphabétique des mots chinois.* Paris: Treuttel et Wurtz, 1811.

——. "Étienne Fourmont: Savant Français." In *Mélanges Asiatiques, Ou Recueil de Morceaux de Critique et de MémoiresRelatifs Aux Religions, Aux Sciences, Aux Coutumes, a l'Histoire et a La Géographie Des Nations Orientales*, 2:291–304. Paris: Librairie orientale de Dondey-Dupré, 1825.

——. *Histoire de La Ville de Khotan: Tirée Des Annales de La Chine et Traduite Du Chinois; Suivie de Recherches Sur La Substance Minérale Appelée Par Les Chinois Pierre de Iu, et Sur Le Jaspe Des Anciens.* Paris: L'imprimerie de doublet, 1820.

——. "Lettre Au Rédacteur Du Journal Asiatique, Sur l'état et Les Progrès de La Littérature Chinoise En Europe."*Journal Asiatique* 1, no. 1 (1822).

——. *Mélanges Asiatiques, Ou Choix de Morceaux de Critique et de Mémoires Relatifs Aux Religions, Aux Sciences, Aux Coutumes, à l'Histoire et à La Géographie Des Nations Orientales.* Vol. 1. 2 vols. Paris: Librarie Orientale de Dondey-Dupré Père et Fils, 1825.

——. *Mélanges Asiatiques, Ou Choix de Morceaux de Critique et de Mémoires Relatifs Aux Religions, Aux Sciences, Aux Coutumes, à l'Histoire et à La Géographie Des Nations Orientales.* Vol. 2. 2 vols. Paris: Librarie Orientale de Dondey-Dupré Père et Fils, 1826.

——. "Mémoire Sur Un Voyage Dans l'Asie Centrale, Dans Le Pays Des Afghans et Des Beloutches, et Dans l'Inde, Exécuté à La Fin Du IVe Siècle de Notre Ère Par Plusieurs Samanéens de La Chine."*Mémoires de l'Institut de France* 13, no. 2 (1838): 345–412.

——. *Mémoires Sur Les Relations Politiques Des Princes Chrétiens, et Particulièrement Des Rois de France Avec Les Premiers Empereurs Mongols.* Paris: Imprimerie Nationale, 1824.

——. "Note Sur La Partie Samskrits Du Vocabulaire Philosophique En Cinq Langues." In *Mélanges Asiatiques, Ou Choix de Morceaux Critiques et de Mémoires Relatifs Aux Religions, Aux Sciences, Aux Coutumes, a l'Histoire et a La Géographie Des Nations Orientales*, 1:452–54. Paris: Librairie orientale de Dondey-Dupré, 1825.

——. "Note Sur Quelques Épithètes Descriptives Du Bouddha."*Journal Des Savants*, 1819, 625.

——. *Observations Sur Histoire Des Mongols Orientaux de Ssanang-Ssetsen.* Paris: Imprimerie Royale, 1832.

——. "Observations Sur Quelques Passages de La Lettre Précédente." In *Lettres Édifiantes et Curieuses Sur La Langue Chinoise: Un Débat Philosophico-Grammatical Entre Wilhelm von Humboldt et Jean-Pierre Abel-Rémusat (1821–1831)*, ed. Denis Thouard and Jean Rousseau, 181–96. Villeneuve-d'Ascq: Presses universitaires du Septentrion, 1999.

——. "Observations Sur Quelque Points de La Doctrine Samanéene et En Particulaire Sur Les Noms de La Triade Suprème Chez Les Différens Peuples Bouddhistes."*Journal Asiatique*, 1831, 3–67.

——. *Recherche Sur Les Langues Tartares, Ou Mémoires Sur Différens Points de La Grammaire et de La Littérature Des Mandchous, Des Mongols, Des Ouigours et Des Tibetains.* Paris: Imprimerie Royale, 1820.

——. "Sur L'Asie Polyglotte de M. Klaproth." In *Mélanges Asiatiques, Ou Choix de Morceaux de Critique et de Mémoires Relatifs Aux Religions, Aux Sciences, Aux Coutumes, à l'Histoire et à La Géographie Des Nations Orientales*, 1:267–309. Paris: Librairie orientale de Dondey-Dupré, 1825.

——. "Sur Quelques Épithètes Descriptives de Bouddha, Qui Font Voir Que Bouddha n'appartenait Pas a La Race Nègre." In *Mélanges Asiatiques, Ou Choix de Morceaux Critiques et de Mémoires Relatifs Aux Religions, Aux Sciences, Aux Coutumes, a l'Histoire et a La Géographie Des Nations Orientales*, 1:100–12. Paris: Librairie orientale de Dondey-Dupré, 1825.

——. "Sur Un Vocabulaire Philosophique En Cinq Langues, Imprimé a Peking." In *Mélanges Asiatiques, Ou Choix de Morceaux de Critique et de Mémoires Relatifs Aux Religions, Aux Sciences, Aux Coutumes, à l'Histoire et à La Géographie Des Nations Orientales*, 1:153–83. Paris: Librarie Orientale de Dondry-Dupré, 1825.

——. "Uranographia Mongolica Sive Nomenclatura Siderum, Quae Ab Astronomis Mongolis Agnoscuntur et Describuntur."*Les Mines de l'Orient* 3 (1811).

——. "Utrum Lingua Sinica Sit Vere Monosyllabica." *Fundgraben Des Orients* 3 (1813): 279–88.

Ahearne, Jeremy. *Michel de Certeau: Interpretation and Its Other.* Stanford, Calif.: Stanford University Press, 1995.

Allen, Amy. *The End of Progress: Decolonizing the Normative Foundations of Critical Theory.* New York: Columbia University Press, 2016.

Almond, Philip C. *The British Discovery of Buddhism.* Cambridge: Cambridge University Press, 2007.

Amar, A. *Monggol-Un Tobci Teüke [A Brief History of Mongolia]*. Vol. 9. The Mongolia Society Papers. Bloomington, Ind.: The Mongolia Society, 1986.

Amiot, Joseph Marie, and Pierre-Joseph Roussier. *Mémoire sur la musique des Chinois: tant anciens que modernes*. Paris: Nyon l'ainé, 1779.

Amiot, Joseph-Marie, Joseph de Guignes, Nicolas-Martin Tilliard, François-Ambroise Didot, and Qing Gaozong. *Éloge de la ville de Moukden et de ses environs; poeme composé par Kien-Long, empereur de la Chine & de la Tartarie, actuellement régnant. Accompagné de notes curieuses sur la géographie, sur l'histoire naturelle de la Tartarie orientale, & sur les anciens usages des Chinois; composées par les editeurs chinois & tartares. On y a joint une piece de vers sur le thé, composé par le même empereur. Traduit en françois par le P. Amiot, missionnaire à Péking; et publié par M. Deguignes*. A Paris, chez N. M. Tilliard, libraire, quai des Augustins, à S. Benoît. M. DCC. LXX, 1770.

Ampère, Jean-Jacques. "De La Chine et Des Travaux de M. Abel-Rémusat."*Revue Des Deux Mondes* III (November 15, 1832): 249–75, 361–95.

App, Urs. *The Birth of Orientalism*. Encounters with Asia. Philadelphia: University of Pennsylvania Press, 2010.

——. *Richard Wagner and Buddhism*. Rorschach, Kyoto: UniversityMedia, 2011.

——. "Schopenhauer and the Orient." In *The Oxford Handbook of Schopenhauer*, 88–107. New York; Oxford: Oxford Univeristy Press, 2020.

Appadurai, Arjun. *Fear of Small Numbers: An Essay on the Geography of Anger*. Durham, N.C.: Duke University Press, 2006.

Arquié-Bruley, Françoise. "L'omnisicient Abbé de Tersan (Charles-Philippe Campion de Tersan, 1737–1819)."*Bulletin de Société Nationale Des Antiquaires de France* 2002: 114–34.

Atwood, Christopher P. "Buddhism and Popular Ritual in Mongolian Religion: A Reexamination of the Fire Cult." *History of Religions* 36, no. 2 (1996): 112–39.

Axel, Brian Keith, ed. *From the Margins: Historical Anthropology and Its Futures*. Durham, N.C.; London: Duke University Press, 2002.

Banzarov, Dorji. "Burqan-u Nom Delgeregsen Ulus-Nuγud-Tur J̌ iγulčilγsan Bičig." In *Travels of Fa HsianTrans. Dordji Bansaroff*, ed. Byambyn Rinchen, 13–40. Corpus Scriptorum Mongolorum Instituti Linguae Litterarum Academiae Scientiarum Reipublicae Populi Mongolici 5. Ulanbator: Mongol Ulsîn Shinjlekh Ukhaani Akademi, 1970.

Banzarov, Dorzhi. *Chernaya Vera Ili Shamanastvo u Mongolov i Drugiya Stat'i D. Banzarova [The Black Faith or Shamanism Among the Mongols, and Other Articles by D. Banzarov]*. Ed. G. N. Potanin. St. Petersburg, 1891.

Baudot, Anatole de. *L'architecture. Le passé.—Le présent*. Paris: H. Laurens, 1916.

Beidavaeus, Abdalla, Andreas Mullerus Greiffenhagius, and Abraham Müller. *Abdallæ Beidavæi Historia Sinensis: Percice e gemino Manuscripto edita, Latine quoque reddita ab Andrea Mullero Greiffenhagio Berolini, Typis Christophori Rungii, Anno MDCLXXVII expressa, nuc vero una cum additamentis edita ab Autoris filio, Quodvultdeo Abraham Mullero*. Jenae: Bielkius, 1689.

Benn, James A. *Burning for the Buddha: Self-Immolation in Chinese Buddhism*. Honolulu: University of Hawai'i Press Kuroda Institute, 2007.

Bentz, A. S. "Being a Tibetan Refugee in India."*Refugee Survey Quarterly* 31, no. 1 (2012): 80–107.

Berger, Patricia Ann. *Empire of Emptiness: Buddhist Art and Political Authority in Qing China*. Honolulu: University of Hawai'i Press, 2003.

Bhabha, Homi K. *The Location of Culture*. London; New York: Routledge Classics, 1994.

Biehl, João, and Peter Locke. *Unfinished: The Anthropology of Becoming*. Durham, N.C.: Duke University Press, 2017.

Bira, Shagdaryn. "Indo-Tibetan And Mongolian Historiographical Mutual Contacts."*Acta Orientalia Academiae Scientiarum Hungaricae* 43, no. 2/3 (1989): 177–84.

Bira, Shagdaryn, and John Richard Krueger. *Mongolian Historical Writing from 1200 to 1700: Shagdaryn Bira; Translated from the Original Russian by John R. Krueger and Revised and Updated by the Author.* Bellingham, Wash.: Center for East Asian Studies, Western Washington University, 2002.

Bjerken, Zeff. "The Mirrorwork of Tibetan Religious Historians: A Comparison of Buddhist and Bon Historiography." Ph.D. diss., University of Michigan, 2001.

Blo bzang rta mgrin [Agvan Dorjiev]. "Bka' Drin Gsum Ldan Rtsa Ba'i Bla Ma Rdo Rje 'chang Mkhan Chen Sangs Rgyas Mtshan Can Gyi Rnam Thar Gsol 'Debs Dad Ldan Yid Kyi Mdzas Rgyan." In *Rje Btsun Blo Bzang Rta Dbyangs Kyi Gsung'bum*, 1:7–19. New Delhi: Mongolian Lama Guru Deva, 1975.

——. "Byang Phyogs Chen Po Hor Gyi Rgyal Khams Kyi Rtogs Brjod Kyi Bstan Bcos Chen Po Ngo Mtshar Gser Gyi Deb Ther." In *Rje Btsun Blo Bzang Rta Dbyangs Kyi Gsung'bum*, 2:43–490. New Delhi: Mongolian Lama Guru Deva, 1975.

——. "Chen Po Hān Gur Gyi Btsun Pa Phā Hyin Gyis 'phags Pa'i Yul Du 'Grims Pa'i Rnam Thar Rgyal Bstan 'Byung Khungs Kun Gsal 'Phrul Gyi Me Long." In *Rje Btsun Blo Bzang Rta Dbyangs Kyi Gsung'bum*, 1:145–244. New Delhi: Mongolian Lama Guru Deva, 1975.

——. "Chen Po Hor Gyi Yul Gru'i Sngon Rabs Kyi Brjed Byang Shāstra'i Zur Rgyan Du Sog Yig Las Bod Skad Du Bsgyur Te Bkod Pa." In *Rje Btsun Blo Bzang Rta Dbyangs Kyi Gsung'bum*, 2:487–546. New Delhi: Mongolian Lama Guru Deva, 1975.

——. "Mtshan Zhabs Mkhan Chen Gyi Dogs Lan Tshangs Pa'i Drang Thig." In *Rje Btsun Blo Bzang Rta Dbyangs Kyi Gsung'bum*, 2:561–72. New Delhi: Mongolian Lama Guru Deva, 1975.

——. "Mtshan Zhabs Mkhan Chen Gyis Chos 'Byung Las Brtsams Te Bka' 'dri Gnang Ba'i Chab Shog." In *Rje Btsun Blo Bzang Rta Dbyangs Kyi Gsung'bum*, 2:551–54. New Delhi: Mongolian Lama Guru Deva, 1975.

Bod, Rens. *A New History of the Humanities: The Search for Principles and Patterns from Antiquity to the Present.* London; New York: Oxford University Press, 2016.

Brag dgon zhabs drung dkon mchog bstan pa rab rgyas. *Yul Mdo Smad Kyi Ljongs Su Thub Bstan Rin Po Che Ji Ltar Dar Ba'i Tshul Gsal Bar Brjod Pa Deb Ther Rgya Mtsho.* 3 vols. Satapitaka Series. New Delhi: Sharada Rani, 1975.

Braun, Erik. *The Birth of Insight: Meditation, Modern Buddhism, and the Burmese Monk Ledi Sayadaw.* Chicago: University of Chicago Press, 2015.

Brown, William A., Urgunge Onon, and B. Shirėndėv. *History of the Mongolian People's Republic.* Cambridge, Mass.: East Asian Research Center, Harvard University: Distributed by Harvard University Press, 1976.

Burnouf, Eugène. "Foě Kouě Ki, Ou Relation Des Royaumes Bouddhiques; Voyages Dans La Tartarie, Dans l'Afghanistan et Dans l'Inde, Exécuté, à La Fin Du IV Siècle, Par Chy Fa Hian. Traduit Du Chinois et Commenté Par M. Abel Rémusat; Ouvrage Posthume, Revu, Complété et Augmenté d'éclaircissements Nouveaux, Oar MM. Klaproth et Landresse. Paris, Impr. Royale, 1836. Un Vol. Gr. in-4; LXVI et 424 Pag., Avec 3 Cartes et 2 Pl. Premier Article."*Journal Des Savants*, March 1837, 160–76.

——. *Introduction à l'histoire du bouddhisme Indien.* Paris: Imprimerie Royale, 1844.

——. *Le lotus de la bonne loi.* Paris: Imprimerie nationale, 1852.

Buswell, Robert E., and Donald S. Lopez. *The Princeton Dictionary of Buddhism.* Princeton, N.J.: Princeton University Press, 2013.

Cabezón, José Ignacio. *Buddhism and Language: A Study of Indo-Tibetan Scholasticism*. SUNY Series, toward a Comparative Philosophy of Religions. Albany: State University of New York Press, 1994.

Cahan, David. *From Natural Philosophy to the Sciences: Writing the History of Nineteenth-Century Science*. Chicago: University of Chicago Press, 2003.

Cakars, Melissa Andrea. "Being Buryat: Sovietization in Siberia." Ph.D. diss., Indiana University, 2008.

Catalogue Des Livres, Composant La Bibliothèque de Feu M. J.P. Abel-Rémusat, Professeur de Langue et de Littérature Chinoise et Tartare Mandchoue Au Collége Royal de France, Membre de l'Académie Des Inscriptions et Belles-Lettres, Président de La Société Asiatique de Paris, Etc. Dont La Vente Se Fera, Le Lundi, 27 Mai 1833 et Jours Suivans, 6 Heures de Relevé, Maison Silvestre, Rue Des Bons-Enfans, n. 30. Paris: Imprimerie de Mme. Huzard (Née Vallat la Chapelle), rue de l'Éperon, n. 7, 1833.

Catalogue Des Livres, Imprimés et Manuscrits, Composant La Bibliothèque de Feu M. Abel-Rémusat. Paris, n.d.

Çelik, Zeynep. *Europe Knows Nothing About the Orient: A Critical Discourse (1872–1932)*. Trans. Gregory Key and Aron Aji. Chicago: University of Chicago Press, 2021.

Chakrabarty, Dipesh. *Provincializing Europe: Postcolonial Thought and Historical Difference*. Princeton, N. J.: Princeton University Press, 2009.

Champollion, Jean-François. *Précis du système hiéroglyphique des anciens Egyptiens*. Paris: Treuttel et Würtz, 1824.

Chang, Michael G. *A Court on Horseback: Imperial Touringand the Construction of Qing Rule, 1680–1785*. Cambridge, Mass.: Harvard University Asia Center, 2020.

Chen, Jinhua. "Pañcavārṣika Assemblies in Liang Wudi's Buddhist Palace Chapel."*Harvard Journal of Asiatic Studies* 66, no. 1 (2006): 43.

Ch'en, Kenneth K.S. *Buddhism in China: A Historical Survey*. Princeton, N.J.: Princeton University Press, 1973.

Chen, Kuan-Hsing. *Asia as Method: Toward Deimperialization*. Durham, N.C.: Duke University Press, 2010.

Chin, Catherine. "Marvelous Things Heard: On Finding Historical Radiance."*The Massachusetts Review* 58, no. 3 (2017): 478–91.

Chittick, Andrew. *The Jiankang Empire in Chinese and World History*. Oxford; New York: Oxford University Press, 2020.

Clark, Imogen Rose. "Is Home Where the Heart Is?: Landscape, Materiality and Aesthetics in Tibetan Exile." Thesis, Oxford University, 2015.

Cohn, Bernard S. *An Anthropologist Among the Historians and Other Essays*. Delhi: Oxford University Press, 1987.

——. *Colonialism and Its Forms of Knowledge: The British in India*. Princeton, N.J.: Princeton University Press, 1996.

Conrad, Sebastian. "What Time Is Japan?: Problems of Comparative (Intercultural) Historiography." *History and Theory* 38, no. 1 (1999): 67–83.

Conze, Edward. *The Prajñāpāramitā Literature*. Tokyo: Reiyukai, 1978.

Cordier, Henri. *Notes Pour Servir à l'histoire Des Études Chinoises En Europe, Jusqu'à l'époque de Fourmont l'aîné*. Leiden: Brill, 1895.

Cowles, Henry M. *The Scientific Method: An Evaluation of Thinking from Darwin to Dewey*. Cambridge, Mass.: Harvard University Press, 2020.

Critical Terms for the Study of Buddhism. Chicago; London: University of Chicago Press, 2005.

Crossley, Pamela Kyle. *A Translucent Mirror: History and Identity in Qing Imperial Ideology*. Berkeley: University of California Press, 1999.

Da Fano, Dominique, and Michel Ange Andre Le Roux Deshauterayes. *Vocabulaire thibetan-latin*, 1773.

"Da Qing Yi Tong Zhi 大清一統志," 1733. Chinese Rare Book Collection (Library of Congress).

Dalton, Jacob Paul. *The Taming of the Demons: Violence and Liberation in Tibetan Buddhism*. New Haven, Conn.: Yale University Press, 2011.

Das, Sarat Chandra, Graham Sandberg, and William A. Heyde. *A Tibetan-English dictionary with Sanskrit synonyms*. Calcutta: The Bengal Secretariat Book Depôt, 1902.

Dashpurev, Danzanhorloogiin, and S. K. Soni. *Reign of Terror in Mongolia: 1920–1990*. New Delhi: South Asian Publ. [u.a.], 1992.

Davis, Natalie Zemon. "Decentering History: Local Stories and Cultural Crossings in a Global World."*History and Theory* 50, no. 2 (2011).

——. *Trickster Travels: A Sixteenth-Century MuslimBetween Worlds*. London: Faber and Faber, 2007.

——. *Women on the Margins: Three Seventeenth-Century Lives*. Rev. ed. Cambridge, Mass.: Belknap Press: An Imprint of Harvard University Press, 1997.

De Guignes, Joseph. *Histoire générale des Huns, des Turcs, des Mongols, et des autres Tartares occidentaux, etc. Avant et depuis Jesus-Christ jusqu' a present; précédée d'une introduction contenant des tables chronologique et historiques des princes qui ont regné dans l'Asie. Ouorage tiré des livres chinois, et des manuscrits orientaux de la bibliotheque du roi*. 4 vols. Paris: Chez Desaint: Saillant, 1756.

De Rauw, Tom. "Baochang: Sixth-Century Biographer of Buddhist Monks . . . and Nuns?"*Journal of the American Oriental Society* 125, no. 2 (2005): 203–18.

Deeg, Max. "Chinese Buddhists in Search of Authenticity in the Dharma."*The Eastern Buddhist* 45, no. 1 & 2 (2014): 11–22.

——. "The Historical Turn: How Chinese Buddhist Travelogues Changed the Western Perception of Buddhism."*Hualin International Journal of Buddhist Studies* 1, no. 1 (2019): 43–75.

——. *Origins and Development of the Buddhist Pañcavārṣika—Part I: India and Central Asia*. Ph.D. diss., Department of Indian Philosophy, University of Nagoya, 1995.

Deeg, Max, and Faxian. *Das Gaoseng-Faxian-Zhuan Als Religionsgeschichtliche Quelle: Der Älteste Bericht Eines Chinesischen Buddhistischen Pilgermönchs Über Seine Reise Nach Indien Mit Übersetzung Des Textes*. Wiesbaden, Germany: Harrassowitz, 2005.

Deleuze, Gilles, and Félix Guattari. *A Thousand Plateaus*. Trans. Brian Massumi. Minneapolis; London: University of Minnesota Press, 2005.

Deshauterayes, Michel Ange Andre Le Roux. "Alphabet Des Tartare Mouantcheoux." In *Recueil de Planches Sur Les Sciences, Les Arts Libéraux, et Les Arts Méchaniques Avec Leur Explication. Seconde Livraison, En Deux Parties. Troisieme Édition*, ed. Denis Diderot, 1:122, plate XXIII. 56. Livourne: L'imprimerie des éditeurs, 1772.

——. *Doutes sur la dissertation de M de Guignes, qui a pour titre, Mémoire dans lequel on prouve, que les chinois sont une colonie égyptienne*. Paris: Praulx, Duchesne, 1759.

——. *Histoire général de la chine: ou annales de cet empire*. Paris: Clousier, 1783.

——. "Recherches Sur La Religion de Fo, Professée Par Le Bonzes Ho-Chang de La Chine."*Journal Asiatique* 1, no. 7 (1825): 150–73.

Di Cosmo, Nicola. "Qing Colonial Administration in Inner Asia."*The International History Review* 20, no. 2 (June 1998): 287–309.

Dibeltulo Concu, Martino. "Buddhism, Philosophy, History. On Eugène Burnouf's Simple Sūtras."*Journal of Indian Philosophy* 45, no. 3 (2017): 473–511.

Dodin, Thierry, and Heinz Räther. *Imagining Tibet: Perceptions, Projections, and Fantasies*. Boston: Wisdom, 2001.

Drège, Jean-Pierre, and Faxian. *Memoire Sur Les Pays Bouddhiques*. Paris: Les Belles Lettres, 2013.

Drocourt, Zhitang. "Abel-Rémusat et Sa Pensée Linguistique Sur Le Chinois." In *Le XIXe Siècle et Ses Langues*, ed. Sarga Moussa, 16. Actes En Ligne Du Ve Congrès de La Société Des Études Romantiques et Dix-Neuvièmistes, 2013.

Droit, Roger-Pol. *The Cult of Nothingness: The Philosophers and the Buddha*. Trans. David Streight and Pamela Vohnson. Chapel Hill; London: University of North Carolina Press, 2003.

Du Halde, J. B. *Description geographique historique, chronologique, politique, et physique de l'empire de la Chine et de la Tartarie chinoise: enrichie des cartes generales et particulieres de ces pays, de la carte générale & des cartes particulieres du Thibet, & de la Corée & ornée d'un grand nombre de figures et de vignettes gravées en taille-douce*. Vol. 3. 4 vols. Paris: P. G. Lemercier, 1735.

Duara, Prasenjit. "Afterword: The Chinese World Order as a Language Game—David Kang's East Asia Before the West and Its Commentaries."*Harvard Journal of Asiatic Studies* 77, no. 1 (2017): 123–29.

——. *The Crisis of Global Modernity: Asian Traditions and a Sustainable Future*. Cambridge; New York: Cambridge University Press, 2015.

——. *Rescuing History from the Nation: Questioning Narratives of Modern China*. Chicago: University of Chicago Press, 1996.

Elisseeff, Danielle. *Moi, Arcade: interprète chinois du Roi-Soleil*. Paris: Arthaud, 1985.

Elliott, Mark C. "Abel-Rémusat, La Langue Mandchoue et La Sinologie."*Comptes Rendus Des Séances de l'AIBL* 2 (2014): 973–93.

——. *The Manchu Way: The Eight Banners and Ethnic Identity in Late Imperial China*. Stanford, Calif.: Stanford University Press, 2001.

Elman, Benjamin A. "Nietzsche and Buddhism."*Journal of the History of Ideas* 44, no. 4 (1983): 671–86.

Elverskog, Johan. "Mongol Time Enters a Qing World." In *Time, Temporality, and Imperial Transition: East Asia from Ming to Qing*, ed. Lynn A. Struve. Honolulu: Association for Asian Studies and University of Hawai'i Press, 2005.

——. *Our Great Qing: The Mongols, Buddhism and the State in Late Imperial China*. Honolulu: University of Hawai'i Press, 2006.

Espagne, Michel, Nora Lafi, and Pascale Rabault-Feuerhahn. *Silvestre de Sacy: le projet européen d'une science orientaliste*. Paris: Éditions du Cerf, 2014.

Ewing, Thomas E. *Between the Hammer and the Anvil?: Chinese and Russian Policies in Outer Mongolia, 1911–1921*. Bloomington: Research Institute for Inner Asian Studies, Indiana University, 1980.

"Extrait du Registre des actes de décès du 2. arrond. de Paris, pour l'année 1832." In *Le Curieux, Deuxième volume, N. 35, Décembre 1886*, 176. Le Curieux, 1888.

Faber, George Stanley. *The Origin of Pagan Idolatry Ascertained from Historical Testimony and Circumstantial Evidence . . . Three Volumes . . .* Vol. 1. 3 vols. London: A. J. Valpy, 1816.

Fa-hsien, and Herbert Allen Giles. *Record of the Buddhistic Kingdoms. Translated from the Chinese by H.A. Giles*. London: Trübner & Co., 1877.

Faxian 法顯. "The Biography of the Eminent Monk Faxian (Gaoseng Faxian Zhuan 高僧法顯傳)." Vol. 51. 2085. Tokyo: Taishō Shinshū Daizōkyō Kankōkai, 1988.

Faxian, and Jean-Pierre Abel-Rémusat. *Foĕ Kouĕ Ki, Ou, Relation Des Royaumes Bouddhiques: Voyage Dans La Tartarie, Dans l'Afghanistan et Dans l'Inde, Exécuté à La Fin Du IVe Siècle*. Ed. Julius von Klaproth and Ernest Augustin Xavier Clerc de Landresse. Paris: Imprimerie Royale, 1836.

Fazl-i-Allámí, Abul. *The Ain I Akbari*. Trans. H. S. Jarrett. Vol. 3. Calcutta: The Asiatic Society of Bengal (Baptist Mission Press), 1894. http://archive.org/details/in.ernet.dli.2015.46757.

Forte, Antonino. "Hui-Chih (Fl. 676–703 A.D.), a Brahmin Born in China." *Annali Dell'Istituto Orientale Di Napoli* 45 (1985): 105–34.

Gagné, Renaud, Simon Goldhill, and Geoffrey Lloyd, eds. *Regimes of Comparatism: Comparatism: Frameworks of Comparison in History, Religion and Anthropology*. Leiden; Boston: Brill, 2018.

Gernet, Jacques. *Die chinesische Welt: die Geschichte Chinas von den Anfängen bis zur Jetztzeit*. Frankfurt am Main, Germany: Suhrkamp, 1988.

Gilroy, Paul. *The Black Atlantic: Modernity and Double Consciousness*. London: Verso, 1993.

Giorgi, Antonio Agostino. *Alphabetum Tibetanum Missionum Apostolicarum Commodo Editum. Praemissa Est Disquisitio Qua De Vario Litterarum Ac Regionis Nomine, Gentis Origine Moribus, Superstitione, Ac Manichaeismo Fuse Disseritur: Beausobrii Calumniae In Sanctum Augustinum, Aliosque Ecclesiae Patres Refutantur*. Romae: Sacra Congregatio de Propaganda Fide, 1762.

Gonpo Kyab. *The Buddhist Canon of Iconometry (Zaoxiang Liangdu Jing): With Supplement. A Tibetan-Chinese Translation from about 1742. Translated and Annotated from This Chinese Translation Into Modern English*. Trans. Michael Henss. Ulm: Fabri Verlag, 2006.

'Gos lo tsa ba gzhon nu dpal. *Deb Ther Sngon Po*. Kun bde gling bla brang gi par khang: International Academy of Indian Culture, 1974.

Guha, Ranajit. *History at the Limit of World-History*. New York: Columbia University Press, 2002.

Guys, Pierre-Augustin. *Marseille ancienne et moderne, par M. Guys*, 1786.

Gyatso, Janet. *Apparitions of the Self: The Secret Autobiographies of a Tibetan Visionary: A Translation and Study of Jigme Lingpa's Dancing Moon in the Water and Ḍākki's Grand Secret-Talk*. Princeton, N.J.: Princeton University Press, 1998.

——. *Being Human in a Buddhist World: An Intellectual History of Medicine in Early Modern Tibet*. New York: Columbia University Press, 2015.

——. "Down with the Demoness: Reflections on a Feminine Ground in Tibet." In *Feminine Ground: Essays on Women and Tibet*, ed. Janice Dean Willis, 33–51. Ithaca, N.Y.: Snow Lion, 1995.

——. "Experience, Empiricism, and the Fortunes of Authority: Tibetan Medicine and Buddhism on the Eve of Modernity." In *Forms of Knowledge in Early Modern Asia*, 311–35. Durham, N.C.: Duke University Press, 2011.

Hallaq, Wael B. *Restating Orientalism: A Critique of Modern Knowledge*. New York: Columbia University Press, 2018.

Hartleben, Hermine. *Champollion: sein Leben und sein Werk*. Berlin: Weidmann, 1906.

Hartman, Saidiya. "Venus in Two Acts." *Small Axe: A Journal of Criticism* 26 (2008): 1–14.

He, Mufei. "Gonbujab མགོན་པོ་སྐྱབས།." In *The Treasury of Lives*, July 2020. https://treasuryoflives.org/biographies/view/mgon-po-skyabs/7473.

Hegel, Georg Wilhelm Friedrich. *Lectures on the Philosophy of Religion*. Trans. Peter Crafts Hodgson. Berkeley: University of California Press, 1988.

Heirman, Ann. "Vinaya: From India to China." In *The Spread of Buddhism*, ed. Ann Heirman and Stephan Peter Bumbacher, 167–202. Leiden: Brill, 2007.

Hikata, Ryūshō. *Suvikrāntavikrāmi-paripṛcchā prajñāpāramitā-sūtra*. Kyoto: Rinsen, 1983.

Hill, Susan M. *The Clay We Are Made of: Haudenosaunee Land Tenure on the Grand River*. Winnipeg: University of Manitoba Press, 2017.

Ho, Engseng. *The Graves of Tarim: Genealogy and Mobility Across the Indian Ocean*. Berkeley: University of California Press, 2010.

——. "Inter-Asian Concepts for Mobile Societies." *The Journal of Asian Studies* 76, no. 4 (2017): 907–28.

Hodgson, Brian Houghton. *Essays on the Languages, Literature, and Religion of Nepál and Tibet: Together with Further Papers on the Geography, Ethnology, and Commerce of Those Countries.* London: Trübner & Co., 1874.

——. *Sketch of Buddhism; Derived from the Bauddha Scriptures of Nipal.* London: J. L. Cox, 1828.

Honey, David B. *Incense at the Altar: Pioneering Sinologists and the Development of Classical Chinese Philology.* New Haven, Conn.: American Oriental Society, 2001.

Hosford, Desmond, and Chong J. Wojtkowski. *French Orientalism: Culture, Politics, and the Imagined Other.* Cambridge; New York: Cambridge Scholars Publishing, 2010.

Huijiao 慧皎. "Biographies of Eminent Monks (Gaoseng Zhuan 高僧傳)." In *Taishō Shinshū Daizōkyō* 大正新脩大藏經, ed. Takakusu Junjiro, 50:0337b19–0338b25. 2059. Tokyo: Taishō Shinshū Daizōkyō Kankōkai, 1988.

Humboldt, Wilhelm von, and Jean-Pierre Abel-Rémusat. *Brief an M. [Monsieur] Abel-Rémusat über die Natur grammatischer Formen im allgemeinen und über den Geist der chinesischen Sprache im besonderen.* Stuttgart: Bad Cannstatt Frommann, 1979.

Humboldt, Wilhelm von, Jean-Pierre Abel-Rémusat, and Wilhelm Humboldt von Freiherr. *De l'origine des formes grammaticales.* Bordeaux: Ducros., 1969.

Hu-von Hüber, Haiyan. "Faxian's (法顯 342–423) Perception of India—Some New Interpretations of His Foguoji 佛國記." In *Annual Report of The International Research Institute for Advanced Buddhology at Soka University for the Academic Year 2010 XI*, 223–47, 2011.

International Association for Tibetan Studies. *Power, Politics, and the Reinvention of Tradition: Tibet in the Seventeenth and Eighteenth Centuries: PIATS 2003: Tibetan Studies: Proceedings of the Tenth Seminar of the International Association for Tibetan Studies, Oxford, 2003.* Ed. Bryan J Cuevas and Kurtis R. Schaeffer. Leiden; Boston: Brill, 2006.

Jacoby, Sarah. *Love and Liberation: Autobiographical Writings of the Tibetan Buddhist Visionary Sera Khandro.* New York: Columbia University Press, 2014.

Jacquet, E. "Examen de La Traduction Du Fo Koue Ki, Ouvrage Posthume de M. Abel-Rémusat, Complété Par MM.J. Klaproth et C. Landresse."*Journal Asiatique* 3, no. 4 (1837): 141–79.

Jampa Tsedroen, Bhikṣuṇī. *Red Mda' Ba: Buddhist Yogi-Scholar of the Fourteenth Century: The Forgotten Reviver of Madhyamaka Philosophy in Tibet.* Wiesbaden: L. Reichert, 2009.

Jasper, David. "The Translation of China in England: Two 19th-Century English Translations of the Travels of Fa-Hsien (399–414 A.D.)." *Literature & Theology* 28, no. 2 (2014): 186–200.

Julien, Stanislas. *Histoire de la vie de Hioun-thsang et de ses voyages dans l'Inde, depuis l'an 629 jusqu'en 645.* Paris: Imprimerie Impériale, 1853.

Kaplonski, Christopher. *The Lama Question: Violence, Sovereignty, and Exception in Early Socialist Mongolia.* Honolulu: University of Hawai'i Press, 2014.

Kapstein, Matthew. *BuddhismBetween Tibet and China.* Boston: Wisdom, 2009.

——. "Just Where on Jambudvīpa Are We? New Geographical Knowledge and Old Cosmological Schemes in Eighteenth-Century Tibet." In *Forms of Knowledge in Early Modern Asia: Explorations in the Intellectual History of India and Tibet, 1500–1800*, ed. S. Pollock, 336–64. Durham, N. C.: Duke University Press, 2011.

Karmey, Samten G. *A General Introduction to the History and Doctrines of Bon.* Tokyo: Toyo Bunko, 1975.

Kaviraj, Sudipta. "Said and the History of Ideas." In *Cosmopolitan Thought Zones: South Asia and the Global Circulation of Ideas*, ed. Sugata Bose and Kris Manjapra, 58–81. New York: Palgrave Macmillan, 2010.

Keane, Webb. "Secularism as a Moral Narrative of Modernity." *Transit: Europäische Revue*, Verlag Neue Kritik, 43 (2013): 159–70.

Kennedy, George A. "The Monosyllabic Myth." *Journal of the American Oriental Society* 71, no. 3 (1951).

Kieschnick, John. *The Eminent Monk: Buddhist Ideals in Medieval Chinese Hagiography*. Honolulu, HI: University of Hawai'i Press, 1997.

King, Matthew W. "Agvaannyam: 'The Origin of Human Beings and the Holy Dharma Kings and Ministers in Mongol Lands,' from the History of the Dharma, The Lamp of Scriptures and Reasoning." In *Sources of Mongolian Tradition*, ed. Vesna A. Wallace, 453–75. Oxford; New York: Oxford University Press, 2020.

——. "Agwan Dorjiev's Questions About the Past and Future of Mongolian Buddhism." In *Sources of Mongolian Buddhism*, ed. Vesna A. Wallace, 416–37. Oxford; New York: Oxford University Press, 2020.

——. "Knowing King Gésar Between Buddhist Monastery and Socialist Academy, Or the Practices of Secularism in Inner Asia." *Himalaya: The Journal of the Association for Nepal and Himalayan Studies* 36, no. 10 (2016): 44–55.

——. *Ocean of Milk, Ocean of Blood. A Mongolian Monk in the Ruins of the Qing Empire*. New York: Columbia University Press, 2019.

——. "Zava Damdin's 'Beautifying Ornament for the Mind of the Faithful: A Praise-Biography of My Root Lama Vajradhara, He Who Possesses the Three Types of Kindness, the Great Mahāpaṇḍita Endowed with Excellent Discipline and Learning Named "Sanjaa." ' " In *Sources of Mongolian Buddhism*, ed. Vesna A. Wallace, 99–122. Oxford; New York: Oxford University Press, 2020.

Klaproth, Julius von. "Vie de Bouddha, d'Après Les Livres Mongols." *Journal Asiatique* 4, no. 1 (1824).

Knechtges, David R., and Taiping Chang, eds. "Sengyou 僧祐 (445–518)." In *Ancient and Early Medieval Chinese Literature: A Reference Guide*, 2:804–804. Leiden; Boston: Brill, 2014.

Körös, Sandor Csoma de. *Essay Towards a Dictionary Tibetan and English. Prepared with the Assis Tance of Bande Sangs-Rgyas Phun-Tshogs*. Calcutta: Baptist Mission Press, 1834.

Lacouture, Jean. *Champollion: une vie de lumières*. Paris: Grasset, 1988.

Laidley, J. W. *The Pilgrimage of Fa Hian; From the French Edition of the Foe Koue Ki of MM. Remusat, Klaproth, and Landresse with Additional Notes and Illustrations*. Calcutta: J. Thomas, Baptist Mission Press, 1848.

Landresse, Ernest Augustin Xavier Clerc de. "Notice Sur La Vie et Les Travaux de M. Abel-Rémusat, Lue à La Séance Générale Annuelle de La Société Asiatique, Le 28 Avril 1834." *Journal Asiatique* 14, no. 2 (1834): 205–31, 296–316.

Landresse, Ernest Augustin Xavier Clerc de, and Jean-Pierre Abel-Rémusat. "Introduction." In *Foĕ Kouĕ Ki, Ou, Relation Des Royaumes Bouddhiques: Voyage Dans La Tartarie, Dans l'Afghanistan et Dans l'Inde, Exécuté à La Fin Du IVe Siècle*, 1–66. Paris: Imprimerie Royale, 1836.

Landry-Deron, Isabelle. "Le Dictionnaire Chinois, Français et Latin de 1813." *T'oung Pao* 101, no. 4/5 (2015): 407–40.

Legge, James. *A Record of Buddhistic Kingdoms: Being an Account by the Chinese Monk Fa-Hien of His Travels in India and Ceylon (A.D. 399–414) in Search of the Buddhist Books of Discipline, Translated and Annotated with a Corean Recension of the Chinese Text*. Oxford: Oxford University Press, 1886.

Leibniz, Gottfried Wilhelm. "A Specimen of the Universal Calculus." In *Leibniz: Logical Papers: A Selection Translated and Edited with an Introduction*, ed. George Henry Radcliffe Parkinson, 33–39. Oxford: Oxford University Press, 1966.

——. "The Principles of Philosophy, or, the Monadology." In *G.W. Leibniz: Philosphical Essays*, ed. Roger Ariew and Daniel Garber, 213–25. Indianapolis and Cambridge: Hackett, 1989.

Lepage, François-Albin. *Recherches Historiques Sur La Médecine Des Chinois; Thèse Présentée et Soutenue à La Faculté de Médecine de Paris, Le 31 Aout 1813*. Paris: Didot jeune, Imprimeur de la Faculté de Médecine, 1813.

Leung, Cécile. *Etienne Fourmont (1683–1745): Oriental and Chinese Languages in Eighteenth-Century France*. Leuven: Leuven University Press, 2002.

Lévi-Strauss, Claude. *The Savage Mind*. Chicago: University of Chicago Press, 1966.

Li, Jianglin, and Susan Wilf. *Tibet in Agony: Lhasa 1959*. Cambridge, Mass.: Harvard University Press, 2016.

Li, Rongxi. "The Journey of the Eminent Monk Faxian: Translated from the Chinese of Faxian (Taishō Volume 51, Number 2085)." In *Lives of Great Monks and Nuns*, ed. Sengaku Mayeda et al., 157–214. Numata English Tripiṭaka Project. Berkeley, Calif.: Numata Center for Buddhist Translation and Research, 2002.

Liu, Yuan-ju. "Stories Written and Rewritten: The Story of Faxian's Search for the Dharma in Its Historical, Anecdotal, and Biographical Contexts." Trans. Jack W. Chen. *Early Medieval China* 2 (2016): 1–25.

Lopez, Donald S. *Curators of the Buddha: The Study of BuddhismUnder Colonialism*. Chicago: University of Chicago Press, 1995.

——. *Elaborations on Emptiness: Uses of "The Heart Sutra."* Princeton, N. J.:Princeton University Press, 1998.

——. *From Stone to Flesh: A Short History of the Buddha*. Chicago: University of Chicago Press, 2016.

——. *The Lotus Sūtra: A Biography*. Princeton, N. J.: Princeton University Press, 2016.

——. *Prisoners of Shangri-La: Tibetan Buddhism and the West*. Chicago: University of Chicago Press, 1998.

——. *The Scientific Buddha: His Short and Happy Life*. New Haven, Conn.: Yale University Press, 2012.

——. *Strange Tales of an Oriental Idol: An Anthology of Early European Portrayals of the Buddha*. Chicago: University of Chicago Press, 2016.

Lopez, Donald S., and Jacqueline Stone. *Two Buddhas Seated Side by Side: A Guide to the Lotus Sūtra*. Princeton, N.J.: Princeton University Press, 2019.

Lowe, Lisa. *The Intimacies of Four Continents*. Durham, N.C.: Duke University Press, 2015.

——. "The Intimacies of the Four Continents." In *Haunted by Empire: Geographies of Intimacy in North American History*, ed. Ann Laura Stoler, 191–212. Durham, N.C.: Duke University Press, 2006.

Luo, Yuming. *A Concise History of Chinese Literature*. Vol. 1. 2 vols. Leiden; Boston: Brill, 2011.

Macfie, Alexander Lyon. *Orientalism*. Oxford; New York: Routledge, 2014.

Makley, Charlene. "Gendered Boundaries in Motion: Space and Identity on the Sino-Tibetan Frontier."*American Ethnologist : The Journal of the American Ethnological Society* 30, no. 4 (2003): 597–619.

Mala, Guilaine. "A Mahayanist Rewriting of the History of China by Mgon Po Skyabs in the Rgya Nag Chos 'byung." In *Power, Politics, and the Reinvention of Tradition*, ed. Bryan J. Cuevas and Kurtis R. Schaeffer, 145–70. Leiden: Brill, 2006.

Mao Jin (毛晉). *Jin Dai Mi Shu/(Ming) Mao Jin Jiao Kan;津逮秘書/毛晉校刊; Tsin Tai Pi Chou/ Mao Tsin Kiao k'an*. 25 vols. 汲古閣刊本, 1628.

Masuzawa, Tomoko. *The Invention of World Religions, or, How European Universalism Was Preserved in the Language of Pluralism*. Chicago: University of Chicago Press, 2005.

McMahan, David L. *The Making of Buddhist Modernism*. New York: Oxford University Press, 2008.

Mgon po skyabs. *Chen Po Thang Gur Dus Kyi Rgya Gar Zhing Gi Bkod Pa'i Dkar Chag*. Beijing: Krung go'i bod rig pa dpe skrun khang, 2006.

——. *Rgya Nag Gi Yul Du Dam Pa'i Chos Dar Tshul Gtso Bor Bshad Pa Blo Gsal Kun Tu Dga' Ba'i Rna Rgyan*. Sde dge: Sde dge par khang, unknown.

Mignolo, Walter D. "Epistemic Disobedience, Independent Thought and De-Colonial Freedom."*Theory, Culture, and Society* 26, no. 7–8 (2009): 1–23.

Mills, Martin A. "Ritual as History in Tibetan Divine Kingship: Notes on the Myth of the Khotanese Monks."*History of Religions History of Religions* 51, no. 3 (2012): 219–20.

Mistry, Freny. *Nietzsche and Buddhism*. Berlin, New York: Walter de Gruyter, 1981.

Mitchell, Timothy. *Questions of Modernity*. Minneapolis; London: University of Minnesota Press, 2000.

Morozova, Irina Y. *The Comintern and Revolution in Mongolia*. Cambridge: White Horse Press for the Mongolia and Inner Asia Studies Unit, University of Cambridge, 2002.

——. "Socialist Revolutions in Asia: The Social History of Mongolia in the Twentieth Century." Routledge, 2009. /z-wcorg/.

Mosca, Matthew W. "Comprehending the Qing Empire: Building Multilingual Competence in an Age of Imperial Rivalry, 1792–1820."*The International History Review* 41, no. 5 (2019): 1057–75.

Moten, Fred. *In the Break: The Aesthetics of the Black Radical Tradition*. Minneapolis, Minn.: University of Minnesota Press, 2003.

Muir, John. *My First Summer in the Sierra: With Illustrations from Drawings Made by the Author in 1869 and from Photographs by Herbert W. Gleason*. Boston: Houghton Mifflin Co., 1911.

Mungello, D. E. *Curious Land: Jesuit Accommodation and the Origins of Sinology*. Honolulu, HI: University of Hawai'i Press, 1988.

Murphy, George G. S. *Soviet Mongolia; a Study of the Oldest Political Satellite*. Berkeley: University of California Press, 1966.

Nakamura, Hajime. *Indian Buddhism: A Survey with Bibliographical Notes*. Hirakata: KUFS Publ. Kansai University of Foreign Studies, 1980.

Nattier, Jan. *A Guide to the Earliest Chinese Buddhist Translations: Texts from the Eastern Han [Dong Han] and Three Kingdoms [San Guo] Periods*. Bibliotheca Philologica et Philosophica Buddhica. Tokyo: International Research Institute for Advanced Buddhology, Soka University, 2008.

Neumann, Karl. "Review of Foe Koue Ki Ou Relation Des Royaumes Bouddhiques: Voyage Dans La Tartarie, Dans l'Afghanistan et Dans l'Inde, Execute à La Fin Du IVe Siècle, Par Chy Fa Hian. Traduit Du Chinois et Commenté Par M. Abel Rémusat Ouvrage Posthume, Rev., Complété, et Augm. d'éclaircissements Nouveaux Par MM. Klaproth et Landresse."*Zeitschrift Für Die Kunde Des Morgenlandes* 3 (1840): 105–51.

Ngag dbang nyi ma. *Chos 'byung Lung Rigs Sgron Me*. Varanasi, India: unknown, 1965.

Nicol, Janine. "Outsiders: Medieval Chinese Buddhists and the 'Borderland Complex': An Exploration of the Eight Difficulties." *The SOAS Journal of Postgraduate Research* 6 (2014): 27–48.

"On the Eras of the Buddhas." *Asiatic Journal* 23 (June 1827): 782–86.

Östling, Johan. "Circulation, Arenas, and the Quest for Public Knowledge: Historiographical Currents and Analytical Frameworks."*History and Theory* 58 (2020): 111–26.

Outram, Dorinda. *The Enlightenment*. Cambridge: Cambridge University Press, 1995.

Ozeray, Michel Jean François. *Recherches sur Buddou ou Bouddou: instituteur religieux de l'Asie orientale: précédées de considérations générales sur les premiers hommages rendus au Créateur: sur la corruption de la religion, l'établissement des cultes du soleil, de la lune, des planètes, du ciel, de la terre, des montagnes, des eaux, des forêts, des hommes et des animaux*. Paris: Chez Brunot-Labbe, 1817.

Padma dkar po. *History of Buddhism. Written by Kunkhyen Pema Karpo (1527–1592) (Chos 'byung Bstan Pa'i Pad+ma Rgyas Pa'i Nyin Byed)*. Ed. Lokesh Chandra. Vol. 75. Śata-Piṭaka Series (Indo-Tibetan Literatures). Delhi: International Academy of Indian Culture, 1968.

Panaïoti, Antoine. *Nietzsche and Buddhist Philosophy*. Cambridge: Cambridge University Press, 2013.

Petit, Jérôme. "Eugène Jacquet and His Pioneering Study of Indian Numerical Notations." *Ganita Bharati: Journal of the Indian Society for History of Mathematics* 31, no. 1–2 (2009): 23–33.

Purevzhav, S. *BNMAU-D sum khiid, lam naryn asuudlyg shiidverlesen ní: 1921–1940 on*. Ulaanbaatar: Ulsyn khevleliin khereg erkhlekh khoroo, 1965.

Quintman, Andrew. "Between History and Biography: Notes on Zhi Byed Ri Pa's 'Illuminating Lamp of Sun and Moon Beams,' a Fourteenth-Century Biographical State of the Field." *Revue d'Etudes Tibétaines* 23 (Avril 2012): 5–41.

——. *The Yogin and the Madman: Reading the Biographical Corpus of Tibet's Great Saint Milarepa*. New York: Columbia University Press, 2013.

Remusat, M., and H. H. Wilson. "Account of the Foe Kúe Ki, or Travels of Fa Hian in India, Trans. M. Remusat [Read 9th March and 7th April, 1838]." *The Journal of the Royal Asiatic Society* 5, no. 1 (1839): 108–40.

Revault d'Allonnes, Myriam. *La crise sans fin: essai sur l'expérience moderne du temps*. Paris: Seuil, 2012.

"Review of the 'Mélanges Asiatique, Ou Choix de Morçeaux de Critique et de Mémoirs Relatifs Aux Religions, Aux Sciences, Aux Coutumes, à l'Histoire et à La Géographie Des Nations Orientales.' Par M. Abel Rémusat. Tom. II. Paris, 1826. 8vo. Pp. 428." *Asiatic Society* 22 (1826): 191–92.

Richtofen, Ferdinand von. "Über Die Zentralasiatischen Seidenstrassen Bis Zum 2. Jh. n. Chr." *Verhandlungen Der Gesellschaft Für Erdkunde Zu Berlin* 4 (1877): 96–122.

Rinchen, Byambyn. *Travels of Fa HsianTrans. Dordji Bansaroff*. Corpus Scriptorum Mongolorum Instituti Linguae Litterarum Academiae Scientiarum Reipublicae Populi Mongolici 5. Ulaanbaatar: Mongol Ulsîn Shinjlekh Ukhaani Akademi, 1970.

Robinson, Cedric J. *Black Marxism: The Making of the Black Radical Tradition*. Chapel Hill: University of North Carolina Press, 1983.

Rochemonteix, Camille de. *Joseph Amiot et les derniers survivants de la mission française à Pekin (1750–1795)*. Paris: A. Picard et fils, 1915.

Rosenberg, Charles E. *The Cholera Years: The United States in 1832, 1849, and 1866*. Chicago: University of Chicago Press, 1962.

Rothman, E. Natalie. *Brokering Empire Trans-Imperial SubjectsBetween Venice and Istanbul*. Ithaca, N.Y.; London: Cornell University Press, 2012.

Rousseau, Jean, Denis Thouard, Wilhelm von Humboldt, and Jean-Pierre Abel-Rémusat. *Lettres édifiantes et curieuses sur la langue chinoise: un débat philosophico-grammatical entre Wilhelm von Humboldt et Jean-Pierre Abel-Rémusat (1821–1831)*. Villeneuve-d'Ascq: Presses universitaires du Septentrion, 1999.

Routray, Bibhu Prasad. "Tibetan Refugees in India: Religious Identity and the Forces of Modernity."*Refugee Survey Quarterly* 26, no. 2 (January 1, 2007): 79–90.

Rupen, Robert A. "The Buriat Intelligentsia." *The Far Eastern Quarterly* 15, no. 3 (1956): 383–98.

Rupen, Robert Arthur. *How Mongolia Is Really Ruled: A Political History of the Mongolian People's Republic, 1900–1978*. Stanford, Calif.: Hoover Institution Press, Stanford University, 1979.

Sacy, Antoine-Isaac Silvestre de. "Notice historique sur la vie et les ouvrages de M. Abel Rémusat." *Mémoires de l'Institut national de France* 12, no. 1 (1839): 375–400.

Said, Edward W. *Orientalism*. New York: Vintage, 1979.

Sandag, Shagdariin, Harry H. Kendall, and Frederic E. Wakeman. *Poisoned Arrows: The Stalin-Choibalsan Mongolian Massacres, 1921–1941*. Boulder, Colo.: Westview Press, 2000.

Schaeffer, Kurtis. "New Scholarship in Tibet, 1650–1700." In *Forms of Knowledge in Early Modern Asia: Explorations in the Intellectual History of India and Tibet, 1500–1800*, ed. Sheldon Pollock, 291–310. Durham, N.C.: Duke University Press, 2011.

——. "Tibetan Biography: Growth and Criticism." In *Editions, Éditions: L'Écrit Au Tibet, Évolution et Devenir.* München: Indus Verlag, 2010.

Schmidt, Isaac Jac. *Forschungen im Gebiete der älteren religiösen, politischen u. literarischen Bildungsgeschichte der Völker Mittelasiens, vorz. der Mongolen und Tibeter.* St. Petersburg, 1824.

Schmidt, Isaak Jacob. *Ueber die sogenannte dritte Welt der Buddhaisten: als Fortsetzung der Abhandlungen ueber die Lehren des Buddhaismus ; gelesen den 21 December 1831.* St. Petersburg, 1834.

Schmidt, Isaak Jakob. "Extrait d'une Lettre de M. Schmidt, à M., Sur Quelques Sujets Relatifs à l'histoire et à La Littérature Mongoles, 10/22 Octobre 1820, St.-Pétersbourg, Dec. 1822." *Journal Asiatique* 1 (1822): 320–34.

——. "Extrait d'une Lettre de M. Schmidt, de St. Pétersbourg, Addressée à M. Klaproth, En Réponse à l'Examen Des Extraits d'une Histoire Des Khans Mongols." *Journal Asiatique* 3 (1823): 107–13.

——. *Forschungen Im Gebiete Der Älteren Religiösen, Politischen Und Literärischen Bildungsgeschichte Der Völker Mittel-Asiens, Vorzüglich Der Mongolen Und Tibeter.* St. Petersburg; Leipzig, 1824.

——. *Grammatik Der Tibetischen Sprache.* St, Petersburg, 1839.

——. *Mongolisch-Deutsch-Russisches Wörterbuch: Nebst Einem Deutschen Und Einem Russischen Wortregister.* St. Petersburg, 1835.

——. *Philologisch-Kritische Zugabe Zu Den von Herrn Abel-Rémusat Bekannt Gemachten, in Den Königlich-Französischen Archiven Befindlichen Zwei Mongolischen Original-Briefen Der Könige von Persien Argun Und Öldshaitu an Philipp Den Schönen.* St. Petersburg, 1824.

——. "Über Den Ursprung Der Tibetischen Schrift." *Mémoires de l'Academie Impériale Des Sciences de St. Pétersbourg* 6, no. 1 (1832): 41–54.

——. *Über Die Verwandtschaft Der Gnostisch-Theosophischen Lehren Mit Den Religions-Systemen Des Orients, Vorzüglich Des Buddhaismus.* Leipzig, 1828.

——. "Über Einige Grundlehren Des Buddhaismus." *Mémoires de l'Academie Impériale Des Sciences de St. Pétersbourg* 6, no. 1 (1832): 89–120.

——. "Ursprung Des Namens Mandschu." *St. Petersburgische Zeitung* 253 (1834).

Schopen, Gregory. "Archaeology and Protestant Presuppositions in the Study of Indian Buddhism." *History of Religions* 31, no. 1 (1991): 1–23.

Schuh, Dieter. *Studien zur Geschichte der Mathematik und Astronomie in Tibet.* Zentralasiatische Studien des Seminars für Sprach und Kulturwissenschaft Zentralasiens der Universität Bonn 4, 1970.

Sengyou 僧祐. "Collection of Notes on the Translation of the Tripiṭaka (Chusanzang Jiji 出三藏記集)." In *Taishō Shinshū Daizōkyō*大正新脩大藏經, ed. Takakusu Junjiro, 55:0111b27–0112b27. 2145. Tokyo: Taishō Shinshū Daizōkyō Kankōkai, 1988.

Sharf, Robert H. "Buddhist Modernism and the Rhetoric of Meditative Experience." *Numen* 42, no. 3 (1995): 228–83.

Shi Faxian 釋法顯. "Fo Guo Ji: 1 Juan/(Song) Shi Fa Xian Zhuan 佛國記: 1卷/ (宋) 釋法顯撰." In *Jin Dai Mi Shu* 津逮秘書, 17:Feuillet 25 ms. Anc. Fourmont 304. Zhong guo 中國: Ji gu ge cang 汲古閣藏, 1628.

Shih, Robert. *Biographies Des Moines Éminents (Kao Seng Tchouan) de Houei-Kiao.* Bibliothèque Du Muséon 54. Louvain: Institut Orientaliste, Bibliothèque de Université de Louvain, 1968.

"Société Asiatique (Séance Du 7 Février 1831)." *Journal Asiatique* 7 (1831): 236–37.

Spence, Jonathan D. "The Paris Years of Arcadio Huang." In *Chinese Roundabout: Essays in History and Culture*, 11–24. New York: Norton, 1993.

Spivak, Gayatri Chakravorty. *A Critique of Postcolonial Reason: Toward a History of the Vanishing Present*. Cambridge, Mass.: Harvard University Press, 1999.

Ssetsen, Ssanang, and Isaak Jakob Schmidt. *Geschichte der Ost-Mongolen und ihres Fürstenhauses; aus dem Mongolischen übersetzt und mit dem Originaltexte, nebst Anmerkungen, Erläuterungen und Citaten aus andern unedirten Originalwerken herausgegeben*. St. Petersburg; Leipzeg: Gedruckt bei N. Gretsch, 1829.

Stoler, Ann Laura, and Brian Keith Axel. "Developing Historical Negatives: Race and the [Modernist] Visions of a Colonial State." In *From the Margins: Historical Anthropology and Its Futures*, 156–88. Durham, N.C, and London: Duke University Press, 2002.

Strong, John S. *Relics of the Buddha*. Princeton, N.J.: Princeton University Press, 2004.

Thouard, Denis. "Humboldt, Abel-Rémusat et Le Chinois: La Recherche de La Correspondence." In *Lettres Édifiantes et Curieuses Sur La Langue Chinoise: Un Débat Philosophico-Grammatical Entre Wilhelm von Humboldt et Jean-Pierre Abel-Rémusat (1821-1831)*, ed. Jean Rousseau and Denis Thouard, 9–28. Villeneuve-d'Ascq: Presses universitaires du Septentrion, 1999.

Thuken Losang Chökyi Nyima. *The Crystal Mirror of Philosophical Systems: A Tibetan Study of Asian Religious Thought*. Trans. Geshé Lundub Sopa. Vol. 25. The Library of Tibetan Classics. Boston: Wisdom, 2009.

Tokuno, Kyoko. "The Evaluation of Indigenous Scriptures in Chinese Buddhist Bibliographical Catalogues." In *Chinese Buddhist Apocrypha*, ed. Robert E Buswell, 31–74. Honolulu: University of Hawai'i Press, 1990.

Trouillot, Michel-Rolph. "Culture on the Margins: Caribbean Creolization in Historical Context." In *From the Margins: Historical Anthropology and Its Futures*, ed. Brian Keith Axel, 189–210. Durham, N.C. and London: Duke University Press, 2002.

——. *Silencing the Past: Power and the Production of History*. Boston: Beacon, 2015.

Tuttle, Gray. "Challenging Central Tibet's Dominance of History: The Oceanic Book, a Nineteenth-Century Politico-Religious-Geographic History." In *Mapping the Modern in Tibet. PIATS 2006: Proceedings of the Eleventh Seminar of the International Association for Tibetan Studies. Königswinter 2006*, ed. Gray Tuttle, 135–72. [Andiast, Switzerland]: IITBS, International Institute for Tibetan and Buddhist Studies GmbH, 2011.

Ulymzhiev, D. "Dorzhi Banzarov—the First Buryat Scholar."*Mongol Studies* 16 (1993): 55–57.

Une société de gens de lettres et de savants. *Biographie Universelle, Ancienne et Moderne*. Vol. 66. Paris: L. G. Michaud, 1839.

——. *Biographies Des Hommes Vivants, Ou Histoire Par Ordre Alphabétique de La View Publique de Tous Les Hommes Qui Se Sont Fait Remarquer Par Leurs Actions Ou Leurs Écrits*. Vol. 5. Paris: L. G. Michaud, 1819.

Uspensky, Vladimir. "Ancient History of the Mongols According to Gombojab, an Eighteenth-Century Mongolian Historian."*Rocznik Orientalistyczny*. 58, no. 1 (2005): 236–41.

——. "Gombojab: A Tibetan Buddhist in the Capital of the Qing Empire." In *Biographies of Eminent Mongol Buddhists*, ed. Johan Elverskog, 59–70. Halle: International Institute for Tibetan and Buddhist Studies, 2008.

Vallega, Alejandro A., and Indiana University. *Latin American Philosophy: From Identity to Radical Exteriority*. Bloomington: Indiana University Press, 2014.

Varisco, Daniel Martin. *Reading Orientalism Said and the Unsaid: With a New Preface by the Author*. Seattle: University of Washington Press, 2017.

Weiner, Benno. *The Chinese Revolution on the Tibetan Frontier*. Ithaca, N.Y.; London: Cornell University Press, 2020.

White, Richard. *The Middle Ground: Indians, Empires, and Republics in the Great Lakes Region, 1650–1815*. Cambridge; New York: Cambridge University Press, 1991.

Wilson, Horace H. *A Dictionary, Sanscrit and English: Translated, Amended and Enlarged, from an Original Compilation Prepared by Learned Natives for the College of Fort William*. Calcutta: Printed by Philip Pereira, at the Hindoostanee Press, 1819.

Wright, Arthur F. "Biography and Hagiography: Hui-Chiao's Lives of Eminent Monks." In *Studies in Chinese Buddhism*, ed. Robert M. Somers. New Haven, Conn: Yale University Press, 1990.

Yayuma, Akira. *Systematische Übersicht Über Die Buddhistische Sanskrit-Literatur*. Vinaya Texte, Erster Teil. Wiesbaden: Franz Steiner, 1979.

Yifa. *The Originsof Buddhist Monastic Codesin China: An Annotated Translationand Studyofthe Chanyuan Qinggui*. Honolulu, HI: University of Hawai'i Press, 2002.

Young, Robert. *White Mythologies : Writing History and the West*. London; New York: Routledge, 1990.

Yü, Ying-shih. "Han Foreign Relations." In *The Cambridge History of China: The Ch'in and Han Empires, 221 B.C.–A.D. 220*, trans. Denis Twitchett and John K. Fairbank, 1:377–462. Cambridge: Cambridge University Press, 1986.

Zhang, Fan. "Reorienting the Sacred and Accommodating the Secular: The History of Buddhism in China (RGya Nag Chos 'byung)."*Revue d'Etudes Tibétaines* 37 (2016): 569–91.

Zürcher, Erik. *The Buddhist Conquest of China: The Spread and Adaptation of Buddhism in Early Medieval China*. Leiden: Brill, 2007.

Zurndorfer, Harriet Thelma. *China Bibliography: A Research Guide to Reference Works About China Past and Present*. Leiden: Brill, 1995.

Джидинский район. "Доржи Банзаров—Первый Бурятский Учёный." Accessed September 26, 2017. http://dzhida.ru/dorzhi-banzarov-pervyj-buryatskij-uchyonyj/.

Index